CORREGIDOR

THE AMERICAN ALAMO
OF WORLD WAR II

ERIC MORRIS

Cooper Square Press

First Cooper Square Press edition 2000

This Cooper Square Press paperback edition of *Corregidor* is an unabridged republication of the edition first published in Briarcliff Manor, New York, in 1981.

Designed by Louis A. Ditizio

Published by Cooper Square Press
An Imprint of the Rowman & Littlefield Publishing Group
150 Fifth Avenue, Suite 911
New York, New York 10011

Distributed by National Book Network

Library of Congress Cataloging-in-Publication Data

Morris, Eric, 1940–
    Corregidor : the American Alamo of World War II / Eric Morris.
        p. cm.
    Originally published: New York : Stein and Day, 1981.
    Includes bibliographical references and index.
    ISBN 0-8154-1085-9 (pbk. : alk. paper)
      1. World War, 1939–1945 — Campaigns — Philippines — Corregidor Island. 2. Corregidor Island (Philippines) — History. I. Title.

D767.4 .M678 2000
940.54'25 — dc21

                        00-056965

DEDICATED TO

THE AMERICAN DEFENDERS
OF
BATAAN AND CORREGIDOR

OATH

To His Excellency, the Commander-in-Chief
of the Imperial Japanese Forces.

I, the undersigned, hereby solemnly pledge myself that I will strictly comply
with the following:

1. I shall never in future resort to any hostile action against the Imperial
Japanese Forces, and I will in no way make any utterance or commit
any hostile conduct against Japan;

2. I will submit to the Japanese Military Administration and do my best to
serve for the realization of the objective of the said administration;

3. I will in no way make any utterance or commit any conduct which may
benefit Japan's enemies;

4. I will in no way make any utterance or commit any conduct which may
be harmful to the tranquility, peace and order, and economic stability of
the country;

5. I will in no way employ or instigate others for the execution of any act
which I have pledged myself not to commit in the preceding paragraphs

6. I will never fail to present myself at an appointed place when I shall be
called up by the Japanese Army.

Prisoner of war

Address: *Trac Cavite*

Signature: *Dalmatia Vasquez*

Guarantor of the above person

Address: _____

Signature: _____

Date:

Sign

誓書

一、將來日本軍ニ敵對セス且一切ノ反日言動ヲ爲ササルコト

二、日本軍ノ軍政ニ服シ進ンテ軍政ノ目的達成ニ奉仕努力スルコト

三、一切ノ利敵言動ヲ爲ササルコト

四、一切ノ人心擾亂、經濟攪亂及安寧公安ヲ害スル言動ヲ爲ササルコト

五、他人ヲ使用シ又使嗾シテ前諸項ノ言動ヲ爲サシメサルコト

六、日本軍ニ於テ召集ヲ命セラレタル場合ハ指定ノ場所ニ集合スルコト

以上ノ條々固ク守リ決シテ違背セサルコトヲ茲ニ謹ミテ誓フ

昭和十七年　月　日

本人現住所

本人署名　*Mair Bureli*

保證人現住所　*Dolmacio Vasquez*

保證人署名

大日本軍司令官殿

知事(市長)又ハ町長ノ署名

Governor, Mayor or Municipal President

The Japanese military government required American civilians to sign an oath of obedience. This is a photograph of an actual parchment document signed by a prisoner.

ACKNOWLEDGMENTS

In writing this account I owe a personal debt of gratitude to so many people.

The Veterans
First there are the veterans of the campaign. It has not proved possible to include everybody I interviewed in the account. To the men and women listed below and to those who are not mentioned by name but who all shared their experiences, my heartfelt gratitude. The veterans entertained me at the convention of their Western States Chapter and subsequently welcomed me, a stranger in the land, into their homes. For this kindness and hospitality, my sincere thanks. Where their memory grew hazy over the details of events that happened forty years ago many veterans sent me articles and newspaper clippings which they wrote in the immediate postwar years, with permission to use them at my discretion.

Malcolm Champlin has allowed me to use four articles he published in the maritime journal *Shipmate*. Others have sent me photographs of the period of the campaign and these appear in the text. Sister Louise Kroeger sent a selection of material from the convent archives at Maryknoll. I am particularly grateful to Sister Coleman for her excellent account of the rescue of the internees at Los Biños. Bill Massello's documentary evidence on the prisoner-of-war experiences provides much of the data in the Epilogue.

The United States
Mrs. Margaret Williams, wife of General Drake's grandson, Duke, an officer serving in the United States Air Force, is the family archivist. Her unfailing support and enthusiasm has allowed me to include in my account material which has never been used before.

Sky Beaven and her husband, Bill, who made me so welcome in Washington and helped in research advice and contacts.

Lt. Col. Mark Gratanas, at the time of my research the commanding officer, 2nd Battalion, 31st U.S. Infantry.

Dr. John Sloanaker, Chief of Historical Research Section, U.S. Military History Institute, Carlisle Barracks.

Brig. Gen. E. H. Simmons, U.S.M.C. (Ret.), Headquarters, United States Marine Corps.

Edward Louden of *Scholastic* magazines and an old soldier who has been so helpful.

The Philippines

Col. Primitivo Milan, Philippine Constabulary, Chief of Historical Archives of the Philippine Army.

Rico José, the University of Manila—a mine of information on the campaign.

Col. Manuel Acosta (Ret.), Philippine Military Shrines Service, a most excellent guide during my excursions into Bataan and on Corregidor.

Col. Christopher Dale, the British Defense Attaché, and his wife, Simone, for their hospitality in Manila.

The United Kingdom

Col. Robert B. Osborn, United States Army Attaché in London.

John Hunt, librarian, and his staff of the Central Library, Royal Military Academy, Sandhurst.

Mrs. Dorothy Fox, assisted by Mrs. Kate Jarman, transcribed the hundreds of hours of tapes, and the typed manuscript and their efficiency, industry, and enthusiasm are beyond praise. It has been a herculean task not made any easier, I am sure, by my almost illegible handwriting.

Publishers

The original idea for this book came from Sol Stein. He has given me inspiration, support, and guidance throughout. Patricia Day has proved to be a magnificent editor; her helpful comments and constructive criticism have improved the manuscript beyond measure.

James Cochrane of Hutchinson in London has been closely involved since I started to produce the manuscript. I am most grateful for all his advice and help.

Last but by no means least, my wife, Pamela, and my family, whose patience and sympathy have proved invaluable throughout the research, the travel, and the writing of this book.

E.M.

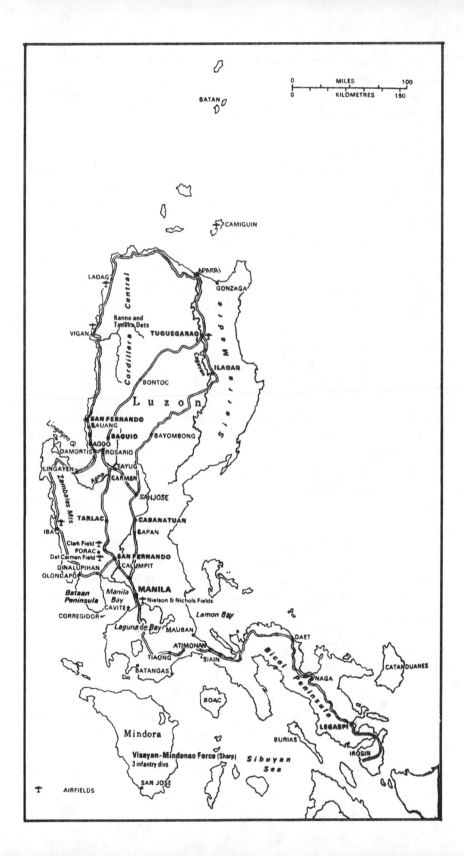

Contents

List of Illustrations

List of Maps

"Cast List"

The following are those veterans of the campaign who were interviewed personally by the author. It is their story that is told in this book:

Armburst, Carl	Lt., U.S.N.	Gunnery officer, U.S.S. *Pecos*; fleet oiler with the Asiatic Fleet based in Manila Bay; engaged to Ruby Moteley
Ashton, Paul	Maj., U.S.A.	Medical officer, 12th Medical Regiment, Philippine Scouts, and later 21st Infantry Division (Philippine Army), Bataan Field Force, and Chief Surgeon, No. 1 Hospital, Bataan Field Force
Bigelow, Edwin	Sgt., U.S.M.C.	Co. H, 2/4th U.S. Marines, Shanghai, and Beach Defense, Corregidor
Boettcher, Arnold	Capt., U.S.A.	Corps of Engineers HQ, Philippines Department, Manila, and HQ, Bataan Field Force
Boghosian, Samuel	Pvt., U.S.A.A.C.	Air gunner radio operator B-17C, 30th Squadron, 19th Air Bombardment Group, Clark Field
Bressi, Arthur	Cpl., U.S.A.	60th (AA) Artillery, U.S. Coast Artillery Corps;

supply clerk, Regiment HQ; and gunner, Battery Chicago, Fort Mills, Corregidor

Broderick, Albert — Cpl., U.S.M.C. — 3/4th U.S. Marines, Shanghai, promoted to sergeant/platoon leader, beach defense, Corregidor

Champlin, Malcolm — Lt., U.S.N.R. — FBI field agent, mobolized 1941; naval aide and flag lieutenant to Rear Admiral Commanding 16th Naval District, Manila Bay. Later naval aide to General Wainwright, HQ, Bataan Field Force

Drake, Charles — Brig. Gen., U.S.A. — Quartermaster-in-chief, HQ, Philippines Department, and USAFFE HQ, Manila and Fort Mills, Corregidor

Erickson, Edward — Lt., U.S.A.A.C. — Pilot 17th Pursuit Sqd., Nichols Field; liaison officer, U.S. Navy, provisional infantry battalion, Mariveles; controller, Kindley Field, Corregidor

Finken, Bill — Cpl., U.S.M.C. — 3/4th U.S. Marines, Shanghai; Marine detachment, Cavite naval base, and beach defense, Corregidor

Fromer, Sol — Cpl., U.S.A. — Battery E, 59th Artillery, U.S. Coast Artillery Corps, Fort Drum, Manila Bay

Garleb, Bill	Pfc., U.S.A.	Company H, 2nd Battalion, 31st (U.S.) Infantry Regiment, Fort McKinley, promoted corporal, Bataan Field Force
Griffiths, William	Sgt., U.S.M.C.	Company B, 1/4th U.S. Marines; squad leader, Shanghai, and platoon leader, beach defense, Corregidor
Hall, William	Cpl., U.S.A.	Battery D, 59th Artillery, U.S. Coast Artillery Corps, Fort Mills, Corregidor
Howard, Frederick	Pvt., U.S.A.	Telegrapher, HQ, 59th Artillery, U.S. Coast Artillery Corps, Fort Mills, Corregidor
Jenkins, Sidney	1st Lt., U.S.M.C.	Intelligence officer, 2/4th U.S. Marines, Shanghai, and beach defense, Corregidor
Jones, Winston	2nd Lt., U.S.A.	Philippine Scouts Field Artillery and later promoted to captain and battalion commander, 41st Division Field Artillery (Philippine Army)
King, Tom	Lt. Cdr., U.S.N.	Engineer supply officer U.S. submarines, Asiatic Fleet, submarine depot ship U.S.S. *Canopus*
Kroeger, Louise	Nun	Order of Maryknoll, convent at Baguio, Luzon

Lay, Kermit	2nd Lt., U.S.A.	Promoted on outbreak of war and commissioned into provisional Military Police; assistant provost marshal, HQ, I Corps, Bataan Field Force
McCann, John	Pvt., U.S.A.A.C.	693rd Ordnance Company, Aviation Pursuit, Nichols Field; enlisted at age of 16 years. Provisional Air Corps Infantry Battalion, Bataan Defense Force, provisional 4th battalion/ 4th U.S. Marines, beach defense, Corregidor
McDavitt, Jerome	Capt., U.S.A.	23rd Field Artillery, Philippine Scouts, Northern Luzon Forces, Bataan Defense Force; Army HQ, USFIP, Fort Mills, Corregidor
McKnight, Roland	Lt., U.S.N.	Commanding officer, U.S. submarine S-36, Asiatic Fleet, and later commanding officer, U.S. submarine Porpoise, Pacific Fleet
Malick, Sam	P.O., U.S.N.	Radio operator, U.S.S. Mindanao, China River flotilla and Manila Bay inshore squadron and finally gunner with 12-inch mortars on Fort Hughes
Massello, William	Capt., U.S.A.	Commanded Battery E, 60th Artillery, U.S. Coast

		Artillery Corps, Bataan Field Force, and later 12-inch mortars, Battery Way, 59th Artillery, Fort Mills, Corregidor; promoted to major
Matson, William	Cpl., U.S.A.	Company A, 194th Tank Battalion, California National Guard, Northern Luzon Forces and Bataan Defense Force
Mills, Loyd	1st Lt., U.S.A.	Platoon leader/captain and company commander, Company C, 1st Battalion, 57th Infantry, Philippine Scouts, Northern Luzon Forces and Bataan Defense Force
Moteley, Ruby	Civilian	Dietician at Sternberg Army Hospital, Manila; later No. 1 Hospital, Bataan Field Force, and General Hospital, Malinta Tunnel, Corregidor
Muther, Frank	Pfc., U.S.A.	Radio operator, Company C, 194th Tank Battalion, California National Guard, Southern Luzon Forces and Bataan Field Force
Osborn, Richard	Pfc., U.S.A.A.C.	Aircrew, B-17C/Link trainer; operative, 19th Bombardment Group, Clark Field, and Del Monte Field, Mindanao

Saccone, Ben	Sgt., U.S.A.	1st sergeant, Company C, 194th Tank Battalion, California National Guard, Southern Luzon Forces, Bataan Field Force
Sakakida, Richard	Sgt., U.S.A.	Nisei born in Hawaii, U.S. Army Counter Intelligence (CIC); undercover agent, Manila interpreter/ interrogator/propagandist, HQ, I Corps; Bataan Field Force and USFIP HQ, Fort Mills, Corregidor
Seitz, (Mrs.) Lilla	Civilian	American housewife resident in Manila; husband, Clay an insurance executive/shipping broker
Sniezko, William	Sgt., U.S.A.	Staff Sergeant, Company B, 2nd Battalion, 31st (U.S.) Infantry; quartermaster sergeant (baker) Philippine Scouts, Bataan Field Force
Son, John	Pfc., U.S.A.	Gunner, Battery G, 59th Artillery U.S. Coast Artillery Corps, Fort Hughes, Manila Bay
Spainhower, John	1st Lt., U.S.A.	Adjutant, 2nd Battalion, 57th Infantry, Philippine Scouts, Northern Luzon Forces and Bataan Defense Force

Taulbee, John   Sgt., U.S.A.A.C.   1st sergeant, HQ squadron, 19th Bombardment Group, Clark Field. Commissioned 2nd lieutenant, provisional infantry battalion, Army Air Corps, Bataan Field Force

Ullom, Madeline   Lt., U.S.A.   Nurse, Sternberg Army Hospital, Manila, and General Hospital, Malinta Tunnel, Fort Mills, Corregidor

Zimmerman, Leslie   Capt., U.S.A.A.C.   Chaplain, 24th Pursuit Group, Nichols Field, and provisional infantry, U.S. Army Air Corps, Bataan Field Force

Prologue

Friday, February 16, 1945
503rd Parachute Regiment, U.S. Army
Corregidor

Maj. Paul Ashton had been a prisoner of the Japanese since the surrender of the American Army in Bataan nearly three years before. A surgeon serving with the elite Philippine Scouts, he had endured hardship, deprivation, and torture at the hands of his tormentors. Now he was going home, or at least he believed he was. His prison camp had been liberated some three days before by the American forces that had landed at Lingayen Gulf. Ashton was in better shape than most and had been found medically fit for transit home. It had been a heady few days, and his mind was still in a turmoil as he saw weapons and equipment that he never knew existed. He saw his first bazooka and marveled at the Sherman tanks. Even the American combat helmet was new; he had used the flat-edged World War I design in "his war."

Early that morning half a dozen men had been loaded in a six-by-six with all their new possessions. Each had been given a footlocker, and for men who for three years had possessed nothing that couldn't be carried in one hand, this was wealth indeed. They were driven to a new airfield on the shore of Lingayen Gulf. Goggle-eyed at the sights that greeted them, they climbed out of the truck as if in a dream. The sheer scale of the war effort left them breathless and also embittered at the shortcomings of their own campaign.

The group were taken out to an empty C-47, and they climbed into the plane and sat on their footlockers. Within a short while a truckload of soldiers arrived, and the ex-prisoners became acquainted with paratroopers for the first time in their lives. The latter scrambled in, sat on their packs, and the plane lumbered into the early-morning sky.

Ashton looked out of the window as they flew low over the Philippine terrain. They followed the South China Sea coast, crossed at San Fernando, and went right over Manila. The plane was low enough for Ashton to see very clearly the fighting going on for the Manila Hotel and the square that contained the Army and Navy Club. Ashton still recognized the gaunt outlines of Bilabid Prison, though little more than a burned-out shell. It was in that "Bastille of the Orient" that he had endured the worst torment, and it was there, even as American forces landed at Lingayen, that he had been sentenced to death by the Japanese for killing a guard. The pilot banked over Bataan, where the jungle still burned from the recent battles, and started to gain altitude. Over Corregidor their plane joined a great gaggle of machines, and Ashton watched as each in turn flew over the fortress. Parachute silks blossomed with each passing. It was only then that he realized that the paratroopers were to be dropped into battle on Corregidor.

Paul Ashton had a grandstand seat at one of the most remarkable airborne operations of the war. The island is such that there were only two drop zones, and these measured no more than 250 yards by 150 yards. Overlooked by the enemy defenses, there were additional hazards in that the undershoot and overshoot areas were bounded by 400-foot-high cliffs down to the sea. So precise were the requirements that not only did the C-47s have to come in one at a time, but, each also had to make three passes over the drop before all the paratroopers had jumped.

Now it was the turn of Ashton's plane. The young stone-faced "paras" stood up and hooked on their static lines. Paul craned his neck to watch out of his tiny window as the first stick made their descent. He couldn't see how any of them were going to hit the island—it was such a little thing. Below he could see the first of two waves of assault craft hitting the beaches around Monkey Point; that was where the Japanese had stormed ashore all that time ago.

On the third pass the last stick of paratroopers jumped, and the pilot set course for Leyte Gulf and the reception camp for POWs. The steady drone of the engine lulled Ashton into a reverie, and his mind slipped back to that last spring before the war began.

I. A SOLDIER'S PARADISE

April 10, 1941
HQ, 60th Coast Artillery
Fort Mills, Corregidor

For the Americans who lived and worked in the Philippines, that island archipelago was like India to the British, a hot and enervating land rich in servants and other amenities of colonial life. Pampered and closeted from the grimy realities of the industrial world, the rigidly stratified society had over the years spawned an imperial aristocracy with a life-style that few of their countrymen at home would have recognized. It was a land where living was opulent yet cheap so that fortunes hard earned need not be squandered in support of "standards." Even those in more humble occupations among the white community could afford servants and the best the island had to offer. Unlike the British in India who lived a Victorian dream, the United States had already granted commonwealth status to the Philippines as a transition to independence. There were those extremists among the ranks of the nationalists who, from sanctuary in Japan, sought to subvert the Constitution in their hot-tempered impatience for immediate statehood; but there was never the undercurrent of ill feeling found among the disaffected masses in India. While Gandhi and his Congress Party sought to obtain a hearing by public protest, Manuel Quezon was well into his first term as President of the Commonwealth and lived as position demanded in the Malacanan Palace in Manila.

There was, of course, the enemy, the Japanese, who even now were rampaging through China and would threaten from across the sea. Hardly a day seemed to pass without Manila newspapers relating in gory detail yet another Japanese atrocity committed on those hapless people. The Orange Plan, devised and studied ever since 1926 by students at the War College, assumed the Philippines to be the principal target for the Japanese. The grand strategy, as simple as it was naïve and more an article of faith than a cogent plan of war, envisaged that Japan would send its fleet against Lingayen Gulf, the most obvious bay for an amphibious invasion of Luzon and a descent on Manila. Thence the battleships of the U.S. Pacific Fleet would sally forth from their sanctuary at Pearl Harbor to succor the Philippines. There would be a grand victory somewhere in the South China Sea. In the unlikely event that the fleet should be delayed, then the garrison made up of American troops and Philippine Scouts would retreat into the mountain fastness of Bataan and onto the island forts until the Navy won through. America, after all, was an optimistic nation that had never known defeat.

Art Bressi, a chunky eighteen-year-old private from the Pennsylvania coalfields, looked forward, as he did every morning, to his long coffee break with the others. Bressi's world, ever since he had been assigned to the Philippines, was the Supply and Commissariat on Corregidor of the 60th Coast Artillery. It was the custom for the regimental quartermaster, Maj. Arnold D. Amoroso, a gunnery veteran of World War I, to hold court before an attentive and select audience: usually Bressi, a long-service supply sergeant named Cramer, and perhaps a couple of cronies who were "visiting" from the batteries on Topside. In the past, the little group had followed the war in Europe. Amoroso, an enthusiastic though amateur historian, had nailed a map mounted on board to the rough hewn concrete of the barrack block wall. They had followed the lightning *blitzkrieg* in the West and the fall of France. More recently their interest had centered on the campaign in the Western Desert and the exploits of the already legendary Rommel. The topic of conversation that morning, however, as elsewhere on the Rock, was the arrival of the *Republic*, an American Presidents Line cruiseship on her first trip under charter to the War Department as a transport. She had raised the Corregidor Light at dawn and was even then docking at Pier 7, Manila. Bressi, like many others, had scrambled onto a vantage point on the Rock to witness this great ship pass through the North Channel. He shuddered at the memories she had evoked. He had "ridden the rails" of that vessel for forty-two days from Brooklyn via Panama to Angel Island in San Francisco. The unremitting bouts of seasickness and the further agony he endured aboard the *Grant* en route to Manila would be his personal nightmare for the rest of his life, he thought. Events and time were to prove him sadly wrong.

"The fellas said I had the weakest stomach on the ship," said Bressi, by way of reminding the others of his anguish, "but hell, I could heave it as far as the next guy." Bressi's wit, already well known on the Rock, had certainly not deserted him in these lesser moments of trial.

"Normally the *Republic* wouldn't make a run from Frisco to the Philippines," Amoroso said, putting Bressi firmly in his place. "She's too damn big. Hell, there can't be much water between the keel and sea bottom at Pier 7." Amoroso relit his cigar stub, which in the heat had become a damp and sorry affair, and then continued. "I for one never took that scuttlebutt seriously about reinforcements for these garrisons. But shit, the *Republic* has got more than two thousand troops on board."

Bressi sickened at the thought of the hellhole of two thousand men living in those cramped conditions. Amoroso moved over to the battered coffee pot. He refilled his blackened and charred pint mug with that evil brew of coffee and rum known only to the "China hands," and then eased his ample and sweaty frame into his wooden, Army issue, revolving chair. He had the floor. The others recognized the signs and sat back as he proceeded to analyze the implications of the new arrivals. Their discussion developed along fairly predictable lines. After all, the war plans were an open secret, and in a peacetime garrison in the tropics there wasn't a great pressure of work. The 60th Coast Artillery was an anti-aircraft regiment, which at that time with eight hundred men had less than a third of its proper complement. It was known that their regiment alone could expect a thousand new recruits off the *Republic* and perhaps more to come from transports rumored to be en route across the Pacific. Though the garrison was right to be impressed by the appearance of the mighty *Republic*, what they could not know was that they were low down on the list of priorities, even in the Pacific. With a war raging in Europe and the Japanese part of the "Axis pact of steel," conflict in the Far East became a possibility too real to be ignored. However, Panama, Hawaii, and Alaska formed a strategic triangle seen in Washington as vital to the defense of the United States. Garrisons there were neglected and run down; their needs had to be met as a first priority. From the first, forces dispatched to the Philippines were grudgingly given.

Bressi, who had been on the Rock since February 1940, accepted the assessments of his betters without question. Not for the first time did he ponder the wisdom of his decision to enlist. His father was an Italian who had immigrated to the States in 1912. There he had met his wife, born and reared in the coalfields. Their mining community, with a population of less than two thousand, boasted two churches—one Catholic and the other Greek Orthodox—a couple of schools, and a half dozen poolrooms. The latter served as Bressi's education and social life. Nevertheless, much to his and the town's surprise, he graduated from the Catholic high school. He then drifted in and out of jobs, all related to mining. For a while he drove a truck hauling raw coal from bootleg mines.

Bressi's fists and the pick handle he carried in the cab came into use on more than one occasion when he crossed the picket lines. Later he drove a truck delivering dynamite, caps, and exploders. He was completely unaware of the deadliness of his load, and in his case ignorance was bliss, especially in a state still ravaged by the Depression. All that seemed to matter at the time was that it paid more than hauling raw coal.

Bressi's mercurial Italian temperament showed no signs of abating with the onset of manhood. He was no nearer to getting a union card. In 1940, out of work and a burden on his struggling parents, Bressi, like so many others destined to end up in Japanese prison camps, escaped into the Army. He really wanted to serve in China, but the Army had been withdrawn from there two years before. The choice for an overseas tour was Panama, Hawaii, or the Philippines, and Bressi picked the Philippines because it was just about as far as he could get from the coal mines of Pennsylvania.

The session over, Bressi walked across the parade ground that separated the Commissariat from his billet in the "Mile Long Barracks" on Topside. He had a deep sense of foreboding, which even the thought of lunch and a free afternoon could do nothing to dispel. "Hell, I haven't joined this outfit to fight a war," he complained to his buddies in the chow line.

As a sentiment it enjoyed widespread sympathy among so many young men, and though he couldn't put his finger on it, Bressi knew that in the arrival of the *Republic* he had witnessed an important event. One of the last things that the major had said still lingered in his mind.

"How are the Japs going to react if we start cramming troops into the Philippines?" he mused. "While we are weak and thin on the ground, we're nothing. But can they stand by and see a strong American garrison across their supply lines into China? Look at the problem the British on Malta are causing the Germans right now."

Bressi just knew that life was not going to be quite the same again.

Bill Garleb stepped off the *Republic* to the sound of the Regimental Band of the 31st United States Infantry. A bright eighteen-year-old kid who had nevertheless flunked out of high school, he joined the Army partly because he wanted to travel but more to escape the pain of an oppressive family life. Garleb had chosen the 31st Infantry because that was as far away from the United States as he could get. He also had a driving ambition to become a writer, and a two-year hitch in the Far East would, he thought, give him all the travel and adventure he needed by way of inspiration for his pen. Except for a couple of weeks of basic training, Garleb had been in the Army for only as long as the journey had taken, and he could hardly wait to start his new life. The music, the cheering, sweating faces of the Filipinos, the sounds and smells of Pier 7 assaulted his senses as he staggered down the gangway and left him totally bemused. This state of limbo did not, however, last for long; harassed sergeants shouted and bawled the recruits into the various units. Eventually, after seemingly endless delays, those destined for the 31st Infantry shuffled off toward the line of waiting trucks. By this time many unaccustomed to the tropics were beginning to suffer from the unrelenting combination of heat and humidity. Manfully they tried to march, but their shouldered packs scoured rivulets of black sweat down their backs. Uniforms specially kept for this occasion became sodden and misshapen, and their soft feet quickly blistered in hard, unyielding boots marching unevenly across the paved yard that led to the trucks. Even so, despite their idle life while in transit, anything was better than another hour spent below decks in the *Republic*.

From the pier the six-by-sixes drove the few short miles to the perimeter of Nichols Field. There a tented "city" had recently been established. This was to be home for the next month while the recruits were quarantined and given training. The journey took them out of the seedy dockland areas of downtown Manila and along the tree-lined boulevard that skirted Manila Bay. They drove through Pasay, where the youngsters gazed in wide-eyed wonderment at the luxuriously appointed homes that belonged to the rich Americans and Europeans. These stood in stark contrast to the dives and hovels of the shantytown barrio that had sprung up along the B Range Road that led in turn to their camp.

The entire 31st Infantry was quartered in Manila. This did not amount to much, because all three battalions were less than a third up to strength. Two battalions were quartered on the military reservation called Fort McKinley, to the southeast of the city, while the 1st Battalion together with regimental HQ were in the Intramuros—the old walled city of Manila.

Even though life was meant to be harder for the GIs in boot camp, Garleb and the others soon slipped into the easy tropical routine of garrison life. The working day began with reveille at 0700 hours. On $21 a month even a private could afford a Filipino to launder clothing, press his campaign hat into the favored style, and keep his barrack space clean. Lunch was at 1130 hours followed by a siesta, and then the men were free for the rest of the day. There were organized sports and team games for those who were interested, but for the most part the soldiers were left entirely to their own devices.

For many on the two-year tour, life in the 31st was a vacation. Some of those on a second hitch had taken a Filipino woman and set up housekeeping in a nearby barrio. In a few units, especially the Air Corps, the enlisted men almost universally lived with Philippine girls. This was considered a good thing and condoned by the authorities, despite the dubious morality. The men could buy a nipa shack or have the natives build one for about fifty dollars. In the barrio they found life easier and certainly cheaper. Living off the base and with one woman helped reduce drunkenness and venereal disease. For these reasons the Philippine Department was even prepared to pay a food allowance for the men to live off the base.

For many more it was the seamy side of Manila, where everything was available at a price, that proved the main attraction of garrison life in the tropics. Consequently alcoholism was endemic in the 31st Infantry, and the medics waged a ceaseless battle against venereal disease.

Richard Sakakida's departure aroused no interest from those

who still lingered around the now silent *Republic*. That was as it should be for an undercover agent. Darkness came with all the sudden finality of the tropics as he scurried on his way into the city. Born in Hawaii of Japanese parents who had immigrated at the turn of the century, Richard had only recently graduated from high school in Honolulu. Then and unknowingly, he was recruited into "the service."

The United States Army Philippines Department had asked the War Department for one or two men who spoke Japanese. In the course of time that requirement was passed down the line to the U.S. Army Hawaiian Department, where it landed up on the desk of Col. Walter J. Gilbert, ROTC instructor and professor of military science and tactics for all the schools in Hawaii. Sakakida was an ROTC cadet officer and along with many others of his background went through a rigorous selection process. Under the cover of simply seeking linguists, boards of Army and Navy officers conducted exhaustive interviews, and the candidates were also subjected to oral and written examinations. By the time this process had run its course it was spring, and Sakakida, having given up all hope of a university education, was working for a furniture company and supporting his widowed mother. On March 13 Sakakida was just leaving home for work when Colonel Gilbert picked him up and drove straight to HQ, U.S. Hawaiian Department.

"Congratulations, Richard," the colonel said as he acknowledged the salute of the Marine sentry who had checked his ID at the entrance to a long corridor off the main concourse. "Washington has just sent back the results of the test. You came out on top."

This news barely registered as Richard realized they were in a part of the HQ he had never visited before. As they walked into the G-2 office, Sakakida felt that something was wrong. Colonel Gilbert swore him in and it was only after he had taken the oath that Sakakida realized he was in "the service." In fact, Richard Sakakida found himself a member of the Counter Intelligence Police (the forerunner of the Counter Intelligence Corps of U.S. Army Intelligence). He was given the rank of sergeant. In bold and simple terms Colonel Gilbert briefed Sakakida on his mission: He was to infiltrate the Japanese community in Manila.

For the next month he received intensive training in codes and ciphers, and especially on how to select and recognize "items of prime interest" to the War Department. At the end of this time he shipped out on the *Republic*. Only his mother and immediate family knew that he was in the Army, let alone leaving Hawaii. Sakakida boarded the ship in civilian clothes with the cover story that he was a crew member who would be assigned a duty after the ship docked in Manila. While Garleb and the others disembarked to a heroes' welcome, G-2 officers briefed Sakakida in the privacy of his cabin. As an undercover agent, his task was to determine which and how many of the more than two thousand Japanese in Manila would possibly be associated with the Japanese military. Given a new identity as a sales representative of Sears, Roebuck, Sakakida booked into the small hotel that his contacts had recommended. Frightened, confused, and very much alone, he learned by heart the details of his new life and prepared to embark upon his mission. He memorized the telephone numbers of his Intelligence controllers, destroyed the evidence, and worked long into the night reading the sales brochures and literature of his cover.

It took just a few days for the *Republic* to be cleansed and prepared for the return trip. The soldiers whose hitch was up boarded for the return trip Stateside. These few hundred men, however, were not the only passengers; there were also Army wives from the East Coast, their children, and baggage. The War Department had ordered them home.

Capt. Bill Massello, a West Pointer commanding Battery E, 60th Coast Artillery, had brought his wife across from Corregidor. They had been in the Philippines since 1939, and this was the first time they had been parted. As they embraced for the last time and the officers were ordered ashore, the ship prepared to sail by way of Shanghai and Honolulu for the Panama Canal and ultimately New York.

Bressi didn't like Wild Bill Massello. Unlike most of the regular officers on the Rock, Massello was convinced that war was coming, and he was determined that his men, in his battery at least, would be fit to fight. There was no tropical routine for Battery E on Corregidor. He worked his men from reveille until dark. Then three times a week he would hold night exercises. These would invariably take the form of night marches around the fifteen miles of shoreline, in which the clerks of HQ Company would be "induced" to partake. Bressi didn't like the night route marches. They would be conducted in absolute blackness to condition the men to the absence of lights in case of war. With full combat pack, rifle, and helmet, the marchers would toil along the island trails, some perilously close to cliffs where it was five hundred feet straight down to the beach below. The night the *Republic* sailed Massello led his men at a particularly punishing pace. Bressi, way back down the line, knew why and sobbed out his curses as he tried to maintain the pace. If this was preparation for war, then all he could do was hope and fervently pray that his tour in the Army would be over before the real thing occurred. It was a sentiment he shared with all the young men in that sweaty and confused column.

May 8, 1941
The Army and Navy Club
Dewey Boulevard, Manila

The U.S.S. *Washington* docked at Pier 9 on May 8, 1941. It was the hottest day of the year. The liner, chartered as a troop transport by the War Department, had left Angel Island, San Francisco, on April 25 with twelve hundred officers and three thousand enlisted men. That was just two weeks before Capt. Leslie Zimmerman's wife gave birth to a daughter. Zimmerman, a Baptist chaplain in the Air Corps, had orders to report to Nichols Field, which had now become the nucleus for the expanding Far Eastern Air Force. This mild and gentle man of God, though wise to the ways of soldiery, was to need all his tact and guile in this new posting. At least Zimmerman walked into this with his eyes open, for he had been warned in the States that the Army's Philippines Department, with its pragmatic approach to public morality and above all its desire for a quiet life, would have scant regard for any chaplain with a crusading disposition!

That evening the Army and Navy Club held a reception. It was in part a *bien venito* for the new arrivals and an *au revoir*, for the wives and families from the West Coast were to return with the *Washington*. The club excelled itself that night. Despite the heat and humidity, the guests enjoyed themselves as the dance band played and the wine flowed freely. Situated about a block away from the Manila

Hotel, and with its back to the bay, this mecca of the social scene had the untarnished reputation that it could produce any dish under the sun.

The MacArthurs made one of their rare appearances at the club that night. Their entry, as always, was nothing less than regal. This Philippine generalissimo, officially retired from the U.S. Army, now in command of the Philippine Army, completely upstaged both the U.S. Army garrison commander, General Grunert, and the peppery Admiral Hart of the Asiatic Fleet. Grunert had known MacArthur for years and understood the private hurt behind the public face. Hart, who at best tolerated anything Army and personally disliked MacArthur, seethed with indignation. MacArthur, flanked by his coterie of aides and chosen Filipino friends, acknowledged the two senior officers, totally unaware of their response to his presence.

Jean MacArthur looked like a million dollars. Not subject to the U.S. Army discipline, and because her husband was in the pay of the Philippine Government, she was under no compulsion to return home. The party did not stay long, but Leslie Zimmerman did get to shake the great man's hand as the immaculate MacArthur mingled with the throng with all the practiced poise of a viceroy before he returned to the privacy of his six-room air-conditioned penthouse atop the Manila Hotel. Once rid of the need to maintain that public face, MacArthur could pace the floor, awaiting the phone call from Washington with an impatience that few outside the room knew he possessed. It was all very well being a Philippine field marshal and serving in this land that he loved; but it wasn't his own country. As the war clouds gathered, MacArthur felt isolated and remote from the centers of "momentous decision making." He yearned for a recall to active duty.

A mile away downtown, deep inside the walled city and close to the Pasig River, which bisects Manila, Richard Sakakida occupied his now customary place at the Japanese Club. By this time he had established his routine. Each morning he would leave his hotel, as befitting a representative of Sears, Roebuck, but then he would while away the hours until the business day was over. Cinemas and discreet cafes together with a little sightseeing filled in the time nicely. Then it was back to the hotel, with time to shower and change before walking the few blocks to the club. Most evenings there were some men of affairs in the Japanese community who gathered there to enjoy the customs and traditions of their homeland. Sakakida was deep in conversation with his "target," a bicycle salesman who had a store close to the main entrance of the Cavite naval base.

June 24, 1941
HQ, 57th Infantry, Philippine Scouts
Fort McKinley, near Manila

The *President Pierce* docked at Pier 7 on June 24, 1941. This was her first voyage as an Army transport, and the old lady still retained all the trappings and opulence of her cruising days. For the three hundred officers and thirty nurses, it had been the trip of a lifetime. Even the five hundred enlisted men had few grounds for complaint. Also on board were thirty-five pilots who were going to China to join General Chennault's American Volunteer Group— the Flying Tigers. These were the first of the one-hundred pilots en route to the AVG training camp at Kyedaw Field at Toungoo, Burma, some 175 miles north of Rangoon.

Lts. John Spainhower and Loyd Mills were from similar backgrounds and were heading for the same regiment, the elite 57th Infantry, Philippine Scouts. Loyd Mills was a young, sharp-eyed Texan. He had been commissioned from the Citizens Military Training Camps and had been on active duty for over a year training draftees at Fort Wallis. Along with three other officers of the 38th Infantry, he had been selected for service in the Philippines. Only one was to come home. John Spainhower at twenty-two years old was the same age as Loyd Mills but had been commissioned via the ROTC in Oklahoma.

The Philippine Scouts was regarded as one of the finest fighting formations in the United States Army. To its officers and men, certainly there was none finer. The officers were American and the enlisted men were native Filipino. Many of the latter were long-service Regular Army men. They were an extremely proud bunch who reveled in the spit and polish of their regiment. The fathers, or at least a relative, most of the soldiers were old retired Scouts. It was encumbent upon whichever family member took a retiring Scout's place to keep up the high standards, and some of the noncommissioned officers in the regiment had seen well over thirty years of military service. The Scouts held an enviable position in Philippine life.

The twelve thousand men authorized by Congress were divided into the 45th and 57th Infantry, the 23rd and 81st Artillery regiments, the 26th Cavalry, and support arms. The cavalry was still horse mounted with saber squadrons, and the only deference to the machine age was made to the reconnaissance troops, who had half-tracks.

The adjutant, 2nd Battalion, 57th Infantry Philippine Scouts, looked resplendent in lacquered mahogany riding boots and gleaming spurs. His shirt had the regulation exaggerated creases in the style of the Scouts. The pith helmet, white and stiff, was tipped just slightly forward over the eyes, the black restraining strap regulation length in a half loop under his lower lip. This military paragon was complete with Sam Browne belt and saber. John Spainhower and Loyd Mills, together with two other newly arrived young officers, felt decidedly unmilitary and uncomfortable in their khaki shirt sleeves and forage caps. Nevertheless, they were taken aback by the easy formality of the greeting and briefing. Having first apologized for the absence of the commanding officer, who was away playing polo against the 26th Cavalry, the adjutant showed them around the lines. Such was their first encounter with that phenomenon of military lore. Elite regiments the world over have one thing in common—an absence of formality among their officers, which in their field formations transcends rank.

Just a few hours later the newly arrived, showered and changed into suits, gathered at the bar in the Officers' Club and compared notes. Already orderlies were hard at work unpacking their bags. Ahead of them lay long hours with hot spoons and layered polish to burnish the new leather into the standard expected of an officer in the Scouts.

"The last thing I need is an alarm clock," said John Spainhower. "My rooms in the BOQ [Bachelor Officers' Quarters] are right under the reveille cannon!" He was right, but within a week was profoundly glad of that room. He was taken into battalion HQ to act as adjutant. As the officer most directly responsible for discipline and order in the battalion, he had to set a good example and appear at headquarters on time every day.

As the light faded, other officers drifted into the bar, and the group broke up as they met their new company commanders. Loyd Mills joined Captain Bessant of Company C and learned about his platoon.

"The battalion is still on peacetime routine," Bessant said, "but for how much longer I can't say. So you better get the most out of this existence while you can."

Mills reckoned he needed no urging on that score!

"Reveille is at 0600," Bessant continued, "and I expect you in company lines with the platoon by 0715. That'll give you time enough for a good breakfast here. And make the most of it, because it's the best time of the day to eat. Duties finish at midday, afternoons and evenings are free."

John Bessant was only a year or two older than Mills, and there were no other American officers in the company. The two quickly established a happy rapport while Bessant regaled his junior with tales of the delights of the Manila social scene—polo, golf, surfing, riding, and pig sticking for the energetic.

"How do we manage for women?" Mills asked. "We were totally outnumbered on the way out, and anyhow the nurses give all their attention to the Flying Tigers."

"Most of the service families have left, but there are plenty of women around," Bessant said. "There are the nurses at Stotsenberg, but the flyboys out at Clark tend to beat us to it. But hell, the local Filipino girls, especially those from the rich families, now they are something else."

The famed beauty of Filipino women had not been lost on the impressionable Mills. Even during his short drive through Manila that afternoon, what he had seen had more than lived up to expectations. Appetites aroused, Bessant suggested they should celebrate Mills's arrival by dining out that evening. He quickly cleared the details with the adjutant, who had no objections, since it was extremely unlikely the colonel would return that night. An hour and three cocktails later the two young officers, now suitably attired in white tuxedoes, cheerfully acknowledged the precision salute of the quarter guard. Bessant turned left onto the B Range Road and accelerated his convertible toward Manila.

The U.S.S. *Grant* docked later that month. Bressi had the duty in the Corregidor Light and watched her head through the South Channel toward Manila. Ed Erickson and a group of other pilots were as glad to get off that ship as Bressi had been. They had drunk her dry of Scotch. Erickson was a "ninety-day wonder." He was part of the first Air Corps class to graduate through the West Coast Training Command. Twenty years of age and bored with college life, this 6-foot, 4-inch Californian joined the Air Corps ahead of the draft. After just a short period of induction and quarantine at Clark Field, some 60 miles north of Manila, Erickson joined the 17th Pursuit Squadron at Nichols Field.

It was at Nichols that Erickson had his introduction to the P-36 pursuit plane. Initially these planes had been intended for Sweden, together with a hundred Curtiss P-40B Tomahawks. Even the hard-pressed British had turned down the Tomahawks because they were inferior to the Messerschmitt 109s, while the Air Force in the States was equipping with the newer, faster, and more heavily armed P-40E Kittyhawks. So some of the Tomahawks were sent to the Flying Tigers in Burma, and the 17th Pursuit got the P-36s. All the dials on the instrument panel were metric, and the air speed indicator showed kilometers. Crew chiefs spent the first couple of days making cardboard cutouts and working on conversion tables.

Erickson's crew chief's name was Whitelow. He was a sad and disappointed man who had been in the Philippines since 1939 with the 20th Air Base Group. After two years he was due to rotate home, but they had just extended his tour for a further year in order to cope with the expansion in the pursuit squadrons. Had he been rotated, Whitelow would have sailed home on the *Grant*. A quiet taciturn man, he accepted his fate and, determined to get the most out of his extra year, turned with a will to servicing the P-36s. Whitelow considered the P-36 to be "a mighty fine little airplane," and he was particularly impressed with its rotary engine.

So while the pilots waited for their Tomahawks, they flew the P-36s and Erickson came, if somewhat reluctantly, to admire its handling, though in ceiling, speed, and rate of climb it was hopelessly outclassed by almost all fighters in service. Also, the plane was sadly undergunned, and there was little armored protection for the pilots.

Lt. Boyd D. Wagner, known as Buzz to his friends, commanded the squadron. Though just a little older than his rookie pilots, he was a born leader and a natural flier. He commanded the respect and admiration of the youngsters and set about welding them into an effective fighting unit. They all sported checkerboard baseball caps with "17th" emblazoned across the front. The pilots wore these whenever they were not actually flying. By these and other means Wagner fostered an *esprit de corps* among his young men.

The flights rotated in turn to Iba Field, a primitive grass strip high up on the western coast of Luzon and overlooking the South China Sea. It boasted one of the two early-warning radar sets in the Philippines. The pilots would spend four or five days at a time operating out of Iba. Here they practiced all the skills of pursuit flying. Occasionally a B-23 out of Clark would obligingly allow itself to be intercepted. Life and living was primitive at Iba; but there was the sea and surfing, the sun and good fresh living for these zestful young men.

And there was Manila on the weekend.

II. Call to Arms

July 23, 1941–
November 26, 1941

July 26, 1941
No. 1 Calle Victoria
Intramuros, Manila

The Japanese descended upon Indochina, and the Vichy French, humiliated, bowed to the inevitable. The Japanese Imperial Navy sailed into Camranh Bay, the finest natural harbor in the Orient. Thirty thousand Japanese soldiers and marines landed at Saigon and Haiphong. President Roosevelt's response was immediate, and thus the fate of the Philippines was sealed.

Presidential decrees froze Japanese assets in the United States, denied the Panama Canal to Japanese shipping, and slapped a crippling embargo on the export of strategic raw materials—rubber, oil, and metals to Japan. Britain and the Netherlands followed suit.

War between Japan and the United States was now a matter of timing. On July 26, the president ordered the American and Filipino forces to combine into a single Army. MacArthur was recalled to active duty and given the high command. Remustered as a major general, twenty-four hours later he was promoted to lieutenant general, and shortly afterward he was given his fourth star.

There were twenty-two thousand Americans in the islands under his command. The only combat unit was the Philippine Division, composed of the understrength battalions of the 31st Infantry, the Scouts, and the horse troopers of the 26th Cavalry. The Philippine Army was in the process of mobilizing and expanding to its planned target of ten territorial divisions. However, in reality the force levels were well below the intended strength, and the quality very disappointing. The profusion of dialects and universal illiteracy among the Filipino recruits presented almost insurmountable hurdles, while the $1 million that was all the near-bankrupt Philippine exchequer was prepared to devote to defense in the year before Pearl Harbor meant that MacArthur couldn't buy his way out of trouble. Except for the paramilitary Philippine constabulary, and that force was little better, it was a paper army with pâpier-maché helmets and guns made of bamboo.

An air of unreality gripped MacArthur at his headquarters in the "House on the Wall" and thence permeated throughout the city. MacArthur's energy was boundless and his optimism contagious. It affected everyone with whom he came into contact. General Grunert briefed MacArthur on the strengths and weaknesses of the American garrison, and then left for home singing his praises. Admiral Hart declared a truce, and for a while at least saw his pitifully ancient and inadequate Asiatic Fleet in a new light.

MacArthur very quickly scrapped the original plans for the defense of Luzon. His was an impossible position for a man of honor, for he had to serve the Presidents of both the United States and the Philippines, and they had conflicting demands. A premature retreat into the fortress of Corregidor and the mountain fastness of Bataan might serve the needs of the Americans—but would mean the abandonment of the Philippine Army and people. Such a move was unthinkable to MacArthur, the officer and gentleman, however expedient militarily. He could not leave Manila to the tender mercy of the Japanese horde while he cowered in Corregidor. And it was against his nature as a "red-blooded American" to give up without a fight. But his instinct and military flair, which had served him so well in the past, deserted him now in his hour of greatest need.

The assumptions upon which he issued his orders from the House on the Wall for the defense of Luzon were flawed, and later, in the opening stages of the war, undermined by the incompetence of subordinates. MacArthur believed that the Japanese would not attack until the hot season. He had therefore until April 1942 to prepare his defenses. By then, he reasoned, his excellent Filipinos, with the promised stiffening of American combat units, would be more than a match for the Japanese, whose fighting qualities, in his arrogance, he dismissed.

The enemy were to be denied the beaches. While Hart's submarines hounded the invasion convoys, MacArthur's divisions would hit them at their weakest point—before they massed ashore in strength. The general ordered the staff of his new command, the

United States Armed Forces Far East (USAFFE), to conduct a thorough study of the likely beaches and how best they could be denied to the invader.

MacArthur's unreality was also reflected in grand strategy and in the corridors of power in Washington. In June 1941, after a series of high-level and top-secret conferences with British officers, War Plan 5 had been agreed to and adopted by Roosevelt's Joint Army-Navy Board. On the assumption of a world war, it was the Allied intention to pursue a "Europe first strategy." So far as the Philippines and the Far East were concerned, the Allies would pursue a "defensive strategy." That was a rather polite way of saying that the Philippines would be abandoned to the enemy.

This was not because the planners believed that a Japanese strike on Pearl Harbor would cut the lifeline to the Philippines. Nobody in authority saw Pearl Harbor as even threatened. From the very first the planners in Washington had anticipated that the Japanese attack on the Philippines would be prepared in the greatest secrecy and precede or at best coincide with a formal declaration of war. The most that the defenders could hope for was just a couple of days' advance warning. The Japanese intention was seen to be the capture of Manila and its harbor defenses in order to occupy the Philippines, sever the American lines of communication, and deny the United States a naval base in the western Pacific.

Against this threat the task of the American garrison was to hold the entrance to Manila Bay and to deny its use to the enemy for as long as possible. The plan optimistically called for the defense to hold out for six months, by which time the Pacific Fleet would have fought its way into Manila Bay to succor the fortresses.

Nobody in Washington believed such a rescue was possible. The Philippine Islands are strategically located in the very heart of the Far East; Manila is over 5,000 miles from Honolulu and less than 1,700 miles from Tokyo. The islands lie athwart the main trade routes from China and Japan through the South China Sea and thence into resource-rich Southeast Asia and the Dutch East Indies. Japanese air bases on Formosa were only 700 miles from Manila. It took three days to fly by Pan American clipper the 7,000 miles to San Francisco. With these distances involved, the resources were simply not available to fight a war on two fronts.

No evacuation plans for the Philippines could be ordered. Instead, those select few in Washington and London privy to the contents of War Plan 5 would have to live a lie. Naval experts anticipated that it would take the fleet at least two years to fight their way across the Pacific. War Plan 5 said nothing but the assumptions were clear: Once their supplies were exhausted the defenders would have to surrender.

The great American public might forgive a defeat in the Philippines after a spirited resistance, but the public outcry could destroy the Administration if they thought their boys had been abandoned. Roosevelt and the Chief of Staff, General Marshall, knew the charade had to be played out to the end. "Sufficient" reinforcements and supplies, suitably packaged in a patriotic fervor, had to be sent to the Philippines and its headline-hungry, ready-made hero.

In the meantime MacArthur and his staff worked around the clock on their plans, blissfully ignorant of War Plan 5. He would remain so until early in October.

MacArthur was recalled to active duty on a Sunday. That day the *Harrison*, a cruise liner, docked in Manila. The ship had sailed from San Francisco nine weeks earlier, and her ports of call had been Honolulu, Shanghai, and Hong Kong.

One of the first passengers to disembark was an FBI field agent. Malcolm Champlin had graduated in 1934 from the U.S. Naval Academy. Three years later, because of poor eyesight, he voluntarily resigned his commission and then studied law at the University of California at Berkeley. Champlin spent just one year practicing law after graduation before being recruited into the FBI as a special agent. His arrival, in the uniform of a naval officer, in the Philippines was a bureaucratic blunder. Still a reserve officer, the Navy had failed to recognize his special circumstances and by the time the FBI had lodged an appeal through official channels to cancel his call-up it was too late.

Champlin had been assigned as aide to the Rear Admiral Commanding the 16th Naval District, Manila Bay. Wearing the regulation white drills and the aiguillettes of his office, he duly reported for duty at the Commandancia in Cavite Naval Yard. The small, cramped yard with its stuccoed buildings, mute evidence of Spain's occupation, was a hive of activity. A number of submarines were being prepared for sea while the tender *Canopus* was warped close in to the jetty and received the finishing touches to her long overhaul.

August 13, 1941
Organization Day, 31st Infantry
Fort Santiago, Manila

On Wednesday, August 13, the 31st Infantry celebrated its Silver Anniversary. The whole day was given over to ceremony, pomp, and pageantry. In the morning there was a parade and a military tattoo on Wallace Field; this was a broad expanse of grass where the moat surrounding the walled city had been covered over. It seemed to Bill Garleb as if all of Manila was there as he marched onto the parade ground with the others in his squad. They went through the drills of the 30mm Browning machine gun with an accomplished precision and to the applause of the vast crowd. For Garleb, Organization Day was simply the happiest day of his life. It was like the graduation he had never had from high school.

Even by the standards of a rookie, Garleb had had a rough passage in Company H, 2nd Battalion. Though a competent soldier, his seriousness and quietly religious ways marked him out as a man apart. One evening he and another man were returning from a movie at the Cuartel de España. Garleb as usual was describing what he saw as the hidden message of the film. The other man turned on him savagely. "Garleb, why don't you knock off that shit," he said, and strode furiously away into the night. The rejection hurt. Garleb could not understand what he had done wrong. Only slowly did it dawn on him that there were things which it was better not to talk of to others.

Nevertheless he was determined to make something of himself as a soldier, if only because he had been such an abysmal failure in civilian life. At first the others were irritated by his search for perfection, then amused, and finally came to respect his skills and knowledge. He became an expert on the machine gun.

Garleb preferred himself as a soldier. It was a new book, a new beginning for a young man who sought to buy himself some respect. That respect took a while in coming; his company commander, Captain Volckmann, thought he was trying to "polish the apple" and for a while was openly hostile. The GIs, and particularly Sergeant Eckhardt, began to think differently. One day shortly before the parade, Garleb was returning to the barracks when he came across Torkleson, the company drunk. In his drunken state he had fallen into the monsoon ditch that surrounded the camp. He was bloody, and he was a mess. He lay there supine in his vomit and urine. Garleb helped him back to the billet, where he washed and dressed his cuts, put him to bed, and had his soiled clothes laundered. The others had been silent witness to this and saw Garleb in a new light.

Garleb earned his nickname of "Prof" by solving the problem of athlete's foot in the company. This highly contagious complaint spreads quickly in the tropics, and the battalion medics had no remedy. The recommended compounds of iodine proved singularly ineffective. Garleb wrote home to his family doctor, who advised a compound of boric acid. It worked, and the company was grateful. Others in the company, the illiterate, turned to "Prof" to write their letters home. In a regiment like the 31st Infantry this service was much in demand.

Despite the monsoon period, the day stayed bright and fine. MacArthur took time off from the House on the Wall and received the salute as the regiment marched by in review order. The sports and athletics followed in the afternoon, and there was a magnificent regimental barbecue in Harrison Park. The day ended with the annual Boxing Festival at Rizal Stadium. Even the old sweats admitted it was the best Organization Day they could remember.

The next day Garleb started a six-week course at the Army Intelligence School in Fort Santiago. The codes and cipher, the map reading and intense study satisfied at least some of his intellectual needs. Though the company had accepted him on their terms, he still felt the loneliness of those who lacked a friend they could talk to as an equal. There was a great deal of Bill Garleb not being used. Yet with all his study and introspection, even Garleb did not anticipate war. For him as for almost everyone else, that was something happening to other people—and thousands of miles away.

August 23, 1941
School of Artillery, Philippine Scouts
Fort Stotsenberg, Clark Field

Washington was playing the charade to the hilt. In late August the *President Hoover* docked in Manila. Among the three hundred reserve officers were many newly trained "specialists," particularly in artillery. George Crane, Winston Jones, and Thomas Harrison were part of a clutch of ROTC officers who had all just finished specialist schools in gunnery or transportation and had had a tour of duty with an artillery battalion in the States. These three officers, assigned to different battalions at Fort Stotsenberg, were horrified by the weapons that awaited them on their first day of duty.

All the artillery battalions were still way below strength. That was to be expected in an army that was still trying desperately to mobilize; they had experienced the same in the States. What they had never encountered were the museum pieces that masqueraded as field artillery. Crane and Harrison were assigned to batteries equipped with the "2.95" field gun, sometimes called the "French 75" because the bore size was the same, more or less. The gun was intended to be carried on pack mules and could be broken down for that purpose. By this time, however, mechanization had arrived, which simply meant that the gun was mounted on the bed of a 2½-ton truck. Two wooden planks were used as ramps to run the gun from the ground into the vehicle.

The little gun stood about 3 feet high and had a wicked recoil—more than enough to send the trail smashing into the cab of the truck if the gun was fired. But the need was for self-propelled artillery, and so the ingenious gunners roped the wheels of the gun to lessen the recoil and then lashed the trail firmly to the truckbed.

So the Philippine Scouts, in the spirit of improvisation abroad at the time, acquired its self-propelled artillery. The only problem was that the trucks had to be reversed into action. The three young officers were aghast at the sight of these contraptions. Later they were to revise their opinions in the close terrain and jungles of Bataan. The short barrels and high angle of fire gave the gun all the characteristics of mortars.

Winston Jones came from Oklahoma. A product of the ROTC, he had been trying to join the Regular Army for a couple of years. The most he had achieved was extended reserve officer training. Even so he had passed through the gunnery course at Fort Sill, attended the famous Louisiana Maneuvers the previous year, and served a hitch with the 6th Infantry Division. Slightly built, with dark, penetrating eyes and a ready air of authority about him, Jones volunteered for Philippine service as soon as the vacancies were announced. He felt a war was coming, and he believed the real enemy to be Japan.

Shortly after arriving at Fort Stotsenberg Jones was appointed the battalion motor officer, 1st Battalion, 11th Field Artillery, Philippine Scouts. This battalion was better off than most when it came to field artillery. The batteries had two types of field pieces. The best was the French 75mm, manufactured in the United States and used by the AEF in France in World War I. They had since been modernized with an improved hydraulic recoil and rubber tires on both gun and limber. Provided the road surface was smooth, the gun and limber could be towed into battle at a sedate 25 miles an hour.

One battery of four guns was so equipped. The other two had the British Model 1911 18-pounder. Worn out from five years on the Western Front, they had been purchased as war surplus by a penny-pinching U.S. Government, dumped in Hawaii, and then shipped to the Philippines just two months before. Jones's first task was to adapt them to be towed by trucks, though where the pneumatic tires would come from to replace the iron-rimmed, wooden-spoked wheels, he hadn't the faintest idea. Events were to overtake him before that problem had been resolved.

Winston Jones very quickly established a rapport with his battalion motor sergeant. A good and thoughtful officer who cared for the men in his charge, Jones soon passed the various initiation tests that it was the custom of the Filipino to set for the American.

Jones purchased a 1934 Packard convertible sedan. It was reputed that there were only two in the Philippines at this time. One was owned by President Quezon and the other by a wealthy colonel on the staff at Stotsenberg. The Army wives had long since gone home, and the colonel had a chauffeured staff car to meet his needs. It was sad to see this gleaming white monster gathering dust and mildew, so he was happy to sell it to Jones. Each Friday at lunchtime the motor sergeant would pick up the Packard from Jones and drive to his home in the nearby barrio. There he and his son would clean and simonize the car.

On Saturday at twelve noon precisely the sergeant would pull up outside the bungalow that Jones now shared with two other officers. Dressed in pith helmet and finest uniform, shining to the hilt in a shining car, the sergeant was ready to chauffeur his officers to a night on the town. After depositing the officers at the club the sergeant would take the car into a compound inside the walled city.

He would stay with his charge all night rather than entrust it to another's care.

At the Officers' Club in Manila standards were changing. Women, who had been unacceptable months previously, were acceptable now. Officers entered, still dressed in the customary white tropical drills, but with White Russians and even mustees, or half castes, on their arms.

August 25, 1941
Clark Field, Central Luzon

Major "Rosie" O'Donnell called the tower and made ready to land at Clark Field. He led his squadron of B-17Cs in three tight Vs of three in a last majestic sweep of the little field before they broke formation and prepared to set down. The gunners at Stotsenberg and the horse troopers of the 26th stared in wonderment as these mighty four-engined giants thundered across the sky. The whole world seemed to explode with the sight and the sound of them as, pterodactyl-like, they swooped in low over the military cantonment.

Two weeks previously at the Newfoundland meeting, Churchill had praised the performance of the "Flying Fortress" in the air war against Germany. Rosie O'Donnell's epic flight from Hickam Field in Hawaii was living proof that the Philippines could be reinforced from the air.

General "Hap" Arnold, the Air Corps chief back in Washington, was convinced that the bombers represented something even more—a physical deterrent against Japanese aggression. More B-17s would be sent until the Japanese would be discouraged from descending on the Philippines.

The British had much the same thought about the need for a deterrent. They dispatched the *Prince of Wales* and the *Repulse* to Singapore.

September 2, 1941
Seaward defense batteries, 60th Coast Artillery
Fort Mills, Corregidor

From the air Corregidor, formed largely of volcanic rock, looks like a giant tadpole with its tail swung to the left, swimming through the mouth of Manila Bay to the South China Sea. It's about 3¼ miles long and just over 1 mile at its widest. The "tail," called "Bottomside," contained the two docks and the barrio San José, a couple of shops and storehouses. Farther out toward the tip, where the island is less than 600 yards across, was the Naval Radio Intercept Station and Kindley Field, a small grass strip capable of handling light aircraft. At the base of the tail is Malinta Hill, high and precipitous, forming a formidable barrier, especially against enemy troops advancing from the tail, where the only landing beaches are located.

The land west of Malinta Hill is called "Middleside." The hospital, officers' and NCOs' quarters, the Officers' Club, and even some schools were spaced out among luscious shrubs and well-kept lawns.

The high and bulbous head is "Topside." The headquarters and the parade ground were complemented by the Mile Long Barracks—a two-story "bombproof" stone building, reputedly the longest barracks in the world. Most of the big sea defense batteries were sited on Topside. The 12-inch rifles of Batteries Wheeler and Crockett dated from 1895, while the 12-inch mortars in Geary and Way were older still.

One thing above all else attracted the attention of the garrison, officers and enlisted men alike: the tunnel complex that had been blasted through Malinta Hill from one end to the other. Heralded as one of the wonders of the age, the main tunnel, constructed in 1932, was of reinforced concrete, 1,400 feet long and 30 feet wide at its base. The walls formed an arch rising to 20 feet above the floor. The island's electric rail system, double-tracked, ran through the concourse. From the main tunnel 25 laterals branched out on either side at regular intervals. The laterals were each 150 feet long and dead-ended, except for the one that led into a further complex containing a 300-bed hospital.

The tunnels were intended primarily for the storage of supplies, equipment, and ammunition to be used by the Harbor Defense

Forces. They were already being stocked with six months' supply for the guns and a defense force of 7,000 troops. None could fail to be impressed with this bombproof labyrinth.

However, the tunnel complex was damp and poorly ventilated and, except for the hospital, never intended to quarter humans. Over the years it had been extended and improved. There was now a quartermaster complex which led in turn to a Navy tunnel. This housed the radios and communications for USAFFE. A long lateral connected with the Malinta Hospital Tunnel from the north; another one, to the naval storage tunnel to the south. Each of these tunnels had its own exit. The Malinta hospital tunnel (north entrance) opened on the dirt road that ran around the north side of Malinta Hill, and the Malinta Naval tunnel on the south road. Another tunnel, dug into the west side of the hill at approximately the same level and to the north of the main tunnel, could store ten thousand gallons of reserve motor fuel.

Capt. Arnold Boettcher was the contracting officer for some of the Army tunnels. He had been dispatched to the Rock in June 1941 from the Engineers' Office of the Philippines Department.

Boettcher together with his surveyors and crew had designed and blasted five new laterals off the main tunnel. His instructions had been precise, even down to the specifications of their furnishings. Unlike the other laterals, they were painted and furnished with cots, tables, even armchairs and carpets. These new laterals were intended to house President Quezon, Commissioner Sayre, General MacArthur, their staffs, and their families.

Corregidor and her sister forts, Frank, Drum, and Hughes, were designed to guard the anchorages of Manila Bay from a threat from the sea, but with guns even older and more obsolete than anything that Winston Jones had to cope with in the Field Artillery back on the mainland.

The island was spotted with huge open gun pits. The main batteries had been completed in 1914 before the onset of the air age, and their improvement had been hampered subsequently by the Naval Limitations Treaty of 1922. Even so, the twenty-three batteries of Corregidor, with their fifty-six different guns and mortars, could give a good account of themselves—provided the enemy played by the rules. That in turn required that he attack from the sea, not use aircraft, and refrain from deploying his own artillery on the opposite shores of the mainland. Particularly crucial were the dominating heights of Bataan; from there one could look down directly *into* the gun pits. Massello knew; he had just returned from a first visit to Bataan to reconnoiter positions for his battery of searchlights.

So perhaps Massello could see the futility of it all, but even he could not fail to be impressed with the enthusiasm of his young recruits. The vast majority of the men who served in his battery were the youngsters who had swarmed ashore as brand-new soldiers from the *Republic* in April; they put heart and soul into their job and were growing more proficient by the day.

Jim Castle, a soft-spoken eighteen-year-old product of a broken home, had arrived on the *Republic*. He was now a fully trained gunner with Battery B, 59th Coast Artillery. His battery with its old and worn-out 3-inch open mounts provided the island's antiaircraft defense.

Cpl. William Hall, who came from the backwoods of Washington State, had been on the Rock longer. He had arrived on the *Grant* at the same time as Bressi. Although only twenty years old, Hall was seen by the new recruits as a veteran if not an "old sweat." Such was the average age on Corregidor.

Bill Hall was a gunner on the fortress's main armament, the 12-inch disappearing rifles of Battery Crockett. These unique pieces had a novel way of operating: the recoil of the fire would sink the gun below the parapet, where it could be loaded and run out. The "disappearing carriage" would then raise the gun above the parapet to fire once more. It took a minimum of 30 men to fire these guns, and a good crew could get a round off every 40 seconds.

Hall was big and beefy—he had to be as the breechblock operator. Cranking that 500-pound monster was not for weaklings. It was all a matter of timing as the breech opened and the gases spewed out. The spongers had the breech clear by the time the loaders had run forward with a 900-pound shell and the 270-pound charge. Both were rammed home, and Hall closed the breech. The fire bells sounded, and the crew ran back, pressing thumbs to their ears to reduce at least some of the concussion.

Hall had made corporal in less than eighteen months. He knew his job, and he liked the life on Corregidor, where he found the air much cleaner than in steamy Manila. It was cooler on the island, and it was free of the plagues of mosquitoes that spread malaria like wildfire on the mainland. There were even servants available; for two pesos a month the Filipino houseboys who lived in the island barrio of San José shined shoes, cleaned belts, made beds, and swept the billets. For an extra dollar a month, the Filipinos would do all the KP duties that came the way of the gunners. Such rates were well within the budget of even the most lowly paid soldier, and when life became tedious he could easily take the picket boat to Manila on a seventy-two-hour pass.

Pvt. Fred Howard jumped off the picket boat heady with the thought of seventy-two hours in Manila. He had arrived on the *Republic* and had spent his time on Corregidor swearing that when he returned to Jacksonville, Oregon, the first thing he was going to do was "punch that lying bastard of a recruiting sergeant right in the mouth." How could anyone describe the Philippine Islands coast artillery as a "serviceman's paradise"?

Notwithstanding his reluctance and naturally rebellious spirit, the service had turned him into a halfway efficient signaler. After two months as the communications man on the 12-inch mortars of Battery Way, he had traded in his 1903 Springfield for a belt and a pistol and a bag of wireman's tools. Repairing and splicing cable beat the sweat and toil that went with serving the heavy guns as well as the shattered eardrums that seemed to be the fate of every coast artilleryman in time.

Howard had teamed up with Nemesio Arzaga, a Philippine Scout corporal from the prison guard detail on the Rock. He kept a spare uniform and "Smokey Bear" campaign hat with Private Barnes of Company K, 31st Infantry at the Estado Mayor. Having showered and changed, the three men (Barnes's "rent" for keeping the uniform laundered was a part share of the Scout's local knowledge) headed for old Manila and those parts rarely visited by the American troops. On their way into the old town they passed groups of servicemen from units that had not been around two months back when Howard last came ashore on furlough. There were engineers and Army Air Corps members, anti-aircraft artillerymen and field gunners by the hundreds. After a beer or two en route the three arrived at their favorite dance hall; the clientele was almost all Filipino. That night it had a quiet and strangely deserted air. There were few customers, and they were all women, for the young men had gone. They had been drafted into units of the expanding

Philippine Army. In the dance hall that night, Howard saw in the Filipino women the first signs of war fear.

October 17, 1941
School of Artillery, Philippine Army
Camp Dall Pillar, Luzon

Winston Jones's easy existence as the transport officer to the 24th Field Artillery did not last very long. He was soon sent as a senior instructor to the School of Artillery at Dall Pillar, about 5 miles from Stotsenberg, close enough for him to stay in his bungalow and for the Packard to continue to enjoy the ministrations of his old motor pool sergeant. The task at the School of Artillery was formidable. As a senior instructor in transport he had to train cadres who would return to the Philippine divisions and pass on their new-found knowledge. The recruits were young and enthusiastic, but none had uniforms, some had tennis shoes, and the majority were either barefoot or wore rope sandals.

The school had some six hundred cotton blankets, but there were no tents available. Motor transport was rudimentary—not that many Filipinos had ever driven a truck. The Army had some Dodge six-by-sixes, but were not about to let a lot of raw recruits loose on those prized possessions. Instead the men trained on charcoal burners, trucks that used alcohol, and the prize possession, a gasoline-powered Model T Ford.

Jones had another American officer working with him. Later he was to reckon this man was the smartest man in the unit—he left before the war started. The man was a chain smoker and an alcoholic. He would drink beer all night long and in the morning by the end of the first hour, he would be a mass of sweat. He perspired so much that his cigarette would become too wet to smoke. Jones had never seen any man sweat so much—even in the humid Philippines toward the end of the rainy season.

The officers would instruct in little "go-rounds," largely wall-less nipa huts with tin roofs. It would sometimes rain an inch an hour for twenty-four hours, and the rain hitting the metal roofs made instruction impossible. It was at about this time that the other officer was sent home—the doctors had declared him medically unfit for the tropics. Even at the time Jones was convinced that he was just smart—that's all.

October 19, 1941
Pier 7, Manila Docks

The tanks arrived in a convoy escorted by a battleship. The U.S.S. *Arizona* stayed for just a couple of days before returning to the Pacific Fleet and "Battleship Row," Pearl Harbor.

The 194th Tank Battalion was a National Guard outfit and the first to be sent overseas. Company A hailed from Minnesota, while C was a California unit and B, which was sent to Alaska, came from St. John, Missouri. For some months they had been training for tropical warfare before coming together in California at Fort McDowell.

Ben Saccone, top sergeant of Company C, was supervising the unloading of the tanks from the *President Coolidge*. They had been issued the new M-3A1s or "Stuarts" at Fort McDowell, and he regarded them with a deep sense of reverence. Along with the other men he sweated and strained, cursed, ranted, and raved at the Filipinos. They had never seen tanks in the Philippines before, and so the longshoremen stood and looked with amazement at the monstrous shapes swinging out of the hold of the *Coolidge*. The tanks swung crazily on their hastily contrived pallets. A stay parted with a resounding snap, and another tank gave the *Coolidge* an almighty clout on its lopsided course to terra firma. "For Chrissake," Saccone yelled, "we ain't come all this way to have our gear smashed by you screwballs."

It was early afternoon by the time the battalion was ready to roll. Saccone dumped the clipboard on the front seat of his Jeep, straightened his cap, and headed toward the small cafe across the square to which the battalion officers had wisely beat a retreat until the unloading was over. There is a time when officers lead from up front, and there are other times when the ground is best left clear for top sergeants. That morning was one of the latter times.

Colonel Miller climbed into his command tank and signaled for the battalion to start up. Blue exhaust filled the air as the big radials whined into top revs. The colonel suspected that there was more pressure on the gas pedals than necessary—but with a lot of people and top brass around, he decided to give his men their hour of glory.

It seemed to the overawed soldiers that the whole of Manila lined the route they followed out of the city that day. The crowd was three deep as the colonel's lead tank, preceded by military police motorcycle outriders and Saccone map-reading in his Jeep, turned onto Dewey Boulevard, past the historic St. James Gate of Fort Santiago.

The processional route followed the line of the wall of the Intramuros past the City Hall and Victoria Road. There MacArthur stood, on a specially erected podium, to review and salute the arrival of his tanks. Miller's lead tank, its guidons whipping smartly from the aerials, traversed the turret left and as the colonel saluted his chief, the gunner below dipped the 37mm in the customary tank salute.

The tanks thundered on by Sternberg General Hospital, where the Army nurses had taken time off from their ward duties to watch the spectacle. The rubber-shod tracks whined past the National Monument and over the Jones Bridge. Now the route lay along the broad avenue and through the old quarter of the city. Bilabid Prison towered above them, a sinister and forbidding shape that cast its shadow over the joy of the Filipino greeting.

It seemed to Bill Matson, as he stood tall on the jump seat of his White half-track, that the whole of Manila was out there to greet them. He struck what he thought was a suitably martial pose with one arm resting on the barrel of the Browning automatic AA mount. Suddenly he was reminded of a newsreel he had seen in the movies at home; it showed British tanks passing through Brussels in May 1940 as they moved up to stem the tide of the *blitzkrieg*.

"Please God we don't suffer the same fate as the British," he silently prayed. Such melancholy thoughts were dismissed from his mind as pretty girls clambered onto the scout car—it was easier than negotiating the sharp protubances of the tanks. As they climbed on board, Matson made the most of his good fortune. They were the most breathtakingly beautiful women he had ever seen, and their kisses were even sweeter. Meanwhile, at the head of the armored column, Saccone had long since given up trying to keep the girls off the Jeep. Once the formality of passing in review was over he left the map reading to the MPs and enjoyed the attentions of a couple of particularly well-endowed raven-haired beauties.

It took another hour to clear the city limits. The gunners and radio operators had joined the commander topside, and the drivers had their visors pulled back. Even with every ventilation grill and hatch open the turrets had become ovens within minutes. Having to fight closed down in these conditions was going to prove next to impossible.

Once clear of the city and on the open paved road between barrios, the battalion speeded up. The Stuarts could comfortably handle 40 miles an hour, and the drivers were skilled. This was in marked contrast to 192nd Tank Battalion, which was to arrive in November: A third of their drivers had never even seen the inside of a tank. Colonel Miller was justly proud of his unit. In the States it had been considered by many to be a better tank battalion than even the regular formations of the 7th Cavalry, reputed to be America's best.

Saccone sped ahead of the convoy to prepare the camp at Fort Stotsenberg for the arrival of the main force. Jeeps by this time were a common enough sight, especially on the 65 miles of highway that linked Clark with Manila. He had few holdups and arrived at their camp an hour after clearing the last sprawling barrio on the outskirts of Manila.

Not so the tanks, for the bush telegraph excelled itself that day. At each new barrio the reception committee awaited Colonel Miller's tank. Even the crews began to tire, for they had gorged themselves on the unaccustomed fruits. Their vehicles bulged with pineapples and breadfruits while on the outside the garlands and flowers made a brave show despite the clogging dust. Eventually it was a weary and very sick battalion that followed the signaled directions of the MPs into Fort Stotsenberg at sundown.

There were other, perhaps less glamorous units that had come in the *Arizona* convoy. The ground mechanics and crew chiefs of the recently formed 19th Bombardment Group traveled third class in wooden-seated buses from Pier 7 to Clark Field. Following on Rosie O'Donnell's achievements, Washington had decided that a full force of B-17s, with P-40s as escorts, would be a sound deterrent to Japanese ambitions—a pious hope on their part, perhaps, that these would be enough of a deterrent to make a defense of the

Philippines unnecessary. Dick Osborn and the others of the 19th Group were to service and maintain the biggest group of B-17s in the Air Force. Their skills and expertise represented in their own way as big a government stake in the Philippines as the tanks. The top sergeant of the outfit, John Taulbee, had described the Philippines to the others from firsthand experience. Some twelve years earlier, before transferring to the Air Corps, he had served a hitch with the 31st Infantry there.

MacArthur was allowed to see War Plan 5 in October. He didn't like it and convinced Washington that he, with his Philippine divisions and heavy bombers, could hold Luzon should the Japanese dare to attack. His staff had identified the likely Japanese invasion beaches, and orders were even then being written for the deployment of the Philippine divisions. Washington later bought MacArthur's ideas, and the general was given complete freedom of action to run his own theater of war.

The implications of this were catastrophic. Under the original plans MacArthur's quartermaster should now have been laying stockpiles on Bataan and Corregidor in readiness for a possible siege. Stockpiles were being established instead in the Central Luzon Plain and near the anticipated beaches.

October 24, 1941
17th Pursuit Squadron
Nichols Field

Ed Erickson and the other pilots touched down. Some of the P-36s sounded distinctly unhealthy to the waiting mechanics; obviously the constant training missions at Iba were taking their toll on these overworked engines.

As the pilots taxied toward the flight line, they discovered that the rumors were true. The long-awaited P-40E Kittyhawks were standing there in line, the squadron emblem already emblazoned on the fuselage. Pilots leaped from the cockpits even as their props feathered, to gather excitedly about the new ships. The Kittyhawks with the big Alison radials were a lot more powerful and faster than anything else in squadron front-line service at the time. What's more, they mounted .6 x .50-caliber machine guns, a formidable armory by any standards.

The squadron commander, Buzz Wagner, climbed onto a wing and quieted the excited young men with the bad news that they could not fly the new planes yet because no Prestone had been sent with them.

Without the special coolant, the planes were effectively grounded. In the rarefied air above 20,000 feet the Prestone prevented the water-cooled Alisons from freezing solid. Some overzealous quartermaster at San Francisco had obviously decided that antifreeze in the tropics was not a priority cargo, and as a result the planes were to blister on the apron for another month.

October 25, 1941
2nd Battalion, 31st U.S. Infantry
San Felipe, West Coast, Luzon

The men of the 2nd Battalion of the 31st U.S. Infantry were on their third three-day exercise since Organization Day. The novelty had long since disappeared. Trucks had carried the battalion more than 100 miles out of Manila, onto the West Coast, beyond San Fernando Province. The troops and their baggage had been unceremoniously dumped on the jungle roadside to make their own way back to McKinley. Though it was still below strength, with the arrival of many new draftees there were now more men in the battalion than at any time in its history.

The troops, rookies and veterans alike, found the 30-mile hikes each day living hell. Garleb noticed that when Sergeant Eckhardt called a break, he would not flop to the ground like the others, but remain standing and keep on his pack. Garleb tried doing the same and found that it worked. He also learned not to drink freely from his canteen, but instead to take a pebble and put it beneath his tongue.

One evening Garleb and a couple of others, together with Eckhardt, walked into the fishing barrio that was close to where they had made camp. The head man was friendly enough and over a beer volunteered the information that there was a Japanese ship out there in the bay. He insisted that it was not a fishing boat. He knew that it was laying mines because his young men in their canoes had been warned away by the Japanese.

This and a hundred other tales of fifth-column activities was duly fed into American Intelligence. The small G-2 staff was swamped by such accounts and could do little other than file the information and investigate some of the more plausible stories. Sometimes G-2 struck it lucky. Richard Sakakida's undercover work paid dividends, for instance, when he was able to pinpoint a Philippine constabulary captain who was feeding information to the Japanese.

At Cavite Lieutenant Champlin's experience as a field agent of the FBI meant that his help and advice were frequently sought by Naval Intelligence. But much of the work was haphazard, and the free-and-easy attitude of his colleagues filled the professional Champlin with horror. Perhaps more vigilance on their part would have resulted in the arrest of the barber in the shop outside Cavite Navy Yard. Far from being a Filipino, he was later identified as a Japanese Intelligence officer who over the years must have gathered a wealth of information from the careless talk of his clientele.

November 10, 1941
41st Artillery, 41st Philippine Infantry
Lake Taal, Batangas Province

Winston Jones and his 1934 Packard were on the move for a third time since his arrival in the Philippines. He had barely seen one cadre through the School of Artillery when, along with all the other American officers, he was assigned as a battalion instructor to a Philippine unit. His place in the school was taken by a long-service American NCO who had hastily been commissioned, along with scores of others, a temporary "3rd lieutenant." Still, thought Jones, as he reflected upon his fortune, life could be a hell of a lot worse. On the credit side it was infinitely better to be assigned to a field regiment, and this one was part of the 41st Division. By all accounts in the Officers' Club, it was a halfway decent unit, commanded by the dynamic Vincente Lim, one of the first Filipino graduates of West Point.

The artillery regiment was located 70 miles south of Manila along the shores of the volcanic Lake Taal. In fact, the HQ and Officers' Club were in the Taal Vista Lodge—a sumptuous branch of the Manila Hotel.

Jones's illusions were shattered when he arrived at his new home. In the whole division, there was but one Dodge four-by-four and a White half-track. There was also a command car for General Lim and a Jeep that had seen better days. So the 1934 Special Packard was pressed into service as the artillery battalion's only vehicle. He did not have to worry, however, about pulling guns with his car, as there were none in the battalion, neither field pieces nor rifles.

Jones spent the next three weeks training the troops on bamboo mockups while they waited anxiously for their field artillery to arrive. Even so the Filipinos, most with no uniform of any type (a lucky few had American-issue coveralls that they had cut down to size), trained enthusiastically.

The Philippine Military Academy in Baguio had recently held its final parade and closed its doors. The cadets who had not completed the full course were commissioned and drafted immediately to command platoons (and in some cases companies) in the new divisions. The seniors who had served their time at the Academy received their first appointments in the field. Those with the political influence in high places were given command of battalions, while those who were not so well endowed were appointed to companies. But even they could hardly complain of the speed in their promotion.

Jones was fortunate at Lake Taal. The battalion commander to whom he acted as adviser had been commissioned out of the Academy two years previously.

November 14, 1941
194th Tank Battalion
Fort Stotsenberg, Central Luzon

The tanks deployed for the first time in accordance with the master plan of operations devised by MacArthur's staff. The southern end of Lingayen Gulf had been identified as the most likely invasion beach in northern Luzon.

The War Game's scenario was an optimistic one. The two Philippine divisions already deployed had held the Japanese and contained them within a shallow beachhead. The tanks were moving forward to deliver the crushing counterattack and thus drive the Japanese into the sea.

Bill Matson had moved ahead in his half-track to his accustomed reconnaissance role. Originally it had been planned that the 26th Cavalry should act as eyes and ears of the tanks, but the horses had long since been overtaken.

Colonel Miller was pleased with the performance of his battalion. From the order to move to the supposed outer perimeter of the beachhead 80 miles away, it had taken the fast-moving tank columns less than 5 hours. The tanks had deployed for battle off the line of march. The 26th Cavalry took a day to make the same journey and arrived on blown horses.

November 20, 1941
Thanksgiving Day
Manila

Lilla Seitz had not returned to the United States; neither had many of the other families of the American business community.

They had received no instructions or indeed advice from Commissioner Sayre's office about returning home. Even if they had, they would have considered such a move unthinkable. Life was too good in Manila.

Clay Seitz worked for an insurance company called American International Underwriters. The Seitzes had a beautiful house in the most fashionable part of Manila. The introduction of air conditioning a few years back had made life so much easier. It was now no longer necessary to spend the summer in the highlands at Baguio.

Across the tree-lined avenue from the Seitzes lived the Japanese consul general and his family. Lilla would return their bow politely if they passed in the street, but she did not call on them.

The pinnacle of society was the Manila Polo Club; Lilla lunched there some days with her circle of friends. Sometimes for a change they would eat at the Army and Navy or the British Club—the latter was also known as the Manila Club. It was their custom to have tea or perhaps meet for coffee at the Ladies' Club, though Lilla had started to curtail many of her social activities; her first baby was due early in the New Year.

Lilla thought it was the saddest thing that all the service wives had been sent home. Manila was such a lovely place to live. It was true that their husbands were probably going to go out and shoot up the Japanese someplace, but the women might just as well wait for them in the Philippines as at home.

Lilla had said as much that evening at the Thanksgiving dinner she and her husband attended in honor of British industrialist and entrepreneur Sir Victor Sassoon. General and Mrs. MacArthur were there too.

Sir Victor, very happy and jubilant, was only too willing to expand on the reasons that had brought him into Manila. He was on his way home, and he thought he had been very clever, which indeed he had, for Sir Victor had liquidated the Sassoon properties in Shanghai. He was convinced he was getting out of China in the nick of time. However, such alarmist talk was not only unsettling the ladies at the table, it was also irritating General MacArthur, who didn't like the limelight swinging away from him.

"Well, war is coming," the general said, "but I can assure you ladies, the time and place will be our choosing."

Lilla and her friends felt much better after those assurances.

November 24, 1941
USAFFE HQ
No. 1 Calle Victoria
Manila

General Sutherland took the signal, which had just been de-coded, into his chief.

> A SURPRISE AGGRESSIVE MOVE IN ANY DIRECTION INCLUD-ING AN AIR ATTACK ON THE PHILIPPINES OR GUAM IS NOW A POSSIBILITY.

MacArthur called in his staff, and together they examined anew both the contingency plans for invasion and the state of training of the new Philippine division.

The lights burned late into the night at the House on the Wall.

November 25, 1941
Pier 7, Manila

The *Henderson* made what was to be its last voyage into Manila. Now the conditions were different; two four-stackers, World War I vintage destroyers, had accompanied her as visible proof of the imminence of war. The convoys were also escorted into Manila Bay. The entire entrance had been mined, and Asiatic Fleet sweepers led the way through the marked channel.

Corregidor was truly *the key* to one of the most formidable seaward defense systems in the world. The electronic minefield, searchlights, and the big guns were all linked into an automatic fire control. Once a ship had been identified as not hostile, the power to the field would be turned off, though there was always the risk of hitting a drifting or rogue mine. For every ship's captain, entry into Manila Bay was now an anxious affair.

John McCann, a private in the 693rd Ordnance Company, Avia-tion Pursuit, and destined for Nichols Field, was on the *Henderson*. He was just sixteen years of age. Twice before he had tried to enlist.

His father was a Marine, and John lived in a Marine town, San Diego. His sister was dating a young Marine, and every time he came to see her he would tell John tales of the service while he waited for his date. John longed to join the Marines, but in order to do so a recruit had to show his birth certificate, and if he was underage a parent had to sign a form giving permission for him to enlist. His mother refused. But eventually he blackmailed her into allowing him to join the Air Corps because the Canadians were in town recruiting for their Army.

"The English use the Canadians as cannon fodder," his mother had said. "It ain't going to happen to any son of mine." Fearful that her son would run away and join up north of the border, she signed the necessary papers.

So on his sixteenth birthday he joined the Air Corps. At least, she thought, by the time her son had learned a skilled trade in the Air Corps, any war could be over. John McCann had joined up as an armorer and had worn a uniform for only as long as it took the *Henderson* to reach Manila.

Cpl. Bob Martinello was in a slightly different position. He had been sent out with the men of his unit, and the equipment was scheduled to come on a later convoy. His unit was the 16th Bomber Squadron, part of the newly constituted 27th Bombardment Group. He was an air gunner in a dive bomber, the SPD-3A Navy carrier plane, which the Air Force had acquired. They were crated and awaiting shipment in Oakland Navy Yard.

However, the *Henderson* did bring a shipment of Prestone. That made a lot of pilots in the pursuit squadrons happy.

November 27, 1941
Company B, 31st Infantry
Fort Santiago, Intramuros
Manila

The *Henderson* had also brought the long-awaited shipment of 81mm mortars for the infantry. Along with the Scouts, the 31st was at the head of the list to receive the new weapons.

With the requisition orders signed, Pvt. Paul Kerchum had been sent by his sergeant to pick up the four mortars allocated to his company. He took a squad of men and a Dodge four-by-four and presented himself with his papers at the service company armory, which was located in the Santa Lucia Barracks. There was a line, but eventually he got the four mortars.

"What about the ammunition, Sarge?" Kerchum asked.

"There ain't any, soldier," was the reply of the overweight, sweating, and visibly frustrated master sergeant. It was the hundredth time he had had this conversation.

"How come?" Kerchum persisted.

"Look, son," the sergeant said, "the ammunition shipment is due on a convoy in about two weeks. It's not up to you or me to judge the decisions of the brass. So pick up your mortars, be thankful for what you got, and haul your ass out of here!"

Kerchum scuttled out of the door, the blast of the master sergeant bellowing in his ear, wondering at the same time how he was going to explain all this to his own top sergeant.

"You know," Paul said to his driver as he reversed the truck carefully out through the old sally port, "life just ain't fun in Manila these days."

Similar sentiments would have been echoed by many of the ground crews at Clark Field at this stage. Not once since he had arrived had Dick Osborn and his cronies been given leave to explore the soldier's paradise of Manila. When they were not working on the flight line servicing the ever-expanding number of B-17s that were arriving (there were over thirty now at Clark), they were digging foxholes and weapon pits and sandbagging in the aircraft parking bays. The base commander was Lt. Col. Lester Maitland, and it was under his express orders that this work was carried out. The men sweated away at what they had come to regard as Maitland's Follies, for they were all convinced there wasn't going to be any war—after all, that wasn't why they had enlisted.

III. Rumors of War

Thursday, November 27, 1941–
Sunday, December 7, 1941

Thursday, November 27, 1941
USAFFE HQ
No. 1 Calle Victoria, Manila

American Intelligence identified a large Japanese amphibious force at sea off the China coast.

The War Department cabled MacArthur:

> NEGOTIATIONS WITH THE JAPANESE APPEAR TO BE TERMINATED TO ALL PRACTICAL PURPOSES WITH ONLY THE BAREST POSSIBILITIES THAT THE JAPANESE GOVERNMENT MIGHT COME BACK AND OFFER TO CONTINUE PERIOD JAPANESE FUTURE ACTION UNPREDICTABLE BUT HOSTILE ACTION POSSIBLE AT ANY MOMENT PERIOD IF HOSTILITIES CANNOT REPEAT CANNOT BE AVOIDED THE UNITED STATES DESIRES THAT JAPAN COMMIT THE FIRST OVERT ACT PERIOD THIS POLICY SHOULD NOT REPEAT NOT BE CONSTRUED AS RESTRICTING YOU TO A COURSE OF ACTION THAT MIGHT JEOPARDIZE YOUR DEFENSE PERIOD.

General MacArthur ordered USAFFE to go on full alert. The troops moved into the field, and the watch over the likely invasion beaches was increased. Colonel Drake, the chief quartermaster at USAFFE, intensified the efforts of his staff to build up the supply dumps in the four defense sectors designated by headquarters. Bataan was not on the list. Corregidor and the other forts received but scant attention. MacArthur regarded dependence on the fortresses as a negative approach.

The general was still convinced that the Japanese would not attack until April 1942 and the onset of the hot season. Admiral

Hart did not agree, and a signal he had received that morning from Admiral Stark, Chief of Naval Operations in Washington, gave all the evidence he needed that MacArthur was wildly wrong in his predictions. It read:

> THIS DISPATCH IS TO BE CONSIDERED A WAR WARNING. NEGOTIATIONS WITH JAPAN LOOKING TOWARD STABILI-ZATION OF CONDITIONS IN THE PACIFIC HAVE CEASED. AN AGGRESSIVE MOVE BY JAPAN IS EXPECTED WITHIN THE NEXT FEW DAYS. EXECUTE AN APPROPRIATE DEFENSIVE DEPLOYMENT PREPARATORY TO CARRYING OUT THE TASKS ASSIGNED IN WAR PLAN.

So Tommy Hart, small, taut, wiry, and irascible, with forty years of sea experience behind him, was convinced that a Japanese attack was imminent. But then the Asiatic Fleet commander had been saying that ever since he had pulled his units out of China in the autumn and concentrated them in Subic and Manila bays. However, he reasoned that so long as the B-17s' reconnaissance missions gave him ample warning, his submarines could be deployed to their patrol stations in time to intercept and destroy the invasion convoys. If the P-40s gave him air cover, the surface units could play their part, too, in the coming battle. Of the USAFFE high command, only Hart seemed alive to the threat from the air.

Having pondered the final alert from Washington, he decided that an additional bit of insurance would not go amiss. He ordered his flagship, the heavy cruiser *Houston*, together with two other cruisers and their attendant destroyers, south to Mindanao, well beyond the range of Japanese air bases in Formosa. In the case of those forces that were to remain, Hart dispersed them, especially his submarine tenders and repair ships, around Manila Bay. The recently renovated but elderly *Canopus* was anchored off Cavite, while the *Otus* was sent to Mariveles, a small dock on the tip of Bataan, and the third submarine tender, *Holland*, was moored just inside the breakwater of Manila. Without these ships his two divisions of submarines would become paralyzed; the repair shops and especially the skilled craftsmen were a vital asset to be protected at all costs.

HQ, 4th U.S. Marines
International Settlement
Shanghai, China

For fifteen years the 4th Marines had protected American interests in war-torn China, and the regiment had been there for so long it had become known as the "China Marines." During this long sojourn it had acquired some unique trappings. Perhaps the strangest was that it had the only fife and drum corps in the Marines. This had been created in 1927 when a leading American citizen in Shanghai, Sterling Fessenden, had donated the instruments. The Fessenden Fifes had been trained by a then resident British infantry battalion, the Green Howards, and the two regiments had maintained close links ever since.

The International Settlement had been coming apart at the seams ever since the outbreak of the war in Europe. The American sector had rivers on two sides of its perimeter—the Whangpoo River and its tributary, the Soochow Creek. Across the former was the suburb of Hankow, which was occupied by the Japanese. From there and other areas of the city that they controlled, the Japanese had been waging a ceaseless campaign to undermine and intimidate the position of the Western powers.

Tension increased in June 1940 when Italy declared war on Britain and France. In July, France capitulated, and the new Vichy authorities ordered their representatives to cooperate with the Japanese.

Since Christmas 1940 an armed truce had existed between the Americans and the Italians. There had been a fight, which started in a downtown night spot called the Little Club, and it had ended up as a battalion-sized brawl between American and Italian Marines; they rampaged through four sections of the city. Five Italians were killed. To prevent any further incidents the two forces were ordered to keep to their own parts of town.

In September 1941 the British contingent left, and the American garrison felt very much alone. Al Broderick, a twenty-four-year-old Marine corporal, stood on the sidewalk and watched first the East Surreys and then the Seaforth Highlanders march down to the jetty at the Soochow Creek. He had made some good friends among the Scots, and his heart filled to the sound of the pipes. Scuttlebutt had it that the Seaforths were to reinforce the British garrison in Hong Kong. They would meet again.

For a young corporal like Al Broderick, Shanghai was paradise. A Regular Marine since 1938, he had been assigned to the Parade Ground Fourth after a hitch on the heavy cruiser *Vincennes*, operating the Neutrality Patrol out of New York. The contrast was immediate and extreme, from the bucking deck of a cruiser uncomfortably riding the Atlantic swell, sentinel to violations of territorial waters by the warring Europeans, to the mystic delights of the Orient. In Shanghai the exchange rate was forty Chinese dollars for one American dollar, and it was almost impossible for a Marine to spend his pay, whatever his desires!

The Marines did guard duty; it was repetitive, boring, and on occasion dangerous. They drew three days out of five manning the machine-gun posts along the front line of the Soochow Creek or the sandbagged emplacement on the bridge that spanned the Whangpoo River and linked Hankow. Broderick and the other Leathernecks found it tedious squinting through the sights of their heavy machine gun at a bunch of Japanese similarly employed or trying to watch the Chinese as they scuttled about their daily business, oblivious to the farce.

Information had been obtained indicating that the Japanese military intended to seize the International Settlement. They staged incidents whereby they claimed the right of hot pursuit into the American sector, and the Marines were alerted to guard against terrorists and to stop the Japanese entering their area. Tension increased, and there had been a number of ugly confrontations along the demarcation lines. The Marines now had to spend their free time in uniform. Despite these petty restrictions the wily China Marine came out on top, for curfew from midnight to daybreak applied to everyone, including off-duty servicemen. Most men found it impossible to make it back to the barracks in time and so were forced to spend the nights in town.

There were other signs to convince the Marines that trouble was brewing. The training program increased, and they spent more hours at musketry practice on the Shanghai police rifle ranges. Many of the older men had been shipped out on the regular monthly transports so that, although the two battalions were understrength, they were now lean and hard. The Marines knew they were cut off and outnumbered, and they were convinced that evacuation by sea was not possible. Consequently the men believed all this training was in preparation for the time when they would have to fight their way out: storm the Japanese positions and force march the ten miles to the Nationalist Chinese lines, before the Japanese could respond. Every morning the battalions marched five miles through the city, and once a week a twenty-mile hike with full pack was organized. All this gave credibility to the widespread rumors about a likely breakout. In the desperate heat and humidity of Shanghai, Broderick felt that for the first time they were earning their pay.

The advance party was evacuated by sea in October. They left in the *Henderson* on one of its routine calls. Private Finken, a truck driver and mechanic of H Service Company, reluctantly bade his farewells to Shanghai. There was no secrecy to the move. All the men had girls or "shackmates," and they got the word before the Marines.

On November 3, orders were received from Washington. The Marines were to evacuate Shanghai. The contingency plan, already thoroughly rehearsed, was put into immediate effect. Two APL transports had been moored downstream for about a week while their holds were being hastily converted to accommodate troops. The work was stopped abruptly, and the ships made ready to sail.

On the morning of November 27, the 2nd Battalion, half of the regimental HQ, and the remainder of the service companies marched to the jetty, and barges ferried them and their baggage out to the *President Madison*. At 1600 hours the ship quietly weighed anchor and, her passage obscured by a monsoon squall, headed out into the East China Sea, southbound for Subic Bay and the Philippines.

On November 28, the Fessenden Fifes led the 1st Battalion and the rest of the regiment for the last time through the International Settlement and down to the President's Line berth. The route was lined by crowds of the silent and passive citizens of Shanghai, resigned in that stoically oriental manner to their fate under the Japanese. At 1400 hours the *Harrison* weighed anchor and cleared the Whangpoo River.

Once they had passed the Yangtze Estuary the ship cleared for action.

Sgt. Edwin Bigelow was first Sergeant of Company H, 2nd Battalion. It was his company that took over responsibility for the anti-aircraft defense of the *Madison*. This meant breaking out the

World War I vintage Brownings and lashing them to deck stanchions. Though by these means and with limited arcs of fire they could give the ship very little cover, it was better than nothing and a defiant show of force.

Conditions on board the *Madison,* which had long since seen better days, were ghastly. Multitiered cots were crammed into the holds, and these soon broke loose from their joints as the ship hit the full force of an East China Sea monsoon. The holds could not be battened down, as the heat would have been intolerable. Consequently they rapidly took on water and, as she rolled wickedly, the end bunks and their occupants were submerged. Everyone was eventually crowded together in the center of the hold in communal and sodden misery.

Toilet facilities were crude, even by Leatherneck standards. A 20-foot-long metal trough hung over the port gunwhale on the foredeck. Its thin canvas screen provided neither shelter nor privacy to the Marines, who squatted, pants around their ankles, along its length. The roll of the ship made life particularly unpleasant for those who lingered at either end of the trough.

Twenty miles out from the Yangtze River, Japanese patrol planes found the *Madison.* The planes would make frequent and menacingly low passes across the ship. Bigelow and his gunners tracked their progress as best they could. Darkness came, the storm abated, and the Marines joined the chow line; in this old tub with her limited facilities it seemed to run twice around the upper deck.

When dawn came the *Madison* was heading south through a moderate swell. There were five big Japanese destroyers for escort, two on each beam, and a flotilla leader a few short ship lengths from their stern. The Marines crowded the rails and stared apprehensively at their unwelcome visitors. The patrol planes also duly appeared, and the pilots repeated the antics of the previous day whenever the mood took them.

In the late afternoon, the Japanese destroyers suddenly increased speed and forged past the freighter. Forming into line ahead, they turned rapidly and headed back on their track. Bigelow rammed his tin hat on his head and called his gunners to arms. The rest of the Marines lined the bulwarks with their Springfields. Ammunition was quickly distributed, and the men prepared to fight, though what they expected to achieve with their small arms against the Japanese batteries is hard to imagine.

The Japanese destroyers sped down the port side not fifty yards from the *Madison*. As each ship passed she dipped her colors in the tradition of the sea and then sailed quickly on her way over the horizon.

Hardly had the excitement died away when a submarine surfaced off the transport's port bow. The Marines again rushed to the rails. This time, however, fear and apprehension gave way quickly to relief as the submarine was identified. The Asiatic Fleet had arrived to escort the *Madison* into Subic Bay.

Just above the horizon a Japanese patrol plane monitored their progress and missed nothing.

Monday, December 1, 1941
Units of the Asiatic Fleet
Manila Bay

It was the day of the Army-Navy football game, and wherever they were stationed it was the biggest day in the sports calendar for both services. Admiral Hart believed the Japanese would use such a golden opportunity for a sneak attack. Consequently he ordered all units under his command to have steam up at dawn, and the ships spent the day sailing around Manila Bay with their crews at general quarters. The Navy patrol planes based at Olongapo and Cavite quartered the South China Sea. An unrepentant but very peppery Hart ordered the ships to their moorings at dusk. Sailors swarmed ashore to the derision of the Army and shore patrols, and the military police were kept particularly busy that night.

U.S. Navy Yard, Olongapo
Subic Bay, Luzon

The *Madison* dropped anchor in Subic Bay, just twenty-four hours behind the *Harrison*. Lighters ferried the men and their equipment to the old Navy Yard. The ancient *Rochester* was tied up at the pier; it looked as if she hadn't moved since the Spanish-American War. The Marines took over an empty warehouse and made themselves comfortable; after the last four days at sea these Spartan conditions seemed palatial. The two transports meanwhile headed south down the coast of Bataan and then into Manila Bay. They berthed at Cavite and unloaded the battalion's stores and heavy equipment. The *President Harrison* put to sea almost immediately and headed northward once more. Her destination this time was the Chinese port of Chingwangloo, where it was hoped she would rendezvous with the Marine detachments and Embassy Guard from Peiping and Tientsin. The *Madison* sailed for the States at a more leisurely pace.

Admiral Hart gave the Marines just twenty-four hours to sort themselves out in Olongapo before ordering them into the field for intensive training. He was convinced that after their years of soft living in Shanghai they needed to be toughened up for war.

Manila Hotel
Dewey Boulevard

That evening Clay and Lilla Seitz attended a private dinner party. Lilla sat next to Admiral Hart.

"Why are you here? You ought to be at home," the admiral said.

"Well the United States Government hasn't told us to leave," Lilla responded.

The admiral was absolutely amazed at this. "But the service wives were sent home months ago!"

It was not the first time that Lilla had questioned the wisdom of their decision to remain in Manila, but then quickly dismissed such cheerless thoughts from her mind. There was the baby to look forward to and Christmas as well. It was ridiculous to imagine any danger to Americans in Manila.

The next morning over their breakfast coffee, Clay and Lilla watched as the Japanese consul general and his family packed their possessions and left. The window frames shook with concussion, and then they heard the sound of distant thunder. It was the third day running that the big guns in the bay forts had sounded; Lilla had never before known them to practice so frequently.

Thirty miles away, Sol Fromer was chief of breech that morning in A Turret on Fort Drum, an island that had been razed to sea level and then rebuilt like the forepart of a battleship. The "hull" was made of concrete 20 feet high and just as thick. There were two superimposed 14-inch gun turrets on the top deck, and let into the walls were embrasures for 6-inch Broadbent guns. The concrete battleship was home to 300 men, and they had been in a state of war for nearly a week. Fromer pressed the bell and signaled the hoist up from the lower handling room. A 14-inch shell weighed 1,560 pounds, and it took 440 pounds of powder to blast it out of the barrel.

Between Drum and Corregidor was Caballo Island, better known as Fort Hughes. Though more conventional than Drum, nevertheless this island was heavily fortified as well. Half a mile long and a couple of hundred yards wide, it was home to 250 Americans and, so the men said, 3,000 snakes and lizards. It also boasted one of the best gymnasiums in the Philippine Islands Coast Artillery, and for three years running the garrison had been the Far Eastern athletic champions. All that was forgotten now as the men began a second week at their guns; they lived and slept at the batteries. The gymnasium gathered dust, and the lizards scurried unmolested.

Tuesday, December 2, 1941
Fort Mills, Corregidor

On Corregidor, too, the men had been living at the batteries. They took turns trekking down to the Mile Long Barracks for a shower and change and, if off watch, perhaps grab a couple of hours' sleep.

Bressi and the supply personnel had worked furiously issuing all the equipment and stores that would bring the gun pits up to requirements. In a seemingly never-ending stream, mountains of supplies, hitherto immobilized by red tape, now disappeared with a hasty and usually illegible signature. Bressi made the most of these days despite the fury and pace of the work, for once the supplies had been issued he would become surplus. Amoroso, newly promoted to lieutenant colonel in the Staff Quartermaster Department, as much as told him so.

Massello had left Corregidor. His command was E Battery, Coast Artillery, a searchlight unit that he had converted from a mob of new recruits off the *Republic* into a team of competent operators and infantrymen. Massello had been convinced that in this coming war his men would have to be responsible for their own defense. He had reconnoitered the jungles of Bataan and knew you could not leave it to the local friendly infantry to defend you. So his men had trained hard, and even Massello had at last admitted he was satisfied. To the gunners that was praise indeed.

On the evening of November 30, Massello had been called in by the regimental commander, Colonel Bunker, who had ordered him to deploy his outfit onto Bataan the next day. Once on Bataan Massello's lights were to be part of the outer arc of anti-aircraft defense for Corregidor and the entrance to Manila Bay. Massello knew where to put the lights; the problem was getting them there.

Massello and his three battery lieutenants worked through the night preparing for the move. It seemed as if everything conspired to make the operation as difficult as possible. The 60-inch-diameter lights had 1 million candlepower, and on their bogies they were big, awkward, and very fragile. Just before dawn Regimental Headquarters called with a change of plan; Massello learned that they were to share the barges with the 3-inch AA guns of another battery. He tore up the loading schedules and started again.

Despite this and many other frustrations, Massello had it worked out to the last detail, and the first barge got away on time for Mariveles. There they hit trouble, for the only unloading jetty available was a rock pier. If that wasn't bad enough, there was another barge ahead of them—full of 250-pound Air Corps bombs, and there were more barges crowding behind.

Massello ordered the Navy crew to bring his barge in on the other side of the pier, and it was only when an Air Corps barge had vacated the pier that Massello was able to bring one of his own alongside and unload.

Siting ten searchlights in jungle-covered mountain terrain with nothing more than mud tracks on which to move the equipment is not a task for the fainthearted. But by the end of the first day Massello had two lights sited. No. 1 Light was on Pooki Hill, and No. 2 looked down on Longoskawayan Point. The remainder were sited into their allotted positions overlooking the South China Sea by the end of the following day. The generators and power units quickly followed, and the cables were laid.

By now there were 50 miles of cable connecting the lights. In itself this was a formidable task in jungle country; and on this occasion it certainly wasn't made any easier by the local Filipinos purloining the wire for clothes lines. The lights deployed, the gunners dug their foxholes and weapon pits.

Wednesday, December 3, 1941
U.S.S. *Holland,* Flagship Submarines, Asiatic Fleet
Manila Bay

Lt. Roland (Mac) McKnight commanded the submarine *S-36.* Already obsolescent, the World War I submarines of the Asiatic Fleet should never have been assigned to a major theater of war. Built as coastal submarines, they displaced 850 tons and so were ideally suited for operations in the shallow shoal waters and lagoons of the Philippine Islands. But for the S-boats to submerge was a complicated and time-consuming business. They had a single shaft connecting the diesel engine and the electric motor to the propeller so that when the boat dived, a clutch on the motor was disengaged, allowing the batteries to take over. A crash dive in an S-boat was not in the manual.

These submarines were so old it was a challenge to keep them going. They had riveted hulls, and they leaked incessantly when submerged. It was so bad in the *S-36* that the watchkeeper had to wear a southwester at the controls; there was never less than a half inch of water slopping around the deck.

However, this was Roland McKnight's first command, and for him there wasn't a finer ship in the Asiatic Fleet. Carefully McKnight conned the *S-36* alongside the *Canopus.* He had spent a frustrating couple of weeks patrolling outside the Corregidor minefield, where his task had been to intercept merchant ships and point them in the direction of the swept channel. Now that was behind him; ahead lay two weeks of refit and maintenance tied alongside the *Canopus*. For the crew this meant decent quarters on the *Canopus* and a week at least tasting the delights of Manila.

McKnight had just ordered "Finish with main engines" when the yeoman of signals appeared. "Signal from flag, sir, you're to report aboard directly. Duty picket boat's on its way over."

The *Holland* was moored inside the breakwater of Manila Harbor, about 6 miles across the bay from Cavite. Mac quickly stepped down into the submarine and changed into his best uniform. At the same time, believing that war had begun, he ordered his young executive officer to stop the refit immediately, cancel all leave, get the new warheads on the torpedoes, and fuel and provision the ship.

Along with the rest of the Navy, McKnight had half expected the Japanese to attack the Philippines two days before.

Twenty minutes later, together with two other submarine commanders, McKnight was in the picket boat speeding across Manila Bay. Once on board, the three eager officers were met by John Wilkes, commander of the 14th Submarine Division. First he allowed them to read the operational orders. McKnight made notes on the small pad he habitually carried. The orders were explicit enough. He was to proceed to Lingayen Gulf and hide out in Port Bilnow until he received further orders. Wilkes then briefed the three officers and urged them to use caution and to feel their way.

"The first patrol will be the most dangerous," he stressed. "It will also be our first appreciation of enemy methods of operation."

Wilkes then went on to explain what their operations were to be on receipt of the news of the outbreak of war.

"Your order of priority must be to sink capital ships, loaded transports, light forces, and finally transports in ballast, in that order. Go easy with the torpedoes," he warned. "Merchant ships only need one to sink them, two at the most. The new magnetic exploder will give you devastating results."

McKnight picked up his charts and returned quickly to the submarine, where he found that the preparations for sea were well advanced.

The *S-36* was the first of Hart's submarines to deploy to its war station. Lingayen Gulf had been identified as the most likely Japanese invasion point on the South China Sea coast. Hart had dispatched one elderly submarine armed with twelve torpedoes to patrol that area. It was assumed that the other submarines would interdict Japanese convoys en route to Luzon so that the *S-36* would have the task of mopping up the survivors.

At 2300 hours Mac headed out through the minefield, picked up his surface escort, and turned north for Lingayen Gulf. Shortly afterward the escort challenged and identified four warships moving south. They were gunboats from the Yangtze River patrol that had made a run for it out of China. Admiral Glassford flew his flag in the *Luzon*; the others were *Oahu, Tulsa,* and *Asheville.*

Thursday, December 4, 1941
U.S.S. *Mindanao*
Royal Navy dockyard
Crown Colony, Hong Kong

The *Mindanao* was the only American warship in Hong Kong. A river gunboat custom built in 1928 with 3 feet of freeboard, she was the least seaworthy of all the China Station gunboats. Glassford ordered her to wait at Hong Kong for news of the fate of the others before attempting the monsoon storms of the South China Sea. The crew knew war was coming. Tales circulated on the lower deck, and rumors flew thick and fast about the Crown Colony, while the Japanese across the frontier of the New Territories made little effort to hide their preparations for war.

Sam Malick was the radio operator on the *Mindanao*. Having monitored the tremendous increase in traffic, he had a fair idea of what was happening even before that afternoon when Lieutenant Commander McCracken piped, "Clear lower deck," and addressed his sixty-seven officers and sailors.

"I've just received word that the *Luzon* and the others have made it all the way to Manila Bay," he announced. As the cheers died away he continued, "There's a storm in the South China Sea, but my orders are to try to make it. Failing that I have orders to return here and to place my ship under the command of the British authorities."

Nobody liked the idea of being bottled up with the British in Hong Kong, and all the men were in favor of making a run for it to Manila.

It was late afternoon when the *Mindanao* put to sea. Once beyond the shelter of the Hong Kong breakwater, the full force of the monsoon hit the little ship, and there was no way the gunboat with its concave bottom and 3 feet of freeboard would make it if the weather worsened. The captain called the radio shack, which was just behind the bridge. Malick, who had the duty, was ordered to broadcast an SOS every fifteen minutes.

He turned his transmitters to the International 500 frequency and began.

The call was answered. Through the fury of the storm, McCracken and the watchkeepers could just make out two ships off their starboard quarter. The squall passed as quickly as it came and there, less than 400 yards away, were two Japanese destroyers. The executive officer frantically looked through the much-thumbed copy of *Jane's Fighting Ships* and identified their silhouettes as Hatsuhara class destroyers, better than 2,000 tons with a main armament of 5-inch guns and quadruple, 24-inch torpedo tubes. McCracken pressed the klaxon, and the discordant gongs for general quarters sounded throughout the gunboat although he knew it was a futile gesture. His main armament was two 3-inch guns built in 1898 and last fired in 1936. The action seemed to have the desired effect, for the destroyers laid back and shadowed from astern. The crew cheered, but McCracken guessed that the reason for this was most likely that the Japanese could not keep station in such heavy seas at the gunboat's speed.

McCracken turned the ship northward, and at his best speed of 6 knots headed into the still angry sea; the Japanese destroyers dutifully followed suit and kept their silent, menacing vigil. McCracken realized there was no way he could turn south in those seas, and so he resigned himself to the only other course of action open to him, if he was to reach Manila—head toward Formosa and then turn south in the shelter afforded by the lee of the island. McCracken ordered the continued broadcasting of Mayday so that the Japanese would think he was in trouble and assume he would sink eventually.

The crew remained at action stations until dark, and Malick

broadcast his Mayday every fifteen minutes. McCracken then stood the men down and ordered Malick to cease transmission in an hour. The sailors had a welcome hot meal and reported back to work. First, McCracken ordered all the life rafts and canvas awning overboard.

"Don't let the boats sink, let 'em float away," he ordered.

The awning was big and white and had a huge Stars and Stripes painted on it for identification. It covered the boat deck where consuls and visiting dignitaries were entertained in what already seemed to be a bygone age; the crew called that part of the ship the Palm Garden. Malick and the others rolled it up, put a load of potted palms inside, and dumped it over the side.

The next task was to paint the ship. Like the awning she was white, so white and gleaming you could spot her at sea, even on the horizon. McCracken consulted the bosun. The only thing in the paint store other than more white paint was a fresh shipment of black shoe polish. The cans were taken down to the galley and diluted in pans of hot water, and the crew set to and painted the ship black. With a speed and dedication that the bosun found entirely laudatory and not a little unique, it took them just twenty-eight minutes to finish the job. In peacetime the crew would take all day to paint the ship. As the sky lightened it was time to return to general quarters.

Dawn found the seas empty. The Japanese destroyers must have come across the abandoned life rafts and figured the gunboat had sunk. McCracken ordered the anti-aircraft gunners to remain on duty while the rest of the crew returned to routine sea duties.

Friday, December 5, 1941
17th Pursuit Squadron
Nichols Field

The pilots now had to contend with construction workers, for they were extending Nichols Field into one of the biggest air bases in the Far East. The original runway lay east-to-west. A new one was in the final stages of completion; its axis was north-to-south, and the two came together in the shape of a "T." The barracks were grouped around the old runway. A new complex of the usual tropical barracks, two stories with a verandah, was taking shape across the field.

In accordance with MacArthur's orders, the troops at Nichols had taken to the field. This meant moving into big pyramid tents near the new barracks. For the Air Corps the concept of getting into the field meant everything close together, neatly organized and close to amenities.

The pilots were becoming accustomed to the Kittyhawks and were exhilarated by the power of the big Alison engines. There was more night flying than before, only this was not for practice; they were flying interceptor missions on Japanese intruders. Large formations had been tracked by Iba's primitive radar off Lingayen Gulf. Though the pilots were never scrambled in sufficient time to allow them to close and intercept the hostiles, it did give a new sense of urgency and purpose to their training.

Wagner was the first to admit to Erickson and the others that there was still too much left to guesswork in their training. He was convinced that they did not know enough about enemy fighters—how good they were or what their weak points were.

And Erickson wondered how the P-40 compared to the best Japanese planes. He knew that if they were in Europe the RAF could brief them on tactics. But as it was they were working blind.

In Washington there was a complete combat manual on the Mitsubishi Zero fighter. The report listed its strengths and weaknesses and how best to use the heavier P-40 to advantage in dogfights. Written in the autumn of 1940 by Claire Chennault, the American "mercenary" in the pay of the Chinese Nationalists and out of favor in the corridors of air power in Washington, the report had been filed and forgotten.

They caught a spy that day at Nichols Field. He was a crew chief from the 21st Pursuit Squadron. Capt. Leslie Zimmerman, besides being a hard-worked chaplain, also spoke German, and so he was recruited to work part time for Counter Intelligence, looking for German agents inside the services. The authorities at home feared the power of the German-American Bund, and there was a sizable German community in Manila, including Catholic priests at La Salle College and a lot of German Americans serving in the forces in the Far East.

Zimmerman caught the crew chief all on his own. It all began with the airman's girl friend, who was a German. She had been seen at the Bund meetings, and so it was decided that the pair should be shadowed. However, on this particular day Zimmerman's surveillance had been spotted. The airman panicked and drove straight back to Nichols Field. The guards on the main gate were not in on the act, and so it was easy for the fugitive to elude his pursuers once he was inside the base. By this time the authorities had been alerted, and when Zimmerman spotted him he was heading for the dispersal bays out on the perimeter of the field. The man ran for a plane and, with Zimmerman and a flock of MPs close behind, attempted to take off, but he crashed even as he taxied. He misjudged the gap between some buildings, clipped the wing, and rammed the plane head on into a retaining wall. Zimmerman yanked the cockpit hood off the crumpled P-26 and pulled the man out of the tangled wreckage. The fugitive had cracked his skull, and his face was an awful mess. A first-aid team appeared on the scene and revived him, and the crew chief was packed off to the hospital, though still in critical condition.

Two days later they put him on the last boat to the United States—as a medical casualty. The incident had caused intense embarrassment in high places, and, with the international scene poised in delicate balance, the powers that be decided that the incident should be hushed up. Adverse propaganda at this stage was the very last thing the government needed, either in Manila or in the United States.

Fifth-column fever gripped Manila. MacArthur ordered the doubling of guards at the air fields and full vigilance against saboteurs. At Clark and Nichols, the parked aircraft were brought in from their dispersal bays, herded together, and placed under floodlights so that they could be guarded more efficiently.

The House on the Wall
No. 1 Calle Victoria, Manila

Vice-Admiral Sir Tom Phillips, Royal Navy, flew in from Singapore to confer with MacArthur and Hart over a joint Allied strategy. Once more the lights burned late into the night in the House on the Wall.

MacArthur reviewed his strategy and force levels. Some 7,000 reinforcements had increased the American garrison to 19,000 men which, together with 11,000 Philippine Scouts and the 60,000 in the Filipino divisions, he considered to be more than adequate to defeat any Japanese forces who got ashore. At sea and en route from Manila Bay was another big convoy, escorted by the cruiser *Pensacola*, carrying troops, crated aircraft, and ammunition.

In the general's opinion no garrison was better prepared to meet an attack. Admiral Phillips was impressed by the statistics and the oratory, though Hart was less convinced by MacArthur's optimism.

High above the South China Sea and about 30 miles out from Lingayen Gulf, pursuit planes at last caught up with a large formation of Japanese fighters. The latter sped northward once they realized they had been jumped, easily outstripping the lumbering Kittyhawks. The frustrated American pilots returned to base and described the mysterious fighters they had espied in the twilight.

The Japanese were putting the final touches to their long conditioning flights. It was a round trip of 900 miles from their bases in Formosa to Lingayen Gulf. They had been trained to fly with great precision so as to allow a further 400 miles of combat flying in a single mission. For much of the time these flights had to be over water, which placed great demands on their navigational skills, and escorting bombers in formation stretched their abilities to the very limit. There was little margin for error. Indeed, no other fighter pilots in the world in 1941 could produce that performance or match that degree of excellence as a normal squadron requirement. Superbly confident red-blooded Americans, and the British too, were shortly to receive the biggest shock of their young lives in the skies above the Pacific.

Saturday, December 6, 1941

In the final round of discussions with Tom Phillips and his staff, Admiral Hart persisted in the view that an attack was imminent and even MacArthur, now faced with the mounting evidence of Japanese air violations, was less sure of his earlier forecasts. Later that day, Admiral Phillips left for Singapore. He had only four days to live.

MacArthur called in General Brereton, who commanded his air forces, and together they reviewed the air defense of the Philippines. After some deliberation, MacArthur ordered all B-17s to be sent south immediately to the sanctuary of Del Monte Field in Mindanao, well outside any conceivable range of Japanese land-based bombers. There was still felt to be a very considerable risk of sabotage from a fifth column, but nevertheless MacArthur ordered the pursuit planes to be dispersed again at Clark, Nichols, and other fighter stations on the main island of Luzon.

Neither order was obeyed.

Over lunch MacArthur held one of his off-the-record sessions with newsmen. The atmosphere was relaxed and friendly in the usual venue for these occasions: an opulent private suite in the Manila Hotel.

"Gentlemen," the general said over the brandy and cigars, "war is imminent. I believe the attack will come sometime after January."

At the same time, 10,000 feet over the South China Sea, Sammy Boghosian was photographing a Zero. He was twenty-one years of age and a radio-operator/waist gunner on a B-17D that was on a reconnaissance flight 200 miles north of Luzon. Ten minutes earlier two fighters had appeared and were now flying in formation with the Fortress, one on each beam.

"Hey, Sammy," the captain called over the intercom, "get a shot of these babies."

Sam scrambled through the plane, awkward and immobile in his flying jacket and boots. The Japanese pilot stayed obligingly near while Sam swung the portside .50-caliber back on its mount and leaned out in the slipstream. He was only a little guy, and the camera seemed to him to weigh a ton.

MacArthur ordered the Philippines onto a full alert.

Sunday, December 7, 1941

It was a normal Sunday in Manila. Despite the orders for alert, the troops were able to relax at the gun positions. Many others had leave. Fred Howard and his friends were enjoying a seventy-two-hour pass on the mainland. Bressi humped his pack up to one of the

3-inch AA gun sites on Battery Chicago, where he had been assigned. There he found the men filling empty ammunition boxes with sand in a rather desultory manner and building an embrasure around the gun pit. It was backbreaking work, particularly in that heat. They had started the job a week back, and they were not even half finished, but nobody seemed unduly worried.

2nd Battalion, 4th U.S. Marines
Olongapo

There was not a lot for the Marines at Subic Bay. The Leather-necks had made the warehouses as comfortable as they could, and by now the floor space had been clearly marked off into company areas. About a mile down the road was a barrio that had half a dozen flea-bitten bars. They were little open-air affairs; most had a dance partition next door and taxi girls who did a brisk trade with the Marines. A little farther along was another barrio called Santa Rosa. Few Marines made it past the first set of attractions; consequently this was less crowded and was preferred by the senior noncoms and junior officers.

Santa Rosa had a nightclub that 1st Lt. Sid Jenkins and Sergeant Bigelow favored. It was quiet and overlooked the river. The two were firm friends, and that afternoon they had strolled out to the club and were quietly sipping the local beer.

"I reckon the Japs are going to strike in the next forty-eight hours," Jenkins said.

Sergeant Bigelow choked on his beer. "What do you base that on, sir?"

"Well, all the Intelligence reports indicate something's up. There have been too many violations of air space in recent weeks for it to be anything else."

Sergeant Bigelow couldn't accept his friend's verdict. They talked long after the shadows had begun to lengthen, each in his own way seeking other explanations for Japan's strange behavior.

At sea three Japanese assault groups headed south through storm-tossed waters. The weather effectively screened their movements from preying eyes above, but for the soldiers it was agony. Their mission was to seize bridgeheads and establish air fields in northern Luzon.

Throughout the towns and barrios of the Philippines the day was one of frantic activity and elaborate preparations. Monday was the feast of the Immaculate Conception, one of the most important holy days in the Philippine calendar. Every barrio boasted its richly ornate statue of the Blessed Virgin. These were lovingly cleaned and decorated by the young girls. The men prepared to carry them in grand procession while others decorated the streets with lights and streamers. The air was heavy with the smells of roasting pigs and fowls. A sense of anticipation and occasion preceded the great festival. The church bells pealed out to call in the faithful to early Mass, and children were taken down to the streams for compulsory baths. In nipa huts and crowded city tenements, proud parents dusted off their Sunday best and prepared to make the most of the coming day.

The feast of the Immaculate Conception was also a public holiday, but not everyone would spend the day in an appropriate Christian manner. Cock-fighting arenas and gambling dens prepared for a busy day. The clip joints and dime-a-dance halls brought in extra staff in anticipation of the numbers of off-duty Filipino soldiers with money to spend, who doubtless would make their way to the bright lights once they had attended compulsory Mass.

The "*Pensacola* convoy," eight freighters packed with men and equipment, was north of the Phoenix Islands, some 5,000 miles and eight days sailing from Manila Bay.

30th Bomber Squadron
19th Bomb Group
Clark Field

There were seventeen Flying Fortresses still at Clark. Though by now they had twice been ordered to fly south, they had delayed their departure, for the air crews were going to a party for Brereton. It was organized by the twelve hundred men of the 27th Bombardment Group, and it promised to be the biggest party the Philippines had ever seen. The Manila Hotel found its resources stretched to capacity to stage such an affair. However, despite the occasion, not all the airmen could attend. There was the question of the alert and the fear of sabotage. A number of isolated incidents had been reported, and so the planes had to be guarded. As he was the youngest and newest crew member, Sam Boghosian was given the guard assignment. While the rest of his crew prepared for the party, Sammy drew the regulation Browning .45 and belt from stores, took a flashlight from his locker, and made his way down to the flight lines. There the big ships were drawn up wing to wing, the arc lights already casting sinister shapes deep into the dark recesses of the Philippine night.

The last truckload of airmen passed noisily out of the gateway, and a strange peace descended across the field. Sammy hitched the holster around from his thigh. The weight of the weapon left a damp sweat patch to mark its place. He had three planes to guard and two-hour watches to keep; the juniors from the other ships would take their turn during the night.

IV. DAY OF INFAMY

Monday, December 8, 1941

1. "Bandits over Clark"

0330 hours
U.S.S. *Canopus*
Manila

Lt. Cdr. George King, U.S.N., an engineer serving as repair officer submarines, Asiatic Fleet, had the duty. He was awakened from a deep sleep by the unfamiliar bump, bump, bump of a ladder. For a moment the source of the noise eluded him. Then he remembered that all the ladders and companionways topside were now fastened only at the top so that in case of war they could quickly be stowed below. Someone was descending the ladder that led past his cabin. This was strictly "officers' country," so it had to be a drunken sailor taking a shortcut to the crew space two decks down. King slipped on a pair of shorts and stormed outside. Ferrell, yeoman of signals, met him at the foot of the ladder.

"Mr. King, we're at war," Ferrell told him.

"You're drunk, Ferrell," King replied.

"Sir, we've just received this signal," an aggrieved Ferrell said as he handed the startled officer a signal pad and board. King moved back inside his cabin and turned on the light. The message read,

JAPAN HAS STARTED HOSTILITIES, PEARL HARBOR HAS BEEN ATTACKED. GOVERN YOURSELVES ACCORDINGLY.

It was just eighteen minutes after the first bombs had fallen on Pearl Harbor.

0340 hours
On board *S-36*
Lingayen Gulf

The officer of the watch pulled back the curtain, shook Mc-Knight awake, and handed him a dispatch that had been sent by Admiral Hart.

> THE JAPANESE HAVE COMMENCED HOSTILITIES. GOVERN YOURSELVES ACCORDINGLY.

Mac went to the radio shack and had the duty watch tune in to Manila Radio, where they learned in detail of the disaster that was Pearl Harbor.

McKnight ordered the crew below. In this tropical heat they had taken to sleeping on deck. The bare steel hulls of the S-boats were like Turkish baths, and men sleeping inside lay in pools formed by their own sweat. This class of submarine had the bare minimum in terms of fans, and no air conditioning; so, in such fetid conditions, even the unyielding deck topside at night was infinitely preferable to life below. Unable to go back to sleep himself, the young lieutenant spent what was left of the night trying to compose a rousing message of war to deliver to his men. In his youth and inexperience he felt it was the very least they would expect from their commanding officer.

On board U.S.S. *Mindanao*
South China Sea

At about the same time, Sam Malick picked up a radio intercept to all ships at sea. The message was quickly decoded, and he hurried to the bridge, where the gunnery officer had the watch. The night lights on the bridge gave the signal pad a strangely sinister appearance as he read,

EXECUTE WAR PLAN 46 AGAINST JAPAN.

Lieutenant Commander McCracken came two at a time up the ladder from his sea cabin below as the officer of the watch sounded general quarters.

Bressi and a couple of friends were playing pinochle at Battery Way. There were not enough gunners to man the mortars, and so the Hommerland Super Probes—considered to be the best long-range radio receivers in service—occupied the magazines. In the small hours of the morning the duty signalers decoded the messages of war that came flooding in. Bressi phoned the officer of the day, who in turn called the Commanding General Harbor Defenses, Maj. Gen. George Moore. The alarm bells sounded throughout the island and her sister forts.

HQ Squadron
27th Bombardment Group
Clark Field

Sergeant Taulbee has been summoned to the group commander's office. He arrived in no time and still managed to look immaculate, setting the example every top sergeant should. In contrast a number of other officers, including the squadron commander and operations officer, with tousled hair, sleep-filled eyes, and uniforms to match, were gathered around the desk. Cigarette smoke hung low below the strobe lighting as the operations officer briefed Taulbee.

Lieutenant Colonel Maitland, the base commander, asked Taulbee if he thought the men should be told.

Taulbee thought for a moment and then advised against such a move.

"Let them have this night to sleep," he said. "It may be the last they'll get for a while. In any event there isn't anything they can do until daylight, sir."

Many had only just gotten their heads down after returning from the party in Manila.

Sammy Boghosian had finished his watch and headed for the operations room, where there was always a strong cup of coffee available for the duty watch. On this occasion he found the room already a hive of activity as officers and headquarters staff reported for duty. Although the top brass had acted on Taulbee's advice, nevertheless the word was out. In five minutes Sammy had heard enough; he scuttled out of the building and down to the squadron lines, all thought of sleep hurled from his mind. He burst into the hut he shared with other noncom air crew.

"Hey, fellas, there's a war on," he yelled. A fusillade of boots, helmets, and bottles, with a drunken chorus of indignation was the response from those who knew the morning held the misery of hangovers. Sam went to his bunk as the ruction subsided, but he was too excited to sleep.

0500 hours
The House on the Wall
No. 1 Calle Victoria, Manila

MacArthur's headquarters was ablaze with light. The duty telephone operators had worked wonders, and staff officers were reporting for duty in a steady stream. Brereton paced the floor in Sutherland's office, fretting at the delay in seeing MacArthur, who was at the time talking with Admiral Hart, and the Chief of Staff had not the slightest intention of interrupting their conference.

Brereton wanted permission to launch a raid by B-17s on the Japanese naval and air facilities at Takao Harbor in southern Formosa, a large base complex situated about 600 miles north of Luzon. Unable to wait much longer and yet unwilling to interrupt his chief, Sutherland ordered Brereton to prepare for the raid. As the air chief hurried away, Sutherland stressed that his was an order to stand by only. MacArthur would have to give his personal approval.

Brereton returned to his own headquarters at Nielson Field, where he found the B-17 squadron commander, Lt. Col. Eugene Ewbank, awaiting instructions before returning to Clark. The staff officers set to and planned the Takao mission in detail. The latest Intelligence data were collated, and "met men" forecast the weather conditions that the bombers were likely to encounter over Formosa. At the same time, orders to stand by were dispatched to Clark, where armorers and other specialists were already waiting to receive instructions. Despite the revelry and carousing that had taken place just a few short hours before, the bombardment group moved into action like the well-oiled and highly professional machine it had become.

It was now three hours after Pearl Harbor.

0600 hours
HQ, 11th Air Fleet, Takao Air Corps
Takao Field
Formosa

The Japanese Air Force was grounded. Thick fog rolled in from the sea and made any hope of flying from the air fields of southern Formosa utterly impossible. Instead the air fields went on alert— all guns were manned and planes dispersed, loaded with bombs, and ready to fly. Air crews sat in the cockpits and fretted away the delay; there was little else they could do under the circumstances.

The Japanese fear was that the Americans in the Philippines, forearmed with the news of Pearl Harbor, would lose no time in launching their own B-17s against Formosa. It was to be another desperately anxious hour before the fog cleared and the Japanese were able to scramble their squadrons of fighters and launch the heavy bombers southward to Luzon.

0715 hours
30th Bomber Squadron
Clark Field

The air crews of the B-17s were called for an early-morning mission. While the rest of his crew finished breakfast, Sammy Boghosian took the Thermos containers into the kitchen. It was the job of the junior man on the flight to organize the coffee, and they were due in the briefing room in twenty minutes. Sammy reckoned he had just about enough time.

General Brereton again strode purposefully into the Chief of Staff's office. His own people had prepared the mission. He had waited two hours for MacArthur to order the attack, but no word had been received from the House on the Wall. Brereton confronted Sutherland—there was little love lost between them at the best of times—and now Sutherland agreed to ask the general.

After a few minutes, the Chief of Staff came out of the general's office, shut the door quietly behind him, and turned toward Brereton. "The general says 'No,'" he said. "We must not make the first overt act."

Brereton argued in vain. "For Chrissake, what do you call Pearl Harbor?" he asked. "Hell, nothing could be more overt than that!"

It was pointless. Brereton, failing either to convince Sutherland or gain access to MacArthur, returned to his Air Corps headquarters at Nielson Field on the outskirts of Manila.

Meanwhile, 60 miles to the north, at Clark Field, the air crews had left the briefing room and on the advice of the operations officer gone down to the flight lines. The early-morning air soon filled to the sound of the Wright Cyclone Radials healthily clearing their throats and covering the dispersal in hazy blue exhaust fumes. Clouds of dust mushroomed from the downdraft of the propellers, and attendant ground crews covered their ears to the deafening sound of the engines. Boghosian stowed the Thermos containers and the sandwiches and tuned the radio. He then moved back down the ship and checked the ammunition feed on the starboard waist

.50-caliber. It began to get unpleasantly hot inside the metal skin of the Fortress, and the crew fretted to be airborne. The pilot ran the engines up to full revs and switched off. One by one, the other ships followed suit.

A strange tranquillity descended over Clark.

Brereton still had not received any order from MacArthur. He could delay no longer if the mission was to be a success, but at least some early reconnaissance of the Formosa fields would be of value later in the day. He ordered two B-17s aloft. Sam watched them leave. By now most of the crews had stripped off their heavy flying suits and were stretched out on the grass beside the planes. Taulbee had arranged for a small pickup with coffee and doughnuts to make the rounds of the flight line. The crews devoured the newspapers it carried, hungry for news, while others gathered around radios tuned to Manila. Somebody had produced a baseball, and a game started among the bored and less concerned. Mid, upper, and nose gunners polished the Perspex of their turrets, for a speck of dirt can become an enemy plane in flight. The British Air Force had already learned the lessons of crystal-clear Perspex in the killing ground that was the skies above occupied Europe. At Clark everybody chewed gum and most smoked incessantly, impatient for the takeoff, while mechanics and crew chiefs made last-minute adjustments. Armorers stood by the long tractor-drawn bomb carts that seemed to stretch in an unbroken line all the way back to the magazines. High explosives and incendiaries, the classic cocktail of air bombardment, would comprise the bomb load for each plane.

0830 hours

Hap Arnold, the Air Corps chief in Washington, called Brereton direct, told him of the disasters in Battleship Row, and warned his shaken subordinate not to be caught napping with the B-17s on the ground. Brereton in turn called Clark and ordered the B-17s to orbit the field. A green signal flare arched across the field, and one by one the giant bombers left their bays and taxied to the end of the runway. Boghosian's pilot gunned the four big motors into life, and the ship trundled down the rutted concrete strip. Without a bomb load she lifted easily into the air. Orders came through from the tower and Boghosian called the pilot with instructions to circle Mount Arayat at 20,000 feet.

The mountain, less than 20 miles east of Clark, was already on their port quarter as the plane clawed for height and joined formation with the others in their formation of three.

Meanwhile, down below tractors towed the bomb-laden carts back to the magazines, where they were parked in neat lines outside the bunkered building. There seemed little point in unloading everything and storing it all away if the planes were to make a raid on the enemy that day. A couple of riflemen were posted to guard against saboteurs or fifth columnists, and the armorers went about their business.

The B-17s had barely cleared Clark when the first tanks arrived. As part of the alert plan the 194th Tank Battalion deployed in platoons along the perimeter of the air field. They were to guard against a paratroop attack. The successful German airborne assault on Crete had set the alarm bells ringing in the corridors of war, and though it did usher in a new era of fighting, in most cases it produced an alarmist and overreactive response. Parachutists were the new bogeymen in the mind of staid military planners.

It was now six hours after Pearl Harbor.

0900 hours

The air warning group at Nielson had word from the coast watchers that Japanese bombers were sighted over Lingayen Gulf, and, shortly after, this was confirmed by the radar plot at Iba. Fighter Ground Control decided that Clark was the target and accordingly scrambled the fighters from the 20th Pursuit Squadron to intercept. The older P-40B Tomahawks barreled into the air, pilots eager for combat, while the 17th Pursuit were scrambled from Nichols to take their place in providing air cover for Clark.

0930 hours
The nuns of Maryknoll Convent
Baguio, Luzon

The nuns had already begun their celebration of the Feast of the Immaculate Conception with the early-morning offices of the Church, and as was their custom this missionary and teaching order had friends to stay. They were all now happily eating breakfast, for the rest of the day was a holiday. The nuns and their guests made plans.

Sister Louise Kroeger felt better than she had for a long while. After years of missionary work in China she had contracted tuberculosis. It had been a long and painful recovery, first at the order's house in Japan and now for the last months in the idyllic surroundings of the convent, set in the cool hills above the summer capital of Baguio.

The telephone rang. It was the Spanish Fathers from their monastery higher up the mountain. They broke the news of the war.

The nuns barely had time to consider what had happened when they heard the sound of planes overhead. Sister Louise led the other Americans outside. There, high above, beautiful silver streaks banked in a wide sweep over the capital. The sun glinted on their wings. The nuns cheered. "They're our planes," they yelled.

They were convinced they were American planes. What other planes could they be?

The Japanese were not heading for Clark, or Nichols; instead they unloaded their bombs on the summer capital even though it was of little strategic value. The Americans had a rest camp at Camp John Hay and a small garrison of sorts. True, the President of the Philippines, Emanuel Quezon, was there, supposedly sulking after yet another public row in his quixotic relationship with MacArthur. But Baguio was a prestigious target, and in Europe that would already be reason enough for it to be razed to the ground.

The nuns saw the bombs spew from the bellies of the planes, and for the first time their ears filled to the terrifying crescendo of their descent. They stood and watched, riveted to the ground in mute horror as Camp John Hay and a nearby barrio disappeared in an obscene blast of smoke and flame. Even before the carnage was complete and the Japanese bombers, unmolested, went on their way, the nuns had rushed inside to organize assistance with bandages and medicines.

Sister Louise led a small group down toward the burning barrio, some 3 miles away. They believed the local people, though superbly organized and drilled to the needs of air raids by their locally appointed captains, would be glad of some help and perhaps spiritual comfort for the wounded.

They were quite unprepared for the sight that greeted them in the barrio; except for the maimed and the dead, the place was empty. The streets were deserted, and buildings burned unchecked. The captains had gone—all the planning and the drills, the training programs were for nothing. They had gone to their families, for they too were being bombed. The civic leaders grabbed what they could, and they ran in blind panic from the burning streets.

The dead lay in grotesque and shapeless forms. Those who like Sister Louise had witnessed war in China, steeled themselves for the worst and set about the grim task with white faces and set lips. Others, the young and the innocent, silently heaved their stomachs into the blood and tissue that littered the streets. For those whose first sight of violent death is the mutilation and human debris wrought by high explosives, the horror can sear the mind.

The Japanese bombers had by now left Luzon behind and were over the open sea. With home over the horizon the crews relaxed a little, for it had all been too easy; and there had been neither sight nor sound of an American interceptor.

MacArthur had his overt act.

1000 hours
Clark Field

Brereton's phone rang. It was Sutherland with the news that General MacArthur would authorize an attack once the reconnaissance photographs had been developed and analyzed. Perhaps the operation could be launched in early afternoon?

Col. Eugene Ewbanks raced for his car and hurtled back to Clark. He could leave his chief to sort out this vague and imprecise instruction, but as far as he was concerned there was enough to order a strike on the Japanese.

It was now seven hours after Pearl Harbor.

1015 hours
HQ, 11th Air Fleet, Takao Air Corps
Takao Field
Formosa

A green star shell soared above the control tower. The first of 54 Nell* bombers trundled down the runway. At 20,000 feet over the South China Sea they rendezvoused with the same number of Bettys† from Tainan Field. Their close escort of 50 Zeros moved into formation. Top cover was given by 34 Zeros, also from Tainan.

The air armada headed south for Luzon.

1030 hours
Clark Field

Sammy Boghosian picked up the message on the group channel, "Return to base and bomb up." He relayed the instruction to the captain, and the crew cheered, for they were heartily sick of circling Mount Arayat.

The big ships came lumbering in one by one. Wheels and flaps down, with fuel tanks half empty they bounced and swayed down the runway and then slowed into the dispersal points. Crew chiefs packed them close so that they could be more easily fueled and armed for the afternoon sortie.

It was 1120 hours by the time that Sam's plane, one of the last to

---

*G-3M Mitsubishi-type 96 two-engine land-based medium bomber.
†G-4M Mitsubishi-type 1 two-engine land-based torpedo bomber.

land, had taxied into its allotted position and the engines had shut down. The crews were ordered to have an early lunch before the first briefing, which for navigators and radio operators was time-tabled for 1220 hours.

Sam collected the Thermos containers and hurried away to the mess hall along with the other noncoms, while the pilots headed for the Officers' Club and their quarters.

Most had less than an hour to live.

1115 hours

The pilots of the 20th Pursuit were now low on fuel. All had been airborne since 0900 hours that morning. They had rushed north as far as the Cagayan Valley, then west in a sweep out to the South China Sea, but they had seen nothing. For the last hour they had flown cover over the bombers and the field. Aloft since the first raid, they were at the limit of their endurance, and so the pilots were instructed to land. The planes were parked neatly alongside the fuel lines waiting for their ground crews to return from lunch. Most of the pilots headed for the Officers' Club, where they joined the bomber crews in a quick drink before returning to their aircraft.

Forty miles west of Clark across the Zimbales Mountains lay Iba; after Nichols it was the most important field in the Philippines. This wasn't because of the contribution that the eighteen Kitty-hawks of the 3rd Pursuit made to the air defense of the Philippines but because it had the only operational early-warning radar on Luzon. The set and its operators lived in a little shack out near the end of the runway, open to the fresh sea breezes and the elements.

The Iba pilots had made sortie after sortie since before first light, always chasing phantoms, turning first one way, then another at the behest of the frantic air controllers.

At 1127 hours the radar screen was alive—the operators had never seen so many blips. Iba informed Nielson Fighter Control, who promptly called out the reserves. Eighteen fighters of the 17th Pursuit were scrambled to patrol Manila Bay. They had been on the ground barely half an hour. Wagner led his squadron in six tight formations of three. Engines strained to gain altitude and the sun, and the air was alive with the excited chatter of pilots. Wagner silenced his men and privately prayed that they would be ready for their baptism of fire. Erickson scanned the sky in the ceaseless search for the enemy. Again he quartered his segment, relying on the wingman to watch his back. In the cramped confines of the cockpit he looked ridiculous; with his six-foot-four frame, his knees were higher than his chin. He tried to ease his back against the unrelenting ribs of the armor plate, but this brought little comfort. Instead he recognized the first signs that marked the onset of cramp, which he had now learned to accept as his private penalty for flying a Hawk.

1145 hours

Nielson Fighter Control was swamped with calls from coast watchers, post- and stationmasters, and the well intentioned. The number of Japanese planes increased with each report until the controllers didn't know who or what to believe.

Nielson called Clark, but the teletype would not respond. Neither did the radio answer, for the operators were at lunch. In desperation the fighter control director called Clark on the civilian telephone network, and even more precious minutes were wasted. Eventually the director, Colonel Campbell, was able to reach some anonymous lieutenant, who promised to pass on the air-raid warning to the base commander.

He never did.

It was eight and a half hours after Pearl Harbor.

1156 hours

The sirens sounded in Manila and over Nichols. At Fort McKinley the gunners swung their barrels skyward and the ground crew stocked the ready use lockers with ammunition. Almost every fighter was either in the air or awaiting orders to scramble—that is, all except the 20th Pursuit at Clark.

The whole base was still at lunch. Mess halls were full, and some men strolled back to the squadron lines or to their billets. The pilots of the 20th Pursuit were now back in their cockpits, eating sandwiches and drinking coffee, which they had brought from the Officers' Club.

1200 hours

Most of the men were enjoying the funniest radio program they had ever heard. In mess hall and barracks, sets were tuned to station KM2H and the lunchtime news from Manila. The announcer, Don Bell, had said that there was an unconfirmed report that Clark Field was being bombed.

Peals of laughter rose above the clatter of cutlery and crockery. In the barracks and tent lines the joke was passed from man to man.

The whole station laughed while Iba died.

The Japanese air armada contained 108 Mitsubishi bombers escorted by 84 Zeros. About half the force peeled off from the main flight and destroyed Iba. The radar shack and its operators were blasted to oblivion by the first bombs, the control tower and its 4 controllers were obliterated.

There was carnage on the ground. The 16 Tomahawks of the 3rd Pursuit fought until they had to land and refuel. Those that survived the hail of bombs fell victim to the strafing Zeros, which chopped them into the ground as they came in to land. It was all over in minutes, and men fled from the field in panic and made their way inland. The Army surgeon loaded some of the wounded into a local bus and headed for Manila.

Iba was abandoned.

Anyone flying into Clark reckons it's one of the easiest fields to find. It lies 20 miles to the east of the 3,800-foot signpost of Mount Arayat. Five miles farther on are the neat white lines of the Army quarters and barracks, standing out among the manicured borders of acacia and mango of the distinctive polo field of Stotsenberg.

While Americans were laughing at Don Bell, the Japanese pilots could already see Clark. The raiders then received their final and very explicit markers to the target, the B-17s themselves. The sun rays reflected like a giant heliograph off the polished and burnished silver metal skin of the closely packed Fortresses.

The Japanese pilots had expected to battle through serried ranks of Tomahawks to deliver their bombs. Not only was the sky clear of planes, but also the enemy had seemingly turned on the lights to beckon them in and then lined up their ships neatly, like lambs for a ritual slaughter.

The men at Clark heard the drone of aircraft. Dick Osborn along with many others wandered outside and looked up. They counted 27 planes in 9 tight Vs. "Gee, look at those B-18s," Dick said.

An older crew chief shook his head. "Nope, we ain't got but ten left in the whole of the Philippines! They can't be ours."

The bombers in majestic flight wheeled north at 20,000 feet. Even the gunners of the 200th Coast Artillery, responsible for the air defense of Clark, took a break from their work to watch the spectacle. They were in the process of resiting their ancient 3-inch museum pieces, and few of the guns were operational.

Sammy Boghosian was walking back to his plane, loaded down again with the Thermos containers.

"Cheers," someone yelled, looking up at the sky. "Here comes the Navy."

The bombs fell first on Stotsenberg and then walked, stick by stick, all the way to Clark.

As the first bomb hit the perimeter—it fell less than 20 yards from the executive officer's tank—the battalion was galvanized into action. Frank Muther, the radio operator, was the last man out as the exec and his crew abandoned the still-ringing hull. The only cover they could find was a monsoon culvert, which doubled as a sewer drain. None of them noticed, at first.

Many ground crew and pilots tried to run toward their aircraft. Dick Osborn realized the futility of the exercise and instead dived head first into one of Maitland's Follies; the breath was knocked from his body as 200 pounds of mechanic landed on top of him.

In the meanwhile, the 17th Pursuit was orbiting over Manila Bay at 10,000 feet. Suddenly a voice came up, loud and clear: "Tally ho, bandits over Clark." Wagner called the Air Warning Group at Nielson—they were responsible for the control of the air defense by pursuit planes—for permission to join the battle. It was refused.

Lieutenant Moore, commanding the 20th Pursuit, was among the first to react. Hurling the remains of a hot dog from the cockpit, he gunned his motor into life and taxied into position for take off. As the bombs first straddled and then obliterated the mess halls, he raced his Kittyhawk along the runway, closely followed by eight more fighters. The planes zoomed away in a desperate bid to gain the height they needed to give battle to the enemy.

A further two fighters gathered speed to run the gauntlet. Tails up, they inched off the ground and flew straight into a stack of incendiaries. The planes, transformed into fireballs, spewed into a line of parked P-26s. The conflagration engulfed man and machine.

John White, a crew chief on one of those P-26s, was in the cockpit running a preflight check. He killed the engine and raced for a nearby slit trench as the flames devoured his machine. He was lucky to make that ditch; many didn't.

The first flight of twenty-seven Japanese aircraft precision-bombed in formation. As at Pearl Harbor they had achieved complete tactical surprise. The AA gunners of the New Mexico National Guard manned museum pieces they had never even fired in practice. The ammunition, manufactured a decade and more ago, was heavily corroded. Shells burst at least 5,000 feet beneath the Japanese.

The bombers hit the runway, the pursuit squadron's aircraft dispersal area, and the mess halls. Many ground crew and troops fled the field in blind terror and ran out toward the perimeter. There was no sanctuary to be found—stray incendiaries fell among the horde, and flash fires started among the acacia trees and cogan grass. Men found what cover they could from the death that rained down from above. Others clawed furiously at the soft rich loam, but the cool earth could afford little protection.

The second flight wheeled in behind the first Nells, unworried by the American interceptors. Those that had made it into the air were overwhelmed by the diving Zeros. Funeral pyres marked the fate of two young pilots. Four more raced for cover; they lived for minutes longer before the Zeros swatted them from the sky.

Moore led two others into battle. Three Zeros fell to their avenging fire before they, too, were forced to disengage and run for their lives. They power-dived their Tomahawks out of trouble and at treetop height sought to elude the vastly superior Japanese planes.

Six ancient P-35s from Del Carmen came screaming into battle. Already low on fuel, they could make but one pass before running for home. Two Zeros were hit by them, but others hounded the impudent intruders from the arena.

Not one American interceptor was able to break through the massed formation of Zeros to get at the bombers; instead they were overwhelmed. The bombs fell on the B-17s, which had all been conveniently refueled. Only a few of the latest model, the series D, had been equipped with self-sealing fuel tanks. Fuel spewed from tanks ruptured by concussion of the high explosives, and the big ships burned unchecked.

Sergeant Taulbee had sought cover in his personal slit trench. He had dug this himself just a few convenient feet from the door of the orderly room. With tin hat on and chin strap in place, this old soldier watched helplessly as the Japanese carpeted the field and, in the most beautiful precision attack, bombed the living daylights out of his group.

Amid the chaos and the carnage, a lone B-17 swooped low over the field, made an apologetic final approach, and came straight in to land. It was one of the pair that had been dispatched that morning on the reconnaissance flight; the pilot had aborted the mission two hours out with generator trouble. Perhaps the Japanese were too amazed to react as the Fortress descended imperiously through the falling bombs. The crew led a charmed life; the young pilot with a deft touch missed bombs, cratered debris, and flaming aircraft as he taxied toward the parking bay. A crew chief with more presence of mind than most batted the pilot. Even before the engines had been killed and the ship came to a stop, the crew was scuttling out of every escape hatch and door.

As the last Japanese bomber droned on its way and the great dust and smoke pall rose above Clark, firefighting crews raced into action. Ambulances ferried the wounded to hospitals, while rescue crews searched among the shattered timbers of the mess halls. Within minutes discipline and order began to be asserted. Those not involved in the relief and rescue of the wounded rushed to salvage what they could from the bombed and burning buildings.

1235 hours

Such endeavor, however, was to be in vain. The Zeros, which had hugged their bombers and flown shotgun over them, were now released from their charges. Only a few of their number had jousted with the American interceptors, and the rest had become frustrated and impatient for battle. With the bombers already setting course for home, the Zeros swooped down on Clark. Now the killing time began.

On the ground men were working furiously to save their airfield, and few bothered to keep an eye skyward for further signs of trouble. Two Fortresses were being run out of the burning paint shop, their pilots at the controls. The planes erupted into flame as the incendiaries and cannon shells from the Zeros tore great chunks from the air frames and burned the fabric beneath.

The Americans fought back, and many acts of personal heroism went unsung. Men manned the guns of their parked planes until their ships burned beneath them. The tanks opened up on the swooping Zeros with their turret-mounted Brownings, but the old water-cooled guns soon burned out, and the crews turned to pistols and rifles to ward off the foe. Bill Matson felt at times that he could reach out and touch the enemy.

Ben Saccone stood on a turret, arms akimbo, and hurled abuse at the Japanese fliers; he had nothing else. The Zeros punched a hole in everything that moved on Clark. They roamed at will just feet above the field. Gunpits were emptied and devastated by raking cannon fire, windows were shattered, and the control tower was abandoned.

The airfield's own close-range air defense should have been able to ward off some of the attacks, as there were a number of emplacements dotted around the field protecting the major installations. Maybe if these anti-aircraft gunners with their .50-calibers had been given ammunition in which the belts had not crumbled and disintegrated from age, they might have put up a more effective resistance. Many Americans were overwhelmed and stupefied by the scale of destruction visited on them by an oriental foe. The truth dawned on men at different times.

Finally, their ammunition expended and their fuel critical, the Japanese pilots reluctantly broke away and headed north for home, well satisfied with the morning's work. The damage wrought by the bombers had been bad enough, but the strafing fighters had destroyed Clark.

1315 hours

The Tomahawks of the 17th Pursuit were ordered down from their empty vigil above Manila Bay, and the pilots returned to Nichols. In their absence a couple of maverick Japanese had shot up the field, although little damage had been inflicted.

A sense of deep shock gripped Clark. It affected men in different ways. Many of the young, frightened and alone, without orders or direction, had fled the chaos. By nightfall they were many miles away in the foothills of the Zimbales; others hid out in the long grass all day. The majority, however, tried to pick up the pieces. Sammy Boghosian stood where his B-17 had been parked. He looked down on a pile of rubble. There were four engines and a heap of melted metal. One propeller blade stood out mute and twisted, like the crucifix of a bombed-out church.

Unwittingly he still clutched a Thermos in his left hand.

Dick Osborn worked on the salvage detail. Taulbee sent him with a group down the runway to the burned-out skeleton of a Tomahawk. The pilot was still in the cockpit, a charred claw gripping the stick. Sick to their stomachs, they cleared the plane off the runway—but no one could touch the pilot.

The men worked on in the late-afternoon sun. By now the stench of death was all-pervasive. With a rag tied around his mouth and nose, Osborn worked at salvaging a B-17. He saw his first cranium cavity open at the top. He threw up and then worked on, without his handkerchief.

The bomber squadron was destroyed. Of the twenty-two Flying

Fortresses only seven escaped complete destruction. Only three ever flew again.

Some men scavenged as well as salvaged. Bill Matson scrounged the twin-.50s out of a downed P-40 and soldered them to a new mount on his half-track.

Capt. Jerry McDavitt's battery of Philippine Scouts were deployed onto the still-burning field. The authorities on high had decided that it needed disciplined regulars to get the dead bodies out of Clark. The official figure was later given as 55 dead, but McDavitt's men logged 189 bodies by the end of the day.

As the funeral pyre burned over American air power in the Philippines, at the polo field in Stotsenberg the adjutant of the 26th Cavalry was pleased to report to his colonel that not one horse had panicked during the raid.

2. War Comes to Manilla

Morning
Company C, 1st Battalion, 57th Philippine Scouts
Fort William McKinley
Manila

Loyd Mills awoke late to a terrible hangover. It had been one hell of a party the night before. He had encountered the "flyboys" at the Manila Hotel and become involved. Now with three hours' sleep and all that alcohol it didn't seem such a good idea. Then it hit him: He had a 15-mile route march scheduled for the company. Loyd took a cold shower, hurriedly toweled, and shaved. At twenty-three years of age the human body can absorb an awful lot of punishment and ill treatment. Even so, he skipped breakfast; his stomach revolted at the thought of bacon and eggs. He reached for a cigarette instead.

Ten minutes later Mills strode across the parade square to his company offices, which were directly opposite his quarters. He squinted against the sun, and his forehead pounded out its protest to the weight of the campaign hat. On the way he met his old company commander, who said, "Hey, Loyd, you heard the latest? The Japs have bombed Hawaii."

Mills was in no mood for humor and passed on his way.

The polished wood of the verandah steps leading to his office was receiving its routine attention from a fatigue party. Even so, Mills soon learned the rumor was true. In short order he was accosted by his newly arrived second-in-command, a fresh-faced youth out of West Point, and his top sergeant.

Mills went into his office, which was like an oven, since the fan had stopped again. An old-fashioned telephone was practically ringing itself off the wall. It was John Spainhower. As adjutant he had arisen at the proper hour and learned of the war in a dignified manner from the newspaper neatly folded in its stand at his breakfast place. He curtly passed on the instructions to his friend to hurry up to regimental HQ, where the colonel was about to brief all company commanders.

Yelling to his West Pointer to alert the company, Loyd ran for HQ. His hangover was forgotten.

Outside the office the fatigue party had moved on to the ornamental cannon. A couple of men polished the brass carriage furiously while the third administered a fresh coat of black paint to the cannon balls. A few well-chosen words in native Tagalog from their company commander was more than enough to send them scuttling for their barracks and to war.

The battalion was ordered to deploy into the field. The received wisdom from headquarters was that the Japanese were almost certain to attempt an airborne drop on McKinley. Mills returned to his quarters; he had just five minutes to pack. Quickly he jammed a few possessions and some changes of clothes into a duffel bag, while his houseboy stood mutely by, unable to grasp the significance of what was happening. Suddenly aware of his presence, Loyd gave him a 10-peso note and told him to pack the rest of the possessions in his cabin trunk. As he went out the door he threw the boy the keys and said, "Take these, kid. If I don't come back, it's all yours."

The company and its transport were drawn up outside. The latter didn't amount to much: a weapons carrier and a four-by-four for the field kitchen. The men marched out of the fort, through the gates, and left down the road that for Loyd Mills and so many generations of young officers had always signaled the start of carefree times. About 2 miles along the B Range Road they deployed into defensive positions and dug their weapon pits.

In the midst of their labors two Japanese fighters appeared low over Nichols and strafed the field. They turned for a second run over the Scouts, who had been ordered not to fire and thus betray their positions. But they opened up with everything they had—rifle and light machine-gun fire chased after the Japanese planes. Loyd Mills joined in with his .45—it made him feel better.

12th Medical Regiment, Philippine Scouts
Fort William McKinley
Manila

Paul Ashton had been a qualified doctor for three years and in the Scouts for three months. He had spent most of his time since arriving in the Philippines administering to cases of advanced venereal disease among the 31st Infantry. This particular morning he was shaving with his pride and joy—a newly acquired electric razor, the latest model. Already the day was hot and humid and his face, wet with sweat, gave the new machine little chance. He gave up after ten minutes and ran some hot water for a wet shave. Angry and frustrated, he turned on the radio and learned of Pearl Harbor.

Ashton finished in rapid time, dressed quickly, and packed. He put all his civilian gear and the electric razor in a big trunk and sent it to the camp theater, where all the officers' heavy baggage was being collected. Paul knew he would never see it again. He set out for the base hospital, where he spent the rest of the day trying to restore some order to the accumulating chaos.

Company H, 2nd Battalion
31st U.S. Infantry

Garleb and his machine-gun squad heard of the war from their company commander. The whole battalion had been out on exercise just a couple of miles from McKinley. Garleb's attitude was one of intense interest and excitement. He had no thoughts of fear, but rather voiced the views of many as he turned to Sergeant Eckhardt, while they worked away mounting the Browning on its anti-aircraft tripod: "How crazy it is for Japan to attack America!"

Similar old-fashioned, heavy wooden tripods were being mounted by Company B on the battlements of the Intramuros.

Pvt. Paul Kerchum formed part of the detail sent off to guard MacArthur's headquarters. Later in the morning the general came out of the building briefly to pose for photographs. Kerchum filled with pride as he stood alongside, his rifle at the "present."

At sea a Japanese cruiser cornered the hunted *Harrison*. Alone and unarmed, there was no way she could outrun the foe. Instead the captain drove hard for the shore of the Chinese mainland and rammed his transport onto a reef. The crew were rescued and interned by the Japanese.

The Japanese were later to salvage the *Harrison* and sail her under their flag until she was sunk by an American submarine.

Pvt. Frederick Howard on the outbreak of war found himself poacher turned gamekeeper. To date the military career of this reluctant soldier had been punctuated by frequent brushes with the law. But soon he was to patrol the Manila waterfront with an MP brassard and a billy club. It all began when he awoke that morning on a table in a girls' business college in Passig. The old *maestra*, or teacher, was madder than a wet hen at him. Typewriters and adding machines lay upended on the floor, and a pair of panties hung from the light bulb. The scene of chaos slowly penetrated through to his booze-addled brain, and Fred began slowly to appreciate the fix he was in. He felt desperately ill, for it was the first time he had ever tried to mix Dobie gin with beer. Thank God, he thought, there was no sign of the two female students who had offered him the hospitality of their dormitory at the dance hall.

More to the point, there was also no sign of his partner in crime, Cpl. Nemesio Arzaga. Fred reached for his pants and tried to make himself decent. That and warding off the blows of the old matron, all with a hangover, was too much. The young soldier gave ground and hopped one-footed onto the verandah. Shit, thought Fred, this is where it becomes public and I get locked up.

Down below in the busy street, children were selling newspapers. Through their raucous Tagalog Fred heard the words "Pearl Harbor" and "Hawaii" over and over again. Even the old woman stopped her assault and in the truce Fred threw down a toston (half peso), and one of the urchins brought up the two-sheet extra.

Despite the Tagalog, Fred knew there was a war on while the matron forgot her peeve and rushed off to make coffee for the brave Americano.

Howard seized his chance and set about trying to find Corporal

Arzaga. Eventually Howard unearthed his companion in arms, entwined with a young beauty at the other end of the verandah, amid the carbon papers in the storeroom. Despite the news Fred had to admire the staying power of his colleague.

The two made good their escape down the back stairs and out into the street. Later over cold beers and a large breakfast in a Chinese restaurant nearby, the Filipino translated the newspaper reports, and the two debated their best course of action. Although they had another thirty-six hours of leave, they knew they had to report to the Rock. Quickly they made their way via the back streets and teeming alleyways of the Passig district to Fort Santiago, where Fred changed into the clean uniform that was in Private Barnes's locker.

It looked like the 1st Battalion was getting ready to move out. There was time for little more than a handshake before Barnes left to join his company. Howard never saw Robert Barnes again. He was killed in the first brush with the Japanese near Calumpit Bridge.

Sobered and subdued by the day's events, Howard and Arzaga made their way to the pier. The two boats available for Corregidor were already overcrowded with officers and senior noncoms. So with no chance of passage for some while at least, they were pressed into police duties in the port area for the rest of the day. It was not until later the following afternoon that they reported for duty on the Rock. Somehow Fred still had his brassard and billy club and also a .45 revolver he had acquired during his police duties.

Lilla Seitz's husband had gone to the office as usual on a Monday morning. She kissed him goodbye, and their chauffeured car sped on its way downtown to the commercial district. Lilla had barely finished dressing when the telephone rang; it was Clay calling from his office to tell her that he was sending Sabino back with the car and $500. He ordered her to go immediately to the grocery store to stock up with everything she would need for the baby and the house.

"What on earth's gotten into you, Clay?" a puzzled Lilla asked. "Are we going on a trip or something?"

It was then that Clay told her about Pearl Harbor.

Lilla remembered an article she had seen in a recent copy of *Life* magazine about the terrible paper shortage in England. So the first things she bought in bulk, along with extra groceries, were rolls of toilet tissue. The next concern was to stock up for the baby's arrival. There was only one good drugstore in Manila, so far as the American community was concerned, and that was owned by a German. Sabino parked the car and Lilla rushed into the store, but the problem was she really didn't know what to buy. It was her first baby, and there was at least a month or more before it was due.

Hans Müller looked up as Lilla approached the counter. "Mrs. Seitz, good morning," he said. "What are you doing here? This is crazy!"

"I have got to have things for my baby," she said.

At that precise moment the air-raid sirens sounded. Müller raised the large trapdoor behind the counter and ushered Lilla and the chauffeur, together with his own family, down the stone steps into the cellar.

"Forget the money, Mrs. Seitz," he said. "I'll get a box and fill it with everything I can think of for a newborn child. Our bags are packed, and this place is going to be closed down any minute."

It then dawned on her that this kindly man and his family were about to be interned, and she had her first experience of the inhumanity of war.

Lilla's enemy alien packed a large carton with medicines and vitamins, diapers, and all the things she would ever need. When the raid was over, Müller helped Sabino load the packages in the trunk of the family Buick.

Lilla's last sight of the Müller family was of them standing dejectedly on the sidewalk, their bags stacked neatly by, waiting for the police to come and escort them to the prison.

Other aliens did not fare so well. Richard Sakakida followed the instructions given on the local radio station and surrendered himself at the local police station for internment. The police slapped him around for a while, and then he was bundled into the back of an open-top truck for the journey to the internment center. Along with three other Japanese and a couple of police for escort, they had to run the gauntlet of the narrow, busy streets in downtown Manila. Abuse, both verbal and the other kind, was hurled at them by angry and frightened groups of Filipinos. The police did little to protect their charges and only intervened on the two occasions in their half-hour journey when the escorting mob threatened to get out of hand.

So, bruised, battered, and not a little bloody, the prisoners eventually arrived at the sanctuary of the internment center. The Philippine Constabulary had strung some wire and set up a guard post covering the entrance to the Japanese Club. Inside, some two thousand Japanese and a few hundred Germans and Italians had been gathered together. All were relieved at the protection afforded them by the more professional Philippine Constabulary and heartily glad to be safe from the callous, indifferent city police and the avenging mobs who were looting alien-owned stores and businesses.

Sakakida squatted against the chain link fence of the tennis court, alone and frightened. He was reasonably confident his cover would hold up, but for how long? If the Japanese started to run their own affairs, even unofficially within the compound, then he would be in real trouble. A number of Japanese businessmen Sakakida suspected of espionage had been arrested just a few days back. If they were placed in the compound, it wouldn't take long for a vigilant inquiry among their own to identify Richard as the common link. He knew he had to be on his guard, but his thoughts and emotions were in turmoil over the war. Kith and kin, race and nation whirled in his mind in conflicting loyalties and a tumble of demands. Sakakida had been born an American citizen, but he could not but feel sympathy at the pathetic sights of families, confused and many physically beaten, who awaited their fate with a quiet dignity. Weren't they his people too? Who wouldn't feel sorry at the ruined lives around him? Richard could only pray that his Control would find some way of springing him before too long— from prison and his dilemma.

Not for the first time that day his thoughts turned to Hawaii and to his mother. God only knew what was happening to the thousands of Japanese caught up in that arena of war. How ironic if his mother and family were now about to bed down in a camp similar to this! What would that do to his loyalties?

The Sternberg

The Sternberg was the general hospital for the Army Philippines Department. Situated in its own beautiful walled gardens just a short distance beyond the battlements of the Intramuros, the hospital was a couple of blocks from Jones Bridge, in the better part of town.

Madeline Ullom, a nurse there since she had first joined the Army in 1940, had been to Mass. A devout Roman Catholic, she attended an early service before going on duty. It was after Mass that the priest had told his little congregation about Pearl Harbor. A hurried breakfast and a quick scan of the newspapers marked the last peace and quiet the nurses would enjoy for some considerable time to come.

The Sternberg under normal conditions was a 250-bed hospital, but ever since the onset of a military alert they had prepared for war. New wards had been opened up and medical teams organized, ready to take to the field at the first alarm. That first morning of war, the hospital became a hive of activity. All the patients who could be discharged were quickly released and their beds made ready for casualties.

The staff had just finished lunch when word filtered down of the attack on Clark. Immediately the first standby medical team, in a commandeered van that now served as an ambulance, left the hospital. A Filipino orderly risked life and limb by standing on the running board, holding on with one hand, while with the other he furiously rang the hand bell that doubled as the ambulance siren. It was crude but effective as the local Filipinos scuttled out of the path of the swaying vehicle.

The first hospital train arrived from Clark in the late afternoon. A fleet of ambulances and flat bed trucks ferried the wounded from the rail terminal across the Pasig River to the hospital. Within an hour two more trains arrived, and the hospital was overwhelmed. Many men lay on their stretchers in the courtyard until the hard-pressed surgical teams could reach them. Civilian helpers did what they could, but for many it was a long and agonizing wait, their suffering aggravated by the makeshift bandages hastily applied in the casualty clearing stations at Clark. There were no field dressings available, and many men had gaping wounds caused by the wonders of war technology. These far outstripped the well-intentioned but amateurish ministrations of frightened friends on the devastated base, whereas the World War I field dressings on hand in Manila, though competently applied, proved totally inadequate for the job on hand—mostly because they were old and flimsy, but also because they were shell dressings and therefore not big enough for the larger wounds caused by incendiary bombs and bullets.

Ullom, trained with the best at Walter Reed in Washington, worked on into evening in the operating theater.

Pressed into the general nursing side was Ruby Moteley, the hospital's civilian dietician. Ullom was small and petite with all the grace of her southern upbringing, whereas Moteley had a beauty that turned men's heads in the streets and made the blood flow faster in their veins. She enjoyed life in Manila and was taking her time in finding a husband though Carl Armburst, gunnery lieutenant from the fleet tanker *Pecos*, was bringing her close to a decision. Their relationship had ripened ever since they had first met on a blind date in November 1940, and they had been going steady for six months.

The *Pecos* was tied up alongside the quay at Manila, and they had spent the previous evening together. Ruby had finally agreed to announce their engagement.

In the late afternoon Ruby was called to the telephone; it was Carl, who had called to tell her that he would not be seeing her for a while. His voice sounded thin and distant.

Illogically she begged him to take her with him.

He told her not to be frightened and promised that he would be back in a couple of weeks.

It didn't help. Ruby, more frightened and depressed than she could ever remember, returned to the wounded in the ward. Five minutes later, with a bedpan in one hand, she helped a young pilot with his bodily functions. Both his hands were gone, and his face was badly burned. Ruby forgot her woes.

With the B-17s destroyed and American command of the air eliminated, Hart ordered the fleet to retreat south beyond the reach of the Japanese.

As the evening shadows lengthened and Manila settled down to blackout and its first jittery night of the war, the *Pecos* backed away from the wharf. Out in the bay she joined her consorts for the dash south. There was the elderly cruiser *Marblehead* and the more modern *Boise*, together with the very old carrier *Langley*; a couple of four-stack destroyers and a fleet submarine provided the escort for the squadron.

Carl Armburst climbed into the gunnery control position high above the bridge of the *Pecos*. He gave himself the luxury of one last lone look back over his shoulder at Manila as the battle gongs sounded out the call to general quarters.

Evening
Nichols Field

Chaplain Zimmerman was feeling utterly frustrated and useless, and he as good as told the base field officer so over dinner in the club. One of the chaplain's chores was to take charge of the Military Amateur Radio Station (MARS). This was a ham radio network through which, for a modest 25 cents, the boys could have messages delivered to home. Ever since he had heard of Pearl Harbor, Zimmerman had been inundated with requests from soldiers anxious to let home know that all was well. So shortly after breakfast, and with a bagload of messages, he had hurried over to the little shack out near the runway where the radio was housed. It was part of the base's radio complex.

The chaplain had found his way barred by a stern-faced and unsympathetic policeman. MARS had been requisitioned for war. Zimmerman and his assistant had gotten around that problem easily enough, for Father O'Brian was a Roman Catholic priest with plenty of contacts outside the base and all the wiles of the Irish. Though the two officers were confined to base, as were all personnel, they had been able to pass their messages to a local priest, who had taken them down to the YMCA, where there was a big radio transmitter that the Philippines Department had somehow overlooked.

Other than that minor victory over officialdom, the war had passed the chaplains by. Thus, angry and frustrated, Zimmerman asked Colonel Maverick, the base field officer, whether there was anything useful that the chaplains could do.

"Yes," the colonel said, "if you two would help man the alert station through the night, that will release one of my flying men in case I need him."

After dinner the colonel took the two chaplains to the scene of their first tour of night duty. They were loaded down with Thermos containers, books, and helmets. Gas masks knocked uncomfortably against their thighs, and Father O'Brian dropped their flashlight, the bulb and glass shattering in the darkness. Colonel Maverick began to doubt the wisdom of his initiative at dinner.

The alert station was in reality a telephone in one of the grubby side rooms in base headquarters. Maverick explained the duty. "It's simple, gentlemen. A message will come in from the Aircraft Control and Warning Group. It's your job to alert three main stations on the base. They are the main guardroom, the Military Police, and Operations Control."

Father O'Brian took the first watch until midnight. Zimmerman bunked down on the camp bed someone had thoughtfully provided, but in his excitement found it impossible to sleep. They changed watch at midnight, and shortly after, the quartermaster and the senior policeman happened by. His duty done, Father O'Brian walked with them for a while; he seemed in no hurry to return to the Bachelor Officers' Quarters.

At 0020 hours the telephone rang, shattering the darkness of the tropical night. Zimmerman grabbed the receiver. A remote, robot-like voice clipped, "Many bombers heading your way," and the line went dead. Zimmerman hastily made the three obligatory telephone calls, but nothing much seemed to happen, so he joined the other officers who had moved outside onto the verandah. It was a beautiful night.

The telephone rang again. As Zimmerman raced back to answer, the base cannon, which was the main air raid alarm, crashed out its warning. At the same time all the lights were killed. The chaplain reached for the pencil flashlight, all he was left with after O'Brian's carelessness. He moved down the corridor and turned in past the typing pool to the alert station.

The voice, remote but now a little impatient, warned, "Air raid imminent."

Though he thought it by now pointless, Zimmerman made the three calls again and then ran for the main door. Fear, unfamiliar surroundings, and an inadequate flashlight resulted in a trail of damage marking his passage out into the night air. Zimmerman stumbled down the steps as the radio shack disappeared under a direct hit. The blast blew a screen from a window in the building, and it enveloped the chaplain like a shroud. He was confused, lost, and momentarily blinded by the white light and heat of the bombs.

Zombielike, Zimmerman staggered forward and promptly fell over the water hydrant. That crunch knocked the breath from his body but rapidly brought him to his senses, and he took cover under the main Signal Corps administrative building. Built on concrete stilts and with a concrete floor, it was as safe as an air raid shelter. There were many others already there, including the quartermaster and policeman, still helpless with laughter at the antics of the chaplain.

The raid was over within minutes, for the bombers had made what turned out to be just a single and unmolested pass across the field. It was enough. There was little left of the radio complex or its occupants. The heat generated had burned the occupants like tissue paper and the only human remains they found were skulls and kneecaps. A second stick had hit the Bachelor Officers' Quarters. Five bombs had struck home, and the building was completely destroyed. One man was dead, and another was trapped. The latter had been in bed—apparently he refused to leave the building. The wooden floor had imploded under the concussion, buckled his bed, and trapped his foot in the process. Zimmerman and O'Brian helped comfort the young officer while a medical team prepared a general anesthetic and made everything ready for amputation.

The other officer had had his head blown completely off. It was strange—there was no fire and the building had been destroyed by the blast of high explosive, but they couldn't find the severed head.

Clark Field
Luzon

Darkness fell over the air field, which was still in a state of collective shock. Ground and air crews worked side by side cannibalizing the remains of shattered aircraft. Sammy Boghosian salvaged radio parts, and Dick Osborn stripped down the .50-calibers pulled out of burning Flying Fortresses.

Around suppertime some men thought about chow; but there

was a poor response to the trucks that Sergeant Taulbee organized to bring food to the squadron lines and makeshift repair shops. Another group of men, filling in the craters on the runway, worked on for a while, until it was too dark to see. A few more drifted sheepishly in from the surrounding countryside, but there were still scores unaccounted for in the chaos and confusion. Records and documents had all been destroyed, and as so many men were newly arrived, nobody in authority seemed to know precisely how many men were missing. Some barracks had burned with such a violent and intense heat that it was impossible to be accurate about the number of those incinerated. Fraternity rings were often all that could be identified among the charred remains.

Most slept where they worked or erected temporary shelters beyond the perimeter, but nobody was prepared to spend the night anywhere near the main barracks complex, or what was left of it, for the sickly stench of death was nauseating and overpowering.

The burned-out shell of the main building, its concrete form skeletal in the moonlight, reminded Dick Osborn of the Alamo.

Fort Mills
Corregidor
Manila Bay

The men on the Rock had spent a quiet day at their guns. No Japanese planes had strayed near enough for them to fire. They were mute bystanders to the tragedy of Clark and the deflowering of American innocence.

V. THE BATTLE OF MANILA

Tuesday, December 9–
Sunday, December 21, 1941

Tuesday, December 9, 1941
U.S.S. *Mindanao*
At sea

Once she had turned into a following sea, the gunboat had made good time. The northeast coast of Luzon was in view when the port lookout sighted a schooner hull down on the horizon. Lieutenant Commander McCracken altered course to intercept and sounded general quarters. It looked as if the crew of the schooner were dumping a lot of things overboard and preparing to abandon ship. The schooner hove to under orders, and a boarding party went across. Sam Malick was among those who searched the little vessel. The crew proved to be Japanese, and they claimed to be fishermen, but it was clear to the American sailors from the wires and aerials that littered the deck that it was radio equipment that had been dumped. The Japanese were transferred to the gunboat, and an attempt was made to take the schooner under tow. The seas, however, proved too rough for the fragile craft and McCracken ordered it to be scuttled.

Shortly afterward a PBY Catalina flying boat on long-range reconnaissance from its base in Subic Bay flew low over the *Mindanao*. A signal lamp flashed the recognition code from the gun blister of the circling plane. McCracken ordered the American flag to be raised, and the flying boat dipped his wings in salute, banked low over the ship, and headed south for home. The *Mindanao* followed suit at her best speed.

Clark Field

The shock of the raid wore off gradually during the day. Clouds hung low, and the base was whipped from the north by frequent bursts of lashing monsoon rain. It looked as if the Japanese air armadas were grounded, but the Americans, though soaked to the skin, cast an anxious eye to the sky every time a break appeared in the cloud layer.

They worked like demons. The runway was bulldozed clear of wreckage, and the bomb craters filled with rock and earth. The aim was to restore Clark to an operational state with a minimum of delay. Hard, physical labor proved the greatest antidote to the traumas of the previous day. By lunchtime they had indeed achieved a miracle. Some 2,000 feet of runway had been repaired, and a number of workshops restored. The base bristled with extra anti-aircraft defenses and machine-gun posts.

Six B-17s flew in from Del Monte. The pilots came in low and fast, buffeted by the monsoon squalls. They dispensed with the more normal landing-approach procedures, as all feared a Zero attack, especially when the big ships were this vulnerable.

Crew chiefs guided the B-17s into their respective parking bays, and a scratch force of mechanics quickly refueled the planes. Within half an hour the six bombers were aloft once more with orders to circle the field until dark. The alternative, leaving the planes as sitting ducks on the ground, prey to the marauding Zeros, was unthinkable. It was better that the bombers should take their chances in the air.

Company C, 2nd Battalion
57th Philippine Scouts

After the bombing of Clark the rumors flew thick and fast. The American High Command, for a while at least, lost all touch with reality and sent ground formations chasing phantoms. As is so often the case when opening moves in a war are dramatic and unexpected, perceptions of the enemy changed from a contemptuously dismissive attitude to one of abject fear. The Americans who had disregarded the Japanese as fighters before the war now ascribed to them almost superhuman qualities. Luzon was gripped with the fear of a fifth-column threat. Although there has never been any official evidence to suggest that the Japanese had an espionage organization in the Philippines, there were dozens of reported incidents. The switchboards of Army bases the length and breadth of the island were swamped with calls from good citizens who reported suspicious behavior and activities of neighbors. To all of these the Army and the police had to respond, especially as so many of these calls, given the mind of the military, were now utterly credible. At the same time as units were responding to these reports, the High Command issued instructions to meet the threat that they now fully expected to materialize, a Japanese airborne invasion. So those reports that were received of parachutists descending over air bases were treated with the highest priority in the House on the Wall, even though they were the parachutes of pilots whose aircraft had been shot down.

Word had reached the 2nd Battalion, 57th Philippine Scouts that Fort Stotsenberg, lying adjacent to Clark Field, was under attack by Japanese parachutists. The battalion was ordered to move to the rescue. However, like every other unit in the Philippines, there was nowhere near the right number of trucks and vehicles to give the battalion mobility. So local buses were commandeered. The window frames were removed by the simple expedient of sawing through the wooden jambs, and the roofs dumped on the roadside. Though open to the elements, at least the troops could keep a more thorough watch for air attack.

Loyd Mills had his company loaded on the stripped-down buses in rapid time. Light machine guns were lashed to makeshift stands to provide some defense from air attack, and the baggage was piled on board. The only intelligence that Mills was given was to expect Japanese roadblocks at any time once he had cleared Manila. He climbed aboard the first bus, ready to lead the battalion out on the rescue mission. Alongside him stood a young corporal, steely-eyed and vigilant behind his .30-caliber Browning. As the convoy moved off, the gunner fed the belt into his gun and cocked the weapon while Mills consulted his Mobil gas station road map as the Scouts drove off to war.

It was the craziest drive Mills had made in all his young life. He didn't know what to expect around the next corner, but he could not afford the luxury of stopping to allow adequate reconnaissance. At the first likely place for an ambush he made the mistake of stopping a bedraggled group of Filipino refugees, their possessions piled precariously on a couple of hand carts.

"Have you seen any Japanese up ahead?" the young lieutenant asked.

At the very word "Japanese," the Filipinos dropped everything and fled in panic as Mills's troops looked on impassively. His only hope lay in the enemy being even more surprised than he: with a little luck he would steamroller his way over a roadblock before any shell could blast the bus and himself to oblivion.

The lead vehicles had reached the outskirts of Clark before the outrider was able to flag them down. John Spainhower, covered with oil and grime and looking less than resplendent astride an ancient ex-Indian Army motorcycle, told Mills that it had all been a mistake and ordered him to meet up with the Regimental Commander at San Fernando, where he would receive new orders.

Mills ordered a break and, with sufficient guard mounted, men jumped down and stretched cramped and aching limbs. The two officers smoked cigarettes and conferred quietly while Mills poured over his tourist road map and worked out the route to San Fernando. A gaggle of children heralded the arrival of some villagers from a barrio, and the Scouts were soon trading cigarettes for chickens. The war suddenly seemed as far away as ever.

It was well after dark by the time Mills parked his convoy in the main street of the vitally important road junction and located the Regimental Headquarters in San Fernando's Town Hall. There he learned that the 2nd Battalion was to dig in and hold the line from Porac, nestling in the foothills of the Zimbales, 12 miles southeast across the flood plain to Guaga, a fishing barrio on the northernmost tip of Manila Bay. Someone in Manila was hedging his bets, for this line was effectively the hinge into Bataan. The Scouts were to hold the door open.

With two companies in the line and a third rotated in reserve, the Scouts remained in San Fernando until Christmas.

If the Japanese were to land in Lingayen Gulf, overwhelm the defenses, and march on Manila, the Americans would have no recourse but to revert to the original war plan and retreat into Bataan. The deployment of the Scouts at that vital point around San Fernando was either an inspired guess or a clever piece of insurance. We will never know the answer, since the records to this and so many other discussions were lost in the confusion of retreat or destroyed before the final surrender.

0513 hours
Wednesday, December 10, 1941

Luzon is a curiously shaped island. It has been likened to a very large mittened right hand laid palm downward. The gap between thumb and forefinger is Lingayen Gulf, while the veins of the hand are the main roads and the mountain spines that reach down to Manila. At the very top of the mitten is the port of Aparri; while another, called Vigan, lies midway up to the forefinger; they were the selected targets for invasion.

The Japanese came with the dawn. Throughout the night the invasion forces had lain uneasily at anchor hoping that a new day would bring a moderate sea, but that was not to be. The elements were to cause the invaders greater problems that day than any defending forces, for both towns were virtually without protection. As the first of the two thousand Japanese troops stormed ashore at Vigan, a high-flying P-40 on the final leg of its lonely night patrol spotted the landings and radioed back the alarm.

General Wainwright was inspecting the deployments of the 21st Infantry Division along Lingayen Gulf when word arrived of the Japanese landings. Both he and MacArthur recognized them as feints aimed to dissipate American strength. They refused to be drawn on the ground, though MacArthur ordered the flight of B-17s at Clark to attack the beachhead at Vigan.

0600 hours
Clark Field

Just 47 minutes after the alarm had been raised, the first of five B-17s lumbered unevenly down the pitted runway and hauled its massive weight into the watery rays of the first sun. Clark was ready to retaliate with the first American bombing mission of World War II. The bombers gained height and over Arayat rendezvoused with the Kittyhawks of the 17th Pursuit, who flew top cover the 150 miles northward to the target beaches.

0700 hours
The landing beaches at Vigan

It was now the turn of the Americans. The sky was clear of Japanese Zeros, so, while the bombers swung out to sea and began their bomb run, the fighters power-dived down from the land side to strafe the packed transports. Belatedly, seven worn-out P-35s of the 34th Pursuit at Del Carmen arrived on the scene and joined in with their gun power.

The bombers made two steady runs across the transports while the darting fighters diverted the air defense; nevertheless, the B-17s failed to score a hit. Three fighters failed to survive the murderous Japanese fire. One was flown by Lieutenant Marrett, the squadron commander of the 34th Pursuit. He rocked one small transport time after time with machinegun fire; he would not leave it alone. While at mast height, the ship suddenly exploded beneath him, and the blast hurled his fighter straight into the sea. The bombers returned to Clark while the fighters, their charges safely home, peeled off south through cloudless skies for Nichols and breakfast.

1120 hours
U.S.S. *Mindanao*
Cavite Navy Yard

The *Mindanao* dropped anchor to a hero's welcome. Though there were pitifully few units of the Asiatic Fleet left around, those that were more than compensated. Whistles blew and sirens sounded in salute to the gallant gunboat. One that was lost had returned to the fold, and there was precious little to cheer about those days. Sam Malick's heart filled with pride as together with his companions they manned the side and stood erect before this age-old Navy custom. Gently McCracken guided his charge inside the breakwater and then dropped anchor alongside the water and provisions barges. Though there was a war on the crew reckoned they had earned a good leave ashore. Thirty minutes later the first bombs fell on Cavite.

1135 hours
Clark Field

Word arrived at Clark of the approach of a Japanese bomber force. There were indeed three separate attack groups, each of 27 Betty twin-engined bombers, heading for Luzon. Ahead of them flew 100 marauding Zeros.

Without a moment's hesitation Colonel Ewbanks ordered the bombers aloft once more. Their mission was to bomb the enemy at the beaches and then fly directly south to the haven at Del Monte. Three bombers were ready, and they took off almost immediately. A fourth followed shortly afterward. The fifth and last ever to leave Clark was a B-17D piloted by Maj. Colin Kelly.

1200 hours
Manila

The church bells sounded in Manila. As the Japanese bombers thundered low over the city the bells had a strangely settling effect on the local people; there was no panic in the streets.

All the nurses at the Sternberg ran out as the planes swept by overhead. Madeline Ullom counted six separate formations, with nine twin-engined bombers in each group. As the bombers banked over the walled city the sun shone on their wings. "Aren't they beautiful," she thought. "It's great to be an American."

All of a sudden the bombs started to drop, and the nurses were stunned. Like the others, Ullom couldn't accept that they were the enemy, yet all her senses told her it was Nichols they were bombing. The head nurse yelled, "Hit the dirt! Hit the dirt!" and the nurses in starched white uniforms dived to the ground in their hospital garden. Ullom was not the only one that day who sobbed her fear and frustration into the dark brown soil.

The Kittyhawks of the 17th Pursuit were scrambled late from Nichols Field. They climbed straight into the waiting ranks of Zeros, which had both height and the sun in their favor. A Japanese pilot in modulated English welcomed the American pilots by name into combat. Ed Erickson's blood ran cold as he heard his name over the air. Forty Zeros blocked the route to the bombers and within seconds the sky over Manila was full of screaming, twisting planes. Though the Americans with three squadrons airborne had mounted their biggest air operation to date, the pilots were overwhelmed by the numbers and superior combat skill of the Japanese.

The only good thing about the P-40 was the half inch of steel plate around the back and under the pilot's seat. It would stop a 20mm cannon shell from a Zero. Erickson soon found that out, for his ship took several as he tried desperately to elude the three Zeros who had chosen him for slaughter. He went through every trick and maneuver Wagner had taught him, but there was no way out. On fire and now in real trouble, he pushed the stick forward and screamed toward the ground in one manueuver that could outfly a Zero—the power dive. Momentarily a Zero filled his sights. Erickson's six .50-calibers hammered out their hate, and the enemy flamed and fell out of the sky.

He saw little more as the hydraulic lines inside the cockpit ruptured and spewed their fluid into his goggles. He couldn't bail out. For a man of his size there was only one way out and that meant enough control to bring the ship up into a stall, throw back the canopy and slide out. Any other way and the tail section was guaranteed to slice the pilot in two. So Erickson rode his plane to the ground.

His undercarriage had failed, and he feathered the propeller as the ground at Nichols Field rushed up to meet him. The Kittyhawk ground-looped into a truck and trailer loaded with gasoline. The ensuing explosion hurled Erickson clear of the plane. Though stunned he had enough presence of mind to roll in the grass and beat out the flames on his flying jacket and helmet. Even so, the hair had been burned from his face; all the pilots sported moustaches. Erickson's had gone along with his eyebrows and eyelashes.

He was one of the fortunate members of his squadron that day. He survived. A couple of machine gunners ran out from their sandbagged emplacement and hauled the young pilot under cover.

On the ground and around him at Nichols, there was pandemonium. The fighter cover had been swept aside, and the anti-aircraft defenses were pitifully inadequate. Many of the Air Corps personnel were caught in their large pyramid tents, resting after an early lunch. There were few slit trenches available, so John McCann and the others had no choice other than to dodge the bombs and run hard for the rice paddies. Japanese fighters spotted the mass migration and came sweeping low over the field, guns blazing. The rice paddies churned and frothed as the defenseless youngsters, in their confusion and their innocence, were slaughtered.

The pattern set two days earlier at Clark was now repeated at Nichols Field. High-level bombers maintained their formation and bombed with precision. Hangars and mess halls, workshops, and the administration block disappeared behind the blast and debris of high explosives. A second formation wheeled in behind and rained incendiaries onto the now exposed woodwork and fittings of the shattered buildings. Nichols, like Clark, burned. Meanwhile, the air defenses brushed aside, the Zeros came in low and completed the devastation. Tracers ripped through everything. Those planes that had survived the bombs now erupted into flames. A stray stick obliterated the barrio of Maricaban just across the perimeter of the field. With the smoke and flames, the Zeros could not discriminate, and they included the village in their agenda of carnage.

Bill Garleb ran, as did the other machine gunners of Company H. Their shallow and irrelevant training had not even begun to prepare them to cope with this Valhalla. Swooping low Zeros blasted their wretchedly inadequate defense lines with their cannons. As if this were not enough, stray bursts of fire from the dogfights above fell among them and caused havoc with the thin veneer of their discipline. As the first ran, the fabric of command disintegrated. Garleb, petrified with fear, jumped into a ravine. At the bottom was a hole, some animal's lair. He burrowed backward, covered his head with his hands, and tried to shut out the nightmare sounds of war.

It was the silence that brought him out. Cautiously he scrambled up the sides of the ravine and peered over the lip. He could see that the Japanese had gone, but there was still much firing as guns of all descriptions punched holes in an empty sky. Not quite; an L-5 came in low over the field. This was an American spotter plane hoping to avoid the fighters. A thousand rifles aimed and opened fire. The pilot bailed out and still they shot at him—he waved his arms frantically as the slugs tore through his canopy.

He was badly wounded by the time he hit the ground; he was also angry, the angriest person that Garleb had ever seen. "You shot me in the air, you shot me on the way down, you sons-of-bitches," he screamed.

Garleb could still hear him mouthing curses and obscenities as the ambulance doors closed and the vehicle headed toward an improvised first-aid station. One had been hurriedly established in the lee of the shattered, already burned-out shell that had once been the main administrative block.

There were some twenty dead and more than a hundred wounded. Many marveled at the relatively low casualty figures, especially since the level of devastation was as severe as at Clark. As soon as the raid was over, men came out of the rice paddies and improvised foxholes and returned to work. One group of carpenters was seen returning to the new barracks block to continue where they had left off before the raid. It was almost as if the raid had never occurred.

Cavite Navy Yard
Manila Bay

Lieutenant Champlin returned to his quarters about 1130 that morning. He had been working since the evening before, supervising the loading of high-octane fuels onto barges. These were to be used by the torpedo boat squadron and dispersed into small secluded coves on the peninsula of Bataan. He had just seen the last barge away.

He telephoned his commander, Admiral Rockwell, to ask a favor. "Sir, if I may, can I shave and shower and grab some breakfast before reporting for duty?"

"Sure, Champ," the admiral replied, "have some sleep and come in this afternoon—there's not very much happening today."

The young officer was midway through shaving when the sirens sounded. Champlin, a face full of lather, rushed outside and looked up into the clear sky. He counted a formation of some fifty-four bombers banking high over the base. A smoke bomb burst. The nine 3-inch anti-aircraft batteries opened up at their maximum range of 24,000 feet. The Japanese bombers climbed a further 1,000 feet and operated unhindered. The formation turned for a second high-level pass over the base. Another smoke canister was dropped, presumably to get the windage. On the third pass the planes bombed in formation and with precision. It seemed to Champlin that not a single bomb missed the base area as the yard erupted into smoke and flame. The ground shook beneath his feet to the concussion of high explosives. The planes now dived into two formations. Each in turn came in at a lower level and dropped their incendiaries. Cavite burned.

Lieutenant Champlin ran for a car and headed for the Commandancia as fast as he could. His progress was halted once he drove in through the main gates as floods of frightened Filipino workers hit his car like a tidal wave. Harassed Marine guards tried vainly to clear a way through the crowds. Champlin turned into a side road, hoping to make quicker progress. Fires raged, and the dead lay in the streets blocking his path, so Champlin abandoned the car and tried to get through on foot.

A four-by-four flatbed drove by slowly; it was piled with dead. As it passed by, Champlin heard a groan. He stopped the truck and, together with the driver, gently moved the dead aside and lifted the man who was groaning out of the tangled pile. Champlin held him in his arms and saw the lower part of his face and jaw was shot away. A bloody, frothing hole marked where his mouth used to be. He looked up and saw the lieutenant's bars on Champlin's collar. "Thank you, Captain, thank you, Captain," he said, and died in Champlin's arms.

Gently, Champlin and the driver lifted the body back on the truck, and the vehicle went on its way. The young officer, badly shaken, picked his way through the chaos of the burning streets.

In between rescue missions some Marines and sailors rushed into the deserted commissary store. They emerged with armfuls of watches and jewelry. Later when a guard had been placed on the building a couple of Filipinos were caught looting. They were summarily executed.

Champlin found Admiral Rockwell in a small shelter near the bombed-out wreck of the Commandancia. He was hatless, with blood all over his shirt from lifting the wounded who had fallen near him.

The first bomb had hit the powerhouse, and the fire-fighting system was out. The admiral told his aide that he had already dispatched an officer to Cavite, where he hoped the telephone lines could still be used, to phone Manila for fire engines capable of pumping water from near the dock and the sea wall.

As the two officers talked, the Japanese bombers came in for another attack. There seemed to Champlin to be fewer of them this time. This was only because they had now divided their efforts and one half sought targets in the bay and along the Manila waterfront.

Sam Malick and the others manned the defenses of the *Mindanao* as the captain warped her out from the base and sought sea room. It was ironic that her guns fired for the first time when sanctuary had seemingly been secured.

A bomber came in low over the wharf where the *Canopus* had tied up. While her few anti-aircraft guns spoke in defiance, Lieutenant Commander King watched the bomb bays open and bombs spew downward, missing the ship but blasting the warehouse farther along the pier.

It seemed as if the entire yard at Cavite was now ablaze. The dispensary, warehouses, repair shops, and barracks all received fresh hits. The wind shifted, and the fire spread out of control through the machine shops toward the Marine barracks and the town of Cavite. The barracks was a two-storied L-shaped building about 200 yards from the main gate. The Japanese tried again to hit the barracks, but they missed and the bombs fell on Cavite.

The town erupted into panic, and dozens were hurt as people

fled. Children, in their confusion, became separated from parents, and some were trampled to death. A hundred family tragedies occurred in the space of a few short moments.

The first fire engines arrived on the scene, and fire parties were organized from the surviving sailors and put to work as the Japanese bombers made their final run over the shambles of the Navy Yard. The oceangoing submarine *Sealion* received a direct hit and quickly sank. The captain of the tender *Pigeon* earned his second Navy Cross by towing the disabled submarine *Seadragon* clear of a burning wharf.

Admiral Rockwell, with his senior staff, established a command post in front of the ammunition depot. Hoses were directed onto the dump to keep the temperature down. Lieutenant Commander Whitney, Captain of the Yard, came limping up with his knee in a bandage to report that some eight hundred gas masks were stored in a loft above one of the machine shops. At that moment another report came in of new fires breaking out near the post office and receiving station. The admiral turned to his aide and told him that the gas masks were his problem to solve.

Champlin flagged down a passing four-by-four and told the driver to turn it toward the raging fires. He intended to find a fire-fighting party and take them with him to the loft. As the vehicle rounded the corner of the commissary store, Champlin chanced upon a group of sailors and shouted to them to come with him. "We've got a job to do, men, and I want volunteers only—but I need you all. How about it?"

They all jumped on the truck.

The driver pulled the truck as close to the burning machine shop as he dared, and Champlin led four men up into the loft to look for the masks. They were easy to find, stored in cans like small barrels, with six masks in each of the sealed cans. The loft was already beginning to fill with smoke. Champlin urged them to hurry, though they needed little urging at this stage. They rolled the barrels down and tossed them over the railing to the ground below, where the other men piled them onto handcarts and ran them out to the truck.

Fearful that the roof would collapse and knowing of no other masks except those that had been in buildings already destroyed, Champlin and his party worked like fury. With a loud crack, a beam directly above him split open, and Champlin ordered his party out of the building. They had saved more than seven hundred masks, ready for the day when the Japanese would surely use gas and chemical weapons on the defenders!

The men scrambled up on top of the gas masks, and the driver edged the vehicle away from the building. As they reversed clear there was a shout, "Get out of there while you can."

It was Lieutenant Commander Granfield, the operations officer. His warning was timely, for, as the truck turned into the street they had used on entering, Champlin found the buildings burning on both sides. In the short time they had been in the loft the fire had jumped the gap, and burning debris littered their path as buildings caved in all around. The driver hesitated, but Champlin ordered him forward. He crashed the gears into low, and the truck ground its way over the burning timbers; the men hung on for dear life with one hand and warded off falling timbers with the other. It was a miracle, but they made it through their tunnel of fire unscathed.

They emerged into an open area, and the truck stopped to let the sailors get down. Champlin turned to thank them for all their efforts. One of them was a bruiser of a stoker, with a face that bore the scars of a hundred barroom brawls. He appeared to be the spokesman for the group and asked the lieutenant for a favor. Champlin told him to go ahead.

"I'm up for a summary court-martial," he said. "Will you testify for me, sir?" Champlin assured him that he would and that his testimony would have considerable effect, whatever his crime. At this point all the men piped up in unison, "Will you do that for all of us, sir?"

Champlin was floored by these requests; then it dawned on him. "Hey, where have you men come from?" he asked.

His suspicions were confirmed. They were prisoners whom the Marine guards had released from the brig as the first bombs fell. "Look, fellas," he said, "remember my name. I am the admiral's aide, and of course I will testify on all your behalfs. But I don't think that will be necessary. The Commandancia is a total wreck, and all court-martial records must be burned to a cinder. Forget the charges because you have proven yourselves today. As far as the Navy is concerned you've got a clean slate. Let's get on with the war."

Champlin shook hands with the men and headed for the temporary headquarters. The sailors continued their interrupted journey to the commissary store.

Throughout the attack, Admiral Hart had watched the destruction of Cavite from the roof of his headquarters in the Marsman Building. There and then he knew that Manila Bay could no longer be tenable as a base for even the few surface vessels that remained. He dictated the executive orders that would send the last ships south. Destroyers, gunboats, and two submarine tenders were ordered out with immediate dispatch. The *Canopus*, *Mindanao*, and *Pigeon* were all the surface units, other than minesweepers and the torpedo boats, that were to remain of the Asiatic Fleet in Manila Bay.

1700 hours

By now it appeared as if the fire was under control. What the bombs had not destroyed, the fire had laid waste. Unlike Pearl Harbor, Cavite was finished as a naval base; there wasn't a repair shop left standing. During the long afternoon, untold acts of heroism had become commonplace, but it appeared that they had failed in their endeavors to save the yard. It was impossible to count the dead, and it was to take the next two days to find and identify many of the bodies.

Admiral Rockwell was horrified by the carnage. By his own estimates there must have been five hundred dead in the base area. Champlin knew they had gotten off lightly considering the damage. There must have been more than eight thousand sailors and Filipinos working in the narrow confines of the base when the first bomb struck. Had it not been for Rockwell's precautions and preparations for air raids, the death toll would have been infinitely greater. Though he told the admiral this, Champlin knew it was cold comfort to a man who had just seen his command reduced to an utter shambles in less than two hours.

1800 hours

Now the news was very much better. The fires were localized and allowed to burn themselves out. The lumber yard had been saved, and so had the main ammunition depot. The latter contained, among other things, some two hundred torpedo warheads.

The Marines had established a field kitchen, and the fire fighters were ordered out, a group at a time, for a rest. A standing patrol was mounted to watch the unburned portion of the yard and check on sparks and small fires. The admiral and his staff relaxed a little for the first time since the raid began as they sat on barrels, eating sandwiches and drinking coffee, trying to take stock of the situation.

They hadn't been there very long before a sailor came running toward the admiral and reported that a very large fire had broken out and was spreading rapidly in the heart of the lumber yard. Champlin was incredulous. He had been with the party that had looked through that area just half an hour before.

Younger than the other officers, he was the first on the scene. He found the fire burning at the bottom, in the center of three large piles of timber, and burning furiously. By the time they had maneuvered a fire engine into position, the fire had a firm grip and was spreading rapidly throughout the lumber yard. The lieutenant's FBI training and instincts told him this was sabotage. He had also learned a lot about fires in the hours since the first bomb fell. It just didn't spread that fast without the aid of gasoline or some other highly flammable substance.

The work began all over again, and the men fought the blaze until after midnight. Then all hands were ordered out of the yard area to be mustered in the open field at the Dalahican School, in the adjacent barrio of San Roque. The reason for this was clear. Despite all their efforts the fire from the lumber yard had spread, and the ammunition depot now lay directly in its path.

Champlin attempted to marshal the men into some sort of order, but it was useless. They were so exhausted that many fell unconscious to the ground. The limits to human endurance had been stretched to the breaking point. Only fresh fire-fighting crews could save Cavite. Perhaps those in authority in Manila could have anticipated the plight, and maybe Rockwell should have sent for extra manpower and assistance long ago. It mattered not, but it is true that nobody visited the scene from the headquarters in the House on the Wall. Manila, the Pearl of the Orient, bore mute witness to the catastrophe at Cavite. Its funeral pyre of thick black smoke had been climbing high into the heavens since the early afternoon.

Admiral Rockwell ordered Champlin to take his car and drive and report to Admiral Hart's headquarters to tell him that Cavite was finished as a naval base, that the radio station and the fuel depot were intact, but that was about all.

Champlin saluted and set off in search of the admiral's Filipino driver. He found him asleep in the admiral's car. Champlin was afraid that he himself might be too exhausted to make the journey so he took another officer, Ens. Tom Suddath, along for company.

After just a couple of blocks it was clear that the Filipino was in no fit state to drive the officers to Manila. Champlin stopped the car, ordered the driver into the back, and took over the wheel. The two officers decided to share the 20-mile drive.

As they approached a bridge near Zapote, on the outskirts of Manila, a police whistle blew. Suddath, who was driving while half asleep, jerked wide awake and skidded to a halt. An excited Filipino came out of the shadows with a shotgun and put the barrel right under Suddath's chin, shouting, "Who you? Where you go?"

The two men told the air raid warden they were naval officers. He didn't believe them. Having no caps, only the shredded soot-stained remains of shirts and slacks, and devoid of rank bars, it was hardly surprising. The Filipino took a lot of persuading as to the officers' identities.

There were four more bridges guarded by equally vigilant wardens on the route into the city. They did their job well, and it was already dawn by the time Champlin was able to make his report to the staff duty officer, for delivery to Admiral Hart as soon as he awoke. The two young officers then made their way across the waterfront to the Army-Navy Club. The building was virtually deserted. They entered through the sandbagged entrance and went down into the basement, where there were plenty of empty cots available. Champlin left word with the guard to wake them in a couple of hours.

4th U.S. Marines
Olongapo, Subic Bay

The Marines had moved into the field on the first day of the war. Unlike the Army and Air Corps units, this did not mean large pyramid tents grouped conveniently around facilities. The Marines, company by company, bivouacked some five to eight miles out of Olongapo. They rotated guard detachments in the Navy Yard and set up a beach defense.

Lieutenant Jenkins had returned from a three-day mission leading a small party south into Bataan. His orders were to trail-blaze a route down the coast to link up with a new Army road then being extended northward. This was to be the Marines' line of retreat through to Corregidor should they be cut off from Manila.

Sergeant Bigelow had established his armorer's shop in the ruins of a Spanish fort about 5 miles inland. He had a couple of days in which to service as many of the machine guns as he was able. Together with the regimental armorers he stripped down the guns and broke out new barrels and bolts. They had received a new shipment directly from the Government Arsenal just a month before the regiment left China.

The shipment had been sabotaged—not in China or the Philippines, but in the United States. The seals were intact until the armorers broke open the boxes; Bigelow also quickly realized that the nature of the sabotage was such that it could only have been undertaken at the source. The threads on the barrels had been tampered with so that they would not fit the breechblocks. The bolt assemblies, still covered in the manufacturer's Cosmoline, had driving rods that had been "notched." There was no way the weapons could be assembled using the new components.

In the late afternoon Subic Bay came in for Japanese attention. A few roving Zeros strafed the base. One fighter headed in to hit the area from the landward side and catch the harbor defenses unawares. Bigelow had his own stripped-down .30-caliber Browning; he had taken the gun's special anti-aircraft tripod and fixed this to a handcart. He opened fire on the Zero as his colleagues, cursing his exuberance, scuttled for cover. It was nothing more than a futile gesture by an angry Marine. The Japanese was too low to get a shot at the gun, and the pilot banked away out of trouble. He waved and grimaced at the lone Marine as he zoomed low overhead.

Clark Field

Sergeant Taulbee was among the first to hear about the downed B-17. Two crewmen, survivors from the wreck, had been picked up and brought into the base. Rescue parties were already out looking for the others, whose parachutes had been seen descending below the cloud layer. The squadron commander sought out Taulbee to tell him that the downed plane was Major Kelly's. The commander and Kelly had been classmates at West Point.

Taulbee nodded in silent sympathy. They were more than that, he thought, for the two officers were of the same height, and that would have placed them in the same company. Taulbee realized that they must have been very close friends.

"Look, Sergeant," the squadron commander said, "I understand that the plane came down just a few miles west of Arayat. I'd like to go to look for it, and I would like it very much if you would come with me. It seems that Major Kelly didn't bail out."

It didn't take them long to locate the wreckage of the Flying Fortress. It had come down in relatively open country, and its descent had been witnessed by many local Filipinos. A short distance from the strewn wreckage of the aircraft the two men came across a huddled heap. At first they did not recognize the remains as those of Major Kelly. There was not a bit of broken flesh on his body, but Taulbee believed there couldn't have been a bone that wasn't broken. Clearly Major Kelly had been hurled out of the aircraft by the force of the impact.

Gently as he could, the squadron commander removed Kelly's wristwatch, West Point class ring, and wallet. Even more carefully the two men lifted the remains onto a stretcher, which Taulbee had lashed across the hood of the Jeep.

By the time they had arrived back at Clark the legend of Colin Kelly had already taken root. What was never in doubt was that

Kelly's ship was jumped by Zeros as it made a final approach into Clark. The ruptured fuel tanks had quickly turned the plane into a blazing torch. Kelly held the burning ship steady so that the crew could bail out. Of such stuff are heroes deservedly made and legends created.

All the other members of the crew survived. They claimed to have hit and possibly sunk a Japanese battleship off Vigan before the Zero attack. From 5 miles up, a Nagara class light cruiser easily assumes the shape of a 30,000-ton Kongo class battleship, especially to an excited crew. But with an Irish American pilot and a Bronx Jewish bombardier, the United States had its first heroes of the war. Headquarters staff in Manila, desperate for some ray of hope, supported the claim that they had indeed sunk a battleship. After some confusion this was identified as the 29,000-ton *Haruna*, which at that time was steaming unharmed off Malaya.

At sunset the remains of Major Colin Kelly were interred in the military cemetery at Fort Stotsenberg. Taulbee had followed the instructions as laid down in the manual for burial with full military honors.

17th Pursuit Squadron
Nichols Field

Ed Erickson had recovered from his ordeal of the early afternoon and was joking with the others down on the flight dispersal.

"Why didn't you bail out?" Wagner asked his young colleague.

"Couldn't, Buzz," joked the pilot. "My chute wouldn't open." Half in fun he held up the singed remains of his parachute.

Wagner grabbed it and examined the parachute closely. The other pilots gathered around their leader, their curiosity aroused. The seals were intact, though some of the straps had been burned. What interested Wagner was that there was no silk inside the harness cover. Other pilots checked theirs, too—many found the same. Further examination showed the chutes had been sabotaged, possibly with a hypodermic needle and acid. The needle would leave no telltale marks and the acid would quietly eat away the silk.

The once carefree group had become grim. They had all heard stories of pilots who had bailed out and plummeted to earth with unopened chutes. Some had apparently clawed through their flying leathers and into the skin beneath as they grappled with what they must have thought in those last frantic moments to have been a faulty release catch.

The pilots split up and searched for new chutes. These were quickly checked and found to be sound. Erickson and the others went everywhere with their chutes from then on—sitting on them in the chow lines and sleeping on them at night.

Later that evening Zimmerman, together with a Military Police unit, visited the now deserted and derelict barrio at Maricaban. He scrambled across the Dilai Ravine, where Garleb and so many of his company had sought sanctuary earlier that day. The village was completely abandoned and the fires long since burned out. In one nipa hut the search party found a complete short-wave radio; ham radio or spy? There was no way of telling.

Throughout that long day the men who manned the anti-aircraft defenses of the bay forts had stood by their guns. No Japanese planes had strayed into their air space. Like the people of Manila, they stood in silent testament to the death of Cavite and watched in numbed horror as the American pursuit planes were knocked out of the sky in the one-sided air battles above the clear blue waters of the bay.

Late evening
The House on the Wall
Manila

Word came in of the loss in the South China Sea of the *Repulse* and the *Prince of Wales*. Tom Phillips, tilting at windmills, had attempted to deny the Japanese invasion force the beaches of

Malaya. These warships, code named "Force Z," had sent up a wall of steel against the skilled Japanese fliers of the 22nd Air Flotilla, but within a couple of hours both ships had been sent to the bottom.

The significance was not lost on the staff in Manila. The Royal Navy had surrendered command of the sea in the vital routes between Manila and the bases in Australia. The nearest capital ships were the shaken survivors at Pearl Harbor. In the East Indies a mixed bag of elderly cruisers from four nations was gathering, hardly a force to dispute the waters of the Far East.

Admiral Hart briefed MacArthur on the extent of the damage at Cavite. He also informed him that the *Pensacola* convoy was not to fight its way through to Manila with its precious cargo of aircraft and tanks; instead it would divert to Brisbane. Once an escort had been mustered, the route to Manila would, it was hoped, be reestablished. So for the immediate future, at least, the main line of naval defense for the Philippines would be the submarines of the Asiatic Fleet. Hart outlined their deployments and his strategy to deny the Japanese armada access to the shores of Luzon.

Thursday, December 11, 1941

There were no air raids on this day. Formosa was closed in by the unseasonably late monsoons while the jittery defenders on Luzon drew breath and made what repairs they could to their shattered bases.

Lieutenant Champlin left Tom Suddath in Manila to report to Captain Wilkes for detached duty with the submarine staff and made the journey back to Cavite alone. His route lay close by Nichols Field, through the Pasay section of the outer suburbs of Manila. Large areas were smoldering from the incendiaries that had fallen off target, and a pall of black smoke still drifted upward from the crippled air base.

As he got nearer to Cavite, Champlin found his route increasingly hampered by crowds of refugees as they fled the stricken base. He encountered mobs of people, many carrying all their worldly possessions on their backs. Others had piled their homes precariously high on little carts pulled by calesa ponies. They spilled across the road in a scurrying, frightened mass, and the only way he could get through was by tooting the horn incessantly and shouting for people to get out of the way. At the entrance to the Navy Yard, he found Marine guards posted and a fire watch mounted on all nearby buildings. The fire by now had burned itself out. The ammunition stores had survived, but the few remaining buildings had been abandoned. In a grove of trees, the Marines had established a field kitchen, outside of which a long line of bedraggled and weary men waited in resigned acceptance for whatever food came their way. Most had spent what was left of that first night huddled along the roadside in San Roque; others were in the open recreation field at Dalahican. A command center was attempting to run some sort of check on missing personnel, but it was hopeless.

Champlin found Admiral Rockwell asleep in the back of a staff car, so he reported his return to Captain Ray, the Chief of Staff. For the rest of that day Champlin played his part in restoring some degree of order and normality to the Navy Yard.

A more robust and heavily sandbagged set of command posts and dugouts were prepared against the air raids that must surely follow.

As at Nichols and Clark fields, most of the men had no clothing other than what was on their backs, so a Marine detail was dispatched with four trucks to the Army stores in Manila. Nobody bothered with the necessary forms for such requisitions; neither, in fact, were they needed.

Members of the American community in Manila now moved into the Bay View Hotel, a solid stone-built structure on Dewey Boulevard. There was no way out of the city for the Americans, but at least the hotel was a safe distance from the air fields and other military targets.

Clay Seitz moved all the more important records from his office downtown and into a rented apartment. This was leased jointly in the names of his two underwriters; both were Swiss nationals. In a city full of rumors other companies sought by similar methods to secure their future against the coming of the Japanese. Although newspapers and radio were naturally reticent about the subject, the landings in the North were freely discussed.

It was not safe to be on the streets of Manila. There was a run on the banks, and people hoarded food. Residents fled the city to seek the safety of the family home in the country, while those in the country poured in to seek the sanctuary of the city walls. The result was chaos. Official vehicles tore through the city at breakneck speeds. The drivers in their officialdom ignored all traffic signals. The road toll of dead and injured steadily mounted. At night sentries, police, and air raid wardens fired at anything that moved, invariably one another.

Manila copied London during the Blitz. The plate glass in shop windows was neatly crisscrossed with adhesive tape and the entrances reinforced with sandbags, stacked in the regulation manner. Inside, however, a number of the larger department stores had bravely persevered with their Christmas decorations.

The first convoys, in commandeered transports of all descriptions, ground their way nose to tail through the city in both directions. Some, like the men of Company C, 194th Tanks, were headed south to reinforce the Southern Luzon Force. They deployed toward the anticipated invasion beaches around Lamon Bay. Other units moved in the opposite direction. Paul Ashton and the Scouts of the 12th Medical Battalion abandoned Fort McKinley in their hastily converted buses and established a command post and clearing station at Orani. They were among the first units to be deployed into Bataan.

Bill Garleb and his company, along with the remainder of the battalion, also abandoned McKinley and headed north to guard the Calumpit Bridge. The roadside was strewn with the wrecks of burned-out vehicles, victims of the marauding Zeros. The roofless buses full of troops passed endless lines of migrating Filipinos.

"Victory, Joe, Victory," their eternally smiling faces said. They raised two fingers to form a V, the symbol of victory. The Americans looked away in embarrassment.

At Sternberg Hospital, the staff were beginning to learn to cope with war. At first they had worked around the clock to clear the backlog of wounded from Clark. They had barely recovered when they were swamped by the casualties from Cavite and Nichols. The nurses worked until they could no longer stand. They grabbed what sleep they could. For Madeline Ullom this meant finding a vacant operating table or convenient corner.

It took them all a little while to realize that this was not a very efficient use of resources, no matter what the urgencies. So the doctors insisted on an orderly rotation and shift system and the nurses worked in eight-hour cycles, but even this proved a punishing pace. However, so long as there was plenty of good, nourishing food, it could be sustained.

That evening Richard Sakakida was taken out of the internment camp. The Intelligence officers who came to pick him up played out a charade for the benefit of others in the compound. They forbade him to speak to anybody in Japanese and made it appear as if he were under arrest. Two hours, a bath, and a good steak later, Richard was a sergeant in uniform once more and already briefed for his new assignment. He stepped into the car that would take him to Fort Stotsenberg. His task was to interrogate Japanese air crews who had been shot down.

Malcolm Champlin was approached by a Marine captain named Clark who had been put in charge of base security. The tall, ramrod-straight Marine had heard the scuttlebutt about the naval officer being an FBI man, and he questioned him closely. When Champlin confirmed that he had indeed been a special agent, the Marine asked if he would accompany him to a house on the base. There were a number of private residences within the perimeter of the Yard. Most of them were located in the compound that had belonged to a small Spanish-owned shipbuilding company; this was just across the street from the Bachelor Officers' Quarters.

The particular house in question belonged to a retired American soldier who had married a Japanese woman. They had a couple of sons, and the old man had stayed on at the base, where he was employed as a caretaker. The house was empty, and there was no sign of the occupants.

The first thing that struck Champlin as he came in through the porch was not just the devastation, but its manner. The building had not been hit by any bombs, but it was clear that someone had taken an ax and gone through the rooms, demolishing all the furniture. This seemed most strange to Champlin.

"Is there a radio in the house?" Champlin asked Captain Clark.

The Marine pointed to a corner of the front room, and the FBI man moved across for a closer look. In front of it, partly broken up, was a large dial with frequencies on the outer rim and a compass rose in the center indicating magnetic directions. Tracing what was left of the wires, Champlin found an aerial fixed to a pole that could be raised up above the house by the simple device of opening an upstairs window, to which the pole was attached. Outside on the back porch was a large wire-netted cage; though now empty, Champlin guessed that it had contained carrier pigeons. The dung on the floor was still fresh.

Captain Clark ordered the family's arrest. The Japanese woman and her sons were easily found, as there were no Japanese left on the streets and there was nowhere to hide. They were taken to the internment and interrogation center at Bilabid Prison. There was no sign of the old man.

Fort Mills
Corregidor, Manila Bay

Art Bressi and the other gunners watched the strangest sight they had ever seen sail past. Close to one hundred merchant ships of all shapes, sizes, and nationalities were heading out through the mine-fields of the South Channel. At the outbreak of war there had been perhaps as many as forty freighters gathered in Manila Bay. None had left, but many more had since sought sanctuary. In the subsequent bombing attacks only one had been hit, but Admiral Hart felt that it would be only a matter of time before the Japanese turned their attention to such prime targets. He ordered them to break out with his blessing, and little else, for there were no warships available as escorts. All the freighters sailed in ballast, as the United States Philippines Department had thoughtfully bought up their cargoes. One ship was the S.S. *Don José*, on lease to the Canadian Government and carrying a shipment of equipment for their two battalions due to be stationed in Hong Kong. The cargo included fifty-seven Bren gun carriers. These were off-loaded together with their civilian agents and dumped in a deserted lot on the edge of Fort McKinley.

Bressi watched the minesweeper turn its charges loose and then head back into Manila Bay. The freighters in an untidy gaggle thrust their bows into the South China Sea and headed south. They all reached their destinations safely. The Japanese had missed a superb opportunity to cripple Allied merchant strength in the southern Pacific.

Early morning
Friday, December 12, 1941
Legaspi
Southern Luzon

The Kimura Detachment, 2500 men drawn from the 16th Japanese Infantry Division, named after their commander, Major General Kimura, and spearheaded by the Kure 1st Special Naval Landing Force, stormed ashore. The nearest defending troops were 150 miles away. By 0900 hours the Japanese had control of the small air field and the Manila Railway Terminal. It was the stationmaster who telephoned Manila with the report of the Japanese landings. A popular but doubtless apocryphal story was told at the time that his call was switched by the exchange from the railroad depot to USAFFE Headquarters in Manila. The following conversation is supposed to have taken place:

> STATIONMASTER: There are four Jap boats in the harbor, sir, and the Japs are landing. What shall I do?
>
> USAFFE DUTY OFFICER: Just hang onto the phone and keep reporting.
>
> STATIONMASTER: There are about twenty Japs ashore already, sir, and more are coming. (A pause.) Now there are about three hundred Japs outside the station, sir. What am I to do?
>
> DUTY OFFICER: Just sit tight.
>
> STATIONMASTER: Sir, a few of these Japs, with an officer in front, are coming over here.
>
> DUTY OFFICER: See what they want.
>
> STATIONMASTER: Those Japs want me to give them a train to take them to Manila, sir. What do I do now?

DUTY OFFICER: Tell them the next train leaves a week from Sunday. Don't give it to them.

STATIONMASTER, hanging up: Okay, sir.*

Though the Japanese were a long way from Manila, they did have troops ashore, and in some strength at two points in the North of the island, Vigan and Aparri. In these beachheads the enemy could now build temporary airstrips, which in turn would allow them to provide air cover for the main landings, which were planned to follow in Lingayen Gulf and later at Lamon Bay. The American commanders, Wainwright in the North and Parker in the South, didn't have the troops to cover every beach, and neither had the intention of being suckered into overreacting. Both knew where to expect the main landings, for the terrain told them much. The light screen of defenders in those areas could do little more than harass these initial Japanese landings as they retreated and offer some resistance where the terrain favored their limited skills. The noose began to tighten on Manila as the Japanese set out in a leisurely fashion to threaten the capital with another line of advance.

Cavite Navy Yard

On December 12 and 13 the weather cleared and the Japanese Air Force returned with a vengeance. Army and Navy bombers struck at targets throughout Luzon. Clark and Nichols were hit repeatedly, while Subic Bay and Cavite, too, received their share of punishment.

Close to the original Spanish shipyard in Cavite was the fuel dump, a large cache of high-octane gasoline and lubricating oils. It was under heavy foliage and had been very carefully camouflaged. Rockwell had even gone to the trouble just before the war had started of sending pilots aloft to see if they could spot the dump. They couldn't.

However, when the Japanese bombers hit Cavite in the late

---

*The Fall of the Philippines, Louis Morton, p. 110.

morning, the first target to be destroyed was the fuel dump. The bombing again came in phases: High-level bombers flew above the flak barrage, and they were followed by fighters and dive bombers, which swooped in low at the fire fighters. Dozens of bombs fell on Cavite, and within a short while the Japanese had completed its destruction. The low-frequency radio tower, used for transmitting to submerged submarines, was straddled by 500-pound bombs. It tottered in the blast and collapsed, in slow motion, to the ground. This was a most grievous loss, for it meant that the submarines could be contacted only on the surface and at night. A paint shop that had by some miracle survived the holocaust of the last raid blew up, spreading fire over the yard. The torpedo repair shop was hit, and warheads exploded in a massive conflagration that enveloped men and buildings within a 100-yard radius of the blast.

On hearing the planes, Champlin hit the dirt. There were no foxholes that he could see anywhere near him. A large bomb hit the road about 80 feet from where he lay. The impact bounced him 2 or 3 feet into the air, and he was bruised from head to foot.

Two Filipino workmen who had been sheltering under a tree suddenly ran out. Champlin yelled at them to get down. One of them did, but the other kept on running. As he crossed a tennis court in front of Champlin, Zeros came in low, dropping clusters of antipersonnel bombs, their cannons raking the ground. As Champlin watched the Filipino, something hit him, and he disappeared, blown into a thousand bloody pieces before his eyes. The sight of a human being blown apart in a split second shook the young officer more than anything else that had happened in the whole campaign.

Champlin picked himself up and walked across to where he had parked the staff car. He got in and tried to start the vehicle, but his hands were shaking so much that he couldn't fit the keys into the ignition. He got out and sat on the running board; his ears were still ringing from the blast, and his eyes, no matter where he centered his gaze, registered only the last moment of the Filipino. It was half an hour or more before he felt fit enough to move. Then he walked across to the dressing station to get the casualty returns. The surgeons were working furiously, mostly on amputation cases. While a medic went to check the figures, Champlin walked out to the back of the building to get some fresh air. There the dead were laid out like tiers of cordwood. On two of them tags were tied to their exposed feet. Champlin read the labels: The word "suicide" was scrawled in large capitals. He cut the labels off and stormed back into the building, where he encountered a surgeon checking the casualty returns.

"Who in God's name has given you the right to judge just how much bombing and exhaustion a human being can stand?" Champlin asked, grabbing the startled surgeon by the shoulders. "Why should these kids be recorded as suicides just because they could take only ten bombings in five days without sleep, while the rest of us can take more?"

Champlin took the casualty returns from the surgeon, and then continued in a quieter tone, "Look, we can't let their families suffer from the stigma of their suicide. What good will that do?" The surgeon took the labels from the aide's hand and ripped them into pieces.

There was another, and just as unpleasant, side to Cavite after the air raids had passed the town and base by. William Griffiths, a sergeant in the 4th Marines (on detached duty at the base), was given a detail of twenty-seven men and ordered to prevent looting. Needless to say, he had the "ape balls" in the Marines, the ones who were always getting into trouble, and he seemed to spend most of his time keeping after them to prevent them from looting. The town by this stage was completely deserted by its usual residents. Only thieves and vagrants flitted in and out of the ruins.

The men collected some bunks from the barracks and set up housekeeping in a church. They all smoked large cigars incessantly—they were the only things at hand that neutralized the smell from the dead dogs that littered the streets of Cavite.

2nd Battalion, 4th Marines
Olongapo
Subic Bay

Seven of the Navy patrol planes had been sent on a fruitless mission; a nonexistent carrier had again been reported off the coast of Luzon. Many of the Marines witnessed the slaughter of the PBYs, the Navy's long-range flying boats. Al Broderick had charge of a machine-gun post on the water's edge and close to the harbor entrance. From the relative comfort of his foxhole, he watched the strange bat-winged float planes come in to land not 100 yards across the bay. Suddenly one of his gunners pointed to the north. A lone Zero had dropped below the cloud layer. As the men cocked and loaded the .50-calibers, the Japanese watched for a while and then darted back into the clouds. By now the whole base area was alerted, and Marines manned their weapon pits along the water-front and harbor wall. It seemed to Broderick that the sense of urgency had somehow been conveyed to the PBYs: One after the other they came in to land in a cloud of spray. As the lead plane was taxiing to his mooring and the last in the flight had settled heavily onto the water, the Japanese struck. A dozen or more fighters filled the sky with their song of death.

Broderick hammered away with the Browning, tears of frustration pouring down his cheeks. It was all over in a matter of minutes; not a single flying boat survived the attack. Two blew up in a spectacular burst of flames, while the others lay brokenbacked and dead in the water. Launches and picket boats rushed to the rescue of the occasional blob that could be seen waving frantically. For a few fliers, surrounded by a sea of flames, there was no hope. The Zeros made a final victory pass low over the water before heading out to sea and climbing hard into the cloud layer. Streams of tracers fell away from the impotent defenses, and the Japanese retired, triumphant and seemingly unscathed.

41st Divisional Artillery
Batangas
Southern Luzon

Some men found that their deployments for battle had taken them into idyllic surroundings, far removed from the squalor of war. Winston Jones and his battery had finally received their guns on the first day of the war. It was surprising how much equipment hitherto unavailable was now released by compliant quartermasters. True, the guns would have been more suited to a museum, but anything had to be better than the bamboo mock-ups they had been practicing with. Jones had eight British 1911 pattern over and under recoil field guns. They had a 75mm caliber and were mounted on their original carriages with wooden spoked wheels. They had last seen action on the Western Front in 1918. To complete the battery, they were given four of the pack howitzers. There was no ammunition available for the guns, and neither had they been equipped with sights. The 1934 white Packard special was still the only transportation available to the battalion—that is, until Jones decided he had had enough and ordered his men to commandeer civilian transport. Even so, their surroundings were more in keeping with a travel brochure. On the first day of war, the battalion had been deployed into the southwestern tip of Batangas from their training base at Lake Taal. Their new location was a half-moon bay, with a lagoon entrance of about 440 yards across. There were sandy beaches and palm trees.

Jones had carefully reconnoitered his sector. There was a little sugar cane refinery nearby, and the sugar cane fields came around until they touched the palms near the beach. The palm grove afforded overhead cover and the chance of some concealment, but moving the heavy guns into their position was another matter. The commandeered trucks could not get across the sand, so the guns had to be unloaded, and their big spoked wheels soon became bogged down in the soft sand. Winston Jones needed boards and timbers, and above all else he needed help. Together with the Filipino battery commander he walked across the headland to the little fishing barrio.

The headman laid on a grand reception for the two weary officers, and there was an immediate response to their request for help.

"Everybody here, he give all the help you need, Captain. We fight Japanese to the death," the headman said in his best English.

They drank a few toasts to victory, to MacArthur, and to President Quezon, and then the two officers prepared to leave. Not a single Filipino made any attempt to follow. Jones looked in amazement and not a little anger at his superior officer.

"You have to understand them, Winston," the Filipino said. "They want to help, but they figure that if there is any army unit in the area, then this is a prime target. They want you to protect them, but they don't want to be hurt."

Jones paused and looked back at the little barrio. Already the first families were on the move to swell the ever-increasing streams of refugees that choked the roads north to Manila.

Somehow by late evening they had the battery deployed in the palm grove. The gunners stood silently by. Looking out to sea, they searched for the first signs of the invader.

Two days later, Jones received the sights for the guns; and on the third day the ammunition arrived.

The battalion rapidly came to terms with its surroundings. Orders were precise and to the point: to stay on the beach, to fight, and to die, if necessary, where they stood. They made the best of things and lived for the moment, though the immediate needs were food and shelter. They were sent some C rations and cans of salmon, but for the most part the troops had to eat at the tables of the local population. A number had stayed in the nearby barrios after the first panic died away, and it didn't prove difficult for the soldiers to be invited, or to invite themselves, to the villages at mealtimes. Jones did establish a kitchen in the battalion area with some clay pots and round-bottom pans he had liberated from the nipa huts that had been abandoned. Men were sent out to forage, but there were many other units in the area with similar problems.

Saturday, December 13
Fort Stotsenberg

Though the key bases had largely been abandoned by their garrisons, men were detailed to stay behind and move the supplies out into the field.

Jerry McDavitt and his company worked furiously at Stotsenberg. The Japanese concentrated most of their attacks on Clark, so McDavitt and his men were only rarely disturbed by the occasional raid or sneak marauding Zero. By this time his men had made some thirty trips into Bataan to deliver supplies to an officially designated dump at Samal. Units were moving into the peninsula to defend its beaches from the Japanese. At the same time, McDavitt, with his reputation as an arch scrounger to protect, saw to the needs of his own men. It looked to him as if everyone was running from hell and high water. There were certainly a number of units, both American and Filipino, that had not been able to restore order and cohesion among the men. But these were base area formations, workshops, and the like, which had been created from raw recruits immediately prior to leaving the United States. There had been little time or opportunity to instill any discipline in the Philippines. So McDavitt established a private dump in Bataan for his own company. Truckloads of food and canned goods were carefully secreted away.

On this Saturday he came to Stotsenberg for the last time and walked into the post exchange. The building was open and deserted. He collected together more than a hundred wristwatches and cartons of cigarettes. At the same time he loaded some boxes of Kotex for the nurses, whom he knew were already establishing a hospital on Bataan.

There were other forms of scavenging. Loyd Mills sent his company top sergeant with a truck and a detail from the Porac line to Stotsenberg. He had heard the rumors of units helping themselves to supplies in the open warehouses at Stotsenberg, and was most anxious not to miss out on the act. The sergeant returned with a dozen extra .50-caliber Brownings, complete with stands and ammunition, and a whole load of other goodies on the shopping list.

12th Medical Battalion, Philippine Scouts
Orani
Bataan

Paul Ashton drove back to Fort McKinley that afternoon. He had already begun to realize that their abandonment of McKinley had been somewhat premature. He had heard of the landings in the North but knew that it would be.some little while before the war reached him in Bataan. So together with another officer and a couple of Scouts they drove into the now deserted fort.

At first Ashton could not believe his eyes. There were great quartermaster dumps full of food and supplies of every kind. There were warehouses crammed with canned goods and flour. The officers went on to the medical supplies. In the dental section they came across gold, thousands and thousands of gold wafers ready to be used for teeth fillings. "Forget it," Ashton said. "Who needs gold wafers?" But they loaded their truck with all the medical instruments they could find.

By now it was evening and really too late to contemplate a drive back to Bataan. Ashton saw his Scouts settled into some empty barracks, and then the two officers drove into Manila to secure their own accommodations in the Army-Navy Club. Later that evening Ashton ran into a couple of Canadian civilians, the agents for the weapons and trucks the U.S. authorities had purchased. The Canadians told Ashton about the trucks and Bren gun carriers that were still parked on the deserted lot at McKinley. The Canadians bemoaned the fact that Headquarters had continued to ignore them. Though they reported every morning to the Motor Transport Service, this department seemed far too busy to bother over the problem of how they should dispose of weapons that were completely new to the American experience. The Motor Transport Service had moved from the wharfside in Manila Bay into the Tondo district of the old city—well away from the bombing and much of the other activity.

"I could use those trucks," Ashton said.

"Jesus, you take them," a Canadian replied. "We've got them here, they're for military purposes, and we're on the same side—though you would have doubted that if you'd seen the way we've been treated."

"Do you want the Bren gun carriers?" the other Canadian asked.

"Guess not," Ashton said, "but I know who could make use of them. The supply base for the 26th Cavalry has moved in close to us. I'll stop by on my way back."

The four men moved into the bar and sealed the transfer over a couple of beers. The two Canadians were obviously very relieved to be rid of the charges. They now hoped to take passage on the first available ship south.

"Have you any drivers for these trucks?" Ashton asked.

There were indeed fifteen locally hired Filipinos who, as the Canadians explained, still had to be paid by the Motor Transport Service. They would probably be found with the vehicles.

The following morning the party drove out to McKinley, and the Canadians handed over the trucks. Ashton also found a fast little car that had been abandoned on the base. This he commandeered for his personal use. They drove the convoy down to the warehouses and began to fill the vehicles with all the supplies they needed. Ashton sent the other officer on ahead with the medical supplies and then distributed his Scouts among the remaining panel trucks. He didn't trust the Filipinos and intended to use his fast little car to ride shotgun over the convoy. Before they set out for Bataan he gave them all a warning.

"Keep in the convoy and the first one of you guys tries to get out of line, we'll let you have it." He loaded and cocked his pistol to prove the point.

It was a hair-raising 80-mile drive back into Bataan. On two occasions a couple of Filipinos tried to make a break for it. Their truckloads of supplies would be worth a small fortune on the now-flourishing black market. The first time Ashton was able to head them off, but one of the trucks careened into a monsoon ditch. Its load of C rations pitched forward, and as the cartons split, tumbled over the cab and hood. The Filipino driver fled. Paul screeched to a halt, leaped out of his car, and tore off across the paddy field after the fleeing man, bringing him down with a fearsome football tackle and then hauling him back to the vehicles.

On the second occasion the convoy had become snarled up with a lot of other trucks as they threaded their way through the bottleneck of Calumpit Bridge, just north of Manila. One truck at the tail of the convoy slipped away in the chaos and confusion. As the vehicle disappeared up a dirt track, Ashton emptied his pistol at the cloud of dust. The truck veered crazily for a moment, and Ashton liked to think he had hit the bastard, but at that range he knew he had probably missed.

Good as his word, he stopped off at the rear-area base for the 26th Cavalry and told their supply officer about the Bren gun carriers and where they could be found.

In the North of Luzon the Japanese detachments from the 2nd Formosa Regiment had consolidated their beachheads, and units from the 5th Air Group now operated out of three newly constructed air fields. This increased the pilots' combat time over the targets in the South.

Ed Erickson had lost count of the number of missions he had flown over these three hectic days. After a while everything seemed to merge into one collage of dogfights against heavy odds, interspersed with hectic activity on the ground. The pilots by now were involved in preparing their planes for battle. They cursed and fumed at the inadequacies of their equipment and the appalling condition of the spare parts. Flying by the book became an expression of contempt for a peacetime Air Corps that had allowed men and machines to mark time. The pilots rewrote the rules of air combat, adding and revising with each mission they survived. They helped the ground crews de-oil the .50-caliber machine guns because with the changes of temperature at altitude the guns froze and the recoil jammed solid. It was against standing orders, but at least the de-oiled guns fired when the pilot pressed the button. The machine guns were World War I-vintage, and so was the ammunition; as soon as the armorers lifted the belts out of the canisters they disintegrated. Many was the evening hour Erickson spent with the ground crews squatting in a circle and, with needle and canvas, fashioning new belts. Erickson forged an even closer relationship with his particular crew chief and mechanics, and they in turn stole and cannibalized to get his ship into the air. Even so he flew a plane that was so patched and worn after three days of almost continuous combat that it really should have been consigned to the scrap heap. By now Erickson, like so many of the pilots, was flying without oxygen. The liquidizers and compressor plant had been early casualties of war at Nichols Field. Instead they flew on a mixture of quinine and atropine. This highly dangerous combination of drugs slowed down the heart- and pulsebeat, allowing pilots to operate more effectively at high altitude.

On the last day of air combat, Erickson was twice forced to crashland. At the end of each sortie the Japanese hit his flight as they were returning to the field, invariably low on gas. On the second occasion, together with Wagner and another pilot, Erickson had been on a strafing mission to the Japanese field at Aparri. They had dropped their 30-pound fragmentation bombs with great accuracy while their strafing of the parked aircraft had further added to the destruction. But a Zero jumped Erickson as he came in for a dead-stick landing. The young pilot came out of the plane before it was through rolling. He had been hit in the leg. Luckily the wound, though painful, was superficial; a young mechanic poured raw alcohol on it and then bound the leg with strips of waste rag. It was all that they had available.

By now the 24th Pursuit Group had really ceased to exist as a fighting force. The 21st and 3rd Pursuit squadrons had no aircraft left at all. Their surviving pilots and ground crew were dispatched into Bataan to help in the preparation of air strips. The 34th was left at Del Carmen, and the remaining pilots of the 17th and the 20th squadrons were given strict instructions not to engage in any air combat. From now on they were ordered to fly reconnaissance flights only and to husband their strength for the day that MacArthur knew was rapidly approaching—the main Japanese landings in, he hoped and prayed, Lingayen Gulf. In between reconnaisance missions, Erickson ferried surviving planes—that meant anything that was at all airworthy, including the obsolete P-26s—onto the dispersal fields in Bataan. The young pilot was credited to date with three Zeros confirmed destroyed. Wagner for his part chose to ignore the instructions on air combat, and a couple of days later downed his fifth enemy aircraft. He became the United States' first fighter ace of the war.

The Japanese aircraft roamed at will across the skies above Luzon. Daily, from 1200 to 1330 hours, the bombers hit Manila. They were so regular that people set their watches by them. Garrisons adapted by advancing the lunch hour to 1100 hours so that the men could eat in peace before diving for the slit trenches.

The quartermasters continued to build up the massive supply dumps in the areas behind the anticipated invasion beaches of central and southern Luzon, but even though the dumps had not reached even half their expected capacity, the supply system began to fall apart. The one exception was the huge government rice granary at Cabanatuan in central Luzon. Commonwealth Department policies and American dumping had resulted in a depot containing more than fifty million bushels of rice, enough to feed an army of twenty-five thousand men for four years.

The Manila railroad upon which so much depended for the

movement of supplies from Manila to the advance depots began to fail. Train and engine crews abandoned their jobs and fled because of enemy strafing and bombing of the railway.

Sunday, December 14, 1941
Washington, D.C.

Directly after Pearl Harbor, Col. Dwight D. Eisenhower had been summoned to Washington from his appointment as Chief of Staff to the Third Army, based at Fort Sam Houston, Texas. His new job was to coordinate the plans for the relief of the Philippines. Eisenhower had been for four years MacArthur's Chief Assistant on detached service with the Philippine Commonwealth in Manila. That experience had given him privileged access to the men, the terrain, and the war plans of the Philippines.

On this Sunday morning, Eisenhower was briefed personally by the Chief of Staff, General Marshall. The latter painted a very gloomy picture both in terms of the strategic priorities of Pearl Harbor over the Philippines and in the details of the loss of the air strength and the destruction of Cavite. The general concluded his briefing by stressing that MacArthur was outnumbered and out-supplied and that, with the forces available to him, the most that could be expected was to deny the Japanese Manila Bay for a while at least.

General Marshall gave Eisenhower an hour to think about the situation and then asked for his recommendations. This brilliant staff officer quickly thought through the issues and identified the major points for consideration. His first recommendation was that every effort be made to relieve the Philippines. The American people, he emphasized, might understand and even excuse failure, but they would never forgive abandonment. He pointed out that the people of China, the Dutch East Indies, and Australia would also be looking for some attempt at relief. Eisenhower proposed that the United States establish a base in Australia, and from there a supply line should be battled through to Manila Bay, at whatever the cost.

The *Pensacola* convoy, with its seven big freighters and their cruiser escort, was expected in Brisbane within the week. This would provide the fighting start for a plan that suddenly burned brightly with optimism. Marshall, light of heart for the first time in a week, gave the staff colonel three days in which to prepare his plans in detail.

2nd Battalion, 4th Marines
Olongapo, Subic Bay

Japanese bombers returned and tore the heart out of Subic Bay. One stick of bombs hit a cock-fighting stadium. As it was Sunday, the stadium was full, and in the excitement of the moment none of the fans heard, or chose to obey, the air raid sirens. Few of the 300-odd Filipinos inside survived. The planes flew on and hit the Navy Yard.

Sergeant Bigelow, along with other Marines, heaved the shattered timbers of the stadium aside and helped pull out the maimed and the dying; it proved a soul-destroying task. As soon as he had done all that could be done, he went to the battalion executive officer and reported the local Roman Catholic priest. This man, a Caucasian, not a Filipino, had questioned Bigelow persistently over the last couple of days as to how long the Marines were staying, what their strength was, and when they intended to leave. The manner and insistence of the questions profoundly disturbed the young sergeant, and when he was approached again during the rescue work, he knew something was wrong.

The battalion Intelligence officer had received complaints against this priest ever since they had arrived in Olongapo, and the local people had been very suspicious of him.

So Bigelow, with a couple of battalion officers, was ordered to make a thorough search of the man's church. It didn't take them long; hidden in the stairs leading into the pulpit they found a short-wave radio. The battalion commander instituted a hearing on the spot, and, surprisingly, the man broke down under questioning.

He admitted that he was a member of the German-American Bund and an agent of Japanese Intelligence.

The agent was taken around to the back of the church, and, before a number of witnesses, he was shot. The details were duly logged. The Marines had neither the time nor the inclination for the charade of a court-martial or the long and protracted routing of a civil court case. In a battalion that had suffered casualties and just witnessed the horror of mass bombing of civilians, there was no voice raised in protest.

0900 hours
Wednesday, December 17, 1941
Kirun, northern Formosa

Twenty-one Japanese transports sailed as part of the first group for the main invasion of Luzon. There were 3 separate convoys, totaling 76 heavily loaded Army and 9 Navy transports. Among them they carried the main elements of General Homma's Fourteenth Army, some 43,110 men. They had a close-in escort of light cruisers and destroyers, while a distant cover of battleships and heavy cruisers, drawn from the Third Fleet, were deployed to meet any Allied attempt to disrupt the landings at Lingayen Gulf.

The Office of the Chief of Staff
Washington, D.C.

Colonel Eisenhower duly presented his plans for the approval of General Marshall. They examined in detail the tables and flow charts that the colonel and his staff had prepared for the creation of the Brisbane base and the onward transshipment of supplies to the beleaguered Philippine forces. The bright-colored lines spelled hope for the beleaguered garrison and a way out of an awkward dilemma for the General Staff.

41st Divisional Artillery
Batangas Province
Southern Luzon

Although Winston Jones now had guns and ammunition, he still had a long way to go to turn his Filipinos into efficient gunners. Very few had received their uniforms and most of the draftees had never seen anything like their artillery before or fired anything bigger than a shotgun. Jones knew, however, they were full of enthusiasm to learn the trade, even though time was not on their side. A field gun normally required a sergeant and up to five gunners as crew, together with additional men for support. But when Jones distributed his men to the guns, the best he could manage was a partially trained sergeant and three newly inducted recruits to each field piece. There were no support elements available.

The night after they had received the ammunition he had devised a plan to improve their training. He found a motor canoe with one outrigger. It had a small inboard engine and belonged to a local fisherman who took a good deal of persuading before he would hand the boat over to the Army. Then Jones had his men build a float with a pole in the center. He tied a white flag to the top of the pole. Early the next morning Jones launched his craft and, with considerable difficulty, made it out through the surf; the medical officer came along for the ride, and they took a Filipino soldier as crew member. At a range of about 300 yards from the beach, Jones towed the target slowly back and forth across the lagoon. Ashore Jones's assistant, Lieutenant Day, and his three American sergeants trained the Filipinos to track and lay the guns in a direct fire role. At the same time they were able to check the guns in their positions to make certain they had a full and unimpeded view across the bay.

After three hours the officers were heartily sick of their chore. There was no protection from the bright glare of the sun, and the fish weren't biting. All of a sudden Jones saw a Filipino soldier on the beach jumping and waving his arms and shouting, but they couldn't tell what the man wanted because of the noise of the breakers.

"It's got to be serious, Winston, for that guy to be going through those antics," the doctor said.

Jones steered the canoe closer to the shore in an effort to hear what he was saying. At that precise moment a huge wave broke about 10 feet away, and their boat rolled in the foaming mass. Jones and his crew swam for their lives, and the boat was pounded into pieces on the shore. The Filipino crewman lost his rifle, and the two officers lost their wristwatches and their dignity.

They finally staggered up the beach and through the barbed wire, and Jones asked the Filipino soldier what he wanted.

"Sir, it's lunchtime," the soldier replied.

Jones could have killed him. If he had had a dry weapon he would have shot him on the spot.

That was the end of the battalion's target practice. The gun crews spent the rest of the day putting ammunition in the breech of the gun, closing the breechblock, and then ejecting it. This loading practice wasn't good for the ammunition, as it damaged the copper rotating band and the grooves, but it was necessary training.

The gunners worked through the night, training hard and changing positions on the gun so they could handle other jobs if the need arose. Jones had set up their newly acquired battery commander's telescope near the two 75mm batteries in the palm trees. It was a very clear night though the moon had yet to rise, and he focused his scope out to sea. Suddenly he saw a shape moving into the bay. He could not tell what it was except that it was large and moving slowly. He followed as it entered the bay and moved across to the southernmost side near the entrance. He heard the anchor drop as the ship came to a stop within what he estimated was 100 yards of the actual rock cliffs. The battery stood to, and the gunners loaded their pieces for real; practice time was over. Jones used the battalion radio and called Division, and headquarters checked with Manila to see if there were any American warships in the area. Jones also called up a battery of 155mm guns, "Long Toms" that were deployed inland, about 3 miles away. He then asked Divisional Headquarters for permission to blow the ship out of the water. Permission was refused.

The ship was still there three hours later. Jones again called Division, this time requesting permission to send a scouting party around by the side of the bay to identify the ship. If they found it to be Japanese, then he would fire on it. Permission was again refused; Division did not want their locations revealed to the enemy. Jones was furious.

An hour later the vessel left the lagoon. It returned the following night, and on two other occasions in the next week. Jones was convinced that it was a Japanese destroyer.

Thursday, December 18, 1941
On board S-36
Lingayen Gulf

Submarine warfare is long periods of intense boredom interspersed with short periods of acute fear. Lieutenant McKnight and his crew had seen nothing; and nothing had happened in the ten days they had been at sea. They received messages from Hart's Headquarters. Some they were supposed to acknowledge, which they did. What McKnight didn't know was that his transmitter was poor and off frequency. None of his messages were getting out of the ship.

That evening McKnight had picked up his recall signal. He was ordered to return to Manila. The voyage south was difficult as the gyrocompass had tumbled, and he had to make most of the voyage closed down on the surface. The old tub was leaking worse than ever as she labored at her best speed.

It was 0200 hours, and the night was fine and clear, even romantic in a sense, McKnight thought, as the moonbeams bathed the sea in delicate tones of light and dark. The pungent perfumes of palm and tropical forest wafted out on the offshore breeze.

The navigation officer, who had the watch, ducked beneath the makeshift canvas screen at the back of the bridge and with a hooded flashlight checked the charts. He told McKnight that he thought they were now in the submarine sanctuary. The submarine sanctuary was an area of coastal waters that was marked as a place where submarines could stay submerged and not be attacked by their own warships.

McKnight grunted in reply; if he were right, that would put them about 10 miles out of the South Channel entrance and minefields to Manila Bay. His orders were to wait for a PT boat to rendezvous with further instructions.

As the submarine turned gently toward the still invisible Manila Bay, the port lookout reported a submarine on the surface, 2 miles away. As there was no way to know whether it was friend or foe, McKnight ordered an immediate dive. He decided that they would stay down until dawn and make contact with the PT boat when they actually sighted it.

It was just about dawn when they spotted the PT boat. McKnight panned the scope across the horizon. There was no other vessel in sight, so the *S-36* surfaced and signaled her identification to the patrol boat. The two vessels came alongside, and the PT boat captain, Lt. Cdr. Buckley, passed across McKnight's instructions to enter the next night at 2330 hours. Then he told McKnight that everyone thought they had been lost and asked where they had been. But with the stray sub about the last thing McKnight wanted to do was make conversation with a torpedo boat commander, so he quickly informed him of the last known position of the other submarine and submerged. Buckley was affronted by what he saw as the indecent haste of the submariner.

The *S-36* entered the following night as ordered and headed for Manila. The minefield was turned off, and a sweeper stood by as escort. McKnight slid past the silent, menacing mass of Corregidor. On his starboard beam the weird, stunted silhouette of the concrete battleship stood out starkly against the night sky. A French freighter passed close by at high speed, in a lone bid for freedom. Her wash rocked the little submarine; she was the *D'Artagnan*, a very distinctive vessel with a square smokestack.

McKnight took his submarine inside the breakwater in Manila Harbor and tied up alongside a camouflaged nest of cargo barges that had been brought down from the Pasig River.

The crew settled down to carry out the necessary repairs. The submarine had sustained some damage to the cells in the set of batteries aft. This required removing much of the top deck plates and replacing the faulty cells with new ones drawn from the *Canopus*. This was a long and complicated business, which took the better part of two days before the work was finished. While the battery cover was open, the submarine couldn't submerge and during the five air raids that Manila experienced in that time, there was little McKnight could do other than sit there and watch them.

When the battery was repaired and the power restored, things improved a little. At the sound of the air raid sirens he would submerge to the bottom of Manila Bay, but the conning tower was still above water. McKnight would stand on his bridge, together with the gunner and the Lewis machine guns, and watch the Japanese fly over.

Thursday, December 18, 1941
26th Cavalry, Philippine Scouts
Along the Agno River
Central Luzon

The news that Wainwright received of the Japanese progress from their landings in the North was bad. His green Filipino troops had done little to stop the enemy. Instead they had fled at the first signs of their approach. At this rate it would not be many days before the Japanese force advancing south from Vigan would be in a position to threaten the main defenses in and around Lingayen Gulf, where already jittery Filipinos were dug in and anxiously awaiting the anticipated main Japanese landings. Wainwright ordered the 26th Cavalry to deploy northward and take up positions along the line of the Agno River. From there the cavalry could move to stop the Japanese advance from Vigan and support the forces in Lingayen Gulf. It was a bold gamble to take, for the cavalry would have to make a forced march of 45 miles against Japanese air superiority.

Sunday, December 21, 1941
The "Battle" of Lingayen Gulf

While the S-36 was undergoing repair, McKnight was a distant observer of the failure of the largest submarine force ever assembled by the United States to prevent or even hinder the main Japanese invasion of Luzon. There were twenty-one submarines at sea. Since it seemed most likely that an invasion force of the Philippines would approach from Japanese bases to the west or northwest of Luzon, John Wilkes dispatched thirteen boats to watch the waters around Formosa, the Pescadores, Indochina, and Hainan. The orders read, "Report the invasion forces and then press home your attacks. Keep to the priority of targets as laid down in standing orders." The Japanese invasion forces were detected, and from December 18 onward, signals trickled into HQ Submarines, Asiatic Fleet.

However, very few submarines were able to close with the enemy, let alone cause damage. A combination of circumstances, in some cases sheer bad luck, for there must always be an element of luck, conspired against the captains. More often than not it was poor training, which in turn led to basic errors in seamanship, often at the most critical point in the move to contact. Those who did press home their attack were robbed of victory by the flawed Mark 6 magnetic torpedo; it proved capable of every trick in the book, except that of striking the target. But it was to take the submarine commanders in the Pacific a long time to convince the naval munitions authorities and the torpedo manufacturers that the weapon was faulty.

Some commanders did not press home their attacks when the opportunity was there; two went to pieces and handed command over to their executive officers. Unfortunately the procedures through which they had been selected for command in a peacetime Navy were not sufficiently good to ensure the qualities of command needed in time of war. One ordered the exec to lock him in his cabin after his submarine had been pounded with depth charges by Japanese destroyers for some hours. He still received the Navy Cross when his submarine docked in a face-saving formula that did the Navy's reputation no good whatsoever.

The large modern fleet submarine *Stingray* had replaced McKnight's elderly *S-36* in Lingayen Gulf. Lieutenant Commander Lamb and his crew had been at sea for a week. Their ship had a number of irritating failures, which had done little to aid morale. On December 21 she developed an air leak. It was small, but nevertheless Lamb was convinced that it was a dead giveaway for any attacking destroyer. He requested and was granted permission to return to Manila for repairs. At 1713 hours *Stingray* was at the entrance to Lingayen Gulf. Lamb came up to periscope depth and prepared to surface for the voyage south to Manila Bay. When he made a last sweep, he spotted smoke on the horizon. Within a few moments his periscope presented him with the submariner's dream (or nightmare, depending upon temperament)—close-packed ranks of fat, waddling transports, approaching bows on, without the room to maneuver or evade.

Lamb sent his sighting report to base. On receiving the message, Wilkes canceled the submarine's return and instead ordered him to press home the attack. Lamb maneuvered until darkness, trying to get into a position to launch a beam attack; at least he so informed his crew. They were more convinced by his obvious lack of aggression and fighting resolve. While the Japanese convoys passed by and the destiny of the Philippines was poised on the threshold of disaster, Lamb and the *Stingray* spent a critical fourteen-and-a-half hours on the seabed, evading detection. He made a couple of attempts to penetrate the Japanese destroyer screen, but these were halfhearted gestures that brought little credit to the man or the submarine service. In the meanwhile Lamb had found several more leaks, which caused him even greater concern. He again requested permission to return to Manila.

The *Stingray* docked in Manila without having fired a single torpedo at the fattest target ever presented to a submariner. Captain Wilkes relieved him of his command.

There was still time to make amends. Though the Japanese invasion force had arrived off its beaches intact, the landings could still be disrupted if the attack was pressed home hard enough. As soon as he had received Lamb's initial report Wilkes had dispatched six submarines from their patrol stations into the gulf. Their orders were: Enter the gulf and attack the enemy. In the three days following, the submarines tried to elude the vigilant destroyer screens. The waters of the gulf are shallow, and all the advantages lay with the surface forces, who drove the submarines to the seabed and terrorized their crews with the pounding of their depth charges. Some captains tried harder than others, but none was able to penetrate the destroyers. All were lucky to escape from the gulf with their lives.

One among the band of gallant exceptions was Moon Chapple, a heavyweight boxing champion. He commanded an S-type submarine and later went into Lingayen Gulf and did his best to get among the transports. Japanese destroyers hounded him out of the gulf. Some of his batteries exploded and killed part of the crew. The submarine barely managed to limp back to Manila Bay.

Despite all the warnings, and the correct assessments by MacArthur that Lingayen Gulf was indeed the logical landing for a march on Manila, the ground forces were singularly unprepared. Beach defenses were in the hands of two raw Philippine Army divisions, one of which had received only ten weeks' training, and the other had no artillery.

The remnants of the Air Corps attempted to interfere with the landings. A few B-17s made the long haul up from the South and caused some damage, but their single sortie was a gesture, nothing else. The heavy artillery ashore also caused General Homma some anxious moments, but in the end it was the swell and the sea that caused the only disruptions to the Japanese timetable. At the end of the day the Japanese were ashore in strength. The raw recruits of the U.S. 21st and 71st Infantry fell back in disorder, while the veterans—Marines, the Scouts, and the 31st—waited passively in the South. They could have turned the beaches red and made the enemy pay heavily had they been committed to battle.

MacArthur in reality had already lost the battle for Manila. His proud promise that the fighting Filipinos would stop the enemy dead in his tracks on the beaches had proved an empty gesture, although the fantasy world in which he and his command staff lived in the House on the Wall was to persist for another three days while he sought to contest the landings.

MacArthur's predicament was made even worse by the failure of the submarines. They had lost control of the waters around Luzon. Eisenhower's plans for a relief convoy weren't worth the paper they were written on; Luzon was surrounded.

Bill Massello was on the wharfside at Mariveles. His searchlights were dug in and deployed for battle, and he was waiting for a barge to come across from Corregidor with some fresh supplies. While waiting he discussed the failure of the submarines in his usual forthright manner with the naval duty officer; the latter in the best traditions of the service sought to defend the honor of his colleagues.

Massello's opening question hit home: "What have you guys done about all those Jap transports out there?"

"It was an unpenetrable wall of steel. The subs just couldn't get through," the duty officer replied.

Massello was furious with this pompous answer. "What the hell did you think it was going to be," he asked, "a game of tag?"

It was just as well that the barge from Corregidor arrived at that moment.

VI. RETREAT

Monday, December 22, 1941–
Thursday, January 1, 1942

Monday, December 22, 1941
Brisbane
Australia

The *Pensacola* convoy docked on the same day that a new command, the United States Army Forces in Australia, came into existence. Brigadier General Clegg, who had commanded the interceptors in the Philippines, arrived to establish the bases and coordinate the airlift to the beleaguered garrison. Major General Brett, who was at that time attending an Allied conference in Chungking, China, was to assume overall command in Australia.

General Marshall in Washington ordered the Australian base to make the relief of the Philippines its highest priority. It was to operate under the command of USAFFE. General MacArthur ordered the planes from the *Pensacola* convoy to be assembled and flown to the Philippines without delay and the freighters rerouted to Manila under escort at the first available opportunity.

Lingayen Gulf

If the Japanese had come ashore where they had originally intended, it might have been a different story. The most obvious beaches were covered by Filipino troops, dug in and seemingly well prepared for battle. Instead a navigational error, caused by their failure to take proper account of wind and tides, produced an accident of war that worked in favor of the Japanese. So they hit the Filipino divisions in the flank, and, though their progress was temporarily halted by the 1st Battalion of the 11th Division, they eventually overwhelmed the resistance, and the Filipinos, ousted from their prepared positions, broke and ran.

The only force immediately available to General Wainwright was the 26th Cavalry. He ordered them to move out of their bivouac at Rosario and advance the 25 miles north along Route 3 to Lingayen Gulf and the small town of Damortis. However, the cavalry, the bulk of which was mounted on horses (the reconnaissance platoons had some motorcycles and light armored cars), hit hard by Japanese troops supported by aircraft, was forced to give ground. The troops fought a brilliant rearguard action, but against Japanese armor they had nothing heavier than .50-caliber machine guns.

As the horse troops slowly retreated under continuing Japanese pressure, Wainwright deployed a platoon of tanks forward of the cavalry to take some of the strain off the exhausted men. At nightfall the tanks were ordered to fall back, and they retreated through the cavalry. The latter, some 600 in number, were drawn up in readiness for a night march when Japanese armor ran into them. It was a narrow road with high banks topped with barbed wire. In the gathering dark there was chaos, confusion, and carnage. Riderless horses bolted into the night, and the casualties from Japanese tank fire were appalling. Many men were trampled by their mounts or crushed to death beneath the tracks of the enemy tanks. The survivors were routed south to Rosario, where only the quick thinking of one of their officers—he blocked the bridge into Rosario with vehicles—gave them respite and the chance to reform.

The roll call that night revealed that there were now only 175 men mounted and still able to fight. Many more who were cut off rejoined their units in the following days. Even so, the regiment had suffered grievously. Nevertheless, they were still able to play their part in the fighting rear guard, and this speaks volumes for their élan and spirit. Used in the traditional role as a rear guard, the 26th Cavalry Philippine Scouts continued to write some of the finest chapters in the annals of cavalry warfare.

With his division falling back in confusion, Wainwright realized that the best he could hope for was to stem the tide along the line of the Agno River, the first significant natural obstacle in the path of the advancing Japanese. The Agno River was only 60 miles north of Bataan. He asked Manila to release seasoned troops to hold the line and perhaps launch a counterattack, but he was refused.

The Japanese in the meanwhile had consolidated their beach-head and were already pushing out along three separate axes. They linked up with Tanaka's forces advancing south from Vigan and threatened the summer capital at Baguio. Once their heavy artillery was ashore, they would be in a position to debouch onto the central plain of Luzon and advance on a broad front to Manila.

Manila

Lilla and Clay Seitz listened to MacArthur's communiqué on the local radio that evening. The baby was due, and Lilla was preparing to go into the hospital. They were heartened by the spirit of the words: "The enemy has landed scattered elements along the shores of Lingayen Gulf. My gallant divisions are holding ground and denying the foe the sacred soil of the Philippines. We have inflicted heavy casualties on his troops, and nowhere is his bridgehead secure. Tomorrow we will drive him into the sea."

Fort Mills
Corregidor

Admiral Rockwell moved to Corregidor and re-established his headquarters in the Navy tunnel on the island. The destruction of the radio facilities at Sangley Point, a promontory on the perimeter of the naval base, had rendered Cavite useless. Now the only contact with the United States was through the big radios on Corregidor.

Champlin had left Cavite in the admiral's barge. The day before, the Japanese had hit the Officers' Club at Sangley Point. They had blown the entire end off the building and exposed the tobacco and liquor stores. Champlin filled a washtub full of fine Scotch and the best Alhambra Corona cigars and took it down to the barge. There was a small watertight compartment in the bows, used to store life jackets, spare cordage, and anchors. Champlin moved some of the gear, placed his washtub full of goodies carefully inside, covered it with life jackets, and left for Corregidor.

After the barge had docked, Champlin waited for a quiet moment and stole down to the wharfside to rescue his secret horde. He printed the word "ADMIRAL" in large capital letters on the tub and then carried it into the tunnel. Beneath the large radio transmitters there were about 20 inches of space, and the tub was 18 inches deep. This proved a perfect hiding place. With the insignia facing outward he reasoned his horde would be safe from prying eyes. Over the following weeks the naval aide dipped into his supplies whenever the need arose.

A number of officers had been left behind at Cavite. Their prime task was to ensure that everything that could be saved was taken away and that which remained was destroyed. Rockwell had been particularly concerned about the store of mines at Sangley Point. After the bombing there were no facilities to move them, yet they were brand new and still on the secret list. There were 102 Mark 12 mines in the store; shaped like a torpedo, they could be sown in the normal manner or fired from a torpedo tube. The mine weighed 1,750 pounds, and it was the new igniting device that was so secret. Rockwell had given explicit orders that these mines must not be allowed to fall into the hands of the enemy. Two demolition experts, a lieutenant and a warrant officer, were charged with this task.

2300 hours
19th Bombardment Group
Clark Field

After the initial raids, the days for Dick Osborn and Sam Boghosian fused into one perpetual nightmare. Without aircraft to fly and fight, they worked hard on the air base at whatever task came their way, maintenance on the few machines still airworthy, salvage of those beyond repair. Whatever their routine, it was punctuated by frequent raids. For them it was still the strafing Zero that held the worst terror. For Osborn the bombs appeared anonymous and indiscriminate, but the raking paths of cannon shells always seemed to be aimed directly at his slit trench. The flak gunners, for a time at least, manned their weapons, and many paid the price of the reckless. The survivors learned how and when to seek whatever cover was available, foxhole or sandbagged emplacement. The men had been moved out of Clark and were now quartered on the golf course at Stotsenberg. Even in this short period of time, the greens and fairways were beginning to show the signs of neglect. Tire marks of the Dodge six-by-sixes would be an additional hazard for any future golfer!

Osborn was roused from the deepest sleep of the exhausted by the raucous yell of Taulbee and a number of other sergeants. Drugged with sleep and bemused, Osborn crawled out of his pup tent. In shorts and undershirt, and with his boots in his hand, he stumbled into line with the others. While the sergeants sorted order out of chaos he pulled his boots on and wondered what had caused this sudden emergency. His whole being cried out for sleep and peace; above all, peace. Like the other 200 men similarly aroused, he was not in the best mood as they were marched squad by squad across the fairway of the eighth green, where they were quartered toward the distant shapes on the skyline of Fort Stotsenberg. The airmen were marched straight down the line of shattered and deserted buildings to the armory. They were now fully awake and Osborn could feel the tension mount as curiosity gave way to fear and apprehension. They were halted outside one of the very few warehouses that remained, and then a squad at a time marched into the building. Inside, it was ablaze with light behind the blacked-out windows. In single file they shuffled down the side of a long table, where each man was handed a Springfield rifle, a bandolier, a bayonet, and a shovel.

When the squadron had been issued these items they were gathered in an open space at the end of the building. Despite the warm, humid night the bare concrete floor and naked light cast a chill over the airmen. Osborn shivered and wished he had had enough sense to grab a shirt.

An officer stood on top of an empty ammunition box and addressed the airmen: "The Japs have landed at Lingayen Gulf, and they are now advancing south toward us. We're gonna take you out to Clark, and we're gonna dig in. Intelligence has gotten word that Japanese are coming in at dawn with paratroopers and gliders. They're gonna try and take the base, and you're gonna stop 'em."

The sergeants separated the squads, and the airmen prepared for war. Armorers showed them how to clean the Cosmoline out of the rifles. Osborn watched fascinated as another showed how to hone and sharpen the bayonets.

"Dear Christ," he thought, "please don't make me have to use this." His guts felt hollow and terribly vulnerable, and he wanted to throw up. The sudden noise of trucks pulling up outside the building jerked him back to reality. He looked about him, fearful that his emotions had betrayed him, but he needn't have worried; most of the youngsters had a strange, detached look.

"We're all the same," he thought, "a bunch of untrained kids who don't know their butt from their face. Any Japanese paratrooper will kick the shit out of us."

An hour later the troop carrier deposited Osborn and his squad out in the middle of Clark. He was convinced that he was in the most vulnerable and obvious part of the field. Along with the others he passed the most terrifying night of his life. First of all, they dug furiously down into the soft loam—fear drove them deep. The gallows humor of Osborn's section sergeant didn't help much, either: "Dig hard, Osborn, and we'll bury you all the easier in the morning."

Osborn was convinced he had been given a death warrant, and as the first gray streaks in the eastern sky heralded the dawn, he knew he had just spent his last night on earth. He jumped down into his foxhole and with nerveless fingers fixed the bayonet, mesmerized by the naked steel. He loaded two five-shot clips into the magazine, correctly applied the safety catch, and rested the rifle on the parapet.

"Keep your shovels handy, fellas," their sergeant advised. "It's the best weapon you've got when it gets down to hand-to-hand combat."

"Oh, Jesus," Osborn moaned as he looked up into the morning sky.

Two hours later they were ordered out of the holes and marched back to their tents at Stotsenberg.

"False alarm, men," said their squadron commander as Osborn's group filed past. "The trucks are needed elsewhere, so you'll have to march back to base."

Osborn didn't mind. In fact, he felt positively lighthearted, reprieved from the very clutches of death.

Tuesday, December 23, 1941
Maryknoll convent
Baguio
Central Luzon

Ever since the first day of the war the American community in Baguio had looked after the nuns. They had called on them almost every day.

The Dominican monastery was farther up the hill, above the convent. The friars from their vantage point could look out over Lingayen Gulf and, with the aid of a battered telescope, pick out the American flag flying over the beleaguered garrison at Damortis. Each morning Sister Louise telephoned the monastery.

"Is Old Glory still waving?" she would ask.

"Yes, still waving, Sister, still waving," they would reply.

Every morning the bombers appeared in the skies above Baguio. On some days the bombs fell close to the convent as they bracketted Camp John Hay; on other days the enemy hit the Military Academy or the municipal buildings. Sometimes it appeared as if they didn't care and just dumped their load indiscriminately over the once-beautiful but now scarred city.

That morning when Sister Louise called the monastery, she had the answer they had all been dreading. The flag was not flying, and the bombers didn't put in their appearance either. The signs were ominous. Then the telephone rang in the convent. Sister Louise answered. It was one of the self-appointed leaders of the American community in Baguio.

"Sister," he said, "we've had a meeting here in the Pines Hotel, and I want to tell you what we're going to do. The Japanese are coming up the mountain and right now are in the outskirts of the city. We've sent out a delegation to meet them. All the troops have abandoned Camp John Hay, and we want to surrender. I'm asking all Americans not to offer any resistance to the Japanese. We're civilians, and we'll seek the protection of the Geneva Convention." He hung up.

The Japanese ran amok in Baguio.

Sister Louise and the other nuns gathered in their little chapel. It was time for Mass. All sought comfort in the soft words spoken by the priest. After the short service, the sisters walked out into the bright glare of the afternoon sun. It was quiet outside, and there was not a sound to be heard. Even the jungle creatures in the nearby undergrowth had stilled their distemperate chorus.

The convent was all in one large building: living quarters, a now deserted school, and the chapel. High on a hill and with a courtyard of tough Philippine concrete, it was built to withstand the force of a typhoon. To a stranger it had the appearance of a fortress.

A bird high in the trees above gave a shrill cry of alarm, and then suddenly they heard howling and screeching; a horde of Japanese soldiers burst into the courtyard. The nuns stood quietly calm, but even with their sheltered lives the intent of the soldiers was clear. For a moment both groups stood their ground.

The nuns' gardener, a quiet, unassumingly devout Filipino, stepped in front of the Sisters; he knew the Japanese had been on the rampage. At that moment the soldiers stood aside as an officer strode into the courtyard. Tall for a Japanese and strikingly handsome, the nuns recognized him as a stallholder from the market in Baguio. They had regularly purchased their fish from him and had never been aware of his nationality; the shock of recognition showed clearly on their faces.

The Filipino seized his opportunity. He begged the officer to explain to his men that the nuns were not like other women. He beseeched him not to harm or molest the Sisters. The Japanese officer spoke to his men, and the Japanese soldiers obeyed. They never touched the nuns, but they did wreck the convent.

Nobody was sure what they were looking for, but they tore the place apart and spared nothing; even the beautifully hand-embroidered altarfront was slashed by Japanese bayonets. The Dominican priest, a Belgian who had been saying Mass for the Sisters, tried to intervene, and he was frog-marched outside and savagely beaten. Half a dozen or more soldiers took turns kicking the inert, frail figure as he lay in the dust and his own blood. After a while they tired of their sport; the priest was barely alive.

The soldiers, their lust for destruction temporarily satiated, went on their way. Sister Louise and two other nuns tenderly carried the beaten priest indoors and bound his wounds. Others tried to repair the desecration of their chapel.

Later that evening one of the Japanese soldiers returned. Sister Louise found him standing at the door that led into the chapel. He asked her to take him to the priest. The soldier was humble and subdued; there was clearly no hostility in his manner as he was ushered to the bedside. The soldier knelt before the bed and in halting English begged forgiveness.

"I'm a Catholic, Father, and I know how I should treat a priest, but in front of the others there was nothing for me to do but beat you as they did. I have come back to ask your pardon. If the others find out I came here, they will send me to an infantry assault company and I will surely die, but I could not live with my conscience and not come back and say I am sorry."

The priest gave the soldier his blessing, and the young man wept unashamedly. As he left the convent he told the nuns not to worry. "Our officer explained that you are holy women and must not be treated like other women. You will be safe."

The young soldier went on his way. The nuns, though often fearful of the Japanese, were never molested though, for good measure, so long as they stayed in their convent, the gardener slept behind the front door at night.

The Office of the Chief Quartermaster
USAFFE HQ
No. 1 Calle Victoria
Manila

It was about 1200 hours when the telephone shattered the stillness in Brig. Gen. Charles Drake's office. Lt. Col. Theodore Kalukaka, his executive officer, answered. "Right away, sir. Very well, sir." Kalukaka replaced the receiver and turned to General

Drake. "The Deputy Chief of Staff would like to see you in his office right away, General."

The Deputy Chief of Staff was Brig. Gen. Richard Marshall, who was a member of the original MacArthur coterie. In 1938 as a lieutenant colonel he had served on MacArthur's staff in Washington.

There was something about that ring of the telephone and the peremptory order that gave Drake a premonition that everything was about to snap. What it could be, though, was a puzzle. Drake, tall and balding, was already at fifty-four years of age one of the older general officers on MacArthur's staff. He had graduated from West Point in 1912 and had been an infantry officer for most of his military career. He was now on his second tour in the Philippines. A wise and thoughtful soldier, he knew something was wrong.

Things had been going along well until then. MacArthur's briefings showed that the troops under Wainwright were still "slugging it out" on the beaches of Lingayen Gulf while, to the south of Manila, Parker's forces were well placed to block the threat from the Japanese beachhead at Legaspi.

"So far as I can see, everything is OK, so what's gone wrong?" Drake wondered. He stopped off on the way and picked up one of his principal staff officers, Colonel Lewis Beebe. Drake was convinced that something was about to break, and whatever it was, they would have to work it out together. The two officers were shown into the Deputy Chief's office; as Dick Marshall rose from behind his littered desk to greet them, his face told them that something big had happened. General Marshall came straight to the point: "How do your defense reserves stand at Corregidor, Charlie?"

They were supposed to have six months of supplies for the garrison of ten thousand men scattered throughout the bay forts. Drake thought about it for a moment before he replied: "Well, there are undoubtedly a few shortages, but on the whole I would guess we are pretty well stocked." He continued: "Besides the prescribed reserves we have a hundred thousand gallons of petroleum in drums stored on the island."

"Check this out for me, and get your quartermaster on Corregidor to come right over to Manila. I want him personally to supervise the drawing of his deficiencies from the base depot."

"OK, Dick, but can you tell me what all this is about?"

General Marshall walked across to a map of the Philippines; it took up the whole of the wall on the far side of the room.

"The general has decided to revert to War Plan 5." He let the significance of what he was saying sink in. The two officers were astounded by the news. Drake felt as if some cruel charade were being played out before him, and the air of unreality was reinforced by Marshall's cold, dispassionate tones as he continued his briefing.

"The beach defenses have crumbled at Lingayen, and the Japs are advancing on three fronts in the North. They have consolidated ashore here at Legaspi, and we have received word that another landing force is about to hit the East Coast. We suspect they will land in Lamon Bay." Marshall's pointer stabbed the axes of advance and the beaches under new threat. "If we can't contain the Japanese on the beaches, then there's no way we can hold Luzon or deny them Manila." Marshall paused for a moment, lit a cigarette, and inhaled deeply in what Drake recognized as the only show of emotion so far.

"General MacArthur plans to retreat into Bataan and onto Corregidor. Wainwright's Corps in the North will retreat through a series of delayed withdrawals." Marshall pointed to six lines carefully labeled D-1 through to D-6 on his map. "The Northern Corps will keep the Japs back and the door open for the Corps in the south to pull back around the bay, pivot on San Fernando, and slip into Bataan. General Parker has been dispatched to Bataan to organize the defense lines, and Albert Jones of the 51st Division has taken his place in command of the Southern Luzon Force."

Marshall paused, stubbed out his cigarette, and immediately lit another. He allowed the quartermasters to think about the implications of the plan. A fighting retreat against a better-equipped enemy with all the advantages of air power is a tall order by any stretch of the imagination.

"You are to treat my words in the strictest confidence," Marshall ordered. "The general will make a public announcement tomorrow. Manila will be declared an open city under the Geneva Convention. That will come into operation on December 26, so all troops must be clear of the city. Otherwise the declaration is violated. You, Charlie, will have to stock Bataan as best you can, but I am ordered to tell you that before you move anything onto the peninsula, the needs of Corregidor must take priority."

"Any questions?" he asked, returning to his desk.

"When will headquarters move, Dick?"

"General MacArthur, his family and staff, together with President Quezon and his entourage, and Commissioner Sayre and his people, will move across to Corregidor during the course of the twenty-fourth. General Moore is being informed right now, and suitable quarters will be prepared. As for the rest of the staff, and your department, Charlie, it is precisely as laid down in the original war plans."

"Well, the first problem, Dick, is the question of supplies. Most of the warehouses in Manila are empty. I have stockpiled at the agreed positions, out in the provinces, and behind the troops watching the beaches. I don't have the vehicles to move the stuff back again."

It was still a sore point with Drake that headquarters had done nothing to stop units commandeering all the available vehicles in the first panicky days of the war.

A central pool of Quartermaster Corps vehicles would be a godsend right now, Drake thought.

"The only supplies held in bulk in Manila are commercial," Drake said. "I have already purchased all the available stocks of canned meats and fruits from the canning companies—Libby, McNeill & Libby, Armour & Company, and Del Monte."

"The only transportation we haven't yet taken over are the river barges," Colonel Beebe spoke for the first time.

General Marshall ordered Drake to commandeer all the water transportation in Manila and the Pasig River.

"How many men will garrison Bataan, General?" Bebee asked.

Marshall didn't reply immediately. When he did, he quietly dropped the second bombshell of the morning.

"I might just as well tell you, but this, too, is in the strictest confidence. All the civilians in Bataan will be moved out of the battle zone. At the same time the Philippine Army divisions," he chose his words carefully, "will not be actively encouraged to retreat. So with our own people and the Scouts, a maximum of forty thousand men for a hundred and eighty days. By the end of that time we expect the relief forces to have broken through to Manila."

Drake privately dismissed the last statement. To this pragmatic career officer such comments were a matter of semantics. He had no illusions about the future.

"How long have I got, Dick?" he asked. "To meet these commitments I need a minimum of twenty-one days."

"You must be out of Manila in three days. As for the rest, well, that'll depend on Wainwright's staying power, but we reckon he can hold the Japanese back from Bataan for about twenty days at the very most.

"Remember, Charlie," the deputy chief concluded as the two officers got up to leave, "Corregidor first, and you can take that as an order from the very top."

General Drake now had to mastermind one of the most difficult operations known to military strategists. To change the base of supply for a whole army at any time is very dangerous; but to attempt to do so in the face of a rapid retreat, one perhaps verging on a rout, is well nigh impossible. He hurried back to his office while Beebe made for the nearest phone; they would need all the departmental heads for a conference immediately. Finally he put in a call to Corregidor; within the hour Col. Chester Elmes and one of his assistants, Bressi's onetime boss, Amoroso, were on a PT boat heading for Manila.

While he waited for his staff to gather, Drake noted down the problems and priorities that lay ahead of them. He was pleased about one thing. Back in the summer he had quietly shipped 500,000 type C reserve rations, together with 1 million gallons of gasoline in 55-gallon drums, onto Bataan. He had anticipated the outbreak of war and the immediate operation of Plan Orange. MacArthur's later decision to fight it out on the beaches had taken him unawares, but he had left the supplies in Bataan. He had planned to build a series of bodegas, or small warehouses, to house the supplies, but he had been overtaken by events. The supplies were all dumped at Limay. Drake got on the telephone and ordered two officers to Bataan to supervise the dispersal of the dumps along the coast road. It would be a disaster if they were spotted by marauding Japanese aircraft and destroyed at this stage of the operation.

General Drake briefed his staff and laid down the tasks and their priorities. They had some 3,000 tons of canned goods, principally meat and fish, together with 100,000 type C rations and 300,000 gallons of petroleum in drums in Manila. Because of the lack of transportation, Drake proposed that the vast dumps behind the present beach perimeters would have to be fired and abandoned. Colonel Beebe spoke up: "Sir, I have a suggestion. We could order retreating units to load their vehicles with supplies at the dumps, especially Stotsenberg—it's only thirty miles from Bataan."

"Good idea, Lewis," Drake said, "but we'll have to station some of our people on the road into Bataan to pick up these supplies. Otherwise there's going to be tremendous inequality among the units and that will cause a lot of trouble."

"I'll see to that right away, General," Beebe said.

"I must emphasize," Drake said, "that we have centralized control. Some units will be moved across by water, and without vehicles they won't be able to forage en route. They'll suffer as a consequence if we are not very careful." Drake turned to his executive officer. "Theo, I want you to select four officers from the staff and a team of noncoms. They will proceed immediately to Orani and establish reception dumps. I will see they have the necessary authority so that incoming units hand over their surplus requirements. That will include vehicles, too."

"That could be a tough assignment, General," Beebe said.

"You're right, Lewis, so you had better get hold of the provost marshal's office and arrange for a detail of MPs to be on hand."

Drake dismissed his officers and they hurried away to their separate assignments.

17th Pursuit Squadron
Nichols Field

The pilots were ordered to ferry all serviceable aircraft into Bataan. In the case of Nichols Field there was little left that was considered airworthy—a few P-26s and P-35s and a couple of Tomahawks that the ground crews had repaired. The story was always the same, improvisation and cannibalism.

Ed Erickson took off shortly after dusk. He had a P-40 to deliver to a newly constructed strip at San Marcellino. The plane veered heavily to port, but Erickson was on to such tricks and quickly compensated. Mouthing a string of curses, he crabbed the machine into the night sky. The ground crew had done a superb job, but the instrumentation was basic and crude. Night flying aids were luxuries the pilots had long since learned to manage without.

Erickson had never before been to this particular field. He had a folded map taped to his knee and by the aid of a pencil flashlight tried to keep his bearings. He knew the field was sandy and that there was a fence around it, but there was no radio there or a control tower. Erickson was on his own.

After ten minutes the field loomed up off his starboard wing. Erickson cranked the undercarriage down by hand—they had run out of hydraulic fluid—checked the gloom for lurking Zeros, and began his descent. It was impossible to make out whether there were any obstacles in the form of parked or damaged aircraft. Erickson passed low over the strip to check the ground. Tracers climbed slowly after him as he banked north of the field and came in again. "Why don't they put on the landing lights?" he wondered. "Shit, it's all I need to be hit by my own side—the silly bastards are just plain trigger happy."

The firing stopped. Somebody had recognized the shape of a P-40 and had his wits about him. Erickson turned on his own landing lights and dragged his tail until he reached the fence, then immediately inside the perimeter cut the engine. He taxied the fighter toward a pair of flashlights, and a crew chief guided him into a dispersal bay.

"They're learning fast," thought Erickson, for the bay was protected by a solid wall of sandbags, and when he stepped high out of the cockpit he sensed the camouflage net above.

The base commander met him in the nipa hut that served as headquarters. Erickson was quite happy to dismiss the gunfire incident as an accident; there had been no damage. Not so the base commander, a tank colonel who, obviously frightened by what might have been, sought to cover his embarrassment by attacking the young pilot. "I am going to report you for buzzing this field and then coming in with your landing lights on. Every Zero within forty miles will have this location by now," he stormed.

Erickson was tired and taken aback by the furor. His leg hurt, it had become infected, and he was due to stop at the hospital in Manila on his way back to Nichols.

"Colonel, sir, your people knew I was coming, and if you had allowed them to light the strip there wouldn't have been any trouble. As for your gunners, it's not my fault they don't know a Tomahawk from a Zero. Now if you'll excuse me, sir, I have a truck waiting to take me back to Nichols."

Erickson made a gesture toward a salute, picked up his helmet and goggles, and limped outside to the pickup waiting to take him home. The colonel's Jeep was parked there, too. Its headlights bathed the field in a white glare and spotlighted the aircraft revetments. Erickson swore loudly, crossed to the Jeep, and turned off the lights just as the colonel came out of the building.

There was no need to say anything. Erickson knew the incident was closed.

Three hours later the truck dropped the pilot off at the hospital. The Air Corps had taken over the Jai Alai, one of the smartest clubs in Manila, as an overflow for the Sternberg. The duty surgeon insisted on Erickson being admitted for a couple of days at least. Besides his leg wounds, he was running a high fever, and the doctor feared the onset of malaria. The Jai Alai was an "officers only" hospital. The patients and staff inherited the chefs, food, and staff of the club. For the first day he was there he dined sumptuously on steak with onions and mushrooms, broiled lobster, fresh salmon, and Viennese pastry, served with snowy white linen and silver by Filipino waiters in natty green uniforms.

On his second and last day in the hospital the authorities heard of the luxury, and everybody reverted to plain Army rations.

Still, Erickson thought as he jumped into the jeep that had come to take him to Nichols, that's one of the best 48 hours I've had for a long while. The leg wounds had been cleaned and stitched, and malaria had not materialized.

"Back to the war," Erickson directed the young Filipino driver. Bombs were falling on the port area as the jeep dodged the rubble and falling masonry on its crazy ride out to McKinley Road and Nichols.

Wednesday, December 24, 1941
0230 hours
Lamon Bay
Southern Luzon Forces, USAFFE

Some 7,000 men of the Japanese 16th Imperial Division, veterans of the China War, began to land on three separate beaches in the southern part of Luzon. The main force, drawn from the 20th Infantry and the 16th Reconnaissance Regiment, landed at Altimonan, while a flank guard in the form of a battalion group with artillery support stormed ashore at Mauban. Though the enemy's route to the capital would not be easy, for the defending troops had the advantage of the mountain passes through the Sierra Madre to help them, the fate of Manila was sealed. There were Japanese columns advancing on the city from four different directions.

The 51st Infantry and the fighting formations of the Philippine Constabulary had prepared their positions in the mountains for battle. Company C, 194th Tanks was ordered in to support. The tanks stayed with the 51st Infantry while the half-tracks were ordered to patrol Route 23 east of Mount Banahao. Their task was to maintain links between the two divisions. Ben Saccone, ever the top sergeant, fretted over his charges as they prepared to go into battle for the first time.

Company A, 194th Tanks
Pozorrubio
Northern Luzon Forces

Advance elements of the Japanese 48th Division caught the tanks by surprise where they had deployed along the side of Route 3, south of Pozorrubio. The company commander, Captain Burke, was cut down by machine-gun fire. In the general confusion—they had been eating breakfast—men ran for their tanks and half-tracks as the first salvoes of the well-aimed Japanese knee mortars burst among them.

Bill Matson pulled the tarpaulin off his twin .50s, which had stood him in good stead ever since he had devised the mount out of the chaos at Clark.

"I thought there was a Filipino battalion up ahead of us," his driver yelled as he gunned the motors of the White half-track into a full-bellied roar. "Yeah, they must have bugged out in the night," Matson shouted back.

He looked across the rice stubble at the broken, inert heap of his company commander and then to Lieutenant Carstin's tank: he would command now. The lieutenant was half out of his turret, his arms semaphoring immediate withdrawal; few of the tanks were equipped with radios. Matson fired a couple of bursts off in the general direction of the enemy, though he could see nothing. The truck lurched forward onto the dirt highway and headed into the great swirling dust cloud. Mortar fire again straddled the road, and the tank in front veered crazily as a bomb burst directly on the turret. Matson knew it was Sergeant Stroboni's tank. As the dust cleared momentarily before the vivid flash of the shell, he saw the fragmented silhouette of the sergeant outlined in death, before the swirling cloud drew down a curtain over the horror.

The survivors of the company reformed a couple of miles farther down the road, and Matson swung out of line to battalion headquarters. Colonel Miller ordered him to head south for the Agno River and locate a suitable position for battalion headquarters to bivouac that night. Matson picked up two motorcycle outriders and headed south. He had no radio in his half-track, so they would have to lead the battalion in. He loaded fresh belts of .50 caliber into the magazines and swiveled the mount skyward. That's where the threat would come from now.

41st Artillery
Batangas
Southern Luzon Forces

Winston Jones and his battalion had spent the morning packing and loading the ancient field pieces onto their commandeered trucks. While the rear guards in the North and the South of Luzon fought their battles 180 miles apart, this particular artillery battalion was ordered into Bataan, where they were to man the first defense line.

When everything was just about ready to go, Jones walked across to the unused shed behind the sugar cane factory where he kept his beloved Packard. Some of his gunners in their off-duty hours had restored the car to its pristine prewar condition. Jones got behind the wheel, and, as always, it purred into life at the first touch of the starter. His mind on a myriad of other things, Winston drove out of the shed over the narrow-gauge railroad that was used to haul the sugar cane. The transmission grounded on the rails and knocked it into low gear. Try as he might, Jones could not release the gear; it was hopeless. With tears in his eyes he drove the car slowly in a wide circle behind the sheds. Then a gunner took his place behind the wheel with orders to keep his foot flat down on the clutch and accelerator. Within a few moments the engine overheated, and then the cylinder head blew apart.

His mind on other things, Jones led the battalion on Route 1 to Manila. Come what may, he was determined to complete the journey in the day. Once through Manila, they made slower time as other units joined the long convoy northward. They followed Route 3 out of the city for 30 miles to the unfordable Pampanga River and the bottleneck at Calumpit Bridge. Ten miles farther on, the road turned left into the busy town of San Fernando, the sugar capital of the Philippines.

San Fernando was the junction of the Northern Luzon Forces with the Southern Luzon Forces. At times that day the traffic jam was so bad that it extended back 10 miles. From San Fernando the road narrowed for the 15 miles to Layac, which in turn marked the entrance to Bataan. The thin macadam crust soon crumbled beneath the pounding wheels of the convoys, and the dust cloud rose hundreds of feet in the sky, a giant spoor for the hunter.

Why the Japanese Air Force did not choose to attack this most inviting of targets must remain a mystery. Jones's battalion, and the others, too, though they continually cast anxious eyes skyward, made the journey into Bataan unmolested by that most feared instrument of death, the marauding Zero. Perhaps the Japanese had their eyes set only on Manila, and in their rigid high command there was no allowance made for individual flair or flexibility in battle. Tokyo had ordered Homma to take Manila, and the fourteenth Army would do just that and no more. Implicit obedience to orders, the tradition of the samurai, may have allowed MacArthur's forces to escape into Bataan.

Not all the troops were able to travel in comfort, commandeered or otherwise. The vast majority of the Filipino infantry battalions marched into Bataan, despite the intentions of the Philippine High Command to leave the Philippine Army divisions to their fate. In single file they tramped down unshaded roads in bare feet, for their oversized American-issue boots were an even worse agony. Their baggy, once-blue denims were now the color of chalk. The dust coated them many layers thick, while their papier-mâché pith helmets were stained black with sweat.

The Filipinos had been totally unprepared for war. They had been outfought and outgunned by a Japanese Army that, even though numerically inferior and itself second-rate, nevertheless enjoyed all the advantages of air superiority. These Filipinos were only kids, and the experience of war, though at long distance, had proved a never-ending nightmare. American lieutenants used sign language to communicate, for the soldiers spoke no English, and the officers no Tagalog. Their ranks were decimated by desertions, but those who entered Bataan were soldiers who, even if they were yet to be blooded in close combat, had loyally stuck to their duty and were, despite their years, determined to see it through to the end. Already their numbers far exceeded anything that Drake and his staff had planned to supply.

It was past midnight when Jones brought his convoy to a halt and pulled the vehicles off the main road into a tree line. They were about 500 yards north of the little East Coast town of Abucay. While his troops slumped exhausted in the trucks, Jones pored over his maps and planned the deployment of the guns. They would move into position at daybreak.

Nichols Field

Leslie Zimmerman had spent the morning visiting the sick and wounded at the Sternberg and the Jai Alai Club. There were plans to evacuate the more serious casualties in a hospital ship, which the

Red Cross authorities were in the process of arranging. The terminal cases were to be left behind in Manila. The medical staff had
drawn lots to see who would leave and who would stay to face
captivity. The chaplain had lunched in the Officers' Club and then
headed back for Nichols. On the way he decided to drop in on Air
Corps HQ at Nielson and discuss the arrangements for the Christmas services.

The headquarters building was deserted. Zimmerman went from
room to room, and there was not a soul to be seen. Desk drawers and
filing cabinets were open and empty; the offices bore all the signs of
a hasty evacuation. He couldn't understand what had happened.

There was a note pinned to the telephone in the duty office. It
was a Manila number that Zimmerman recognized as the provost
marshal's extension at USAFFE Headquarters. He got through on
the third attempt and spoke to the officer of the day, who told him
that Manila was about to be declared an open city and that he was to
be evacuated with the Air Corps to Bataan. He was to report to Pier
7 at 1700 hours that evening.

The phone went dead before he could reply. It was the first that
Zimmerman had heard of any return to Plan Orange. He jumped
into his car and drove furiously to Nichols. The base was largely
empty by the time he arrived. At his quarters, he found the Catholic
priest waiting for him. Zimmerman had never been so glad to see
anybody in his life. Grabbing a musette bag from his footlocker, he
jammed inside his shaving gear, and a photograph of his wife and
their baby. There was just enough room for a New Testament and a
small prayer book, and the two chaplains headed for Pier 7 on the
Manila waterfront. They arrived with about ten minutes to spare,
to find chaos and confusion everywhere.

"We needn't have rushed, Father," Zimmerman said as he surveyed the milling crowds of Air Corps men. Officers with meg-
aphones attempted to keep units together, but it was proving
difficult.

Eventually they reported their presence and received a boarding
pass for the interisland steamer *Mactan*, due to sail just before
midnight.

"You won't need those where you're going, Chaplain." A military
policeman pointed to the Red Cross armband on Zimmerman's left
arm. "There'll probably be Jap snipers on Bataan. I'd advise you to
throw those in the bay and draw some sidearms."

An Army captain came up to them. "He's right, Chaplain," he said. "If you'll come with me, I can take you to the armory, and you can draw some weapons." The two chaplains meekly followed the soldier.

"What about the Geneva Convention?" Father O'Brien asked.

"That's the last thing the Japs have heard of, believe me, Father," the captain said, leading the two chaplains into the armory.

Another column of men marched down to the pier. It was the 693rd Ordnance Aviation Company. They had left Nichols Field over a week before and bivouacked in one of the better but empty suburbs of Manila. The trees along the pavement arched over and covered the road, effectively screening them from the air.

John McCann celebrated his seventeenth birthday on that street. The youngster from San Diego had never seen such grand homes as these before. With a couple of friends he had gone exploring, being careful not to touch anything. The houses were built high off the ground, on what seemed to be 6-foot pillars. The soldiers used the space underneath to keep their gear and footlockers, and they set up field kitchens on the pavement. The men worked at Nichols salvaging the last of the aircraft, and returned to their opulent suburb to eat and sleep.

The heavy vehicles, repair-shop trucks, and stores had already left for Bataan. The men had hung around until it was time to march down to the waterfront. Each man had been armed and carried only his personal pack and rifle. The local people flocked into churches, and the haunting carols greeted them as they passed the cathedral. The city streets rang to the hollow tramp of their boots. It was a cool, dark, peaceful night, and each man was lost in his own memories of a better Christmas. Occasionally their reverie would be interrupted by a lone prostitute optimistically touting for trade. One garishly painted creature of the night accosted John McCann.

"Ten pesos Joe, last time ten pesos." The seventeen-year-old blushed furiously at the ribaldry and banter of his comrades while the whore screeched her curses after the departing troops.

The *Mactan* dumped them at Mariveles in the early hours of the morning. Military police met each boat as it came in and identified the units.

A sergeant reported, "Six hundred and ninety-third Aviation Ordnance."

"Yeah, well, you're now provisional infantry, Second Battalion. Walk north," the policeman ordered.

It was the first these Air Corps men had heard about the infantry. The unit walked north all night. A jeep met them in the early morning and led them to their allotted position at Orion, some 14 miles north of Mariveles. The exhausted troops, unaccustomed to marching, were immediately ordered to dig their foxholes. For them Christmas went unnoticed as they dug trenches and erected the concertina wire to their front. Daylight revealed that they were on a wooded knoll that commanded a good field of fire northward across a rice paddy; eastward they overlooked the beaches of Manila Bay.

Clark Field

Clark was abandoned about the same time as Nichols Field. The crew chiefs and senior mechanics of the pursuit squadrons were ordered to an airstrip outside Cabcaben; there they would service the surviving Tomahawks. The air crew and ground specialists of the 19th Bombardment Group, still clutching the Springfields, were loaded into trucks for the journey south. Before they left, the troops pilfered the store; the rest was burned down.

Dick Osborn and Sammy Boghosian made the whole journey in daylight in the back of an open-topped six-by-six. They had liberated two cases of beer and were determined to make the best of their part in the retreat. Ever since the scare a couple of nights ago Dick Osborn had been convinced he was living on borrowed time.

They had passed through the bottlenecks at San Fernando and Layac, and it was beginning to get dark. The dust on this part of the journey was as crippling as a desert sandstorm. Even though they covered their faces with handkerchiefs, it got in everywhere.

Then Osborn looked up and through the dust spotted three fighters with rounded wings. "Zeros!" somebody yelled. One plane peeled off and came in low over the convoy. Men started to jump out of the trucks; the vehicles themselves speeded up as fear was transmitted to the drivers. Some who jumped were horribly injured. Osborn decided he would stay with the truck. He figured he would rather be shot than run over, and besides, there was the beer. The plane turned out to be a P-35; the pilot waggled his wings and climbed to join his comrades, oblivious of the harm he had done.

The bomber crews were dumped at Limay and like everyone else dug trenches. John Taulbee, who had traveled on ahead of them, detailed their instructions and kept them busy, but even he could not deny the rumors that they were due to be evacuated south to Australia as soon as a ship became available.

2000 hours
Fort Mills
Corregidor

The interisland steamer *Don Esteban* docked at Corregidor. MacArthur and his entourage stepped ashore onto the North Dock. General Moore, the garrison commander, escorted them to the dank, stinking tunnel where they were to spend the night. The flittering lights from their candles cast strange and ominous shadows on the tunnel wall. The main tunnel was packed with Filipinos celebrating their Christmas Midnight Mass.

President Quezon and his wife were given accommodations in the hospital lateral. Even in such clinical surroundings, the dank atmosphere played havoc with his tuberculosis. The walls rang to the wracking sounds of his persistent coughing.

General Moore escorted General MacArthur and his wife, Jean, together with their small son and his nurse to a curtained-off portion of Lateral No. 3. Some Army cots had been prepared and a few items of furniture, Army issue chairs, and a desk had been moved into the cubicle. General MacArthur made it abundantly clear that something better would have to be found for his family and quickly! He took over General Moore's cottage on Topside the next day.

It had been a long and difficult day for the Commander-in-Chief.

Besides all the heartache and emotional turmoil over abandoning Manila, MacArthur had also parted with some of his top aides. General Brereton had departed south for Australia in one of the last available flying boats. Though he had protested at MacArthur's order sending him south, there seemed little point to his staying. The B-17s, or rather the few survivors, had already left, and Brereton could be of more use organizing advanced bases from where the lines of communication could be protected from Australia to Mindanao.

There had been two bitter and acrimonious meetings with Admiral Hart. The latter had rightly been furious, for MacArthur had failed to inform him of the return to Plan Orange. The admiral had learned of it by chance only the day before, and this had left little time to evacuate his people or redeploy the *Canopus.* Hart had agreed eventually that the submarines would remain to the limit of their endurance before sailing south. This meant the defenders could rely on submarine cover until the New Year.

Admiral Hart had been at wharfside in Manila to see the MacArthurs on their way to Corregidor. The two men shook hands and stood quietly talking while a special cargo was delivered to the *Don Esteban.* It was the gold and silver bullion of the Philippine Treasury. The gold bars themselves were worth more than $41 million; the silver coins were carried on board in large metal boxes.

Although Corregidor had yet to be attacked, the men had lived with that fear ever since the war began. They stayed at their batteries, worked long hours of duty, and the tension was beginning to show. Fred Howard was looking forward to Christmas dinner; the whole garrison had been promised that it would be the real thing— turkey with all the trimmings.

So that they would not be interrupted by an air raid, the troops had elected to have the special dinner on Christmas Eve; for many that had been their family custom at home. But an hour before the meal, Howard was ordered by his platoon sergeant to report to the North Dock. "There's a special detail just come in, but don't worry. Your turkey dinner will be waiting for you when you get through," he said.

Five men had been detailed from each of the six gun batteries of the 59th Regiment. The official parties had left, and the troops were quickly divided into squads and marched onto the silent *Don Esteban.*

Howard was soon staggering down the gangplank with a load of silver coin. Philippine Scouts, armed with Thompsons, lined the 300 yards to the tunnel entrance and into the vaults. This made Howard furious. "Hey, Joe, what's the matter with you? Do I look like a Jap or something? Put that damn thing away," he shouted.

The Scouts looked on impassively and ignored the outburst.

After a while, the members of the work party became very tired. The silver boxes weighed 40 pounds each and the gold bars, bound in fours, were even heavier. There was an American woman at the foot of the gangway with a clipboard and checklist, counting the bullion as it was unloaded. Howard went up to the lady and said, "There happens to be an old wheelbarrow over there, ma'am. We could probably find even better ones to haul the bullion off the boat." He walked across and returned with the old barrow.

"No, we want the bullion carried by hand." Her shrill, high-pitched voice seemed to jar through his aching head.

"We aren't going to steal the silver, ma'am."

"You'll do as you're told, soldier," she replied tartly.

"Say, ma'am, pardon me for asking, but what rank are you?" Respectful as ever, he was determined to hold his ground.

"I am from the High Commissioner's Office, and I'm in charge of this detail. Get back to work, soldier."

"Old cow," he murmured as he moved back onto the boat for another load.

They called a break shortly after, and the men gathered around a small truck. There were some buckets of crushed papaya and Dixie cups of cold coffee.

The woman ordered them to hurry up with their dinner.

Nobody said anything. They returned to work, and it took until the early hours of the morning before the detail was finished.

Howard and the others hurried back to the battery. He knew he was wrong, but nevertheless he had this blind faith that the turkey dinner would be waiting for them.

"Sorry, boys, it's all gone," the duty sergeant said.

"Well, that's fine, Sergeant," Howard said. He knew if he said any more he would spend the rest of Christmas in the brig.

"Say fellas, did you guys get some food on this detail?" The sergeant, perhaps with a twinge of conscience, exuded bonhomie and concern for the welfare of his men.

"Oh, yes, thank you, Sergeant. We got papaya for our Christmas dinner." Howard led the group away before there was trouble.

Not all the sea traffic was sailing out of Manila that night. Rockwell had ordered Champlin to take his barge and return to the capital. He was to seek out the district supply officer, Captain Morsell, to give him a number of instructions. First he was to speed up the evacuation of all the remaining naval personnel, except the hospital staff, from Manila. Then Morsell was to find the civilian agents for the oil companies and arrange for the destruction of all the surplus oil in the base and at the companies' storage depot. The latter was a couple of miles inland on the banks of the Pasig River. Captain Morsell had been left behind specifically for the task; he had dealt with agents in the past and knew them all personally.

Before he sailed, Champlin checked with the inshore patrol to see where the best place to land would be. They advised him to use the Yacht Club landing. The duty officer reminded him to be out of Manila as soon as he could, since it would be an open city soon. Champlin picked up the crew of the admiral's launch, a Navy coxswain and three Filipino sailors, and set a course for Manila.

The minesweeper guarding the swept channel hailed the launch. As Champlin came alongside he could make out the shapes of three much larger vessels behind the warship.

The minesweeper's captain picked up a megaphone and leaned out over the wing of his open bridge. "Can you lead these ships through the minefield?" he asked.

"No," Champlin promptly replied. He didn't have the time, not if he was going to deliver his messages and get out of Manila before the deadline. He had been through the minefield only once, and that was in the *President Harrison*, when he had first arrived in the Philippines. That seemed a lifetime ago, he thought.

The captain called back, "Well, you can spot the marker buoys leading into the swept channel, can't you? These ships have Army on them, and they cannot stay here much longer. Come daylight the Japs will have them for sure. I'm ordering you to take them through if you possibly can. They must get moving. I will pass across the bearing of the marked channel, and then you'd better get a move on, sailor."

Champlin had no choice. "Aye, aye, sir," he replied. "Tell the lead ship to follow me but to stay well back. I'll try to find the buoys, but for God's sake ask those boats to give me room."

The minesweeper's captain passed across the compass bearings and relayed Champlin's instructions to the waiting steamers.

Champlin moved up into the bows of the launch and began to look for the marker buoys. He couldn't help but remember the steamship *Corregidor*, loaded with refugees. She had blundered a week ago into the minefield. There had been heavy loss of life. He glanced behind him. The lead ship, instead of keeping its distance, was closing fast. Champlin cursed, ordered an increase in speed, and peered intently into the night. Suddenly one of the Filipino crewmen cried out. He had spotted spray breaking over something— could it be the marker buoy? Champlin ordered the coxswain to alter course for a closer look. It was the buoy marking the edge of the minefield. All he had to do now was find the gap that meant the entrance of the swept channel into Mariveles.

The channel opened up ahead of them. Marker buoys led the little convoy on a wide arc into Mariveles Harbor. As they approached the entrance, the boom defense vessel lowered the anti-submarine nets, and Champlin hauled back to allow the steamships into the harbor. He reversed course and as he passed each ship, the troops lined the rails and cheered the launch. Champlin waved back; only he knew just how close to death they had come.

An hour later, the launch docked at the Yacht Club and Champlin stepped ashore. He found a Navy shore patrol who informed him that the Japanese were rumored to be in the outer suburbs.

"Can I borrow a car?" Champlin asked.

"Help yourself, Lieutenant." There were a number abandoned on the wharf. He took a little British-made sports car and headed for naval HQ in the Marsman Building. He found one officer there who had been left behind to ensure that all the confidential books had been destroyed. He had finished his task and was just about to leave by road for Bataan.

"Captain Morsell left a few hours back, Lieutenant," he was told. Champlin reckoned he must have been on one of those three steamers he had escorted into Mariveles.

Champlin knew what had to be done. The oil stores had to be destroyed. But how on earth could he accomplish the mission? The other officer was in no hurry to offer his services and quickly left for Bataan. Champlin drove back to the Yacht Club, parked his sports car, and walked over to the launch. He could see the mast above the wharfside and realized with alarm that it was already dawn.

The first thing he had to do was find some oil executives. Then was the time to worry how a mere lieutenant could order the destruction of the oil stocks. He gave the coxswain some instructions. "Take the launch around to the jetty beneath the Officers' Club. If you stay hidden you should be reasonably safe. I can't give you a time when I'll be back. You'll just have to use your own judgment."

"Aye aye, sir," the coxswain replied. "Don't forget the deadline, sir."

"Thanks," Champlin said as he hurried up the steps into the Yacht Club. Despite the early hour there seemed to be plenty of noise and activity.

Champlin walked into the members' bar and at first felt as if he had walked onto the set of *Gone with the Wind*. The bar was full of civilians attempting to cram as much into their last hours of freedom as they could. A number lay sprawled in a drunken stupor at the tables. Eurasian women, those who hadn't lasted the night, lay asleep in the armchairs, but there were still some standing, determined to wring the last drop of life before the cold onset of occupation.

Champlin ducked into the men's room. A man was stretched out under the washbasins. As Champlin felt too conspicuous in his naval uniform, he pulled the man out and yanked his shirt off. Putting it on quickly, he felt more like a civilian, even though the shirt was none too clean. He returned to the bar, where he noticed one man, a newspaper reporter for one of the American magazines, who was viewing the party with a look of contemptuous amusement. Champlin had met him on a few occasions before the war. As soon as the reporter had recovered from his surprise at finding an American officer still in Manila, Champlin quickly took him into his confidence.

"The man you want, Champ, is a guy called Rock," the reporter said. "He works for Standard Oil, and you'll probably find him at the University Club. I saw him there a couple of hours ago, and he said then he was waiting for the Navy." Champlin wished him well and hurried out of the building.

The University Club was two blocks away on Dewey Boulevard. Inside there seemed almost as many revelers as in the Yacht Club. A waiter introduced Champlin to the waiting oil man.

James Rock, a tall, distinguished-looking man in his midforties, was obviously relieved to see Champlin. "Thank God you've come," he said. "I've been waiting here all night. I was just about to give up and go home."

"How much oil is there in Manila?" Champlin asked. The answer astounded him.

"There are enough petroleum products in the Pandacan area of Manila to operate the Asiatic Fleet for the next two years." The oil man continued, "Don't worry about the fuel oil. I know just what the Japs will be after, and that's all the lubricating oil. And they also need alcolate."

"What's alcolate?"

"Alcolate is a volatile and specially refined liquid that is mixed with ordinary gasoline to make the high-octane fuels used in aircraft. It takes just a small amount of alcolate to make a tremendous amount of high-octane fuels."

"How much alcolate do you reckon there is?"

"Difficult to say offhand," the oil man replied. "Certainly more than two-and-a-half million gallons."

Champlin realized that this was a prize worth more to the Japanese than Manila itself.

"Can we destroy this stuff?" he asked.

"Yes, but the chances are that you'll burn down half of the old city with it and, if the wind is right, a major part of the waterfront to boot."

The lieutenant pondered for a moment. "What if we were to cordon off the area with all the police still in uniform and mobilize the fire services?" he asked.

"Yeah, that'll do the trick, but we will need to bleed some of the fuel oil off first. The great risk is of burning globules flowing into the Pasig River and into the bay. If that happens the damage will be considerable."

"Well, we will just have to take the risk," Champlin replied.

"I'll be delighted to destroy all the oil under my control," Rock said. "But I must warn you that it cannot be done without destroying everybody else's oil as well. Now, I believe the other American companies will play ball, but there's the Dutch, the French, and the British to consider. I'm not sure they'll cooperate."

"Can we call a meeting, do you think?" Champlin asked.

"Right. You order some breakfast for us, and I'll make some calls," Rock said as he left the bar.

The two men were in the middle of their meal when a French oil executive sought them out, and Champlin quickly explained his mission.

"As of now, *monsieur*," the Frenchman said, "we are part of Vichy and therefore neutral. We will not destroy our oil, but we welcome it to the Japanese. I must warn you, *monsieur*, that if you attempt to sabotage the property of France, then I will personally see that the Japanese try you as a war criminal." The Frenchman bowed stiffly, turned abruptly on his heel, and left the room.

"We'll ignore that crap," Rock said. A waiter came up with a note on his tray. Rock read the message and laughed out loud.

"I'm afraid that my British colleagues are enjoying a game of tennis and won't be available for at least another hour," he said.

The other oil executives, representing the major American and Dutch oil corporations of the day, gathered in the lounge, and Rock explained the plans and the needs of the operation. The ensuing arguments dragged on for an hour or more, and Champlin became increasingly exasperated.

Eventually Rock picked up the telephone in front of him and called his foreman. He issued clear orders to gather all the workers around and to destroy the Standard Oil products, beginning with the alcolates and the refined lubricating oils. The gesture was dramatic but it was enough. The others, one by one, followed suit. Rock arranged for the fire and police services to report to his foreman; the others had agreed he should coordinate the operation.

Rock shook Champlin by the hand. "Well done, Navy. Now you run along back to the war and leave the rest to us, but before you go, come and have a drink. It is Christmas, after all!"

They went down to the bar with the other executives. Champlin felt that the least he could do in the circumstances was to buy the drinks.

Rock took him to one side and warned him that they could expect trouble from the two British oil men and their Shell Oil Company.

"Don't these guys realize this is a British war too?" Champlin asked. He remembered an Intelligence report he had seen a couple of days earlier. Something like 180,000 barrels of oil that had been captured intact in Hong Kong had been used by Japanese tanks in Malaya a few days later. He made his mind up. "Tell your people to be ready to blow the Shell oil to kingdom come, whether the executive tennis match is over or not."

Champlin was on the point of leaving when the two Englishmen entered the room. With bucket shorts held up by old school ties, and tennis racquets, that bizarre appearance, typical of the breed, added to the air of unreality.

Having explained his mission again, Champlin asked, "Have I your permission to destroy your facilities?"

"'Fraid not," replied the older and presumably senior of the two. "We need the approval of our principals in Singapore first."

"Hell, are you in this war?"

"Sorry, old boy, but company rules are company rules, don't you know."

Champlin was having difficulty holding onto his temper, but he persevered. "Would you rather see this oil fall into the hands of the Japanese rather than violate company rules?" he asked.

"I am sorry, old boy, but I'm afraid our hands are completely tied in this affair." It was the younger one's turn to speak.

Champlin nodded to Rock, who moved quietly to the nearest telephone.

"Let me at least buy you two gentlemen a drink," Champlin said.

"Well, that's deuced decent of you, old boy. Let's drink to Uncle Sam and an end to this wretched war."

Champlin downed his Scotch quickly and headed for the door. Rock joined him on the way. He shook hands with the oil men and wished them well, and turning to the British representatives, Champlin said, "Oh, by the way, *old boy*, your oil is now in flames."

He left the building before they had a chance to reply.

Five minutes later Champlin ran up the steps and into the Officers' Club. He intended a last check around to see if anybody had been left behind. In the ballroom the Filipino servants had laid out all the suitcases belonging to American officers who lived in the club. Tennis racquets and records, clothes and treasured possessions, even girlie pictures awaited the arrival of the Japanese. It was the saddest sight Champlin had ever seen.

Waiting for him down on the little dock was his coxswain. It was plain to see that he was overjoyed at the sight of his officer. They cast off at once and headed out across the bay for Corregidor. Champlin looked back at Manila and the Pasig River estuary. It was a terrifying sight. Flames leaped hundreds of feet into the air, and heavy smoke covered the sky to such an extent that it dimmed the sun all their way to Corregidor.

The fire was to burn for five days. Some buildings were damaged and a few warehouses on the immediate waterfront destroyed, but the fire fighters under Mr. Rock's direction did a superb job.

Champlin reported his return to Admiral Rockwell. It had been an uneventful trip as they sped across the bay, unobserved by Zeros.

"Did you do that, Champ?" the admiral asked, pointing toward Manila, now a glorious red glow; it was difficult to believe the intensity of the fire.

Champlin, for the first time awed by his act, nodded silently.

"If that's the oil burning you've got the Navy Cross, son. But if the city is burning, too, then I'll defend you at your court-martial!"

U.S.S. *Mindanao*
Manila Bay

Ever since her arrival at Manila Bay, the *Mindanao* had spent the war dodging Japanese bombs in the course of her duties as part of the inshore patrol. Hart had considered her fortunate to have survived this far, and a further long sea voyage south to safety was seen to be beyond her capabilities. Consequently the *Mindanao* had been left behind to languish as part of the naval presence in Manila Bay. The old lady was expendable.

On Christmas Eve the gunboat bunkered for the last time in Manila. The crew had scrounged some additional .30-caliber machine guns and had mounted them in pairs along the promenade deck. Sam Malick had a couple on the port and starboard rails. He was there on that last hectic afternoon and twice manned the starboard mounts as Zeros came boring in on their strafing attacks. They oiled in rapid time. A detail armed with fire axes stood by, ready to cut its "umbilical cords," fuel lines and everything, should the Japanese put in an appearance.

From Manila the *Mindanao* sailed across to the North Dock at Corregidor. The island fortress still had not been attacked, and it was generally believed that the reason for this was that the Japanese feared the strength of her defenses. North Dock became, for the

Mindanao and other small ships, a haven and a sanctuary from the all-powerful Zero.

U.S.S. *Canopus*
Manila Bay

The submarine repair ship made her last voyage on Christmas Eve. Leaving a burning Manila behind, the *Canopus* moved across the bay and anchored in Mariveles Harbor, at the very tip of Bataan. Her duties were to equip and maintain the submarines for the final patrols southward and then to become a repair shop for the Army. The High Command believed that Mariveles, sheltering under the anti-aircraft umbrella of Corregidor, would prove a safe haven for the venerable old lady. The ship was moored in a secluded cove and as close to the shore as possible. Camouflage nets were broken out and spread above, and the men made preparations for painting the ship. Their aim this time was to blend with the jungle. A mottled green paint was daubed liberally on her upper works, and an intricate pattern of branches was woven into the rigging and netting. As Lieutenant Commander King was not convinced that even these elaborate precautions would save the ship, he sought and achieved permission to move much of his stores ashore and set up shop in some abandoned huts on the wharfside.

Christmas Day
The White House

Winston Churchill was spending Christmas with President Roosevelt. Churchill had arrived in the United States a couple of days previously at the head of a large and superbly briefed staff. The purpose of the visit was to cement Anglo-American relations and coordinate a joint war strategy against the Axis. Britain feared that in the wake of Pearl Harbor the United States might renege on the earlier commitment to a Germany-first policy. The British had been fighting the war for two-and-a-half years and were extremely professional in their approach to strategy conferences; they threatened at first to overwhelm the more amateur Americans. In what became known as the Arcadia Conference, Roosevelt pledged his country's war effort to a German-first strategy, though both Allied leaders were alarmed by the threatened collapse in the Far East.

The most difficult moment of the conference occurred on Christmas morning. General Marshall and his staff learned that, at a private meeting with Churchill and his advisers the previous evening, Roosevelt had agreed to turn over to the British "certain American reinforcements" destined for the Philippines if it proved impossible to reach the beleaguered garrison. Marshall showed the document to Eisenhower, now a brigadier general in the War Plans Division. The latter interpreted it as a British plot to write off the Philippines in favor of Singapore. Secretary of State Stimson was informed, and he threatened to resign if the paper was not withdrawn. Roosevelt later called his advisers together and in a charming and adroit manner dismissed the paper as a piece of nonsense. Nevertheless, Marshall was determined never again to allow the president to have any formal sessions with the British unless his advisers were present.

Christmas afternoon was devoted to the problems of the war in Asia. General Marshall proposed that a number of theaters of operations should be established, each with a supreme commander. In the Far East the Allies created ABDACOM (American, British, Dutch and Australian Command) under the British Commander-in-Chief for India, General Wavell. His responsibilities included all the Allied forces in Burma, Malaya, the Dutch East Indies, and the Philippines, though his orders effectively excluded him from exercising that high command. He had no power to dismiss a subordinate commander; neither could he interfere in the command structure of the troops under his control. Wavell was specifically charged with the "coordination" of the defense of Malaya, Burma, and Australia. Such a compromise suited the British, who believed that the United States might try to make them responsible for a theater of war that showed all the symptoms of disaster and, worse, public humiliation.

The compromise, though politically palatable to both sides, did little to improve the prospects for relief of the Philippines or to ease MacArthur's predicament. Nor did the arrival that day of Admiral Nimitz in Hawaii to assume command of the Pacific Fleet offer much hope of succor. He laid down two primary tasks for his forces. The first was to protect the Midway-Johnston-Hawaii triangle and second to maintain the line of communications through Samoa, Fiji, Australia, and New Zealand. There was no consideration given to using the depleted Pacific Fleet to defend or relieve the Philippines.

There was worse to come. Eisenhower now felt that the United States could make no strategic commitment to help the Philippines beyond public statements. Once the weight of the Japanese assault on Luzon was appreciated in Washington, and the American High Command had assessed the full damage to the fleet after Pearl Harbor, they were privately prepared to write off the archipelago. The president was later told by the War Plans Division that in order to mount an offensive northward from Australia to Manila Bay, the United States would have to assemble a fleet so huge that Navy units would have to be transferred from the Atlantic. Roosevelt concluded to Stimson that the diversion of forces from the principal theater of the Atlantic for aid to the Philippines was entirely unjustified.

4th U.S. Marines
Bataan

Admiral Hart's parting gift to MacArthur was the 4th U.S. Marines—a noble gesture, no doubt, though it was not appreciated then or later by the fiercely independent Leathernecks. Few could imagine a worse insult than to come under the command of an Army general, no matter what his pedigree. The general ordered that they should be brought without delay to Corregidor. A new Praetorian Guard, they were to man the beach defenses of the island fortress. The hitherto separate Marine detachments from Cavite and Bataan were brought together to form the 3rd Battalion of the regiment.

In the early hours of Christmas Day, Marine convoys threaded their way south through the mountains of Bataan and deployed into staging areas until barges could be spared to move them to Corregidor. Al Broderick was not sorry to be on the move. He had spent the whole war to date manning the beach defenses at Olongapo, a lonely and exposed detail for the squad, separated from the rest of the company.

There weren't enough trucks provided, so Broderick used his own initiative and commandeered the vehicles from a local trucking concern, together with the drivers. The company stores and packing cases were stacked to provide cover and seating, and the convoy started on the road to Mariveles. The company commander sat up front with the driver while Broderick manned a BAR (Browning automatic rifle) mounted on the cab; another was fixed to the back of the truck. The driver was useless; every time he changed gear, the vehicle lurched toward the ditch. Broderick thumped the cab roof in loud disapproval, and eventually the company commander could stand it no more. "Knock it off, Sergeant," he yelled, and the driver, now completely unnerved, lost control. The vehicle careened into the ditch. It took them half an hour of sweat, toil, and a tow from another truck before they were on the road again.

The company commander ordered Broderick to take the wheel, and the Filipino driver scampered gratefully away and disappeared into the night. This was the leading truck in the convoy, and the only light Broderick had to see by came from ships burning in Manila Bay. It was a wild drive, and everyone, not the least Broderick, was relieved when an MP directed them into a bivouac in the hills above Mariveles.

Sergeant Bigelow formed part of the Marine rear guard in Olongapo. With a squad of armorers he set about blowing the naval stores at the base. Everything that could not be moved they destroyed: Submarine fuel, spares, maintenance shops, and even the old *Rochester*, sentinel of a happier day, capsized into the mud. Those sea bags that they could not take with them were unceremoniously dumped into the harbor. Bigelow pulled back behind the motorcyclists of the outpost line just as the first Japanese troops moved into the town from the north.

Mariveles Harbor

The first barges began to arrive from Manila. They were about 100 tons gross weight, and the tugs could pull three at any one time, but at a maximum speed of 3 knots for the 60-mile round trip. This was a slow process, and further delays occurred at Mariveles, where there were only three small piers, each capable of accommodating five barges. Marines were detailed to the harbor, where they spent the first Christmas of the war hard at work on the wharfside.

Manila, in the meantime, received the undivided attention of the Japanese Air Force. They concentrated in particular on the port area. The bombing became so heavy that the locally recruited stevedores deserted in droves, and work came to a standstill. General Drake was so desperate that he broadcast for volunteers on Manila Radio. The Luzon Stevedoring Company, the largest commercial concern in Manila, responded immediately to the call, and so did many civilians. Gangs of Filipinos, Americans, British, Scandinavians, and Czechs worked day and night without thought of reward to help an army about to leave them and their families to the tender mercy of a barbarian foe.

Drake was able to move supplies from the main bases by road into Bataan. Some forty trucks from Stotsenberg and another fifty from McKinley carried much-needed stores to the quartermaster stockpiles, but this represented a very small portion of what was available. That which wasn't pilfered was later burned.

The Abucay Line
Bataan

Troops began to dig in along a line that stretched from Abucay in the east to Morong on the South China Sea coast. The coastal regions were strongly defended, but inland among the mountains the line petered out into nothing. It was intended that these positions should delay the Japanese for as long as possible while more defenses were prepared some 7 miles to the south.

The 57th Infantry, Philippine Scouts, deployed from the Porac line during the day, despite the risk of air attack. The move was completed without interference from the enemy. Loyd Mills and the 128 men of Charlie Company became the right flank of the Abucay line. They had some 600 yards of ground to defend; it extended from the main road to the beach, and this meant all three rifle platoons in the line. Except for company HQ, there were no troops in reserve. The Scouts compensated for this by working to improve their positions. There was an abundance of concertina wire, and this they laid in depth to their front while Mills took great care positioning the additional machine guns he had acquired from Stotsenberg.

Artillery support for the Scouts was provided by Winston Jones's battery. At daylight he had realized that the tree line in which he had bivouacked the battery gave him ample overhead cover but a very poor field of fire. He knew his gunners would be incapable of anything more than direct fire. To his front was the rising ground of a rice stubble field; it would provide a commanding arc of fire, but the guns would in turn be horribly exposed. Then Jones saw the answer in the newly harvested rice, stacked in the fields ready for shipment. He ordered his gunners to build a wooden frame for each gun, and dig gun pits. Then one by one the pieces were moved into position. The frame was placed over the gun and the sheaves of rice stacked around; within the "hide" there was enough room for the crew and ready use ammunition. Work stopped on the occasions that a high-flying Japanese reconnaissance plane passed overhead, but mercifully they were not spotted. The final touch was the construction of a trapdoor to cover the muzzle; this could be lowered on a rope from inside the gun position.

Most of the work was completed by nightfall, and the gunners were able to retire to the tree line, where the battery administrative base had been established. The quartermaster and cooks had done their best with the meager rations available, and the gunners settled down to enjoy their Christmas dinner. Jones was pleased with the way the Filipinos had developed, and though they were still little more than raw recruits, he felt a close affinity with his soldiers. They had earned his respect and responded to his leadership. The young American recognized that during the course of the past 24 hours some of the mystique of command and comradeship had been revealed.

Captives of the enemy
Maryknoll convent
Baguio

The nuns had repaired some of the damage that the enemy had inflicted on their convent and restored the chapel in time for Mass.

The Japanese had placed the Sisters under a form of house arrest; they were forbidden either to leave the convent or to communicate with the local population. There were no guards at the convent, though patrols visited them and sometimes searched the premises at irregular intervals. The nuns would have starved had the local population not taken the risk and kept them supplied with food. Help also came from another and very surprising source. A soldier revealed that he had been a Protestant minister and knew of the Sisters in Japan. He came at night and gave the Sisters some rice and a little meat.

There were pine trees in the courtyard. Gregorio the gardener had cut down a limb, and the nuns decorated the tree with the trimmings that they kept aside for each year. The Japanese allowed one Dominican priest to visit the convent and say a Christmas Mass. The mother superior had saved a supply of candy bars; there were enough for the Sisters to have one each. Earlier that morning Sister Louise had seen the chocolate on the tree, and counted the bars, one for each of them; unable to resist the temptation, she ate a bar.

The mother superior had called the nuns together around the tree. They sang carols, and then she distributed the chocolate. "There is a bar missing, Sisters," she said. "Can anyone explain the mystery?"

Sister Louise confessed her weakness and broke down and wept; for her it seemed the final straw. Other Sisters wept too. The chocolate bar became the escape valve for all their fears and the strain of the past days of occupation and humiliation. The remedy was good, and they all felt better afterward. The nuns sat around the tree and talked of a happier Christmas and they shared their chocolate with Sister Louise.

Manila

It was the saddest Christmas Lilla and Clay Seitz could ever remember. Some families had made an effort to have a tree and presents, if only for the sake of their children, while others caroused away the last hours of freedom. Lilla still had not left for the hospital, the baby was now overdue, and the doctors were concerned. She had chosen the Seventh-Day Adventist Hospital because it was new and, built of concrete, she thought it safer from bombs.

Most civilians spent Christmas Day sheltering frequently from the sequence of savage air raids. The walls of the old city were breached in half a dozen places, and for the first time Zeros flew low, machine-gunning the streets. Law and order began to break down as many policemen wisely saw first to the protection of their families. When the Japanese arrived, a man in police uniform could expect scant mercy. Looters dodged the raids and Zeros, and, as the word spread, the larger department stores were ransacked. All the while convoys of trucks bumped their way, nose-to-tail, through the streets; some soldiers stared in wide-eyed amazement at the scenes around them; most were too tired to care.

Friday, December 26, 1941

"*MANILA ES CIUDAD ABIERTA.*" So proclaimed the banner headlines in the two surviving newspapers in Manila, and the people learned that their city had been declared an Open City under the Geneva Convention. This required the enemy to respect the proclamation that there are no military activities or garrisons and to refrain from bombing. The newspapers published the full text of MacArthur's message, and the radio station broadcast the news throughout the day. Many of the public buildings had placards and banners with the words, "OPEN CITY" or "NO SHOOTING" printed in bold letters. Others had white bed sheets hanging from windows or ledges.

American truck convoys breached the convention, however, and barges still loaded at the wharf. The Japanese bombed the port area and then later in the evening acknowledged receipt of Manila broadcasts declaring the capital an Open City.

As dusk fell the lights came on; the blackout was over.

Elements of Company C, 194th Tanks, entered Manila. Frank Muther manned the radio, though it had long ceased to function, in the executive officer's tank. That officer led the convoy in a half-track. The tank crew were feeling the additional strain of being one man light. They had been falling back ever since the battalion had been blooded in battle the day before, and the crews were exhausted. They had been given specific orders not to drive through Manila, but nobody knew the detour around the city, and they had not been given any maps.

Muther's tank was last in the headquarters group, and he was driving. All he could see through the driving slit were the taillights of the tank in front. All of a sudden the lights disappeared, Frank increased speed, and the abrupt surge of power woke the others from their slumber.

"What the hell, Frank!" yelled the gunner above the whine of the gears.

"I've lost the convoy! Have a look out the top for Chrissake, Joe!"

Frank vaguely recognized the landmarks, and he thought he was on Roxas Boulevard. Yes, there was the old statue, its silhouette quite unmistakable even in that light. Muther relaxed a little. "No sweat, fellas," he said. In a few moments he would cross Jones Bridge and then take the main road for Calumpit.

Muther's attention wandered, and that's when disaster struck. What he failed to see until it was too late was a crowd of Filipinos gathered around the base of the Roxas statue. There was no way he could stop in time; with a cry of alarm he pulled hard on both levers. The tracks locked, and the tank started to slide toward the crowd, which scattered in terror. The regular driver was now awake and thoroughly alarmed at what was happening. "Let go of the left lever, Frank!" he yelled. Muther released the lever, the track gripped, and the tank went into a violent spin. The charging tank missed the crowd but hit the statue a mighty blow. The left rear overrider neatly hooked onto the small ornamental pillar at the base of the statue, and the tank stopped dead and threw the crew forward in a welter of curses, cuts, and bruises. Locking pins snapped under the strain, and the tank shed its track.

"Thank God we didn't hit anyone," Muther said, trying to look on the bright side. "The mood that mob's in, if we had hit them they'd have lynched us."

It took them the rest of the night to jack up the tank and unhook it from the statue. They spent the morning laboriously replacing the track. By midday, tired but triumphant, they had finished. The driver started the tank engine, allowed it to warm up for a moment, and then released the levers. The machine jolted forward and shed its track again.

The crew cursed and fumed, and a Filipino crowd gathered and laughed merrily at their predicament, which hardly helped the Americans' morale. The driver, a more phlegmatic man than the others, took a closer look at the damage and spotted what they had earlier missed in the half light of dawn. The front bogie had a buckle—slight, not enough to be noticed at a quick glance, but more than sufficient to throw the track once the gears were engaged. "That's a workshop job, fellas," he announced.

Muther, technically in command in the absence of the executive officer, decided the only thing to do was to immobilize the tank and hitch a ride with a convoy. The gunner removed the breech from the main armament, and carried it the short distance to Jones Bridge, where he dropped it into the Pasig River. The driver smashed the controls with a heavy hammer, and Frank dismantled the radio and scattered the parts. The vehicle was as effectively immobilized as time and resources allowed.

The crew then picked up their packs and trooped off in the direction of the bridge; there they reckoned they could thumb a lift easily enough. They had just arrived when a column of Bren gun carriers came trundling along the Boulevard.

"Gee, what's these—tankettes?" the driver asked.

"No, I seen pictures of these things in France—British Bren gun carriers," Muther said.

Waist high and slung low like a sports car, the open-topped vehicles were named after the Czech-designed Bren machine guns with which they were armed. They normally had an inadequately protected crew of three; such vehicles had no place in a modern war.

Headquarters Company, 26th Cavalry, had gone to pick up their "remounts" from the deserted lot at Fort McKinley, and these were the last of the detail en route to their base on Bataan. The tank crew scrambled gratefully on board, and the carriers jolted off across the bridge.

Company A, 194th Tanks
The Agno River line
Northern Luzon Forces

A platoon of tanks from Company A were trapped on the far bank of the Agno River, behind enemy lines. They had been in support of the rearguard and were stranded when jittery Filipino engineers blew the bridge. Some of the crews disabled their tanks by throwing vital parts into the river and then swam over to the far bank under the cover of darkness, only to find the troops already in retreat. They commandeered a bus, drove hell for leather down the highway, and rejoined their company at San Miguel.

The platoon leader, Lieutenant Arch, and his crew refused to abandon their tank. Instead they fought through Japanese lines, broke free, and linked up with one of the early guerrilla bands in the forests around Banbam. Arch was killed in action with a guerrilla unit in September 1943.

Bill Matson moved out to establish a new battalion bivouac north of Tarlac, but he found the road blocked by a stationary truck. They were under air attack, and the Filipino driver could be seen running hard for the cover of the trees across the rice stubble. Matson left his .50 caliber and jumped out of the half-track. "Drive around me through the ditch," he yelled to his driver. "I'm gonna get this truck outta here."

He pulled himself up into the cab as his own vehicle ground its way past, the tracks churning their way through the soft earth as the bank collapsed behind it. The Zero made another long raking pass and then zoomed off in search of fatter targets. Matson crashed the big Dodge into gear and took off after his half-track, which he then followed into their new bivouac. He drove the vehicle under cover and scrambled up behind the cab to inspect the cargo. He dragged back the tarpaulin to find a full load of 5-gallon cans of gasoline and cases of .50-caliber ammunition.

"No wonder the Filipino took off," Matson thought. "With this load on board he would have fried if one of those Jap incendiaries had found its target." He decided the battalion could make better use of this newfound horde than the unit for which it was intended.

They were in action again that night. The Japanese employed a favorite ruse that had worked before in the campaign. They used Filipino civilians to screen their advance. On this particular evening the human shield wore red shirts and yelled out, "Don't shoot, Joe, we're Filipinos, don't shoot!" The defenders knew there were Japanese behind the shield even though they caught only an occasional glimpse of the enemy. Grim-faced, the American tank crews made ready for battle; engines started, and Matson cocked his twin .50s. There were eight tanks and half-tracks forward, and they had been joined by the self-propelled artillery of the 71st Philippine Scouts.

The human shield came out of the sugar cane about 300 yards to the American front. The only thing they could do was to open fire. The gunners with zero fuses blasted great swathes in the packed ranks. The shield melted into oblivion, and the Japanese infantry was exposed. Matson opened up with the twin .50s; he didn't aim, there was no need. He just raked the gun back and forth across the cane until there were no more Japanese or Filipinos left standing; then he leaned over the side and vomited onto the mound of empty cartridge cases on the ground below. After a while the tanks were ordered to fall back, the retreat continued anew, and Bataan came ever nearer.

The order of march followed a familiar pattern among the exclusive club that now comprised the rearguard of the Northern Luzon Forces. It always seems that troops who have to undertake that most difficult of tasks, the delay of the enemy as a rear guard, quickly form an *esprit de corps*. They hate and fear their task because of the risk involved, yet would change positions with no man.

Units slotted into place as the column passed designated points. Ahead that evening moved the 2nd Squadron, 26th Cavalry, followed by their regimental HQ and then Troops A and B of the 1st Squadron. The tanks and self-propelled artillery in mutually supporting groups came next, and bringing up the rear were the cavalry scout cars. They blew the bridges and the culverts behind them, thereby effectively shutting the door on the enemy.

The Japanese were in no great haste. After all, where was there for the Americans to go except the cul-de-sac at Bataan?

Bataan

Massello was down at the wharfside in Mariveles with about forty men from headquarters unloading a couple of barges. He was a good scrounger, only this time he had undertaken a little more than even he could handle. The barges contained radar, which was just what he needed for the searchlights, for it could detect movement without revealing their own positions. The problem was the size of the equipment. There were two separate units, and each came complete with two trailers, one for the control cabin and the second for the generator.

By the time the men got around to unloading the trailers it was a black tropical night, and there were neither arc lights nor derricks to help them. It took hours, but they did it; by sheer muscle power the trailers were hauled onto the jetty, and trucks backed up to tow them away. The weary gunners scrambled aboard with thought for little else except sleep.

But Massello had other problems to face on his return to the battery headquarters. Now that the peninsula was beginning to fill with troops it seemed that every Tom, Dick, and Harry hooked his field telephone onto his wire; this overloaded the generators, and then there was trouble. He had a repair crew out that night trying to restore power to one of the outlying searchlight sites. Massello could not rest until the problem had been rectified.

Early the next morning Massello was called to the telephone. Dawn had been breaking when he had eventually gotten to bed, and he was not in the best mood. He picked up the telephone. "Yeah, who's that?" he asked.

"I want to tell you that your wire is on the ground out here."

Massello thought it was another one of those damned interlopers. "Well, now," he said, "how do you hear me?"

"Fine," came the reply.

"Well, what the hell are you kicking about?" he asked.

There was a pause from the other end of the line, then the voice replied, "This is General Aitken."

"Well, General, we'll come right out there and get our wire right off your ground," Massello hastened to say.

He had never heard of General Aitken; but then by this time there must have been twenty or more generals on Bataan.

Fort Mills
Corregidor

The last two destroyers remaining with the offshore patrol, the old World War I-vintage four-stackers *Peary* and *Pillsbury*, sailed past Corregidor in the fading light and headed south for the Java

Sea. Earlier in the day Admiral Hart had taken passage, and his leave of Manila Bay, in the submarine *Shark*.

Art Bressi had joined Battery Chicago, located high up on the most exposed part of Topside. The gunners had worked hard to improve the defense positions around the weapon pits. They had built a circle of 55-gallon drums, filled with sand, two barrels high, one on top of the other. There were four 3-inch 50-caliber anti-aircraft guns to the battery. Fairly modern weapons, unlike many of the other batteries, they were centrally controlled from the director unit, which in turn electrically operated the dials on the guns. The battery had its own generator, and the whole area was festooned and littered with high-voltage cables.

On Corregidor anti-aircraft gunnery had become a very exact science. Bressi had been finding this out as he tried to cope with the problems of range finding by triangulation. Sergeant Swanson, the gun captain, taught Bressi all he knew, and he learned his trade quickly. Swanson was a typical career sergeant; he babied the youngsters who served his gun and showed them how to make life tolerable in the field.

They had to live in the gunpits, though this was less of a burden now that the weather had improved as the monsoon season came to an end. The men had shelter halves. Two made a pup tent, which they suspended from the oil barrels. Their need was for shade as much as shelter. The gunners fashioned camp beds, and some even carried their footlockers up from the main barracks. Swanson encouraged them to do this, for it all added to the extra weight and cover around the gunpit.

Elsewhere that night and especially on the Rock men talked of the fall of Hong Kong. The short-wave broadcasts from San Francisco confirmed and described in gory detail the capture of the British bastion. Hong Kong had been British seemingly forever; it was a part of that Empire on which the sun never set. Now it was the rising sun of Japan that had confounded the white man with his own weapons. The onward march of the "Japanese barbarian" was quite incomprehensible to the young Americans. If the might of the British Empire could be humiliated, first the *Prince of Wales* and *Repulse* and now Hong Kong, what chance did they stand? The garrison knew the size of the disaster at Pearl Harbor; the San Francisco station had again reeled off the names of the mighty ships. They felt even more exposed and deserted by their nation. A week or so before it had seemed utterly incredible that the United States would not move heaven and earth to rescue the thirty thousand American soldiers and civilians; now they were no longer quite so sure. Their perceptions of the Japanese began to change as the foe assumed the proportions of supermen invincible in battle.

By this time the Rock had absorbed a considerable influx of military refugees of one sort or another, but there was no overcrowding yet. The Marines were still on the mainland in Bataan, and the regular garrison, though they had moved out into the field, were still able in the off-duty hours to return to their barracks for a shower and rest. Rations had been reduced a little, but the little stores down in the native barrios and the soldiers' canteens still seemed to be well stocked with the essentials as well as some of the luxuries of life. Perhaps the only sign of shortage was in cigarettes, and this was exaggerated as soldiers bought in bulk and hoarded their stocks. Except for the occasional stray bomb jettisoned by a Japanese bomber, the island hadn't been attacked yet. The garrison was still an observer, albeit with a grandstand seat in the front line—to the war. Morale was good, too. It was common knowledge among the soldiers that the abandonment of Manila, and the retreat into Bataan and the bay forts, were in accordance with the original war plans. In a matter of weeks the first rescue convoy would break through the Japanese blockade, and they would all return home heroes!

There was some evidence of extra defense works on Corregidor. Many of the soldiers were employed in laying barbed wire, digging foxholes, and constructing tank traps. But very few took this to mean that the Japanese might invade the island.

Corregidor, like Bataan, was already full of Filipinos. Many of them were civilians, either the servants of officers or well-to-do refugees from Manila. There were probably spies already ensconced on the Rock. Sometimes at night strange lights flickered in the sky, and occasionally a Japanese rocket seemingly answered from the south shore below Cavite. Maybe much of this was imagination, but even so the office of the provost marshal was extremely lax about such matters. There were no regular sentries at the various docks, so theoretically it was easy for anyone to land on or leave the island. To add to the general confusion, there were a large number of troops, American and Filipino, who were not allocated a task or duty. Every army since the dawn of history has produced its shirkers and malcontents. Corregidor had more than its fair share. Some of these were already beginning to concentrate in the main concourse of Malinta Tunnel. Others, the majority, preferred to camp out among the verdant and lush greenery of the island. These men drifted down to the tunnel only for their food, or they raided the cupboards of the abandoned officers' quarters. There were very few patrols of Military Police to interfere with their nefarious activities.

There was also another alarming trend for the future. There were far too many service and headquarters troops in comparison to the fighting formations. Even the arrival of the veteran 4th Marines a few days later was to do little to redress this imbalance.

Saturday, December 27, 1941
Bataan

Troops poured through the narrow bottleneck of Layac Junction, which marked the entrance to Bataan. In a compact and never-ending stream, convoy after convoy thundered down the road until it seemed as if the overcrowded peninsula would surely tilt into the South China Sea. Intermixed with the fleeing horde came the refugees. Thousands fled before the Japanese advance, placing intolerable burdens upon quartermasters. The latter had not been able to secure the expulsion of the local civilian population from the battle area, and now with swollen numbers came the attendant risks of starvation, disease, and epidemic. The medical services were no better prepared than the Quartermaster Corps to cope with the problems of the besieged in Bataan.

General Drake signaled all unit commanders in the field to forage in their retreat. Especially plentiful in the provinces were rice and sugar. Even so, many units entered Bataan empty-handed. Drake's quartermasters noted the arrival of convoys with trucks carrying nothing other than troops. The supply points that had been established behind the delaying positions were pilfered or abandoned. The government rice granary at Cabanatuan was left intact to the advancing Japanese.

Napoleon once said that an Army "marches on its stomach." On Luzon the retreating Americans obligingly left storehouses of rice intact for the Japanese to replenish their supplies.

Company C, 194th Tanks
Manila

While the tanks of the rear guard in the Northern Luzon Forces were bivouacking at Fort Stotsenberg and preparing to move up into the line, Ben Saccone led the last scattered elements of Company C through Manila. He was in command, for the officers of his detail were either dead or missing. He had lost all of his maps and overlays when his jeep was destroyed in an ambush. It had happened two days before, and Saccone knew that he had been lucky to escape with his life. The Japanese had deployed along the edge of a rice field and caught him in a vicious crossfire. Later that day five tanks were lost in another ambush. The Japanese allowed them to enter a ravine, blocked the road behind, and then pounded them with artillery.

Saccone led in a half-track. Behind him came two tanks, and another half-track brought up the rear. He stopped the convoy outside a gas station. He knew he was in Panay, an outer suburb of the city, but he was hopelessly lost. The station was deserted, so they refueled their vehicles, used the men's room, and helped themselves to candy bars. Saccone kept a careful account of all they took and left a promissory note on behalf of the United States Government before rejoining the others. He did take a tourist road map, and with this he led his men through Manila and to the rendezvous at the important road junction of Plaridel, about 25 miles north of the capital. He knew he had no right to drive through the city, but there was no other choice open. For a soldier like Saccone, "declarations of open cities" did not belong on his battlefield; what mattered most were his beloved tanks and the welfare of the surviving men under his command.

The last units of the Southern Luzon Forces streamed through

Manila. Their commanders, too, universally ignored the requirements of international law in their retreat.

HQ, 16th Naval District
Queen Tunnel
Corregidor

Lieutenant Champlin was sadly disillusioned by what he found on Corregidor. Since returning from Manila he had toured the island, and he realized now that it was anything but a mighty fortress. The powerhouse, water supply, oil reserves, and all major communications were above ground. The biggest anti-aircraft weapons he had seen were the 3-inch guns of Battery Chicago. The ancient coastal defense guns were set in cement and had arcs of fire limited to the open sea. Most if not all the battery positions were crude gunpits wide open to bombs or plunging artillery fire.

There were four Navy tunnels on Corregidor, each about 150 feet long, 15 feet wide, and perhaps 12 feet high. They were approximately the size of the Malinta Tunnel laterals. One contained the vital radio equipment and the operators. Two more were used primarily as living accommodations for the relatively small naval staff on the island.

A long lateral connected Malinta to the naval storage tunnel to the south. At the same time the Navy tunnel had its own exit on the south road. The basic accommodation was fairly sparse: two- or three-tier bunks and Army-issue furniture.

Servicemen the world over are great improvisers. Over time, more and more of the comforts of home began to appear, carpets and armchairs, even the occasional picture or more likely a pinup. There was, after all, an abundance of quarters and barracks that had largely been abandoned on Topside.

The fourth, Queen Tunnel, housed the headquarters of the 16th Naval District, the Inshore Patrol, and later the 4th Marines, some food, and a reserve supply of torpedoes and warheads for the submarines. "The office" of the 16th Naval District consisted of a desk each for Admiral Rockwell, his chief of staff, and one for the yeoman of signals. Stretched out on a pile of empty tomato crates that reached to the ceiling were charts of Philippine waters, spreading all the way across the width of the tunnel from the admiral's desk to the head of Champlin's bunk on the other side.

Champlin had hurried back to Queen Tunnel from Mariveles, where he had been to deliver some documents. He had learned from the dockyard staff there that the mines in Cavite were still intact. The demolition experts left behind had failed to carry out their mission.

"Bad news travels fast," Champlin thought as he found that the admiral had already learned of the calamity. The aide joined in the staff discussion of what course of action they might usefully pursue. Most of the schemes that were proposed seemed to have immediate drawbacks; if they tried to blow up the mines the town of Cavite would be destroyed as well as half of Rosario, for stored nearby were another five hundred of the older mines. Another alternative was to load the mines onto a barge and dump them at sea, but this the experts calculated would take at least a week; and Intelligence reports indicated that the Japanese had already passed Cavite in their advance on the capital. As he listened to their talk, Champlin became more and more incensed. The other officers were older and more senior, but it seemed that their whole approach was from the "can't be done" angle. Eventually, unable to keep quiet any longer, Champlin intervened. "It seems to me that it's got to be done. The military necessity for this operation is the vital factor, not whether it can be done or not. I just don't see what choice we've got."

"Okay, what would you do, Champ?" asked Commander Wilson, an old and rather senior engineering officer, a trace of irritation in his voice.

"I would take some handpicked men and go into Cavite at night."

"What then?"

"Once I got into the base I would decide on a plan of action."

"Good luck, Champ. You can try tonight."

Champlin spun around. Unbeknownst to any of them, the admiral was standing in the doorway—he had been there long enough to get the drift of the conversation.

"Take whatever you need, Champ." the admiral said.

Champlin saluted and walked out of the tunnel into the fresh evening air, his mind a whirl of plans and schemes. He chose as his second in command a young reserve officer, Lieutenant Henry; he had had two weeks of military service. In peacetime he had been working in public relations for a large American corporation in Manila. Henry had been locally recruited into the censorship office in Manila, but Champlin had worked with him when they had sited machine guns as additional defense for the tunnels. Champlin liked what he saw—a natural talent for leadership and a daredevil spirit. Champlin sent Henry to the mess tunnels to get twenty-five volunteers for the mission. As it was after five and the men had already eaten, he instructed Henry to have the party armed and ready to go on the North Dock in forty-five minutes.

Champlin organized their transportation. He had already decided on the Navy tug *Pigeon*; she doubled as a tender for the submarines and was moored just inside the minefields.

There were more than sixty sailors waiting for Champlin when he arrived at the wharfside. Drawn up in ranks, they were armed and ready to go. "I'm sorry, Champ," Henry said apologetically, "but they all insisted on coming. You're going to have to choose!"

Champlin, choked with emotion, walked down to the front rank and stopped dead in his tracks. "I might have guessed," he said. There, grinning broadly, were his sailors from the Cavite brig.

"Hi, Lieutenant, sir," said the Brooklyn stoker with the lived-in face. "When we heard you were in charge of this mission we passed the word that it might be kinda interesting."

There was nothing that Champlin could say or do except get on with the difficult decision of selecting his crew. He took "his convicts"—somehow they seemed to be a good-luck omen, and in any case were proven fighters. He thanked those who had to be left behind, and the party boarded the launch.

The *Pigeon* was waiting with steam up beyond the minefield. They clambered aboard, took the motor launch in tow, and swung toward Cavite. As the tug left Corregidor behind, it began to get dark, so Champlin felt relatively safe from air attack. On the run in, Champlin gathered his band together on the fantail and outlined the mission.

Champlin had decided to use the launch and land at the small, secluded jetty at Sangley Point instead of Cavite, then, if it was all clear, to signal the tug into the harbor. The raiders blackened their faces with engine-room soot and checked their weapons. The two young officers discussed possible courses of action and agreed that if it was at all possible they would attempt to dump the mines in the bay.

An hour later, the rhythmic pulse of the tug's engines slowed, and as it came to a stop, the sailors brought the launch alongside. The landing party climbed quietly aboard, and under the puny cover afforded by the tug's 3 inch and .50-calibers, nosed their way into the little harbor.

With fenders out, the launch bumped gently against the wall. Champlin signaled, and everybody waited, ears straining for the first sounds betraying the presence of a vigilant enemy. There was nothing. Two men with Thompsons poised moved cautiously up the steps, peered over the top, and then ran across the deserted wharf to the cover of a wrecked warehouse. A low whistle signaled all clear, and the rest of the party went ashore.

"Champlin's commandos" quickly split into their prearranged groups. Three men mounted a machine gun and stayed behind to guard the boat and act as a rear guard. In this manner, should they have to fall back quickly, the party's line of escape was secure. The truck party left to find some transportation, and the rest of the men fanned out in a line to check the yard as far as the main gate. Champlin walked ahead on the wide gravel path while the rest kept their distance and moved to the crunch of his boots. He figured that if there were Japanese around, this noise would flush them out and save them from having to check every nook and cranny in the wreckage.

"When I move, you move; if I stop, you stop," Champlin had ordered, "and if the Japs open fire, then double back to the boat."

It was the longest 400 yards the sailors remembered, but they made it to the gate with nothing worse than frayed nerves. Champlin, who had set himself up as bait for the enemy, couldn't stop shaking.

"Say, Lieutenant, would you like a slug of brandy?" "Brooklyn" asked, handing him a silver hip flask. Champlin didn't bother to inquire into its ownership; he gratefully drank the fiery liquid.

A small patrol was sent to check the Navy buildings opposite the main gate, and the remainder took cover and waited. Twenty minutes later the group signaled their return. They had with them three extra men—two Filipinos and an American. The former were police whom the patrol had discovered in a liquor store, and they were very drunk. Champlin could get no sense out of them but, afraid to let them go lest they raise an alarm, placed them under guard. Finding the American proved a real stroke of luck. He was an ex-Marine and was now foreman for a construction company that had been building some extensions to the Navy Yard. He had a Filipino wife, but he had packed her off to her family until the war was over and had moved into his office. He had been asleep when the patrol found him. Champlin decided to take the old man into his confidence and told him the purpose of their mission. The foreman's chief concern proved an answer to Champlin's prayer. Each morning some 200 Filipino laborers reported to the yard for work. They had been paid to the end of the month and were determined to honor their contract, even though there was nothing to be done.

"How many of your laborers can you get right now?" Champlin asked.

"Oh, at least twenty, Lieutenant," he replied, "and I know where there is a mobile crane—it's old and slow, but it will do the job."

"Where are the nearest Japs?" Champlin asked.

"They came through Cavite this morning with a tank column, but, according to my boys, they didn't set foot in here because they thought it might be mined and booby-trapped."

"Are there any outposts in the neighborhood?" Lieutenant Henry asked.

"Yep. Apparently they got a roadblock about a mile south of town."

"Okay, Henry," Champ said, "you take five men and get down there, have a look, and then meet us at Sunset Beach."

Henry picked his men and the party doubled off into the night.

Shortly afterward the truck party appeared on the scene. They had a Buick, a jeep, and a six-by-six, all with flat tires, but better than nothing. The men scrambled aboard and drove down to the stockpile of mines on Sunset Beach; it was about 5 miles from Sangley Point. The foreman met them there with his Filipinos and the mobile crane.

The next problem was to find a barge, so while the sailors and workmen loaded the mines onto the truck and took them to Sangley Point, Champlin went in search of a telephone. Many times in the past he had arranged for barges from the Luzon Stevedoring

Company. He found a phone and the exchange answered; Champlin could hardly believe his luck as he asked for the home number of Chick Parsons, the company's Manila area manager.

"Sure I can help, Champ," he replied. "I've got a couple of barges left and a tug. Most of my boys have gone, so labor I can't provide. Getting anything to you tonight is impossible, but I promise to have the barge alongside Cavite by ten tomorrow night. I'll do that if I have to stoke the tub myself."

What more could Champlin ask of a man who faced such an uncertain future, internment at best, and worse if the Japanese were to learn of his part in the operation?

Champlin called a halt to the work just before five in the morning. Time was running short if they were to make it back to Corregidor before the Zeros' dawn patrol. Despite all their toil and backbreaking work, less than a third of the mines had been moved to the dockside. They heaved some old netting over the mines and erased all signs of their labor, the trucks were dispersed, the outposts called in, and the laborers scurried away to their homes as Champlin had a final talk with the foreman before boarding the launch.

"Don't worry, Lieutenant," the old man said sympathetically, "I'll have a full crew here tomorrow night, and we'll soon move all this."

"I appreciate that, sir," Champlin replied, "but please, no activity here during daylight. If a Jap reconnaissance plane spotted this, then it would all be for nothing."

They hitched the launch to the *Pigeon* and the tug chugged out across the bay on its 30-mile run to the haven at Corregidor. At dawn the tug's crew and the "commandos" manned the anti-aircraft weapons and prepared for battle, but Lady Luck smiled on them and the short voyage proved uneventful.

The *Pigeon*'s return to Sangley Point proved as uneventful as their crossing earlier that morning. Nevertheless, all the weapons were manned as she neared the entrance to the dockyard. There was movement on the base, and for a moment Champlin thought they were heading into an ambush until they identified a tug pulling away from a barge, which was in turn secured to the wharfside. Chick Parsons had kept his word. Champlin exchanged greetings as the tugs passed. He couldn't help noticing that instead of Filipinos, Parsons' crew were white-shirted Caucasians. The office staff had been mobilized for their last contribution to the war effort.

The foreman and his laborers were hard at work by the time Champlin and his party stepped ashore. Lieutenant Henry detailed the outposts when the foreman chided him. "Give an old Marine credit, mister, I got some of my best men watching the Japs. They haven't moved since yesterday."

Henry smiled ruefully and hurried away with the sailors.

By 0400 hours the last of the mines were loaded into the hold of the barge, and Champlin carefully checked the manifest. Henry had sent two parties of sailors around the yard to ensure that everything of value had been sabotaged. They found a partially repaired PBY standing intact on its slipway and a set of airplane engines from the Pan American clipper base swinging from their jigs. These together with a store of high-octane fuel that had been overlooked were quickly destroyed. In the case of the latter, afraid to start a fire, the enterprising Henry and his crew emptied buckets of sand into the tanks.

The *Pigeon* came alongside and secured a line to the barge. Champlin jumped down into the barge and, with an ax, hacked some holes in her bottom. They bade farewell to the gallant foreman and his crew and, as the *Pigeon* took the strain, pulled out into the deeper water of Manila Bay. The barge began to settle slowly by the bows. Midway between Cavite and Corregidor the charts showed deep water and a muddy bottom; the only trouble was that the barge showed no signs of sinking, although her gunwales were awash. Then Champlin realized that Chick Parsons, ever helpful, had given him one of their newest barges made of the best wood available. Champlin discussed the problem with an anxious skipper of the *Pigeon*; it was already dawn.

"The only thing is to capsize the bastard," he suggested.

So the *Pigeon* began to tow the barge in a wildly veering course at 12 knots, but nothing happened except that the barge took on a little list; some of the cargo had shifted. The *Pigeon* ran alongside the barge, and a couple of seamen scrambled aboard the slippery, buckling deck. This time the tow lines were fastened to a bollard amidships on the port side of the barge, and the *Pigeon* took up its position on the starboard side and at right angles. When all was secured and the seamen were safely back on board, the *Pigeon* went ahead at full steam. The barge began to shudder violently. At 10 knots the barge, with its entire load of a hundred mines, flipped over like a pancake. There was tremendous turbulence as the mines went to the bottom, where the mud was many feet deep; they were beyond recovery. The lines were cut loose, and the barge drifted away on the tide, bottom side up.

The *Pigeon* sped back to Corregidor without being spotted. Champlin fretted the whole way. He had forgotten the name of the foreman.

Monday, December 29, 1941

Champlin returned to Fort Mills to find the island fortress even more crowded. During his absence, the 4th Marines had been shipped across and settled into the barracks in Middleside. They provided their own work details for the barges, and it had taken the whole night to move men and stores to Corregidor. The Marines, proud of their independence, brought with them rations for 2,000 men for 6 months, 10 units of fire for all weapons, 2 years' supply of summer khaki, and 100-bed hospital. The regimental quartermaster, Major Ridgely, carefully dispersed his supplies under Marine guards; interunit pilfering had been rife on Bataan.

The Regimental Commander, Colonel Howard, reported to General Moore for orders as the Commander Beach Defenses at Fort Mills. He called an officers' conference for midday to discuss the deployments and ordered that the Marines be allowed to sleep late in the bombproof barracks. Deployment into the field would begin after lunch.

Sergeant Swanson briefed his crew in the gunpit. "Remember, you guys, what I taught you." He pointed with his arm into the sky. "Read the signs of an air attack and you'll be okay."

It was a hot, beautiful day. The sky was clear and blue right into the heavens, and the sea lapped the shoreline below. It wasn't the thought of a swim that caused Bressi to daydream—in any case, he was frightened stiff of the sharks—rather it was the convoy that was rumored already on its way to their rescue. Was that a haze on the horizon—or the funnel smoke of many ships?

"What does that mean, Bressi?" the sergeant asked, catching the young soldier gazing out over the sea.

"Watch the gun barrel, Sergeant," he replied promptly. You won't catch me like that, he thought.

"Right, Bressi," the sergeant said. "If the barrel rolls in elevation, doesn't traverse right or left, but stays on a steady line, then we've got trouble with that incoming flight. It's a zero-zero approach." Even Bressi listened carefully to the words of wisdom as the sergeant described their nightmare, a bomber flight that had their battery as target.

"Even if it's a zero-zero approach, you still man the gun and get off the six rounds for the box barrage, no matter what!" he emphasized. "On my word of command, and only then, do you hit the deck, fast. But don't look so worried, fellas," he concluded. "A gun pit is so small that the statistical odds on us getting hit, even by fragments, are small."

Sergeant Swanson dismissed the men, and they picked up their mess cans and trooped the short distance down the hill to the battery headquarters and the chow line that was already forming. Bressi looked out over the sea again; it was heat haze after all. But they all knew a convoy was on its way. The San Francisco station had broadcast the news only the night before. They had made but scant progress toward the steaming cauldrons of stew when the air raid alarms sounded.

"If this is another fucking exercise, I'll goddamn well resign," panted Bressi as he pounded up the hill to the gun.

It was no exercise. Eighteen twin-engined Japanese Navy bombers of the 14th Heavy Bombardment Regiment had the privilege of opening the air war on Corregidor. At a height of 18,000 feet, they pounded the HQ and barracks of Middleside with 550-pound bombs.

The Marines ran for cover as the bombs blasted aside the concrete barrack's cover and shattered the interior. Those on the ground floor were safe, but there were casualties among those Marines caught in the upper story.

Sgt. Al Broderick had been standing out on the parade ground talking to the colonel when the air raid sounded. As they stood there and watched the bombing, an aide rushed out and advised the colonel that he ought to take cover, if only to set a good example.

"Damned busybody," Broderick mumbled as he stumbled over the fallen masonry and cowered inside a doorway. He was convinced they were safer out in the open.

Half an hour later Japanese Army bombers put in their appearance. Twenty-two Bettys smothered Topside in high explosives while eighteen dive bombers of the 16th Light Bombardment Regiment, screaming down below 2,000 feet, dropped their bombs on selected targets. They ran into a solid steel wall of .50-caliber tracers, and four of them corkscrewed into the ground. The Japanese didn't risk their dive bombers again over Corregidor for many a day.

When General Drake arrived on Corregidor, he found that USAFFE headquarters had been planted on the very top of the island, on Topside, as it was called, the most conspicuous point. It was a juicy target for the Japanese. No camouflage was attempted; despite all that had happened in Manila and at Clark, the American High Command was still not sufficiently air-minded and placed too much faith in the ability of anti-aircraft guns to ward off bombers. The fact that these gunners were caught unawares at Clark seemed at the time to lend strength to their argument.

The headquarters area was made even more conspicuous by the staff cars parked near the entrance. Thus it took little intelligence for the Japanese to select General MacArthur's headquarters for this first mass bombing raid on Corregidor. Why they were not all killed and the entire headquarters wiped out can never be explained. Drake was convinced that God must have had them by the hand.

The Japanese bombardiers, luckily for the defenders, cut their fuses long for deep penetration. This had the effect of creating a delayed-action bomb; the velocity of its fall would cause it to penetrate deep before the fuse burned through and the warhead exploded in the heart of the target. However, the Japanese fuses were too long, and the bombs were penetrating 20 to 25 feet through volcanic rock before exploding. In this case the ground had the effect of cushioning the blast and concussion.

In the first salvo on that memorable day, one 550-pound bomb struck the ground directly in front of the headquarters, not 30 feet from the main entrance. With the explosion, the whole building seemed to rise and then slowly settle again. Plaster, dirt, small pieces of concrete, and bits of volcanic rock rained down upon those who were still inside. The concussion was terrific. Drake could feel his whole insides turn over, and his eyes bulged from their sockets. At any moment he expected to be buried under the collapse of the building, but it withstood the shock masterfully. Had there been a shorter fuse on the bombs, it might have been a different story.

Almost before the dust had settled, the second salvo came. Another 550-pounder struck off the southeast corner of the headquarters with the same awful thundering effect. They had hardly come through this when a third bomb struck. A 550-pounder came directly through the roof and penetrated three concrete floors into the basement of the central section of the headquarters, which was used as the post exchange. There the bomb exploded, blowing out the entire middle section of the headquarters. A fourth bomb struck the ground about 100 feet from the northeastern corner.

Following the third salvo Drake picked himself up from the floor of the barracks and looked across the room. The only other person there was his chief clerk, Sergeant Dean Smith from Denver, Colorado, who had jammed himself under a concrete washtub before Drake could. The rest of the entire headquarters staff, as one mind, early in the bombing had decided that Malinta Tunnel was a much safer bet and had taken off like a covey of quail in that direction—a good 1½ miles away. Drake now followed suit; he pounded down the path as fast as his long legs would take him, and close on the heels came the chief clerk.

At 1300 hours the Japanese Navy returned and 60 Nells continued the bombardment. There were no pursuit planes to contest the Japanese sky, and the whole weight of the defense fell to the flak gunners. Bressi and the others sweated away stripped to the waist replenishing the ready-use ammunition trays beside the gun. Throughout the raid he kept a wary eye on the barrel, and three times the crew ran for cover. In what proved to be the last Japanese sortie, the bombers passed over the tip of Bataan and wheeled high over the North Channel. Once again it was the turn of Topside.

"Zero-zero approach!" Swanson yelled suddenly between the sharp, ear-splitting bark of the gun.

The crew fired their six rounds at the incoming flight in record time, and Swanson yelled, "Hit the deck!"

Bressi got about 20 yards out of the pit and threw himself behind some crates as the whistle of the falling salvo in crescendo blotted out his senses. The ground heaved and buckled beneath him, the "whang" of the shrapnel immediately followed by the heavier rattle of cascading debris.

Bressi lay there momentarily stunned; a cry jerked him back to reality.

"Swanson's hit!"

He looked up and saw the sergeant sprawled motionless across the entrance to the gunpit. Bressi crawled across and, with the other youngsters, watched his gun captain die. A single bomb fragment had caught him under the jaw.

They called for a medic, but there was nothing anybody could do. Bressi bent low over the prostrate sergeant. All he could see was a mark under the chin and the jugular vein turning blue and then black. The sergeant, paralyzed with shock, died within a couple of minutes. It was the first battle casualty of the battery, and that and the fact that it was the popular Swanson caused a particular sadness and sense of loss among the men. The man they had placed their trust in, the seemingly indestructible Swanson, was dead. What chance did they have?

Corregidor's baptism by fire had lasted for two hours, in which 81 medium and 18 dive bombers had dropped more than 60 tons of bombs on the fortress. Damage to the surface structures was considerable: The barracks and wooden buildings were destroyed, and the electric railroad track was shattered in a dozen places. There were some 20 dead and 80 wounded among the garrison. The Japanese, however, had not gotten away completely unscathed. Besides the dive bombers that fell to the .50-caliber guns, the heavier batteries on Corregidor, in the forts, and those on southern Bataan put up a lethal barrage. Communiqués at the end of the day claimed that 13 Japanese bombers had been destroyed.

U.S.S. Canopus
Mariveles

The last squadron in the attack wheeled high over the smoke and flames of Corregidor, set course for Mariveles, and bracketed Canopus with a perfectly placed pattern of bombs. Tied up as she was, there was no way they could miss damaging the helpless ship. The concussion of near misses sprang a dozen leaks and buckled her keel out of alignment. Only one bomb hit the *Canopus*, but that nearly proved to be enough. An armor-piercing 250-pounder cleaved its way through the thinly plated afterdeck before its delayed-action fuse exploded on top of the propeller shaft and under the magazines. Fires broke out immediately.

Even before the rain of rocks thrown from the craters on the cliff face subsided, fire fighters and damage-control parties sprang into action. The executive officer's crew attacked the blaze from the top deck. They found smoke pouring from the ammunition scuttles leading to the magazines below and directed their hoses straight down the hatches.

Commander King had rushed back on board during the raid, and he helped direct the effort from below decks. Stokers and mechanics fought blistering heat and choking smoke to the very source of the damage: the passage outside the magazine. They pulled wounded and dying men away from the blast area where they had fallen. The chaplain led another rescue group into the engine room, where more casualties had been caused by bomb fragments, some of which had severed the steam lines. A number of engineers and stokers had been horribly scalded. The chaplain knelt and gave comfort to the dying.

The ship was saved by a miracle. After the fire was out, damage-control parties found crushed but unexploded powder charges in the magazine, mute evidence of how close to complete destruction they had indeed come. The bomb fragments that had wrought such havoc among the sailors and ruptured the steam lines had also sent the steam into the magazine, where it cooled, condensed, and helped douse the flames.

Just four hours after the raid, *Canopus* was operational. Someone had painted a sign, "Business as Usual," over the entry port.

On board *S-36*
Mariveles

McKnight was called alongside the *Canopus* and given sailing orders for his last mission out of Manila Bay. He was to patrol south of Verde Island Passage, about a day's sail from Corregidor, and once his endurance was reached, was to sail south for Surabaja and the Dutch East Indies. McKnight was given four valuable specialists to take to safety.

One of the casualties of the bomb damage to *Canopus* had been the records in the supply office. They had been burned to a crisp. The supply officer, with the burden of bookkeeping lifted, issued anything and everything to all comers. The word quickly spread, and the sailors on the *S-36* trooped across to satisfy their needs. They came back with arms full of clothing, boots, shoes, and shirts. On a small, cramped submarine it got to be more than a joke, and eventually McKnight put an officer on the gangway. The chart store had also been destroyed, and so the navigator had to manage with what he had immediately on hand. They had no charts for the Malay Barrier and the Dutch East Indies.

The *S-36* went out through the North Channel. Fires still burned as they passed Corregidor to port, and a great pall of smoke hung low like a sea mist over the water. McKnight took a final look at the dark mass of the battered island, cleared the little bridge, and prepared to submerge into the South China Sea.

Tuesday, December 30, 1941
Fort Mills
Corregidor

A rather bizarre ceremony occurred outside the main entrance to Malinta Tunnel. Before the MacArthurs and a hundred witnesses, Emanuel Quezon was inaugurated for his second term as President of the Philippines. The simple but moving ceremony ended with the oath of office and the national anthems. Then the audience listened to a message dispatched earlier that day by President Roosevelt:

NEWS OF YOUR GALLANT STRUGGLE AGAINST THE JAPA-
NESE AGGRESSORS HAS ELICITED THE PROFOUND AD-
MIRATION OF EVERY AMERICAN CITIZEN. I GIVE TO THE
PEOPLE OF THE PHILIPPINES MY SOLEMN PLEDGE THAT

THEIR FREEDOM WILL BE REDEEMED AND THEIR INDE-
PENDENCE ESTABLISHED AND PROTECTED. THE ENTIRE
RESOURCES IN MEN AND MATERIALS OF THE UNITED
STATES STANDS BEHIND THIS PLEDGE.

These words of hope were soon common knowledge among the
garrison. Soldiers, young and old, found new faith and strength
from the promise of their president. In the excitement and in their
naiveté, they failed to notice that there was no mention of when
they could expect the help to arrive.

Wednesday, December 31, 1941
With the rear guard in the field

The last elements of the fleeing Army poured onto Bataan. There
were no military policemen to keep a check on numbers, and so
nobody was very sure just how many troops, let alone civilians, had
moved onto the peninsula. There were very few road signs or unit
markers. The Filipinos in the barrios and fishing villages that had
suddenly become dumping grounds for thousands of men stared in
wonder at the incredible number of trucks, guns, and equipment of
an army that covered their homes in thick layers of dust. Until a
month ago they had probably never seen a soldier in their lives.

The Japanese continued the drive on Manila from north and
south, with Homma paying very little attention to the lines of
vehicles disappearing into the jungles of Bataan. The staff of the
Japanese Fourteenth Army considered it to be nothing more than
the frantic, disorganized flight of scattered and unimportant elements of the Philippine Army. They could be mopped up and
Corregidor bombarded into submission when the capital had been
secured and the fruits of a triumphal entry had been savored.

In the meantime, the Japanese advance had reached the outskirts
of Baliuag, a barrio north of the important road junction at Plaridel. While they deployed for an attack, the defending elements of
the 71st Philippine Army Infantry Division abandoned their positions prematurely.

The tanks of Company C, now less than two weak platoons in strength, were ordered in to counterattack. The position was crucial, for if Baliuag fell the Japanese could detour at Plaridel and seize Calumpit Bridge. There were still troops to cross, and the engineers had not completed laying the charges for its demolition. The Stuart tanks, supported by a few of the self-propelled half-track 75mm guns, waited in concealed positions as Japanese engineers, protected by a squadron of tanks, came forward to inspect a small bridge about 900 yards out of the town.

Lt. William Gentry in the lead tank surged forward. Saccone in another followed suit, and they hit the Japanese in the flank. For once surprise and initiative lay with the Americans, and they weren't about to waste such a golden opportunity. A bitter fire fight ensued at point-blank range in the narrow, nipa-lined streets of Baliuag. In the tank battle, the Stuarts, though heavily outnumbered, had the advantage. The armor plating on the Japanese tanks was so thin that the armor-piercing shells went right through. They changed to high explosive and blasted the Japanese tanks apart. The nipa huts burned as if they were made of paper, and the Japanese fell back in confusion.

In ten minutes it was all over. The Americans had achieved a most complete tactical victory, and as the tanks pulled back unscathed, the 75mm guns opened fire, covered their withdrawal, and leveled the town.

On New Year's Day, the tanks were one of the last units to cross Calumpit Bridge, and then it was destroyed. The armor retired through San Fernando and passed the outpost line manned by Company B, 31st U.S. Infantry, outside Guagua. The road to Bataan was secure.

Sternberg Army Hospital
Manila

Ruby Moteley and Madeline Ullom had been left behind in Manila as part of the small medical team who administered to the terminal cases in the hospital. A couple of days after Christmas a hospital ship had sailed, and for a brief moment hopes flared that they would be among the ten nurses selected to sail. They weren't, and each had become resigned to the arrival of the Japanese. Moteley had other worries, too, for she had no word of her lover on the *Pecos* since the tanker sailed on that first awful day of the war.

The nurses were reprieved. The very few men left in the hospital were moved quietly out to another civilian hospital, and the nurses were told to pack and be ready to leave. They traveled to the wharf in a covered truck and boarded the steamer *Mactan*. The little ship had a difficult trip across to Corregidor. The Japanese bombed and strafed, but eventually she arrived with little more than her dignity ruffled and a few more scars to add to her battle wounds. The half dozen nurses and a doctor landed on Corregidor just as the island prepared for its now daily air raid. The party scampered quickly along the pitted jetty of North Dock for the nearest cover. A truckful of soldiers came by. As it slowed, willing arms reached down and swung the nurses into the back.

The last of the nurses had arrived on the Rock.

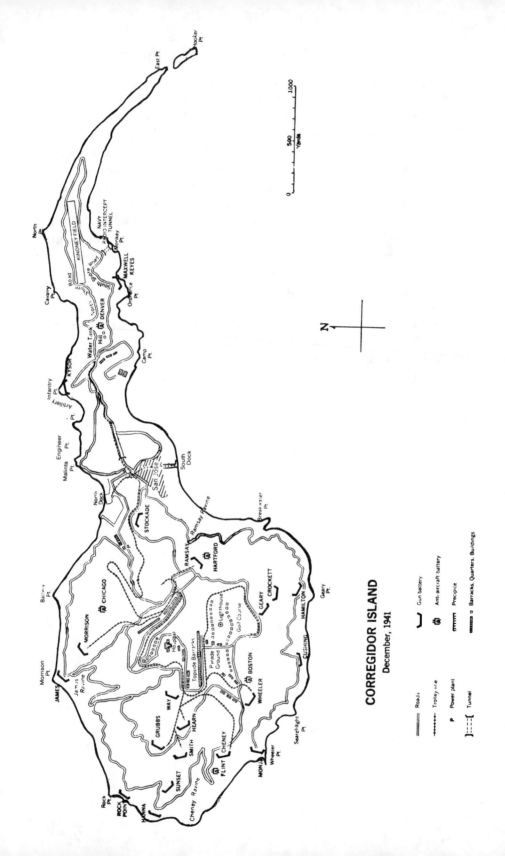

CORREGIDOR ISLAND

December, 1941

VII. The Battle of Bataan

Thursday, January 1, 1942–
Tuesday, February 10, 1942

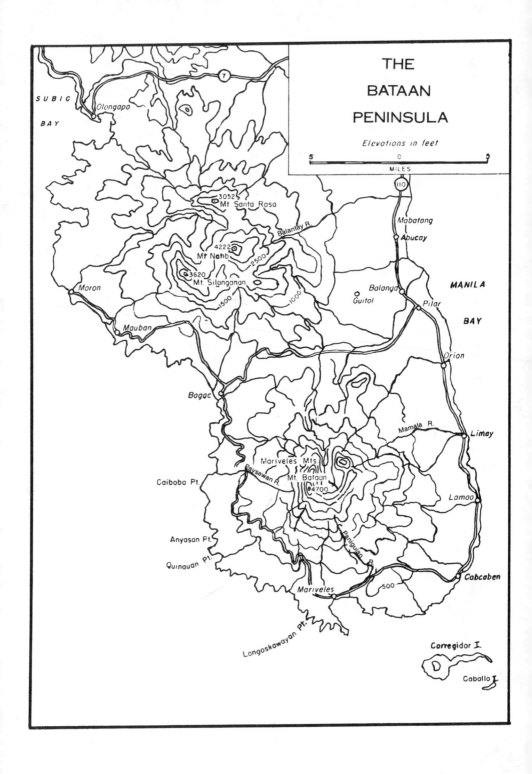

THE
BATAAN
PENINSULA

Elevations in feet

SUBIC
BAY

Olongapo

7

3052
Mt. Santa Rosa

Balantay R.

Mabatang

Abucay

4222
Mt Nahb

2500

Moron

3620
Mt. Silanganan

1500

1000

Mauban

Balanga

Guitol

Pilar

MANILA

BAY

Orion

Bagac

Mamala R.

Limay

Caibobo Pt.

Pavsawan R.

Mariveles Mts.
Mt. Bataan
4700

Lamao

Anyasan Pt.

Paniguian R.

Quinauan Pt.

Mariveles

500

Cabcaben

Longoskawayan Pt.

Corregidor I.

Caballo I.

1. Prelude

April 1980
Department of War Studies and International Affairs
The Royal Military Academy Sandhurst, England

The military situation at the year's end

The reversion to Plan Orange, namely a last-ditch defense of Luzon by the withdrawal of forces into Bataan and onto the island fortresses guarding the entrance to Manila Bay, was a complicated operation. For success it required adherence to a strict timetable, absolute trust and understanding by the two corps headquarters involved, and nerves of steel on the part of their respective commanding generals.

The operation is best seen in two phases. The first was to effect the juncture of Wainwright's troops (the Northern Luzon Forces), who were retreating south from the main Japanese landings in Lingayen, with Parker's troops (the Southern Luzon Forces), who were moving northwestward around Manila and the bay toward Bataan. As a map of the area reveals, the vital ground that had to be held if the operation was to succeed was around the towns of Calumpit, Plaridel, and San Fernando. Calumpit and Plaridel were important because they controlled the only route for Parker's troops, while San Fernando held the key to Wainwright's retreat into Bataan.

The second phase was the fighting retreat along the last 45 miles leading from San Fernando through the neck of Bataan and into the peninsula proper.

The main pressure fell on the divisions commanded by General

Wainwright. It was their task to delay the Japanese for as long as possible while the soldiers of the Southern Luzon Forces retreated from the very extremities of the island, force-marched around Manila (the capital was now an open city and thus its boundaries could not be violated), threaded their way through the bottleneck at San Fernando (made so because that was where they met up with Wainwright's corps), and then on into Bataan. Wainwright, by denying the Japanese San Fernando, became the "hinge" that held open the door for Parker. Once the last of the troops were through, the door could be slammed shut in the face of the Japanese, simply by blowing up San Fernando's one and only bridge.

But this is not to imply that by comparison Parker's troops had it easy. They had long distances to cover, some 100 miles or more in makeshift transportation or walking, and under a hostile sky. Once past Manila their troubles really began, for up until then, and with the exception of the rear guard, none of them had been under attack from Japanese soldiers. But the Japanese were advancing through northern Luzon on a number of fronts toward Manila. This meant that the retreating Allied forces were actually moving toward the enemy! Hence it became necessary for the Southern Luzon Forces to throw forward a defensive corridor, in reality a series of hastily erected roadblocks, manned by ad hoc formations, which checked the Japanese advance along the more likely routes to the capital. Had any one of these failed to hold them, the way would have been clear for Homma's troops to fall upon the open and exposed flank of a retreating army that was already in some disarray. The result I leave to your imagination.

In the midst of this operation Major General Parker relinquished command of the Southern Luzon Forces to his ebullient senior divisional commander, Maj. Gen. Albert Jones. This small, chubby, fire-eating Welshman with enough of his ancestry left for the "coal to be on his face," believed in leadership by example. It was only his energy and drive coupled with that canny skill of always being in the right spot at the right moment, that was to save his new command time after time in the succeeding days.

General Parker was sent by MacArthur to be in charge of the last part of this intricate jigsaw. Parker was ordered to prepare the ground in Bataan. This meant preparing and stockpiling Bataan for a long siege and moving troops into the main defensive positions.

This was to become known as the Abucay line. In addition, "homes" and campsites had to be found for the scores of retreating formations that poured in a never-ending stream into Bataan. These locations had then to be recorded and logged onto the campaign map so they could be fed and quartered. Defensive positions had to be dug, strays sorted out, and order restored from chaos.

Parker was ideally suited to this role. He had arrived in the Philippines in 1941 as a brigadier general and been very quickly promoted and thrust into a key combat command. He had made his reputation as a planner and coordinator. An excellent staff officer, it is clear that when he subsequently reverted to his corps things did not go well. In the latter stages of the campaign in Bataan his divisional commanders became increasingly exasperated and angry with the irrelevance of the instructions they were given. Unlike Wainwright, who was forever visiting the front-line units, or the swashbuckling Albert Jones, who led from the front, Parker kept his headquarters well to the rear and sought to direct the battle from there. His was a totally different style of leadership and undoubtedly best suited to his own personality and preference.

1745 hours
Thursday, January 1, 1942
Intramuros, Manila

Japanese troops formally marched into the city in accordance with the instructions detailed by their commander, General Homma. Three battalions from the 48th Division entered the city from the north, and a larger force from the 16th Division came in from the south. Much of Manila was in flames. The Pandacan oil fields, Fort McKinley, and Nichols still burned, while other fires raged unchecked from the indiscriminate Japanese bombing of the old city, which had continued until the day before. It would seem that neither side had paid more than lip service to the declaration of an open city.

The three thousand American and other Allied civilians had

prepared as best they could for the internment they knew was to follow. The only advice that the high commissioner's office had given before it left in unseemly haste for the sanctuary of Corregidor came in the form of a newspaper article. Women were advised not to wear trousers, and the men were told to destroy all the stocks of liquor they could possibly find, each in its way seen as a deterrent to the oriental horde going on a rampage.

Lilla Seitz was admitted into the Seventh-Day Adventist Hospital on Calle Donada in one of the more fashionable quarters in Manila to await the birth of her child. Her husband, Clay, together with the rest of the American and Allied civilians, was taken in open trucks to an internment camp that had been established on the sprawling campus of Santo Tomas University.

As the light began to fade, a group of Americans looked down from the windows of the Bay View Hotel on the ceremony taking place on the lawn of the High Commission. Two companies of Japanese sailors and another of infantry were drawn up. The American flag was lowered and it fluttered to the ground. A Japanese sailor stepped onto the crumpled banner, unhooked it, and in its place fastened the emblem of the Rising Sun. As the Imperial Japanese standard was raised, the officers saluted, troops presented arms, and a small band played the national anthem, the *Kimigayo*.

On board *S-36*
Calapan Harbor
Mindoro

McKnight celebrated the New Year by sinking his first enemy ship. It was a fat freighter moored against the wharfside. Commander Wilkes would have approved of his textbook attack. From periscope depth, McKnight watched the activity on the quayside as the ship's derricks swung what appeared to be gun limbers out of the hold and onto the dock. A column of infantry had, he assumed, just disembarked; they were drawn up farther along the quay, ready to march into the town. He ordered the depth setting on the torpedoes for 10 feet, and the navigator called the final bearings off the attack periscope's dials.

McKnight allowed himself the luxury of a last look at the target and a final sweep around the bay. Except for the freighter, the harbor appeared deserted.

"Down 'scope," he ordered. Compressed air hissed out as the periscope slid noisily into the deck housing.

"Fire One." The submarine gave a slight jolt as the torpedo left the bow tube.

"God, we can't miss this," the navigator said. "He's only four hundred yards away."

Their torpedo missed, as almost every other Mark 41 had missed in the war to date; like the others, it ran deeper than expected. However, the result was the same as if they had hit the target plum center. After the shock wave of the explosion had rocked past the submarine, McKnight returned to periscope depth and anxiously surveyed the damage; the crew as a man held their breath. The torpedo evidently had passed under the keel of the freighter and exploded with devastating effect against the wall of the wharf. The periscope showed a freighter already listing heavily against the quay, on top of which there was the most terrible confusion and chaos. The column of infantry had taken the full blast of flying debris, and fires mushroomed in a dozen places. McKnight relayed the glad tidings to the crew, and they cheered the captain and their first kill. The submarine left the port before the Japanese could begin a search and headed for what they hoped would be even happier hunting grounds in the Sibuyan Sea.

19th Bombardment Group
Del Monte Field
Mindanao

Some 650 airmen had been evacuated from Bataan and had successfully negotiated Japanese infested waters in an unarmed interisland steamer. In the late evening the S.S. *Mayan* tied up at the Del Monte pineapple cannery dock and her passengers stepped gratefully ashore.

Dick Osborn still couldn't believe the phenomenal luck that had allowed them to make good their escape. The incredible journey started on New Year's Eve on Bataan when rumors began to circulate among the men that crew chiefs were drawing up a list in conjunction with the squadron commanders. It was supposed to include the most highly qualified men, and it caused considerable anxiety and tension as the hopefuls compared qualifications. Osborn, for one, didn't want to stay behind; he was no infantryman, as that night in the foxholes at Clark reminded him; so it was with considerable relief that he was told his name was on the list. Sammy Boghosian found that he, too, was scheduled to leave Bataan.

The selected men left their bivouacs in the late afternoon. It was a pretty drive down to the wharfside at Mariveles, and now that he was leaving, Osborn sat back in the truck, and with only one eye open for the enemy, enjoyed the luxury of the majestic mountain scenery. The scuttlebutt was that the whole outfit was to be shipped first to Mindanao; there B-17s and transports would be waiting to fly them on to Australia and an air force that could not exist without their irreplaceable talents. Like many rumors, it was true in part. The airmen were indeed to be shipped to Mindanao, but there most were to stay. MacArthur's intention was to establish a forward base that would be used as a springboard for the relief of his beleaguered fortress.

The line of trucks rolled into Mariveles in the early evening, and the troops embarked immediately onto the *Mayan*. The little inter-island steamer was soon crammed to capacity. The Filipino crew stretched a tarpaulin over the top deck, partly to provide shelter and shade, but more importantly to screen the human cargo from prying eyes in the sky above. The ship carried no guns, and so the only weapons on board were the rifles and small arms of the passengers. The lucky men, other than the officers who were four to a cabin, were the last to board, for they were accommodated on the upper decks. Osborn was jammed down below against the hull, judging by the water he could hear lapping up against the thin plate, about a foot above the waterline. The hatch covers were hauled back but even then it was unbearable below decks. The hot, airless hold reeked of body odors and, after a short while in the South China Sea, vomit. A couple of strategically placed buckets were the crew's gesture toward sanitary arrangements. Many in their discomfort didn't bother to make it that far, and it was only the thought of escape from the horrors of war that prevented a mutiny.

Daylight found them off the island of Mindoro. Word was passed that the ship was to anchor throughout the day and continue the journey by night. In this way the captain hoped to elude the Japanese blockade. Thus, seemingly secure in the sheltered cove, those below decks sought to clean up the mess from the night before and waited their turn for a breath of air. There was food available but the chow line stretched so many times around the deck that Osborn decided to live off what he had brought with him from Bataan—some fruit and a couple of cans of C rations.

They dozed throughout the day and waited with inward impatience for the sun to set. At about three o'clock in the afternoon the hubbub of noise on the ship stilled as if by an unseen hand; they heard the drone of aircraft engines. An aircraft appeared low over the lagoon, and somebody yelled out, "It's a Kawasaki float plane."

Osborn knew the type, a four-engined long-range reconnaissance job. The news did little to cheer those jammed in the hold. Their discomforture was not eased either by a man on the top deck who insisted on giving a running commentary.

"Here comes the bomber now, his bomb bays are open! He's making a run at the ship!"

Everybody below remained silent.

The first bomb missed the ship. As the hull vibrated to the concussion and those on the top deck got a soaking from the spray, the men in the hold remained absolutely still. There wasn't any talk. Nothing.

"He's turning, he's making another run, he's coming back!"

This time Osborn saw the flash from the bomb's blast through the open hatches, heard the roar of the blast and the tinkling of glass. The bomb had missed by no more than 30 feet, and the hammer blows of the sound waves vibrated against the hull. The plane made three more runs over the ship; each time he dropped a bomb, and on each occasion he missed. By then the ship had sprung a leak around the stern plates, and every pane of glass and piece of crockery was smashed. Signs of panic spread among the passengers and some of the men were for jumping overboard. The squadron adjutant, an elderly lieutenant, rushed around the top decks warning everybody not to jump because their best chance of survival was to stay with the ship because the concussion from the bombs would kill anyone in the water.

As the plane came in for what proved to be his fifth and final pass, one man jumped overboard anyway. The near miss stained the sea with his intestines; it was about all that anybody could see that remained of Lieutenant Brown. Except for frayed nerves, he proved to be the only casualty. Thereafter Lieutenant Brown achieved immortality in the gallows humor of the GI, for the slogan of the 19th Bomb Group became, "Jump in and drown with Brown."

When the Japanese patrol plane had lumbered off into the distance, the captain of the *Mayan* decided that it would be better for the men to wait ashore until dusk, and the order was passed to lower the lifeboats. Many believed that the Japanese Air Force would soon be back in strength, and so there was an undignified scramble. Some couldn't or wouldn't wait; throwing aside their rifles and packs, they jumped overboard and swam toward the shore. One young airman near Osborn had found an old life jacket. He fastened it and then stood on the ship's rail.

"I can't swim. What will I do?" he pleaded.

"Jump in," an anonymous voice advised. Osborn watched as the kid jumped and he hit the sea 20 feet below, head first. It was a wonder he did not break his neck. He just quivered as he hit the water, surfaced, and a willing hand reached out and hauled him to a lifeboat.

Osborn decided that jumping was not for him. He realized that the lifeboats would have at least two more round trips before he could secure a place, and he was hungry, and there was now an opportunity to remedy at least one need. He sought out his buddie Woodie Stefanson among the throng pressing against the rails.

The two friends could see little point in remaining with the crush of men around the lifeboats, especially as the action seemed to be over, so they went below decks and, working their way through the midships section, found the supply room unlocked and deserted. They loaded the pockets of their fatigue coveralls with all the canned foods they could carry. Anything that was worth stealing they took before they caught the last boat ashore. Together with a few friends, they found a quiet spot on a hill overlooking the cove and feasted the hours away to sundown.

The ship sailed that night and by morning anchored in a secluded cove on the island of Panay. The men draped the *Mayan* with branches and foliage, trooped ashore, and waited for nightfall. The following night saw them on the final leg of their journey to Del Monte.

With the rear guard
On the road to Bataan

In the first desperate week of January the select brotherhood of units that had come to form the rear guard fought hard to deny the Japanese Layac, the "Gateway to Bataan." Behind them the town was a seething mass of marching troops, trucks, tanks, and horse artillery as all jockeyed for position to cross the single steel girder bridge that spanned the river.

On the Borac-Guagua line the decimated remnants of the 11th and 21st Philippine divisions, Wainwright's valiant rear guard, fought a desperate action against two regiments of Japanese assault troops. A few tanks from the 194th bolstered the defense and were witness to yet another battlefield atrocity by the enemy. An attacking column, which the tank crews estimated at eight hundred strong, was led by three Filipinos carrying white flags and beseeching the defenders not to fire. The tank crews had no choice. They opened fire, cut the column to pieces, halted the Japanese attack, and then fell back in orders to the next holding position.

Below Layac General Wainwright moved the 71st Infantry back into the line reinforced by elements of the 31st (U.S.) Infantry and the 26th Cavalry. Their orders were to buy more time; the main battle position at Abucay was not yet complete.

Company B, 1st Battalion, 31st Infantry deployed for battle. They had the dubious privilege of fighting their regiment's first engagement of the war. As Paul Kerchum lay in his machine-gun pit just off the main Bataan highway at Culis, surveying the scenes around him he thought it was a very strange war. After the last of the shattered rear guard had marched through their position, enterprising Filipinos appeared on the scene with crates of beer and ice. These they sold at a peso a bottle to the soldiers in their foxholes and weapon pits. Throughout the rest of that long, hot day the Filipinos, in their horse-drawn carts, unconcernedly crossed the line and went about their daily business. It all seemed so unreal to the young Americans. Many had thought about going into action for the first time, but none had ever imagined it would be like this.

At dusk the Japanese hit the 31st Infantry with everything they had. A torrent of heavy shells hammered at the American position. The Americans had no answer to this long-range artillery other than to sit tight and ride with the blows. As a baptism by fire it was overwhelming. Company B wavered in its resolve: A trickle of men drifted back and ran the gauntlet of fire to safety; others followed suit, and this soon became a flood.

Most of the company were still civilians at heart for, as we have seen, their training in the prewar days had done little to prepare them for the demands of modern combat. The unit had also suffered when so many of the good noncoms, together with the cream of the corporals, had been commissioned as officers into the new and hastily raised divisions of the Philippine Army. Nine went out of Company B alone, and they had had only twelve corporals. It was at the squad level that the steadying influence of the good noncom was missed, and that was where the rout began.

Paul Kercham hoisted the .50-caliber onto his shoulder and ran with the others. After about 100 yards of this panic-stricken, headlong flight, he stopped and looked up at his corporal, Tom Bridges. Loaded down with a tripod and swathed in the ammunition belts, Bridges ran alongside him.

"What the hell's going on? We aren't supposed to be doing this, Tom!" he said.

Bridges simply grunted and pushed the little guy on. Shortly afterward they bumped into an officer from the 3rd Battalion who had been sent up to attempt to make some order out of chaos. They eventually re-established a line, and somewhat sheepishly the men sorted themselves out into squads and dug in. Most hoped for a chance to make amends, but later they were pulled back to Bataan.

The 31st Infantry in the ensuing confusion lost contact with the 26th Cavalry, who were holding the line with them on the left flank.

The cavalry now found its own retreat blocked by the Japanese, who pursued the 31st Infantry. The only way by which the cavalry could regain the safety of the main defense lines was to march overland and cut their own route across the jungles and mountains. This forced march was an extraordinary affair, if only because the Filipinos took their horses through places where they had no right to be. However, in a campaign that saw so many unusual acts, it passed almost unnoticed. This incredible feat of arms also marks the end of an era, for this march by the 26th Cavalry, Philippine Scouts, was the last such action of its kind by horse cavalry in the history of the United States.

Despite the losses and the confusion, General MacArthur had masterminded an operation that has rightly entered the gallery of classic fighting retreats. In the space of three short weeks he had drawn in the two quite separate parts of his Army and fed them into prepared positions in Bataan.

It is true, however, that the Japanese did not seek a decisive engagement, and it was largely Homma's tactical misconceptions that allowed MacArthur's forces to have a relatively easy time in the retreat. If the Japanese Air Force had intervened at any stage during those critical weeks there would have been carnage and chaos among the long lines of retreating convoys.

Considering the training and equipment of the Filipino troops, it is surprising that not a single major unit was cut off or lost during the withdrawal. This is a tribute to MacArthur, his commanders, and the junior leaders in the field. Even more, it is a tribute to the Filipino who, lost, bewildered, and scared out of his wits by a war for which neither his culture nor his short period of training had even begun to prepare him, nevertheless stuck doggedly to his duty and to his flag. Many deserted and returned to their homes, but the vast majority marched into Bataan to at best an uncertain future alongside the Americans.

Though they were comrades-in-arms, there was an essential difference between them. For the Filipino it was his country that had been invaded and now largely occupied. While he retreated into Bataan he left behind his mother, wife, sweetheart, and sister to be ravished and defiled by the Japanese soldiers. As for the American, his family was safe and sound thousands of miles away, so all he had to care about was himself. He was a professional soldier and he was in this mess because of his government. That is the lot of the professional soldier; as servants of the state they are by definition expendable. Despite his lack of training and unpreparedness for war the American soldier in the Philippines was a professional: There were no draftees in the islands. Nevertheless, from these two contrasting positions MacArthur had to bond a strong and resilient defense until rescue could be effected.

If an army has to make a last-ditch stand, then the terrain of Bataan is in many respects ideally suited. The peninsula is 30 miles long, at its very widest 25 miles, and it tapers to an average width of about 15 miles. Numerous streams, ravines, and gullies, all coated with a thick growth of tropical rain forest, dissect the interior and impede forward advance.

A spine of mountains running northwest to southeast effectively splits Bataan in two. To the north the dominant mountain is Mount Natib (4,222 feet); it is connected by a saddle ridge and high pass to Mount Silanganan (3,620 feet). To the south, the base of Bataan is dominated by the Mariveles Mountains, of which the highest peak at 4,700 feet is Mount Bataan.

A motor road runs down the Manila Bay coast to the small seaport at Mariveles. On the South China Sea coast the roadways are little more than fair-weather tracks. There is a lateral road that connects Bagac on the West Coast with Orion. This metaled highway midway down the peninsula dictates the lines of defense.

MacArthur had established the main battle position along the Morong-Abucay line, with a reserve position just forward of the lateral road from Bagac to Orion. He divided Bataan into three main areas of responsibility. On the South China Sea coast he established Wainwright's I Corps; difficult terrain dictated this to be a secondary theater of operations.

The Japanese were expected to put the main thrust of their assault on the Manila Bay side of the peninsula, where the terrain was more open and flat. Consequently in Parker's II Corps, MacArthur concentrated his better though still unblooded battalions of Philippine Scouts. Directly behind the reserve battle position, the remainder of the Philippine division was deployed. Finally, to the south of Mount Bataan MacArthur created the Service Command Area in which an amalgam of units—provisional Air Corps elements and Navy battalions—guarded the likely beaches and coves against an enemy attempt to outflank the main defense lines from the sea.

Richard Sakakida worked at Wainwright's headquarters on Army Intelligence. The Japanese soldiers kept voluminous diaries, and these provided a rich harvest of information on Japanese mood, morale, and intentions. Sakakida frequently traveled to the front and collected the items that had been gathered from Japanese dead. On these occasions he took a couple of American soldiers with him for protection, not from the Japanese but from the Filipinos. The latter, nervous and excitable, probably would have shot him for a Japanese. Such escort details were the responsibility of Kermit Lay, a lieutenant commissioned from the Air Corps. He had spent two hitches in the infantry and one in the horse cavalry before the war, so when the Air Corps had been assigned an infantry role, it was Private Lay who had shown the captains and the lieutenants standard weapons drill.

It was about a week after the unit had moved into Bataan that Private Lay was ordered to report to his company commander.

"Let me be the first to congratulate you, Lieutenant," Captain Maxwell said, extending his hand.

"What do you mean, sir?" the startled private asked. "I'm not a lieutenant, and I don't want to be an officer."

"What's wrong with you, Lay?" Maxwell asked.

"Okay, I'll tell you straight, sir. I don't like officers. I'm an old soldier, and I ain't qualified to be anything else . . . sir."

"Well, you're sure not bashful about it." Maxwell put his arm on Kermit Lay's shoulder and said, "Now, why don't you do your part? We want officers out there with your experience and your background. Hell, you saw the way the officers in your own unit couldn't even clean the Cosmoline out of the Springfields."

Lay did not really have any choice in the matter.

Maxwell took the reluctant Lay down to the Philippines Department administrative base at Little Baguio. It was next to No. 1 Hospital, and so they called in to see some of their men who had been wounded in the early days on Nichols and evacuated to Bataan. The hospital's CO had his office in an old bus, behind which was a barbed-wire fence. This was used as the cage to house Japanese prisoners; all were severely wounded.

Kermit Lay was sworn in as a second lieutenant and immediately assigned to the 11th Philippine Infantry Division. This was something that neither he nor Maxwell had anticipated; the understanding had been that he would return to his old unit.

Lay found a truck that was heading for the 11th Division. It was already full of other replacements, both American and Filipino, so he crammed himself into the back, and as the truck jolted out of the base and headed north, brooded about his fortunes and his future as an officer.

He must have dozed off, for he remembered little of the journey before the truck stopped at I Corps headquarters and two signal corps radio operators clambered down. An officer stuck his head around the back of the truck. "I need a lieutenant," he said.

Lay crouched low in the front corner, for he had no desire to serve in a corps headquarters—all that spit and polish sent shivers down his back. However, one brash young American with brand-new sergeant's stripes on his faded shirt pointed toward Lay. "Here's a lieutenant sitting right here! Wake up, Lieutenant, sir."

Kermit Lay, cornered and alone, surrendered to Fate and scrambled off the tailboard and probably saved his life. He was taken into the corps headquarters and appointed assistant provost marshal.

"Shit," Lay thought, "if only my old buddies could see me now. Ten years of undetected Army crime, and I wind up a policeman!" His first assignment was to go up to the front line as escort to Richard Sakakida while he collected Japanese documents.

Air Corps Provisional Infantry
Bataan

Life had assumed an air of normality at Kermit Lay's old outfit, and John McCann started to enjoy his service life again. Although he had only two meals a day, the provisional Air Corps had their own field kitchens, and the food was good and filling. There was a little barrio just north of them where the Filipinos had, overnight, become the most astute traders. The price of canned goods and other small luxuries rose considerably.

It was all an adventure again as the young man, far from the front line, listened to the rumors of war and convoys en route across the Pacific. Sergeant Farmer, an old soldier, would sit and tell the youngsters of his days in the infantry.

McCann had taken ROTC in high school, and this stood him in good stead, for nobody had thought of giving the Air Corps any organized basic infantry training. The nearest they got was when they took their Springfields, went down to the beach, and used empty coconut shells for target practice. In a way it served its purpose, for they "got the feel of the gun."

There were still small groups who wandered past the position, lost and looking for their parent unit; and many men were still coming in from the North.

"Have you guys seen the seven hundred and twenty-eighth?"

"No, we're the six hundred and ninety-third."

"Aw, shit! Well, do you mind if we join you a while?"

"Sure, go ahead."

They saw occasional reminders of the war as the casualties came back from the battles raging around Layac and the "Gateway to Bataan." On most days a bus, in which the seats had been ripped out and the roof taken off, would stop with its load of stretcher cases.

"Have you guys seen Number One Hospital?"

"Have you got some gas you can spare?"

McCann would take some water to the wounded and stare in wonder at these men from another world.

To take their minds off the more serious side of war, McCann and his companions would hunt carabao, a type of local water buffalo. There were a couple of farm boys in the group who knew how to stalk and butcher. Life was an adventure to the impressionable teenagers.

Monday, January 5, 1942
U.S.S. *Canopus*
Mariveles Bay

The Japanese sent another squadron of planes to finish the *Canopus*. Anti-aircraft shells stitched pretty patterns in the sky at their maximum altitude while the bombers flew 2,000 feet higher, unhindered and in perfect formation. Again the pattern of falling bombs bracketed the ship, but only one bomb, a 250-pounder, hit the old lady. The bomb plowed into the smokestack and sprayed the upper decks with a lethal fusillade of fragments and splinters. The gun crews had little protection behind their inadequate shields at the best of times, and their open gun tubs afforded no cover to plunging debris. Jagged metal scythed through them causing some fearful injuries, though on this occasion there were no deaths. The damage to the upper decks and superstructure was minor, even though they were pitted with holes. The *Canopus* resembled a giant colander. The near misses had caused the more severe damage. Underwater concussion stove in hull plates, loosened rivets, and buckled the stern.

The captain decided that since it was quite apparent that the Japanese knew precisely where the *Canopus* was moored, their camouflage would have to take on a completely new dimension if they were to deceive the enemy and stay in business as a depot and supply ship. The engineers deliberately listed the ship, derricks were left askew, and the cargo hatches were ripped open. Smoke pots were placed over the damaged upper works. The Japanese reconnaissance aircraft—"Photo Joe," as he had been nicknamed by the defenders—would, they hoped, report a listing, burning, and abandoned ship. Except for a skeleton crew, the sailors moved ashore. Some set up housekeeping inside some half-completed storage tunnels, but most preferred the fresh air of the open hillsides. The more enterprising slung hammocks among the roots of the giant trees and dug foxholes conveniently near in case of air raids. The light air-defense machine guns were also moved off the *Canopus* so that the ship would not provoke retaliatory fire in future air raids. The gunners set up their weapons on the hills above Mariveles, but very few Japanese aircraft were so bold as to swoop in low. Even the Zero kept his distance over the port.

The Office of the Chief Quartermaster, USAFFE
Fort Mills
Corregidor

On the advice of General Drake, General Sutherland, MacArthur's Chief of Staff, ordered that all troops in Bataan and Corregidor were to go on half rations immediately.

Drake had spent three days collating all the information available about the supply situation, and the picture was not at all optimistic. He had some grave misgivings as to the amount of food that had been accumulated, and his figures served to reinforce his doubts. It was estimated, and they could do no more than guess, that there were more than 100,000 people on Bataan; of these perhaps 70,000 were troops and the rest civilians, mostly refugees. Drake had been told to anticipate and cater for 43,000 troops and such civilians as were needed for labor. Reports on the amount of food available proved equally alarming. Between Bataan and Corregidor, in the North Channel, and along the shore of lower Bataan were some 150 barges still to be unloaded. There were also 5 small freighters that had been unwilling or unable to make a dash for freedom. Drake ordered the freighters to be moored close to Corregidor and under the protection of its heavy batteries until their holds could be emptied. They had been extremely fortunate with the barges, and so far only 10 had been lost, either to bombing or drifting out to sea due to insecure anchorage. The latter was a particular problem caused by the rip tides, strong winds, and cross currents in the North Channel.

They unloaded the barges at night. Drake found that if barges after unloading were returned to their original anchorage before daylight, the enemy would leave them alone, no doubt in the belief that they were not being used. To change anchorage, however, was fatal, as undoubtedly "Photo Joe" kept an accurate account of all their locations.

The survey that took in the food dumps in Bataan, the stores in Corregidor, and the cargoes still to be cleared from the barges allowed Drake to calculate that the garrison had 30 days' supply of a very unbalanced diet. In detail it broke down as follows:

Fifty days of canned meats, and fish—mostly stored before the war.

Forty days of canned milk, most of which had been taken off freighters in the harbor.

Thirty days of canned vegetables, mostly string beans and tomatoes.

They had a shipment of flour that had largely come from a barge load of ground wheat that had been unloaded from a freighter in the harbor for the American Red Cross in Manila. In the hurry and excitement of moving barges to Bataan, this one had somehow become mixed up with the evacuation.

There was some sugar, oleomargarine, syrup, very little salt, and some pepper. Worst of all, the Americans had only 15 days' supply of rice, the main and staple diet of the Filipino. There was little or no coffee, vinegar, fresh fruits, fresh meats, potatoes, onions, or cereals.

They had some 600,000 gallons of gasoline in storage, and a large British collier full of Welsh coal. On checking the gasoline, Drake's staff found that some of the tank barges had been sabotaged with sugar, and a gum that the chemical warfare people could neither identify nor remove. So seriously did they take this particular threat that a sample of the gasoline was sent to Australia for analysis.

Armed with these reports and his facts and figures, Drake went to General Sutherland's office.

At first the Chief of Staff was not prepared to believe the reports made by the units of the numbers of men they had to feed—these were called ration strengths. He had calculated that there were not more than a total of 70,000 people on Bataan, and he thought that units were undoubtedly "padding" their strengths in order to get more rations.

Drake agreed that this was possible but pointed out that there was no way he could check this out, and even so he doubted whether the exaggeration would produce such a distortion.

Sutherland asked him what he would advise.

Drake believed that at the current rate of consumption, the food would last for only another 20 days, and he recommended going on half rations immediately. In reply to Sutherland's question as to how much food this would be, he said that it would be in the region of 30 ounces, or 2,000 calories, a man a day.

Sutherland agreed to recommend this to MacArthur, but promised that the order would take effect immediately.

At the end of the conference, Sutherland informed Drake that General MacArthur had decided to stock Corregidor with enough food to supply a garrison of approximately 20,000 troops up to July 1, 1942.

"To meet this requirement I shall have to draw the extra supplies from Bataan!" Drake protested.

The protest was in vain. The items were approved for transfer, Drake made the necessary arrangements, and for three nights supplies were shipped across quietly from Bataan. General Drake, for his part, was very angry that he had been overruled, so he established a complicated system of ration credits and just as quietly shipped a large portion of these foodstuffs back across to Bataan.

Even with all these preparations and contingencies, Drake knew that unless help arrived quickly, the beleaguered forces would starve. Before leaving, Drake outlined his plans for foraging for foodstuffs immediately available in and around Bataan. His first thought was the rice supply. The rice had been harvested but was lying unthreshed on the very dry rice fields. In this condition it is known as "palay."

The main concentration of rice fields lay in the northeastern corner of Bataan, and these were already in Japanese hands. Nevertheless, foraging parties were hard at work, and as much palay as possible was collected. Drake had also called on the local population to surrender their stores of rice to the military authorities. They were paid $1.75 a cavan (about 115 pounds), which was a fair market price. The rice had to be threshed and milled before it became ready for delivery to the troops, so Drake arranged for three rice mills close to the front lines to be dismantled and resited to the south along Mariveles Road. The mills were functioning by the middle of January and operated for a month until the palay ran out, by which time they had produced some 30,000 pounds of rice. It was worth the effort.

The next consideration was fresh food, in particular meat and fish to augment the canned foods and C rations. There were the carabao, and when necessary they could slaughter the artillery mules and then the horses of the 26th Cavalry. There were also two mule trains, but Drake decided to keep them in existence as long as possible. They were invaluable to pack food and much-needed supplies over the trails to the troops on the front line.

There was an abundance of fish in Manila Bay and many small fishing villages along the eastern shoreline. The local population had in the past set out fishing traps and indeed supplied Manila with fresh fish daily. Drake's quartermasters rounded up as many fishermen as they could find and set them to work. All fishing was done at night, the catch of fresh fish exceeded 12,000 pounds, and there were prospects of even more. Then the bottom fell out of the fishing market when the villagers suddenly refused to fish. Some of their number were caught by the Japanese. They were tortured and then allowed to return to their communities, a mutilated warning to others. As if that were not bad enough, the Air Corps provisional infantry battalions on beach defense, and others, fired on the fishing boats, despite all attempts to prevent them. Finally, the beach troops stole a large part of the catch before it even got to market; they took what they required on the beach or hijacked the trucks on their way to the supply dumps.

For slaughtering carabao Drake enlisted the support of the Army Veterinary Corps. They improvised a slaughterhouse, a platform over a mountain stream, complete with block and tackle. Parties were dispatched to drive the carabao onto corrals that had been built near the abattoir. The butchers slaughtered between 30 and 40 animals a day. The meat had to be delivered quickly, by truck and mule train, for if it was allowed to stand exposed to the heat, it started to spoil. There was a tropical fly that produced maggots from its eggs in less than half an hour when laid in fresh meat. Even so, for a while at least they slaughtered enough meat to give each man, on paper, a daily ration of 4 ounces. Those in the front line, however, rarely saw such luxury and so had to fall back on their own devices and expertise. Of course they, too, organized carabao hunting parties, but it was more usual for them to eat what was immediately on hand. The Filipinos pointed out the wild bananas, which the men picked green, covered with leaves, and placed on the bottom of the foxhole to ripen. The forests contained an abundance of wildlife. The men shot monkeys and made stew and trapped lizards—the iguanas were considered a luxury, especially the tail, which was white meat not unlike chicken. The connoisseurs of the infantry found pythons too to be especially good eating.

One item whose shortage concerned Drake greatly was salt. They had very little in stock and no way of obtaining more. There were many saltbeds in the lagoons around Manila Bay. Before the war this had been a major industry, but there were no beds on Bataan. The only way to increase the salt supply was by boiling seawater. The quartermasters found a number of very large cast-iron cauldrons that even the locals had long since abandoned. These were set up over large open ranges, but the best they could manage was about 400 pounds of salt a day. This was not sufficient to issue to the troops, but it did give the bakery salt and some of the messes a small amount for cooking.

The bakery on Bataan was an elaborate and highly successful operation. Its sergeant major was Bill Sniezko, who had transferred as a very young sergeant from the 31st Infantry into the Quarter-master Corps of the Philippine Scouts. The unit had 3 officers, 2 sergeants, and 240 Scouts. They had World War I-vintage ovens, which they dug into the clay bank of a ravine so that the only part showing was the oven door. The men also fashioned more ovens out of dobe mud and rice straw, a sort of Dutch oven. All these units operated continuously, with the Scouts working an 8-hour shift. At this rate they produced some 20,000 pounds of bread daily, but for the soldiers it meant at best 6 ounces of thin bread, with the front-line units again coming off worse. The fresh bread found its way to the nearest formations, the headquarters and rear-area troops.

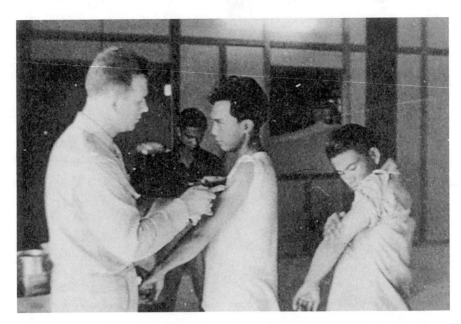

Lt. (later Maj.) Paul Ashton giving tetanus shots to Philippine Scouts at Lubao shortly before Pearl Harbor. He was captured by the Japanese and imprisoned in Bilabid until liberated.

Pvt. William Garleb, a school dropout, who sought haven in the Army in the spring of 1941.

Pvt. Garleb's unit, Company H of the 31st Infantry, in the spring of 1941 at Nicholas Field. Very few survived the war.

The U. S. S. *Mindinao* immediately before she made her dash for freedom. It took 28 minutes for the crew to "paint" her black with shoe polish. The awnings were dropped at sea to make the pursuing Japanese believe that she had sunk in a tropical storm.

Three pictures of an American hero. *(upper left)* 2nd Lt. Winston A. Jones, Field Artillery, U.S.A. Reserve, five years before Pearl Harbor. Jones escaped from the Bataan death march and became a leading figure in the guerilla resistance movement.

(upper right) At right he is seen in guerilla uniform on February 3, 1945.

(below) Maj. Jones upon his return in April 1945. Meeting him are his parents who throughout the war thought he was dead.

2nd Lt. Loyd E. Mills of the 57th Infantry, Philippine Scouts, in full dress uniform. He arrived in the Philippines on the eve of Pearl Harbor. The dress uniform became a casualty of the war.

Lt. Malcolm (Champ) Champlin, U.S.N. An F.B.I. field agent, who was called up by mistake and who ended up a hero by blowing up the oil refineries in Manila in the path of the oncoming Japanese.

Lt. Roland McKnight, U.S.N., commander of submarine *S-36*, built for a previous war, was assigned to thwart the Japanese landings in Lingayen Gulf. He ended his naval career as a rear admiral.

The 4th Marines, having escaped from Shanghai in the nick of time, on their arrival at Subic Bay. On December 29, the 4th Marines were sent to Corregidor; one of only 3 combat trained units in the Philippines, they were consigned to protect General MacArthur's headquarters on Corregidor. In the front, Sgt. William E. Griffiths.

Brig. Gen. Charles Drake, Quartermaster, who, when confronted by Japanese troops armed with flame-throwers, surrendered the survivors in the Malinta tunnel. Neither he nor his aide knew Japanese, and the Japanese knew no English. The lingua franca for the surrender was Russian.

The pilots at Clark Field went off to have lunch while their planes, waiting to be refueled, would wind up like sitting ducks when the Japanese strike force hit.

A poor snapshot from General Drake's collection showing the *Canopus* in the north channel between Corregidor and Bataan.

In front row, right, Pvt. Dick Osborn, who was ordered to load pineapples instead of people onto MacArthur's airplane. Nevertheless he managed to get one stowaway aboard the plane.

A somewhat blurred snapshot of one of the "angels of Corregidor," 2nd Lt. Madeline Ullom, an army nurse who was evacuated to Corregidor where she worked endless hours in the Malinta tunnel ministering to the wounded. She was taken prisoner by the Japanese.

Mounted in the 1890's, these relics of a bygone age were intended to deny Manila Bay to an invading fleet. Partly because of Capt. Massello's heroism, these mortars inflicted massive casualties on Japanese troops hitting the beaches of Corregidor.

The author standing on one of the mortars in Massello's battery, 1979.

Capt. Bill Massello was a soldier's hero of Corregidor. Though badly wounded he kept his guns in action to the very end. He survived imprisonment, the hell ships, and forced labor in Japan, his ordeal ending only after Hiroshima. This photograph was taken in January 1946.

Petty Officer Sam Malick on return to active duty from Prisoner of War camp. He was liberated in Manchuria by Soviet troops in August 1945.

収容所 Camp 収容年月日 Date Interned	Santa Tomas Jan. 6, 1942 昭和　年　月　日	番　　　號 No.	
氏　　名 Name	Evans, Arthur Henry	生 年 月 日 Date of Birth	May 25, 1888
國　　籍 Nationality	American	本　籍　地 Place of Origin	Battle Creek, Mich
身 分 職 業 Position or Occupation	Tarif Administrator	抑留前ノ住 所又ハ居所 Address before Internment	Manila Hotel
父　ノ　名 Father's name	Evans, Irwin H.	通　報　先 Destination of Report	1003 Golden West Ave. Arcadia California
母　ノ　名 Mother's name	Evans, Emma Ferry	特　　技 Speciality	
妻(夫)ノ名 Wife's (Husband's) name	Evans, Ruby	特 記 事 項 Remarks	

An identity card of an American civilian prisoner in the Santa Tomas internment camp.

This is a very rare example of a photograph taken on X-ray film, inserted in the dark into a camera that was smuggled in to the Cabanatuan prison camp. This picture shows the chaplains with the hospital commander. Four of these men died in hell ships en route to Japan. Only Chaplain Zimmerman, second from right in the front row, is alive today.

2. The Battle of the Abucay Hacienda

Friday, January 9, 1942–
Friday, January 23, 1942

April 1980
Department of War Studies and International Affairs
The Royal Military Academy Sandhurst, England

A Foreword to the Battle

The Battle of Bataan is a collective title that I have used to describe a month of very confusing Japanese offensives, from January 9 through about February 10. To set the scene:

Although the Americans and Filipinos began the battle in good heart along the Abucay line, yet had to give ground and defend their second line of resistance from Pilar to Bagac, they nevertheless fought the Imperial Japanese Army to a standstill. Elsewhere in Asia the forces of the Emperor swept all before them. In the Philippines the Japanese Army suffered its first major defeat of the war. General Homma never recovered from the shame and humiliation of his failure and indeed was destined to hold no further position of high command for the rest of the war.

In a complex and often overlapping sequence of offensive operations, Homma tried every trick in the book, and many that weren't, to break the spirit of the defenders. He began with sustained offensives against the Abucay line (which I have called Abucay Hacienda, since that battle became the focal point of the front). At its height Japanese troops in a series of disastrous operations sought to outflank the line with amphibious right hooks (the Battle of the Points). Finally, while these were still in progress, the defenders withdrew behind their new line, and the Japanese attempted to bounce through before the Allies could dig in (the Battle of the Pockets). At last it was Homma who called a halt and appealed, cap in hand, to Imperial general headquarters for fresh men and materials with which to complete his allotted task.

What of Corregidor? The fortress was bombed and bombarded though not invested during this month. It succored and directed the titanic struggle of Bataan; it was the source of hope and relief and the center of intrigue and pragmatism in the double dealings that transpired from Washington to Malinta Tunnel.

Friday, January 9, 1942
Abucay line

The troops were about as ready as they ever were going to be in their weapon pits and foxholes along the Abucay line. Loyd Mills walked his sector of front with his senior Filipino Scouts and for the umpteenth time checked the field of fire of his .50-caliber guns as they looked out over the flat coastlands, swampy fish ponds, and rice paddies. He still felt uneasy about the failure of Company A on his left to clear the bamboo and sugar cane to their front. He had remonstrated on a couple of occasions that they should have fired these fields, but regimental headquarters had paid little heed to his words.

The untried 41st Philippine Infantry Division held the center of the line, rising ground from the sugar cane to the foothills of Mount Natib. Much of their front was heavily scarred by innumerable lava ravines from the now-extinct volcano. About 1,000 yards behind the foremost infantry, Winston Jones and his gunners waited for battle. He had moved the bulk of his ammunition into a drainage ditch between the rice field and the creekline and covered them with straw and brush. Ordered to provide fire support for both Scouts and his own infantry, Jones had established a fire direction center. In cooperation with the infantry, he had quartered the maps and numbered the squares in such a way that he would be able to shift fire quickly from one location to another. The fire direction center in the battalion command post was in the drainage ditch alongside the ammunition dump. Jones had piled sandbags up to about 4 feet above ground level and camouflaged the bunker with rice sheaves and brush.

To Jones's left, and holding the foothills of Mount Natib, was the tired and dispirited 51st Infantry Division. They had been given what General Parker considered to be a quiet part of the front. No one anticipated a Japanese attack through such difficult terrain when the easier ground of the coastal plain was available.

Abucay Hacienda nestled in among the foothills. A now deserted group of nipa huts, which had once housed the sugar cane workers, clustered around the hacienda, a large house left over from the Spanish colonial days. It had a quaint courtyard and a few outbuildings typical of the architecture of the period.

The Japanese opened the Battle of Bataan with a massive artillery barrage directed against the II Corps front. General Homma had already withdrawn his veteran 48th Division for new deployments in the East Indies. In their place he moved the 65th Infantry Brigade under Lt. Gen. Akira Nara. The 6,500 men of this misnamed force (it was known as the "Summer Brigade") were overage and medically unfit. They were intended as a garrison and occupation force and had no combat experience. Indeed, they were in pretty poor condition even before the battle. The march south from Lingayen Gulf in the scorching heat of the Philippine summer had thinned their ranks of the elderly and infirm.

Nevertheless, General Homma and his staff, from their headquarters in the old Scout barracks at Fort Stotsenberg, were not unduly perturbed by the loss of the better combat troops to another theater of operations. Homma was convinced that the Americans would offer little more than token resistance in their present positions before making perhaps a more spirited stand in the southern tip of the peninsula under the protection of the guns on Corregidor. Thus in what he saw as a pursuit rather than an assault, General Nara, who was given tactical command of the battle, split his force into three columns. A regimental combat team based on the 122nd Infantry would attack down the West Coast, while the main weight of attack would hit the eastern side of Bataan and Parker's II Corps. The 141st Infantry, suitably beefed up with additional artillery and armor, was to advance out of Hermosa astride the coastal highway. Nara's hopes for a quick victory lay with his third column, the experienced 9th Infantry, which he had borrowed from the 16th Division. Reinforced with extra artillery, the force was ordered to exploit inland, probe for a weak link in the defense lines among the foothills, strike south and then east, and thus outflank the American line.

General Nara had been reliably informed by Army HQ Intelligence that MacArthur had less than 40,000 American troops, of which some 25,000 were on Bataan. There were perhaps another 10,000 Filipinos, but he was told to discount any possibility of resistance from such units, as they were plagued by wholesale desertions.

The Intelligence staff worked with tourist maps very similar to ones the Americans had used to find their way into Bataan. They had no detailed knowledge of American deployments and in their assumptions guessed wrong. The Japanese placed the main defense lines some 3 miles north of their true position. The result was that the terrifyingly heavy artillery bombardment that at 1500 hours that afternoon signaled the Battle of Bataan punched mighty holes in empty ground.

After half an hour the Japanese bombardment lifted, and the infantry advanced into plain view. Some were wheeling bicycles, and none had moved into open and extended lines ready for battle. The defenders held their fire until the last moment, and then a hundred cannons spoke as one, and the densely packed column withered before the unexpected and deadly accurate fire. Winston Jones's gunners sweated at their field pieces pouring round after round onto a road they had carefully zeroed a week before. Except for short periods when the weary gunners stopped to allow their barrels to cool, the guns fired through the evening and into the night at an enemy who had quickly run for cover.

Saturday, January 10, 1942
Bataan

General MacArthur, accompanied by a small retinue and a couple of zealous photographers, toured Bataan and the battlefront. He first visited Parker's corps headquarters, where he chatted amiably with the staff, and then drove by way of the Pilar-Bagac Road across the peninsula to meet with General Wainwright. Kermit Lay in his military police Jeep escorted the entourage into corps headquarters.

MacArthur stayed for only a short while, talked to a few soldiers, and paid a quick visit to the hospital before returning to his island fortress. To those men who met him, the message was the same, full of optimism and hope for the future. "Help is on the way," he assured everybody from his generals to the lowliest private in the field.

MacArthur never visited the troops on Bataan again. Although the Filipinos adored him and revered his name, it was something that the American soldiers never forgave. The general was to carry the epithet "Dugout Doug" with him to his grave, a stinging reminder from the campaign in Bataan which no amount of subsequent glory could purge.

Sunday, January 11, 1942
57th Philippine Scouts
Abucay line

The Japanese infantry attack built up in pace and tempo through the day. Initially the main thrust came straight down the coastal highway. Loyd Mills and the Scouts had never seen such a spectacle and could only assume that these Sons of Nippon had never before encountered seasoned infantry dug into strongly defended positions.

The Japanese battalions first debussed in plain view amid highly accurate artillery fire and then advanced slowly along the road. They made a frontal attack carrying their rifles at the high port and just occasionally loosened off a couple of rounds at the defenders.

The enemy pressed home the attack to within 150 yards of the trenches when the Scouts' machine-gun and rifle fire decimated their ranks and piled the dead high before the wire. It was the most ridiculous infantry fighting the American officers had ever seen. Charlie Company brushed the enemy aside.

Survivors from the Japanese assault sought refuge in the sugar cane field, whence at dusk they joined with others in a frenzied assault on Able Company's foxholes. Mortar flares turned night into day, and the Scouts fired point blank at the enemy but the cane field gave the Japanese the cover they needed. Using the bodies of dead comrades as ladders, and at fearful cost, they leaped the wire and at bayonet point prized Able Company from its position. The Scouts counterattacked with the dawn and drove the Japanese back through the wire and into the cane field beyond. Every foxhole had to be fought for, and it was the turn of the Scouts to take casualties. Alexander Mininger, a second lieutenant just graduated from West Point, won the first Medal of Honor on the battlefields of World War II; he died in the act of wiping out a Japanese machine-gun nest.

The Scouts fired the sugar cane, and as the field burned they shot down those Japanese who tried to run from the flames. Later in the afternoon Charlie Company sent out a couple of fighting patrols; they counted more than 250 enemy dead on the battlefield.

The Japanese continued the pressure past the following week, though the axis of their advance swung inland as they sought both the elusive weak link and safety from the withering and steadfast accuracy of the Scouts and their field artillery.

41st Field Artillery
Abucay line

Most of the Japanese attacks on the center of the line and those positions defended by the infantry units of the 41st Division came at night or early in the morning. Winston Jones's guns shifted fire concentrations as requests came in from the infantry. He also had a Filipino observer in a tall tree immediately to the rear of his command post. One afternoon he reported on his field telephone that the Japanese were sending carabao across the line.

Winston called his gunners to arms and warned the infantry. The Japanese had been sending carabao across the front lines to see if the ground was mined. The Filipinos busily prepared for what was likely to be the first round in another frenzied night assault.

The field telephone jangled noisily in its housing. It was the observer again reporting that it was not carabao but horses, and he thought they were pulling guns.

Jones trained his battery commander's 'scope on the ground in question. There about 1,000 yards to their front, the powerful magnification identified what was a Japanese horse-drawn battery moving its guns into position. In the world of counter battery fire it was a gunner's dream.

Jones gave his orders. The gunners let down the trapdoors to the rice hides and bore-sighted the guns; this allowed each gun captain to train the barrel on the movement he saw. On the word of command they opened a devastating fire on the Japanese, and men and horses were hurled aside by the fury of the shelling. Through his 'scope Jones watched the complete destruction of the enemy battery; limbers exploded, and horses bolted in all directions. But even in the heat and excitement of victory his gunners remembered their drills; gun captains, once they had the range, traversed a few mils left and right to complete the destruction. By the time Jones ordered the cease-fire, there was nothing left of the Japanese battery.

Unfortunately at the end of the engagement, a couple of gunners moved back from one of the guns just as Photo Joe put in an appearance. A flight of Zeros appeared as if from nowhere, and for the next ten minutes attacked the Command Post—it was all they had identified in the rice field. They dropped 50-pound antipersonnel bombs, and one hit the edge of the command bunker. There was a loud crashing noise and a cloud of dust and smoke, but neither Jones nor the battalion commander were wounded; the latter, however, was quite upset and shaken by the experience. He was evacuated out of the position, and Jones was ordered to assume temporary command. The battalion commander never returned. In the meantime, more Japanese bombers appeared, and they began to bomb the rice fields about 900 yards back from Jones's bunker. Obviously they didn't believe that the guns could be so close to the front line, for they never bothered with anything in their field except for the first attack on the bunker.

Japanese retaliation for the destruction of their field battery took another and more horrifying form. The next morning artillery observers and infantry in the front line saw young Filipino women who had been buried alive up to their necks near to where the battle had occurred the day before. A loudspeaker taunted the Filipinos as the girls slowly died. A distraught lieutenant begged Jones to put the girls out of their misery; the Japanese must have smeared their faces in sugar, for the ants were eating them alive. Jones couldn't bring himself to give such an order. Yesterday's engagement now seemed a hollow victory.

12th Medical Battalion
Casualty clearing station
Abucay church

Paul Ashton had helped establish the main casualty station in the Abucay church. Made out of stone and covered with mud, it had walls between 4 and 6 feet thick, which made it practically "artillery proof." The team of a dozen doctors and some twenty orderlies worked around the clock as the casualties poured in from the battlefront. Ashton utilized the nave of the church as the registry and the main ward, while the chancel became the operating theater. A patient would be brought in on a litter, and a doctor would make the first preliminary examination. Ashton and the others never knew what awaited them until they pulled back the blanket.

In so many respects it was the strangest medicine he had ever practiced. Because of the dust and heat of the tropics, the worst problem was secondary infection. The doctors used the same treatment that had been pioneered during the Spanish Civil War. Once the wound had been dressed and cleaned, bullet or shrapnel extracted, the area was encased in plaster and immobilized. They would open a hole to dress and wash the wound with antiseptic fluids, and, though in time it might become flyblown and full of maggots and drive the soldier nearly demented with irritation, it remained surprisingly clean.

A Filipino came walking up the hill to the Church one day with his arm and shoulder in his hand; except for a few strips of sinew and flesh, it was practically severed. It was a fearful wound, everything had been torn with great force, but fortunately the blood vessels had been smashed and obliterated, so there was little bleeding. Ashton sat him down and trimmed away the dead stuff, the arm and shoulder fell away, and an orderly picked it up and took it outside to the pit where they buried all the amputated limbs. Paul cleaned the space where his scapula had been and dressed the gaping wound. The Filipino soldier, without the slightest display of emotion or pain, then went outside and joined the other walking wounded in the ambulance that waited to take them the 20 miles to the main surgical hospital.

Another man, a Filipino sergeant, was shot in the stomach. Ashton's examination revealed that the bullet had gone through the liver and was arrested in the stomach wall. The surgeon gently bathed and bound the wound and gestured to the orderlies. There was nothing that could be done; they didn't have the facilities for such an operation, and the sergeant would never survive the rough ride to No. 1 Hospital. They placed the litter in a secluded corner of the church along with the other terminal cases. The orderlies had rigged up some screens out of Army blankets so that in death the men might have a quiet dignity and peace. Half an hour later the Filipino started to vomit violently, and an orderly hurried down the aisle to find Ashton. By the time they returned, the man had vomited up the bullet and was lying there on his stretcher, his face creased into the biggest grin. He developed a slight case of jaundice later when they moved him down to No. 2 Hospital but made a complete recovery.

The remarkable thing that those surgeons who were receiving their first experience of battle casualties learned was the ability of the human body to heal from even the most horrific wounds. Other men also survived the "terminal ward." Had they been at home with all the facilities of modern medicine, surgeons would have been obliged to operate, and the chances are the men would have died on the table. And there was the reverse of the coin. Young men succumbed from wounds that were superficial and minor. In these cases what the surgeons could not diagnose let alone cure was the searing experience of battle on the human mind. In such instances the man had lost the will to live.

Thursday, January 15, 1942
Fort Mills
Corregidor

The single hope that fortified the men on Bataan and Corregidor was their belief that somehow large reinforcements, shiploads of food and supplies, would break through the Japanese blockade and come to their rescue!

San Francisco radio stations, in particular William Winter, a newscaster on station KGEL, were listened to avidly by the beleaguered forces. Winter told them of the newspaper headlines, eight columns high in *The New York Times*, "ALL AID PROMISED—PRESIDENT PLEDGES PROTECTION," and of similar stories. The morale of the garrison soared after hearing such words of comfort from a caring outside world. General MacArthur's headquarters was inundated with encouraging words of imminent rescue. At the end of the Arcadia Conference, General Marshall, the Chief of Staff, sent USAFFE that part of the communiqué that referred specifically to their plight:

A STREAM OF FOUR-ENGINE BOMBERS, PREVIOUSLY DELAYED BY FOUL WEATHER, IS EN ROUTE. . . . ANOTHER STREAM OF SIMILAR BOMBERS STARTED TODAY FROM HAWAII STAGING AT NEW ISLAND FIELDS. TWO GROUPS OF POWERFUL MEDIUM BOMBERS OF LONG RANGE AND HEAVY BOMB-LOAD CAPACITY LEAVE NEXT WEEK. PURSUIT PLANES ARE COMING ON EVERY SHIP WE CAN USE. . . . EVERY DAY OF TIME YOU GAIN IS VITAL TO THE CONCENTRATION OF THE OVERWHELMING POWER NECESSARY TO OUR PURPOSE.

MacArthur translated this optimism from home into a communiqué to the troops which did more than anything to sustain those who chose still to believe that their country would not abandon them to the enemy. From the mighty guns on Corregidor to the platoons slugging it out on the Abucay line, MacArthur ordered the following message to be read to all troops:

> HELP IS ON ITS WAY FROM THE UNITED STATES. THOU-SANDS OF TROOPS AND HUNDREDS OF PLANES ARE BEING DISPATCHED. THE EXACT TIME OF ARRIVAL OF REIN-FORCEMENTS IS UNKNOWN, AS THEY WILL HAVE TO FIGHT THROUGH JAPANESE. . . . IT IS IMPERATIVE THAT OUR TROOPS HOLD UNTIL THESE REINFORCEMENTS ARRIVE.

General Drake, in anticipation of relief, had signaled the new headquarters in Australia with detailed lists of their requirements. At the same time, this cautious soldier went ahead and planned to run small blockade runners from beyond the Japanese lines in the southern islands. He knew that running in supplies to a be-leaguered garrison was not impossible; after all, the British were doing something similar to relieve their garrison in Malta. What he didn't know was that an American carrier, the U.S.S. *Wasp*, was already en route to lend support in the Mediterranean.

Drake selected Panay, less than a day's sailing to the south of Corregidor, as the likely southern terminus; there was plenty of rice on this fertile island. He calculated that they should be able to run the blockade and feed the Bataan garrison, he hoped for some months to come, without draining the resources on Corregidor. The island had in Capiz a small coastal port ideally located on its northern shore from which ships could make the round trip to Corregidor in two nights.

On Tuesday, January 20, the specially chartered ship, the inter-island trader *Legaspi*, made its first successful run into the South Dock on Corregidor.

Drake also decided to send some of his Filipino officers as agents into the provinces of Batangas and Cavite, to the south of Corregi-dor, across the South Channel. These provinces could supply the garrisons with rice, bananas, coconuts, and livestock, especially cattle, pigs, and chickens. He selected Looc Cove in Batangas as the loading point. The area was mountainous, had few trails, and was infested with Japanese patrols—but these could be checked and monitored. The run to Looc Cove, a distance of about 15 miles, meant that the ships could leave Corregidor after dark, proceed through the minefields, move well out into the South China Sea, and then head directly into the cove. There would still be time for them to load supplies, negotiate the minefields, and dock at Corregidor before daylight. It all required careful timing and a clearly understood system of signaling. Drake chartered two ships for these hazardous missions, the *Bohol II* and the *Kolambugan*, each of about 500 tons' cargo capacity.

In the next month the vessels each made only two successful round trips to Looc Cove; there were a number of abortive missions when they failed to make contact with the agents ashore.

In the southern Philippine Islands, Drake had opened up, prior to the war, a supply depot at Cebu, on Cebu Island. It was intended at first to supply the garrisons in that region. However, it became apparent following the isolation of Luzon that Cebu could be a base for the assembly of the supplies routed north from Australia.

Cebu was to become of primary importance in the lifeline, their hope of salvation. Drake notified Australia to route all vessels destined for Bataan and Corregidor to Cebu for unloading. There his agents chartered local interisland steamers in readiness to make the run into Corregidor.

In Brisbane two officers arrived from Washington with $10 million to bribe mercantile captains to make the run to Cebu. Even at that price there were very few takers.

4th U.S. Marines
Beach defenses
Corregidor

While the battle raged along the Abucay line, the Marines deployed to their allotted defense sectors, dodged the daily bombing raids, and dug in along the beaches and clifftops of Corregidor. The Rock may not have been in the front line, but it had become the nerve center of the American effort, the citadel of American hopes, and the Marines were the only beach defense troops the fortress had. Colonel Howard established regimental headquarters in the Navy tunnel and directed the operation. Howard had at first questioned the wisdom of moving a crack infantry regiment away from Bataan and the main battle. However, from the first there was no doubt. MacArthur's Chief of Staff, Richard Sutherland, was adamant that they should provide the beach defenses for Corregidor.

The 1st Battalion covered the most likely invasion beaches from Malinta Tunnel to the island's tail. The beaches from Bottomside west to Morrison Hill and Ramsey Ravine were given to the 3rd Battalion, and the rest of the island, the high cliffs and shoreline of Topside, became the concern of the 2nd Battalion. Regimental reserve, HQ, and service companies bivouacked in Government Ravine, directly below batteries Geary and Crockett. Shelters, weapons pits, and pillboxes assumed the separate identity of their owners as Marines scrounged what local building materials they could find.

From December 30 until the end, the Marines bivouacked, slept, worked, and ate in the foxholes, caves, and trenches to which they had been assigned. A considerable amount of work had been done on the west and middle sectors before the Marines had arrived on Corregidor. But very little had been attempted in the vulnerable eastern sector, that part of the island most accessible from the sea, except for a line of concrete trenches along a "final defense line" on the eastern side of Malinta Hill. In other places veteran Marines were less than happy with many of the positions that had already been prepared. So many artillery and machine-gun posts were relocated and new ones were established. Marines turned to the backbreaking toil of stringing mile upon mile of barbed wire while others, in scenes reminiscent of a medieval siege, built makeshift bomb chutes over the cliffs.

Corporal Finken was out on Geary Point. The gunners donated some 12-by-12 timbers, and with these his squad constructed a pillbox. There was no great hurry as they fashioned a lean-to and roofed their home with timbers and sandbags.

Sgt. William Griffiths was at the opposite end of the island, at Monkey Point. Here he built a command post large enough to accommodate his men and from which they could observe across the bay to Cavite. Griffiths soon understood why Corregidor was called the Rock; it took his squad days of hard digging to make a hole 3 feet deep.

Al Broderick was much in demand. He was one of the few Marines who had done a course on field fortifications before the war. There was plenty of wire available but no stakes, so he had to improvise these out of rocks. Broderick worked his way along the beaches showing the companies how to fashion their own concertina wire and defend their front. It took him ten days to lay a double apron of wire along the beaches, but there were no land mines available to make the positions secure.

For all the Marines, life on the beach defenses soon settled into a daily routine. They had sleeping holes and just before dawn moved to their weapon pits for "stand to," when a duty NCO did the rounds and ensured that all the positions were manned and ready for action. "Stand to" usually lasted for about an hour; then the majority of men were dismissed for breakfast. A small patrol from each company searched the shoreline, coves, beaches, and wire to check that there had been no enemy infiltration during the night. They spent the day improving the gun positions and staying under cover. The days were long and boring, with little to break the monotony except an occasional weapon drill and, of course, the air raids. Sometimes the senior noncoms held school, but instructions had to be carried out in small groups. Once it got dark and the men had been given the second and main meal, the real work began. Wiring details headed down to the beach to improve or perhaps repair the damage caused by the bombing. Loading parties moved stores from the dockside to the tunnels, and fighting patrols watched for indications of invasion, though most reckoned that Bataan would have to fall before the Japanese hit Corregidor. Marines off duty visited their buddies or gathered around the nearest radio tuned to the United States.

Enlisted men are a lot harder to fool than most generals think. The Marines on Corregidor had a fair idea of just how desperate their predicament was. The word drifted down the line from Bataan, and many recognized that the propaganda coming out of the headquarters in Malinta Tunnel bore no relation to the situation as they saw things. The scant respect that the Marines had for the Army was also influenced by what many of these regular troops saw as the pack of lies they were being fed.

Food was already scarce and rationed, though the amount and quality varied considerably from one position to another. Sergeant Bigelow had a platoon from the service company composed of new draftees, almost all of whom were Air Corps graduates from the

Philippine Military Academy at Baguio. These young aristocrats, taught to fly aircraft that no longer existed, were drafted into the Marines to be trained as infantry, and because they were Filipinos their diet was based on rice. Each morning at about 0500 hours they received a couple of large spoonfuls of rice and some prunes. At about 1700 hours they had the same quantity of rice, this time supplemented with a little meat or vegetables.

Al Broderick, in common with most other Marines, had a bottle of cold coffee and a canteen cupful of cracked wheat for breakfast. In the evening the ration was an ice-cream dip of rice with a little corned-beef gravy; an 8-ounce can of corned beef was shared among ten men.

At least where Broderick was they were well off for water. A little creek came down from the galleries above on Topside. They had a fair flow of water, as it was still near the rainy season. It was enough to keep a little rock pool full.

The Marines on Corregidor probably had more to eat than the troops on Bataan, and as the Marines on Corregidor were not physically involved in battle, their needs were less. However, there were few places to forage on the island; it was largely devoid of wildlife. Corporal Finken was close enough to the bakeries on Bottomside to be attracted to the smell of freshly baked bread and was not above stealing an occasional loaf whenever the opportunity arose. An air raid would often result in large numbers of fish floating belly side up, casualties of the bombs that fell in the bay. For those Marines who were prepared to take their chances with sharks and Zeros, those were a welcome addition to the daily diet.

For a while there was another source of forage. The Japanese had sunk a couple of barges close to Geary Point. Some of the cargo floated out of the holds, and the current carried the flotsam fairly close to the beach. While their comrades stood watch, others swam out to the wreck. There were a few barrels of flour, corn, and sugar, and these gave the cooks in the 2nd Battalion the opportunity to practice their culinary arts making fritters.

Corporal Finken swam out and bagged a barrel of raisins and another full of syrup. His squad rigged up a still behind a searchlight battery. They filled a barrel—one third raisins and another of syrup—some water, and a little rice to start the fermentation. After a couple of days they drew off the liquid into some smaller barrels, placed them under shady ferns, and put a piece of glass over the top. They let the brew cook for about a week and then tapped the bottom. The liquid was rather cloudy, but it was the unanimous opinion of those invited that it was "a delicate vintage and tasty to the palate."

Broderick had already made two trips to the barge when he spied a large crate floating out to sea. He was not the world's greatest swimmer, but he reached the case, kicked out, and pushed hard against the current for the shore. He had learned as a California boy never to fight currents but to let them help, so he saved his strength, kept a firm grip on his find, and waited to drift in farther along the beach. Even so, it was almost too much. Finally he got close enough for two Marines to jump in and help him, exhausted, to the shore. He lay on the beach and recovered his breath while the others carried the crate to the galley. Eventually he felt well enough to stagger after them and see what treasures he had rescued.

The crate contained four 1-gallon jars of ink. Broderick, wet and bedraggled, came close to tears as he surveyed his find. The mess sergeant demanded to know what he intended to do with them.

"Well, maybe we can trade them for something," Broderick spluttered as he coughed up yet another lungful of seawater.

The guns suddenly opened fire. Broderick heard a whistle and as he ducked, a piece of shrapnel came between them and shattered two of the jars. He left a speechless mess sergeant to clean up the ink; he much preferred to take his chances with the barrage and the bombs.

Wednesday, January 14, 1942
41st Field Artillery
Abucay line

Unremitting Japanese pressure was at last beginning to tell on the forces holding the Abucay line. Units were falling back, and a number of dangerous salients had formed. One was a small arrowhead ravine, about 150 yards long and perhaps 60 yards at its widest, in which a Japanese company had established foxholes and thrust out the defenders. Though the Filipinos of the 41st Division held the sides, the Japanese were able, especially at night, to pour a devastatingly effective fire into their flanks. Two attempts by the defenders to rout the enemy had ended in bloody failure, and the Filipinos were beginning to wilt under the pressure.

Winston Jones directed his guns onto the ravine and produced some of the most accurate artillery fire of the campaign. There was no margin for error, so he personally laid the first gun of Battery Able onto the target and dropped the shell plumb into the center of the ravine. Very deliberately his subordinates brought the other three gun sections to bear, and the battery followed with a sustained barrage. So accurate was the fire that the Filipino infantry lined the ravine and picked off the disconcerted Japanese as they were forced out of their foxholes. After half an hour a battalion group swept through the ravine, mopped up the last of the enemy resistance, and restored the line.

The divisional commander, Gen. Vincente Lim, who had personally witnessed the engagement, wrote a citation for the Legion of Merit for Winston Jones and awarded him a field promotion to major.

Saturday, January 17, 1942
Abucay Hacienda

Though the 41st Division in the center of the line, largely due to the efforts of Jones and his artillery, was now holding firm, disaster struck on their left flank.

In an effort to recapture lost ground, battalions of the 51st Division disintegrated in their own counterattack. The Japanese 141st Infantry had found the weak link for which they had sought so diligently and wreaked havoc at what had now become the center of the defenses. At the same time the 9th Japanese Infantry, which had set out a week before on its long outflanking march and had remained undetected by the defenders, suddenly burst out of the foothills of Mount Natib and caught the exposed and unsuspecting Filipinos in the flank. The 51st Philippine Infantry Regiment fled to the rear and in so doing presented the enemy with the opportunity to roll up the Abucay line from the left flank. The 2nd Regiment of the 51st Division, the 53rd Infantry, was forced to give ground and eventually started to retreat in some disorder westward across the lower jungle-covered slopes of Mount Natib and all the way into the thinly held right flank positions of Wainwright's I Corps.

General Parker had recognized the gravity of his position almost as soon as the 51st Division gave way. He ordered up his corps reserve, the 31st U.S. Infantry and the 45th Philippine Scouts, to counterattack the Japanese at Abucay Hacienda. The critical point of the battle had been reached. If General Nara pressed home his advantage, he could envelop the entire II Corps and hem it in against Manila Bay. Already he had driven a wedge deep into the defense line, and against such pressure Wainwright on the West Coast would have no alternative but to withdraw to keep in step with the other corps.

The Japanese paused for a few hours to reorganize. Colonel Takechi's 9th Infantry was, despite its success, in considerable disarray, and he was hopelessly lost and unaware of the disaster he could inflict upon the defenders. This gave sufficient time for the American infantry and the Scouts to complete their long approach march and prepare to counterattack at dawn.

The American infantry dumped their heavy packs at the assembly point and then headed through the jungle, led by jittery Filipino guides. Bill Garleb still retained his gas mask pouch but had long since discarded the mask; like the rest, he used it to carry other things—a few pieces of shrapnel, a small Bible, and photographs of home.

After four hours of forced marching the company stopped for a rest. Garleb eased the shoulder straps of his webbing, took off his tin hat, and reached for the mess cans into which he had packed some boiled monkey bananas. He peeled one and started to eat.

Shortly after the noncoms gathered the men into line, they continued the march through the jungle. Since the majority of his life had not been very satisfying to Garleb, he had developed the knack of turning off to the reality of his surroundings and daydreaming, and his thoughts turned to the coming battle, his own baptism by fire, and he tried to analyze his own feelings. He felt neither fear nor apprehension, but rather a detached, almost scientific curiosity: How would he handle the coming battle? How would he behave? He realized that for the first time in his life there was no turning back—he couldn't ask his parents what he should do. He was on his own, and whether he survived would depend very largely upon his own behavior.

Early the next morning, they moved through the artillery lines and came across signs of the previous battle. Clothing was scattered all over the place, ammunition pouches and weapons littered the empty foxholes. The attack was due to start at 0815 hours. While the troops waited amid the debris of the last battle, officers checked their watches and made their plans.

The regiment was to advance astride Trail 12, which was about a mile to the east of Abucay Hacienda. The 1st Battalion was to move to the left of the trail, and the 2nd Battalion along it and to the right, with the 3rd Battalion in reserve. On the regiment's right, the 45th Philippine Scouts were due to launch their attack, but they had gotten lost during the night approach. The objective was to secure the line to the Balantay River and, in the case of the American infantry, recapture the hacienda.

The battle lasted for five days without a break, and by the end of that time the Americans and the Scouts were drained. They had little or no sleep and very little hot food, and most of the troops sustained themselves by eating raw sugar cane.

The Japanese counterattacked at night and invariably won back the ground they had lost. By day their snipers played havoc among the unsuspecting Americans. Climbing into clumps of bamboo and onto the limbs of trees, the sniper would camouflage his position and stay there for days on end. He would eat a little rice and then drink some water; this caused his stomach to swell and helped to dampen the pangs of hunger. More than one American ration party had been ambushed by snipers on its way up the line.

Bill Garleb was a company runner when the 3rd Battalion moved into the battle on the second day. The regiment was still short of its objectives as the Japanese fiercely contested every yard of ground. His machine-gun company deployed in support of the assault launched by F Company of the regiment's 2nd Battalion. They had made little progress through the closely packed trees and dense undergrowth before they were pinned down by accurate Japanese small-arms fire.

Garleb rolled into a deserted foxhole, and a man with a Garand followed. The young soldier, who was shaking with fear, threw the rifle at him. "I can't stand it anymore!" he cried. "My buddies are dead!" He begged Garleb to shoot him through the hand. Garleb felt disgusted and revolted; he wanted to shoot him through the head.

Just at that moment Garleb heard a noise behind him and the fire of a heavier-caliber weapon. Garleb grabbed the Garand, turned to the back of the foxhole, clipped off the safety catch, and curled his finger around the trigger. In close country such as this the Garand was an ideal weapon; it didn't have the bolt action of the Springfield but instead could be pumped like a submachine gun. Garleb saw the undergrowth to his left move; he took careful aim, settled more comfortably into the textbook prone position, took the first pressure on the trigger, and prepared to enter the war. The soldier beside him blubbered in the bottom of the trench, Garleb held his breath, shut his mind to the whimpering, and waited for his moment.

The bushes parted and out stepped two American officers and a Philippine Scout. The latter wore a canvas vest that had pockets bulging with drums of ammunition; in his hand he carried a .45-caliber Thompson.

Garleb scrambled from his foxhole and asked them what they were doing there. "We're hunting snipers," one of the officers replied, somewhat taken aback by Garleb's sudden appearance.

Garleb, who was very angry, told them they were about to fire into their own troops.

The younger of the lieutenants thanked him for the warning, obviously relieved that their adventure had not ended in disaster.

The other officer pointed to the man in the bottom of the foxhole and told Garleb to take him back to his command post before he did any damage.

Garleb saluted, pulled the soldier out of the trench, and prodded the bundle of human misery in the general direction of battalion headquarters.

Garleb handed the man over to a medic and waited outside the command post for reassignment. After a short while a runner staggered in and Garleb, out of curiosity, followed him inside the bunker. He listened as the runner reported that his outfit was pinned down on the left flank out by the sugar cane, and that Lieutenant Magee needed a volunteer and a sack of grenades. Major Moffat looked around him. "That's me," Garleb said before he realized he had spoken. Some officers opened up a fresh box of grenades; there were a dozen of the old World War I vintage and four new pattern grenades. Garleb piled them into a haversack and followed the runner out into a ravine, at the base of which they came to an aid station. One of the men lying there had his head swathed in bandages, and his thumb had been shot off. As the corpsman bandaged his hand he was singing, "God Bless America."

"Gee, how corny can you get?" Garleb asked, embarrassed by his display of excessive patriotism.

They climbed out of the ravine, followed the sound of battle, and came across Lieutenant Magee and his platoon pinned down on the edge of a field of sugar cane. Garleb took up his position next to a soldier he knew as Henderson; he was armed with a Browning automatic rifle.

"Okay, you guys, give me covering fire," Garleb shouted above the clatter of small arms. "I'll count to three each time and then throw a grenade."

He was lying in a shallow shell scrape, so he had to rise to his knees to get enough impetus for the throw. The machine-gun fire was so heavy that sugar cane fell as if it were being reaped.

Seven times Garleb risked his neck; each time he hugged the earth as bullets stitched the ground in front of him. All the grenades he threw were duds. "Fucking old ammunition," he wailed as he reached deeper into his bag for the more modern grenades.

Henderson was even more frustrated and stood up straight. "Get outta here, you dirty yellow Jap sonofabitch," he yelled, the BAR bucking and kicking as he let off a long burst in the direction of the enemy machine-gun nest. Garleb seized his opportunity and hurled two of the new grenades at the Japanese position. Sugar cane flamed to the explosions.

There was silence.

"Okay," Magee said, "we'll go around and come into the cane from the left. You two," he pointed to Garleb and Henderson, "keep up a covering fire until I blow my whistle."

Garleb and Henderson did as they were ordered and when the whistle blew moved forward through the cane. It was like trying to walk through a brick wall. They came to a small trail and met up with the rest of the party. Carefully they worked their way forward, passed a dead American on the way, and came to what had been the machine-gun nest. The position, a mound of earth thrown up around a shell hole, was deserted; the enemy had departed, though in their haste they had left behind a smashed tripod and some ammunition. Magee checked the area and then led the platoon back the way they had come. They passed the dead American; he was lying face down on the trail, a gaping red hole in his back.

"Get his dog tags," Magee said.

Garleb reached down, grabbed the collar, and turned the body over. He recoiled in horror. Instead of the usual tape the man had a gold chain supporting his tags, but under his throat was a small hole about the size of a dollar piece, and it was ringed with ants.

"Pick him up and we'll carry him back," the lieutenant ordered. Henderson handed Garleb his BAR, picked up the body, and slung it over his shoulder, head down. The nose started to bleed, and sightless eyes stared at Garleb as if in reproach.

Company B, 31st Infantry
In the sugar cane, below Abucay Hacienda

Company B had lost sixteen men dead and many more wounded, and they were pinned down just below a ridge line before the hacienda. A field of sugar cane separated them from their objective.

Paul Kerchum was in the heavy weapons section. He and his machine-gun squad had set up their gun in a grove of acacia trees that lay close to the field of sugar cane. From there, machine gunners were able to give covering fire to the rest of the company who had taken cover around them. Just across what seemed to be the fields, and in clear view on the skyline, stood the hacienda, the battalion's object in the counterattack. The Japanese, however, had spotted the position of the machine gun and had opened up one of their deadly barrages of mortar shells. American casualties were mounting, but nobody seemed willing to make the first move to continue the advance and sustain the momentum of the counterattack.

Now, there is a species of large red ant that nests in the acacia tree; they rear up on their hind legs and growl at their prey. Somehow Kerchum must have disturbed their nest, for some had gotten into his pants and were biting him hard. Eventually he could stand it no longer and in the midst of the barrage jumped to his feet. "Let's do something! Let's go ahead or go back, but let's do something!" he pleaded, and he began to run toward the hacienda.

The company charged out of the grove and into the sugar cane, bayoneting those few Japanese who were foolhardy enough to stand their ground. The impetus of the attack might well have carried the company all the way to the hacienda had not a deep sunken valley, which had hitherto been hidden from view, suddenly emerged to block their way. The last of the Japanese who were able scampered down the valley sides and were soon lost from sight in the thick undergrowth. The Americans dug in along the crest and awaited developments. Even Kerchum felt there had been enough excitement for one day, and he was no more anxious than the next man to pursue the Japanese into the unknown valley. So they dug their foxholes and awaited what they believed would be the inevitable counterattack.

There was a man in the outfit called Lineberg. Later that afternoon he was looking down over the valley from his foxhole when he spotted a small Japanese patrol moving through a glade in the valley floor below. It was strange because the Japanese didn't look up and obviously had no idea the Americans were there. Before the rest of the company could react, Lineberg grabbed his Garand and shot them all. Lineberg was beside himself with pleasure at his achievement. In great glee he jumped out of the hole and ran down to his kill, where he quickly looted the bodies and returned to his own position unscathed.

Kerchum thought he was lucky, but Lineberg was now convinced that the war was "a real picnic" and the Japanese "suckers." That evening he grabbed a bag of grenades and announced that he was going off "to hunt some Japs."

Private Lineberg headed out into the sugar cane and was never seen again.

Company B had now reached the limit of their advance. Perhaps if some officers had been able to capitalize on the initial momentum caused by Paul Kerchum's private agony, more could have been achieved; but that was not to be the case.

Regimental headquarters of the 31st Infantry tried to attack through Company B's positions and take the next ridge line across the valley, but the assault failed. Company L of the 3rd Battalion passed through and launched their attack; they relied heavily upon grenades to clear a path through the sugar cane and dense jungle scrub. Like Garleb they found the majority of them were duds and paid heavily for their government's parsimony. They fell back in considerable disorder through Kerchum's position; some were badly wounded. Kerchum helped one man whose leg was bloody. The knee was shattered, and his thumb was hanging by a thread. He didn't seem to notice his leg. All he could say to Kerchum was, "Watch my thumb, watch my thumb."

Headquarters now decided to set fire to the cane field. They detailed the 81mm mortars of the heavy weapons section with the task. The correct ammunition for these weapons was in the holds of the *Pensacola* convoy now thousands of miles away in Australia; but the armorers had attempted to adapt and improvise. They used spare 75mm shells. The only thing they had in common with the mortar was vintage.

The experiment failed disastrously. Though a number landed in the sugar cane and had the desired effect, the majority wobbled in flight and fell short, the salvoes bursting with devastating effect along the ridge line held by B Company. By the time the company commander, hollering "Don't fire! Don't fire!" on the radio had stopped the barrage, the damage had been done, and there were another dozen names to add to the regiment's Honor Roll. As if that weren't enough, the wind changed direction. Flames and smoke swept back into the American position and made the foxholes untenable. It had been a costly battle for the battalion. The shaken survivors were forced to evacuate their positions and move back about 900 yards to the next ridge line. The Japanese followed up and launched a number of heavy attacks against the position, but Kerchum's machine guns, massed along the ridge, beat them back, though they were able to infiltrate snipers through the lines.

The next morning Kerchum returned to his post from the battalion headquarters leading in a Filipino labor detail with fresh supplies of ammunition. Kerchum crouched low and moved quickly, and the Filipinos followed as best they could. Once they had reached the safety of their own lines, he relaxed a little and chewed on a long stalk of sugar cane. He bounced the cane playfully on the helmet of his chum Red Brown as he passed Brown's foxhole and was about to distribute the ammunition to the guns.

"Get down, get down," Sergeant Sutton hissed.

Kerchum looked up to where the sergeant was taking cover behind a tree.

"There's a sniper out there. They've just shot Red."

Kerchum looked back in dumb horror to his friend's stand-up foxhole. He had thought he was bending forward, resting; now from this position he could see he was dead.

Monday, January 19, 1942
Company H, 31st Infantry
The ravine on Trail 12
Abucay line

Bill Garleb found that in combat he was good at something at last. In the five days of battle he experienced success as a soldier. He was really alive, and his senses were alive. He found no joy in killing, but his intent was to stop the enemy from killing him, and in that he discovered both excitement and confidence in his own training and abilities.

They had driven the Japanese out of the cane field on their part of the front and pushed them down into a ravine, from where the enemy had defied all attempts to dislodge him. Eventually, in a three-company attack, the battalion engaged in a vicious fire fight which won them some ground, but at a fearful price. The Japanese retreated to a hill about 440 yards away. From that commanding position they were able to pour a withering fire down on the Americans. The latter took the rest of the day to negotiate the precipitous ravine and a small stream at its bottom and then deployed along the trail on the other side that led to the jungle-covered slopes. By that time they were ordered to dig in and wait for the dawn. The plan was to attack the hill at daylight.

Lieutenant Magee placed his men at 10-foot intervals on either side of the trail. He carefully pointed out their arcs of fire and warned them to be on their guard against Japanese infiltrators. Corporal Piper was sent out to scout the ground ahead. The scout had been gone for some time, and it was quite dark when they heard a movement on the trail ahead of them. A soldier on the opposite side of Garleb was the point man in the platoon. He jumped up and Piper yelled, "Don't shoot! Don't shoot!" Garleb watched frozen with horror as the soldier put six rounds into Corporal Piper.

Before the squad could react to the tragedy, the Japanese straddled the trail with an accurate mortar bombardment. The deadly little knee mortars worked their way through the American positions with pinpoint accuracy. One shell, luckily a dud, hit Garleb on the side of his tin hat; the force slammed his head into the ground and broke his glasses.

Magee ordered the platoon to fall back; he could see no value in staying in such a vulnerable position and taking casualties. It was pitch black, the undergrowth flaring only to the burst of the mortar shells. Magee led, followed by a staff sergeant and the now hysterical soldier who had killed Piper. Garleb came next, then Henderson and the rest of the platoon. Each man grabbed the belt of the one in front. As they entered the little path that wound its way down the precipitous side of the ravine, Garleb suddenly realized that there was no one behind him. By now the knee mortars had been outranged, but their place had been taken by equally accurate field artillery. In these circumstances there was little the four could do but press on until they found some cover. The little group reached the bottom of the ravine, splashed through the stream, and tried to find the pathway that led out of the ravine on the other side. It was hopeless in the dark and Magee, finding a sheltered overhang, decided that they should wait for daylight. The four of them clambered onto the ledge; their legs dangled in the water.

It became apparent that the Japanese were launching an attack and that they were in the middle of the battle. American Stokes mortars began to explore the ravine bottom, and then a 75mm field battery joined in, too. Heavier-caliber shells whanged overhead as the artillery duel reached a crescendo.

The soldier who had killed Corporal Piper lost control of his bowels and whimpered pathetically, "We're going to get killed, we're all going to be killed. My God, don't let us die."

They heard Japanese assault troops splash through the stream and move ever nearer to their position. Magee pulled his pistol and turned to the whimpering wreck.

"Shut your goddamn mouth. If you don't keep quiet I'll blow your fucking head off."

The Japanese passed within feet of their position but amid the thunder and noise of the barrage they were not detected, not even when the enemy moved back through the ravine after their assault had failed.

With the first gray streaks of dawn, they found the path to safety and scuttled quickly back to their lines.

Major Moffat greeted them at company HQ with the words, "We thought you were dead."

The rest of the platoon had scrambled across the ravine and made it safely to the lines before the Japanese had launched their infantry assault.

Thursday, January 22, 1942
141st Japanese Infantry
Abucay line

It was now the turn of the Americans to defend. Leaving enough troops to contain the 41st (PA) Division and the Scouts on the coast, the Japanese concentrated the bulk of their forces across the Balantay River, just to the northwest of Abucay Hacienda.

The attack began at noon with a heavy air attack and then, behind a rolling artillery barrage, a thousand Japanese infantry hit the exposed battalions of the 31st U.S. Infantry. After the incident on the ravine, Garleb and the others had dug foxholes in the sugar cane field and prepared for the Japanese attack. The American infantrymen were near the end of their tether. The asinine tactics of their officers had caused needless casualties, while their disregard for the requirements of life had meant that the men had gone without adequate food for days at a time. Even if he was a high school dropout, Garleb could see the futility of foxholes in a field of sugar cane. From the air the fresh black earth against the green background of the sugar cane was an easy indicator for the dive bombers. They withstood the dive bombers and the artillery for as long as they could, but in their already weakened state this called on their last remaining shreds of reserve and courage. On more than one occasion that terrible day Garleb was lifted 4 or 5 feet off the ground by a near miss and slammed back into the earth. They screamed and prayed and burrowed deep into the earth, they called on God, their president, and their mothers to save them from the torment; but to no avail. Toward late afternoon a break occurred in the bombardment, and the troops fell back. Though they moved quietly and in good order, they had taken enough. By dark they were back where they had been days before, at the very start of the counterattack.

General Parker reported that the counteroffensive by the leading elements of the Philippine division, the 31st U.S. Infantry, and the 45th Philippine Scouts, had failed.

Though Wainwright's forces had fared better on the West Coast, they had been sorely tried, come under considerable pressure, and been forced to give some ground.

General MacArthur preferred to send his chief of staff across to Bataan to see and report on the situation personally. Upon Sutherland's recommendation MacArthur ordered a phased withdrawal to the reserve line along the Pilar-Bagac Road, where he planned to make his final stand. He wired Washington:

I HAVE PERSONALLY SELECTED AND PREPARED THIS POSITION, AND IT IS STRONG.

3. The Battle of the Points

Thursday, January 22, 1942–
Tuesday, February 10, 1942

Thursday, January 22, 1942

General Kimura sent the 2nd Battalion, 20th Infantry by landing barge to outflank Wainwright's forces. They were ordered to land at Caibob Point, some 5 miles below Bagac. The operation was a complete shambles. The Japanese had not been able to make an adequate reconnaissance, except from the air, and had no detailed maps or charts of the area. By pure chance the barges were caught by a patrol of American motor torpedo boats and dispersed in the confusion and darkness. Those who survived drifted far to the south. Some made a landfall at Quinauan Point, while others ended up in a cove at Longoskawayan Point, just a couple of miles from Mariveles.

The Americans had had prior warning of the operation. A courier traveling from the Japanese Fourteenth Army headquarters at Fort Stotsenberg to the command post of the 20th Infantry in Bataan became lost and strayed into an American patrol. In the skirmish that ensued, he was killed. His documents were sent back to I Corps headquarters, and Richard Sakakida translated them. The papers provided detailed information about the operation, except the landing beach, which was in code. The defenders now had some idea as to Japanese intentions and could plan accordingly. Two torpedo boats were dispatched each night to patrol inshore along the coastline of the South China Sea.

A second warning, though one that went unheeded, was provided by Massello's radar operators. The night of the landings, the telephone rang in Massello's command post. It was the searchlight and radar unit on Pucot Hill, directly above Mariveles. The operators reported they had a contact on their screens.

Massello asked if they were sure.

They told him they had checked the set out that afternoon, and it was working perfectly.

Massello immediately informed Col. Guy Stubbs, who was their artillery coordinator between Bataan and Corregidor, and Stubbs promised to let the Air Corps know. The Air Corps radar, higher up in the Mariveles Mountains, was a more modern set, and it was reputed to have first-rate operators. They searched but could find nothing, so Stubbs telephoned Massello to tell him that his men must be mistaken, since according to the Air Corps there was nothing out there.

Massello checked again with his own people. They were in no doubt and still had a contact. The battery commander thought for a moment and then ordered his No. 1 light to illuminate and sweep the area where the contact had been reported. The telephone at the command post rang immediately; this time it was the angry regimental commander, Colonel Chase on Corregidor, asking Massello what he meant having his lights on to search the ocean.

He explained that they had picked up a blip on their radar, although the Air Corps couldn't find anything, and that he thought there was a possibility of a landing party out there and was using the light to verify the radar.

The colonel firmly reminded Massello that he was anti-aircraft and ordered him to turn the lights off before slamming the receiver down in Massello's ear.

Massello turned to Lieutenant Colson in the command post, and they discussed what they should do next. Massello decided to ignore Chase, even though he was the regimental commander, for he was safe and sound on Corregidor while they were on Bataan. He felt that he could not afford to take the gamble that the Air Corps might be right. So he ordered his No. 2 light, located farther north, to make a sweep out to sea. This time the telephone nearly fell out of its cradle, so persistent was the ring.

It was Chase bellowing at him about the lights.

"What lights?" Massello asked innocently.

"There are lights on out to sea," said a confused Chase.

Massello soothed the colonel by suggesting that the lights might belong to the 515th, who were north of them. The colonel hung up after reminding Massello not to turn his lights on anymore.

They continued the search throughout the night, and though the radar continued to report the contact, the searchlights found nothing. It was a dark, moonless night with low, heavy clouds rolling in off the sea and a mist that the lights could not penetrate.

Early the next morning the No. 1 light post came on the phone again to report a Japanese landing party on the beaches below them.

Massello ordered them not to get involved but to protect themselves and their equipment while the Army took care of the Japanese.

In this instance it was the newly formed naval battalion that was sent in against the Japanese landing. The men on the *Canopus* dropped everything and quickly organized an ammunition party and reinforcements to move up to help their hard-pressed comrades.

Pilots and mechanics from the grounded 3rd Pursuit Squadron joined in the battle and helped contain the three hundred Japanese until regular infantry could arrive. In this action they were doubly fortunate, for the cove was within range of the mighty guns on Corregidor. After some delay and confusion the 12-inch mortars of Battery Geary came into action for their first real shoot of the war. The bombardment was also the first time that American heavy-caliber coast artillery had fired in anger since the Civil War.

The bulk of the Japanese battalion, some six hundred men, had landed farther north at Quinauan Point, about midway between Mariveles and Bagac. As with the southern landing, the thick, jungle-covered terrain made organized fighting impossible. By the time the Americans had reacted to the situation, the Japanese had dug in and, with all the advantages of terrain on their side, prepared to resist stubbornly. They were not eliminated until a battalion of the 45th Philippine Scouts with armor and artillery in support mounted a costly assault on their positions. It was February 8 before the last resistance had been overcome.

USAFFE HQ
Malinta Tunnel
Corregidor

In the meantime, a crisis of a different sort was developing on Corregidor. President Quezon had listened to another one of Roosevelt's fireside chats in which he had discussed at great length the scale of the American war effort against Germany. There had been no mention at all of the Philippines, and the old man, now very sick and failing fast, was filled with righteous indignation. Without MacArthur's knowledge he cabled Roosevelt. He said:

THIS WAR IS NOT OF OUR MAKING. NO GOVERNMENT HAS THE RIGHT TO DEMAND LOYALTY FROM ITS CITIZENS BEYOND ITS ABILITY TO RENDER PROTECTION.

Though he ended his message with an eloquent plea for help, the intent was thinly disguised: The Philippine President was clearly contemplating capitulation. It is impossible to offer either an explanation for or to excuse Roosevelt's reply. It was a complete fabrication and a travesty of truth:

ALTHOUGH I CANNOT AT THIS TIME STATE THE DAY THAT HELP WILL ARRIVE IN THE PHILIPPINES, VESSELS FULL OF THE NECESSARY SUPPLIES HAVE BEEN DISPATCHED TO MANILA. OUR ARMS, TOGETHER WITH THOSE OF OUR ALLIES, HAVE DEALT HEAVY BLOWS TO ENEMY TRANS-PORTS AND NAVAL VESSELS. A CONTINUOUS STREAM OF FIGHTER AND PURSUIT PLANES IS TRAVERSING THE PACIFIC. EXTENSIVE ARRIVALS OF TROOPS ARE BEING GUARDED BY ADEQUATE PROTECTIVE ELEMENTS OF OUR NAVY.

Sunday, January 25, 1942
Navy headquarters, Queen Tunnel
Corregidor

Admiral Rockwell called Champlin into his improvised office, swore him to secrecy, and then told him that in the vaults on Corregidor there were about $40 million in gold bars. The Treasury official in charge of the gold, a man named Willoughby, was very concerned about the possible capture of the gold and had, with the blessing of the high commissioner, Francis Sayer, the senior U.S. government representative in the Philippines, appealed to the Navy for help. The commissioner's office had contemplated sinking the gold in relatively shallow water at some definitely fixed points with a view to recovery after the island had been liberated. This confirmed in Champlin's mind that all talk of rescue was merely propaganda. Though he long suspected this to be the case, it still came as a considerable shock to be confronted with the hard truth of their predicament.

"Champ," the admiral said, "I want you to go to Willoughby. I have mentioned your name already to him, and he is expecting you. You will offer him the complete and full cooperation of the Navy and speak as my representative. You are to work and plan with him to any extent necessary to carry out his desires and to preserve this money for the future use of the Philippine and United States governments. This is a matter of utmost secrecy."

Champlin hurried across to Malinta Tunnel and sought out Willoughby. Sinking the gold in carefully selected points in Manila Bay Champlin saw as presenting insurmountable problems. "In the first case, it would have to be a large-scale operation involving a considerable number of men," Champlin said.

"That's bound to raise the question of security," Willoughby agreed.

"Second," Champlin said, "there are problems over location. There are few places where the bottom of Manila Bay is sandy, much of it is mud. It wouldn't take the Japanese long to work out the location."

Willoughby agreed.

"Finally," Champlin said, "there is the question of the containers to be used. How long will it be there? What effect will salt-water corrosion have on the containers?"

The two men agreed to meet again the next day after they had given some more thought to the question.

When they met the next day Champlin was astounded to hear Willoughby announce that the problem had been solved. "There's nothing to worry about, Champ," he said. "The high commissioner presented the problem to General MacArthur at dinner last night. He has offered to take full and complete responsibility on behalf of the Army."

Champlin, somewhat in a daze, returned to Queen Tunnel. He couldn't see how the Army could solve the problem but nevertheless reported this latest development to Admiral Rockwell.

"That's just big talk, Champ," the admiral said. "Don't worry, the problem isn't solved yet."

Monday, January 26, 1942
Anyasan Point

General Homma sent Lieutenant General Morioka, who had been commanding the 16th Division in southern Luzon, into western Bataan to assume command of the operations against Wainwright's I Corps. Homma gave Morioka just two additional battalions and a directive for some decisive action quickly. Morioka dispatched another company, drawn this time from the 1st Battalion of the luckless 20th Infantry, to reinforce the bridgehead at Quinauan Point. Like the other before, this force lost its way at sea and eventually staggered ashore in a cove to the north called Anyasan Point.

Ed Erickson and the rest of the redundant members of the 17th Pursuit Squadron had spent the past two weeks on beach defense along the cliffs above Anyasan Point. The pilots and mechanics, fully alerted, were ready and waiting for the Japanese landing. The methods adopted by the fighter pilots were nothing if not original. As the barges floated in on the tide, the Air Corps dug holes 3 feet deep along the cliff, then stuffed them full with sticks of dynamite, rocks, nails, and anything else they could find. When the barges beached on the shingle below, they pressed the plunger and the whole cliff face fell in on the Japanese. The surviving Japanese sought what cover they could among the debris and rocks that dotted the shoreline.

In the meantime, the withdrawal from the Abucay line had been completed. This move released the Scouts, and Wainwright secured their services from the USAFFE Reserve. The 45th Philippine Scouts moved across Bataan and down into Aglahoma Valley to move against the Japanese at Quinauan Point, while the 2nd Battalion, 57th Infantry was hurried south to relieve the naval infantry and mop up the Japanese bridgehead at Longoskawayan Point.

The following afternoon Ed Erickson was ordered to deliver a dispatch to Wainwright's headquarters. He jumped onto the British Indian Army Enfield, a motorcycle that the squadron had "acquired," and roared off down the jungle trail. Late that evening he returned to the unit. By now he had learned to master the heavy machine and reveled in its power and speed. He was traveling a good deal faster than the conditions warranted when disaster struck. In the twilight, and without lights, he failed to spot a jungle creeper that lay across his path. It caught him under the chin, jerked, and flung him down onto the spinning rear wheel of the motorcycle. Rider and machine careened into the ditch in a tangle of limbs and metal. The force of the crash knocked him out, and when he came to, Ed found he could not move his legs. He lay there for an hour or more, trapped in the wreckage of the bike, before he was found by a passing patrol. An ambulance rushed the now thoroughly frightened Erickson into the hospital—he was convinced he had broken his back and that his flying days were over. Luckily the surgeons found nothing more than strained and torn muscles, and they put him into traction for a couple of days. Erickson's relief knew no bounds. He would be able to fly again!

2nd Battalion, 57th Philippine Scouts
Longoskawayan Point

The Scouts relieved the naval battalion and prepared to reduce the last elements of the Japanese resistance. Once again the Americans learned the lesson that was now so often demonstrated in the campaign: Trained troops can accomplish easily and quickly what untrained men find difficult and therefore costly.

At 0700 hours John Spainhower, the battalion adjutant, ensured that the Scouts were ready on their start line, contacted Battery Geary and gave out the coordinates. Within a couple of minutes the first of the 670-pound land-attack projectiles burst with devastating effect among the Japanese positions. The mortars were firing at a range of some 12,000 yards, only 2,000 yards short of their extreme range; nevertheless, the shells landed right on the target.

The bombardment lifted after an hour and the Scouts moved forward into what was for this battalion their first real action. They behaved superbly, with two companies in the line and a third in reserve. They swept all before them at bayonet point. The shattered and demoralized Japanese fell back in disarray and confusion to the very edge of the cliffs. In the final phase of the action no quarter was asked or given, and by the end of the afternoon the few shattered survivors sought sanctuary in caves along the cliff face.

The Scouts handed the mopping-up operation over to the naval battalion and marched out to their bivouac area. It had been a relatively easy operation for a trained battalion, and they had few casualties. The reduction of the northern beachheads was later to prove a more costly affair, however.

The few Japanese survivors in the cliff at Longoskawayan Point could no longer offer any effective resistance. They had no alternative to surrender save death, and that could serve no useful purpose. Richard Sakakida was summoned from Wainwright's headquarters. He arrived the following morning and broadcast an appeal to the Japanese. Their response was a fusillade of shots that sent the sailors deploying along the beach and running for cover. The crew of the *Canopus* introduced their secret weapon into the fray. They had welded some spare armor plating onto two naval launches, mounted a quick-firing cannon in the bows, and included a couple of .30-calibers for extra punch and air defense. The sailors had nicknamed these strange craft "Mickey Mouse battleships." One of these came chugging into the cove and proceeded to pour round after round into the caves. There was nothing particularly glorious about the last acts of defiance by the Japanese. Unlike the Spartans at Thermopylae or the Texans at the Alamo, no heroism was involved. The sailors regarded this resistance in the caves of the South China Sea as an act of obscenity, one that degraded and befouled human dignity. When they eventually climbed into the last cave they found one crazed and wounded soldier, too badly injured even to take his own life.

693rd Ordnance Company/
Air Corps provisional infantry
Ordnance Supply Dump
Little Baguio

John McCann had spent the last week on detached duty from his unit as part of a guard detail for the huge ordnance and supply dump in the foothills above Mariveles. With two other men, he had set up a guard post in a grove of huge trees outside the perimeter wire of the dump. Brodemeyer, a private first class, was technically in command of the detail, and the third member of the team was Earl Craig. Still only sixteen, he and McCann had enlisted together in San Diego.

Their job was to prevent vehicles from entering the dump at that point and to direct them to the control point on the main gate about a mile down the road. They pitched their pup tent under the roots of a large tree and surveyed their domain. They were right on the bend of a very steep incline, so it was easy to control the traffic. The boys hung a crudely painted sign outside their post which read, "No Japs Beyond This Point"—McCann was still enjoying the war.

At night the trio would rob a truck or two as they left the camp. After a few days, they became quite proficient. As soon as the truck hit the curve, the driver had to shift into bottom gear. The boys took it in turn to run out and jump into the back of the truck and throw out as much stuff as they could before it reached the top of the gradient. When daylight came they recovered their loot from the ditch.

The first night that McCann tried it, he nearly got caught. A second vehicle rounded the bend, and its headlights picked him up as he vaulted for cover into the ditch. When McCann went out the next morning to collect his ill-gotten gains he found the ditch full of saddles and bridles. It was a long time before the other two stopped teasing him about that night's escapade.

Another night yielded four boxes of Australian raisins. They divided them up, using an empty C ration can as a measure, and then started to play poker. By the end of the day, McCann had lost all his raisins to the other two.

The platoon's first sergeant visited them every other day with fresh rations. McCann had heard of the landings at Longoskawayan Point, and he asked if they might go up and see what was happening; he was bored, especially since he had lost all his raisins.

As a matter of fact, the sergeant was looking for a detail to go up to the beaches, for ordnance needed men to look for Japanese weapons. He took McCann and Craig with him, promising to send Brodemeyer a relief detail.

McCann found that they had been detailed to act as porters for an ordnance specialist, an old soldier who had been up and down the ranks with the years. They climbed down onto the beach and had soon collected a pile of weapons. Then they wandered off on their own and met two Scouts who showed them where the Japanese had jumped off the cliffs. After a while McCann noticed that Craig wasn't with them. Slightly concerned, for the occasional shot was still to be heard, they retraced their steps and came upon Craig kneeling beside the body of a dead and very ripe Japanese. He was prying the gold teeth out of his mouth, working them loose with a couple of sticks.

McCann turned away, sickened, and headed back to their stockpile.

The Scouts fed them and then helped carry their weapons to Mariveles Road; there they hitched a ride to Little Baguio and returned to the guard post.

Craig had the teeth in a C ration can, soaking in salt water. It was late evening, and during their absence Brodemeyer had been boiling up some of the raisins into a pretty heady mixture. They waited for the concoction to cool. A patrol came by and joined the group, and they put the coffee pot on. The C rations contained soluble coffee in a little tin with a cellophane seal, which was meant to keep the coffee airtight and fresh, but the rations were so old they found the coffee had congealed into a solid lump. The technique was to heat it slowly and work the coffee down with a spoon.

Brodemeyer pronounced his "liqueur" ready and invited the others to have a drink while they waited for the coffee to brew. One of the visitors looked around the little camp site for a cup. Nobody noticed as he picked up the C can with the teeth, heard water swishing about, and threw the contents out into the bush. While they sat and drank, Craig told them about his teeth and looked across to where he had left the can. He jumped up and started to raise hell.

"Who's got my teeth? Which of you lousy jerks has stolen my teeth?" he yelled.

Everybody wondered what on earth he was screaming about, and then realization dawned. With a look of horror and disgust on his face, the guilty soldier threw down the cup and ran into the bush, where he was violently sick.

Craig spent hours thrashing about in the jungle undergrowth but to no avail. He never forgave the man who threw away his teeth!

Friday, January 30, 1942
St. Joseph's Hospital
Tandnay
Manila

Only a few days after the Japanese occupied Manila, a high-ranking naval officer came to the Seventh-Day Adventist Hospital and ordered that all the patients were to leave at once. The hospital was being taken over by the Japanese Navy.

There was an immediate exodus of the sick; many of the Filipinos were picked up by their family or friends and sought what medical treatment they could elsewhere. But for Lilla there was nowhere to go except to the internment camp. The doctors at the hospital had told her that the birth was imminent, and rumors had already reached her of the primitive medical facilities at Santo Tomas.

Lilla plucked up courage and asked the ward nurse if she could speak with the Japanese officer. After a while the officer appeared at her bedside. He was polite and courteous, not the barbarian she had envisaged, and he even spoke some English. Encouraged by his demeanor, Lilla explained her predicament. The officer was sympathetic but firm. If she could find a hospital that would take her, the authorities would provide a car to take her there. This was quite a concession, since Lilla already knew that all motor cars had either been commandeered or hidden by their owners. Until the end of the war all movement in the city was by foot, bicycle, or *caramata* (horse and cart). But that still didn't solve the problem of where Lilla was to go to have her baby. No one was eager to have an enemy American under his roof. The Japanese had given the hospital staff twenty-four hours to clear all the civilian patients out of the wards, and indeed it was close to that deadline before some Spanish friends (Spain was, of course, neutral) arranged for her to be admitted into St. Joseph's. It was in this hospital, run by a Spanish Catholic nursing order, that Lilla gave birth to a girl. Her parents named her Cynthia.

Clay saw his baby daughter the day after she was born. Dr. Moreta, the Spanish doctor who delivered her, went to Santo Tomas and implored the commandant to permit Clay to have a pass for a few hours. The Japanese authorities released Clay Seitz into the custody of Dr. Moreta, just long enough for him to pay a very short visit to the hospital.

It was to be almost a year before Clay Seitz was to see his wife and new family again. Lilla remained at St. Joseph's close to a month. With the shortage of drugs and food it was a long, slow recovery from childbirth. The Spanish friends in the meanwhile went to Santo Tomas and persuaded the commandant to allow Lilla and her child to convalesce in their home. The authorities had enough problems at Santo Tomas without a mother and newborn child adding to them, so Lilla was paroled into a form of house arrest.

However, the Japanese were less than happy with this arrangement, and after a few months they moved Lilla and her baby into a house that was owned by Americans. The latter, an elderly couple, had been allowed out of Santo Tomas for reasons of ill health. With Lilla there as well, the Japanese were able to concentrate the aliens under one roof and thus keep an eye on them. It was still a form of house arrest.

The Americans were not allowed out, even to shop. They had to rely on the charity and sympathy of Filipinos, friends, and onetime servants to bring them food. Separated from Clay, Lilla found this house arrest nearly as miserable an existence as life inside the internment camp later proved to be. She was not sorry when eventually the baby was considered strong enough by the authorities to share in the rigors of internment behind the barbed-wire stockade of Santo Tomas.

Fort Mills
Corregidor

After the first air raids, when the magnificent garrison headquarters had been flattened, MacArthur had all his staff and their organizations moved into various laterals in Malinta Tunnel, despite the fact that these had never been intended for human occupation. But MacArthur, with his gift for improvization and love of detail, had overseen the move, and he personally allocated the accommodation. The desk that he and General Sutherland, his Chief of Staff, shared was in Lateral No. 3, about 150 feet from the east entrance to the main tunnel. This also placed the generals conveniently close to the main communications center. Diagonally across but nearer the entrance, in Lateral No. 2, was the headquarters of the Harbor Defense Commander, Gen. George F. Moore. Col. Ted M. Chase, Commander of the Coast Artillery and Massello's chief, located his headquarters in Lateral No. 11, while other laterals were used by supply and technical services, ordnance, signal, finance, etc. Drake used No. 8 as the quartermaster lateral.

Many of these headquarters formations could be identified only by the signs of cryptic initials chalked at the entrance to laterals or hanging, in crudely fashioned wooden frames, above a cluster of clerks. So the storage and supply tunnels of Malinta had been transformed into a gigantic beehive, which while being the nerve center of the campaign had also become a hotel for nearly all the noncombatant forces on Corregidor. It clearly illustrated the American talent for overorganization and top-heavy command structures. The same Churchillian paraphrase that later was applied to the Allied headquarters in North Africa—"Never in the course of human history have so few been commanded by so many"—could certainly have been applied to Corregidor.

Along the sides of the main concourse, and even in some laterals, wherever there was space, crates were piled 6 feet high. These not only contained precious food, but also the lifeblood of the headquarters—paper and stationery, tons of the stuff. Overhead was a maze of wire, pipes, and ducts, and at the end of each lateral, beyond the office space, double- and triple-tiered bunks were slotted against the only available bare rock face.

Some men grew accustomed to their tunnel existence. Drake never could. Constantly surrounded by bedlam, he found it absolutely bewildering. Life was not quite real; one moved, worked, tried to eat, tried to breathe, but always in a dream. By now engineers had rigged neon lights that cast a bluish glow throughout the laterals and added to the air of unreality. Naked bulbs created shadows on the stone cave of men working at their desks like bewitched beings. It was a macabre scene.

In the beginning, there were no washing or lavatory facilities except in the hospital and naval tunnels. After General MacArthur moved his headquarters from Manila, two washrooms with lavatory facilities were placed in the laterals, one for officers and the other for enlisted men and civilians.

Whenever Drake returned from a visit outside, it was the smell of Malinta that hit him like a blow in the face. The air within the tunnels reeked of damp. It was everywhere, like a graveyard smell of wet rock. Even in the dry season it was hot and foul, and the walls constantly dripped moisture. The smells of mildew, urine, and sweat mingled with the fumes from the diesel engines that powered the generators. Overall was the heavy stink of creosote hanging like a blanket in the air that moved sluggishly, when it moved at all.

The first air raids also had another dramatic effect on Malinta Tunnel. It became a permanent air raid shelter and refuge for the civilians and for those military who were faint at heart. Expressions such as "tunnelitis" and "tunnel rats" gained currency and notoriety among the more disciplined members of the fortress garrison who treated those who hid from the war with contempt and disdain.

MacArthur passed the civilians who hid in the tunnel, the well-to-do refugees from Manila, and the poorer inhabitants of Corregidor barrios, daily whenever the air raid alarm sounded. When the siren wailed, MacArthur in company with an aide would make his way out through the crowded civilians seeking shelter in the main passageway, huddled silently in that hunched-down, age-old oriental squat of patience and stolid resignation, out into the open to watch the weaving pattern of the enemy bombers.

MacArthur did not see this as an act of bravado, but rather his simple duty. Leadership is often crystallized in some sort of public gesture, and in war it can take the form of a fraternity of danger. A bond can be forged between a commander and his men when the bond is of sharing the risk of sudden death. MacArthur was convinced that the gunners in the batteries and the Marines in the foxholes liked to see him at such moments.

The effects of gestures such as these are difficult to gauge, but clearly they had little effect on those who sought to evade the war by skulking in the tunnel. At first the numbers of these men were small, but the rot did set in early and it grew in volume when the Japanese later began the artillery bombardment of Corregidor. It certainly wasn't difficult to hide among the thronging mass of people who milled around the main tunnel or move with more purpose from one lateral to another.

There were some who tried to prevent the rot from spreading. Sergeant Bigelow would accompany his company commander, Major Shaffner, on his almost daily trips to roust out those Filipinos and Americans who had been directed to work on beach defenses and who had no right to be in the tunnel; but it was an uphill struggle.

Life was pretty miserable for everybody who lived and worked in Malinta Tunnel. Air shafts had been sunk through the solid rock from the surface above and then carried horizontally along to the rear ends of the laterals. This was supposed to force the air coming through the tunnel entrances into the laterals and then up to the air shafts, but this sytem was devised when the tunnels had been intended for storage purposes only. The swollen population overwhelmed the ventilation facilities. Engineers installed suction pumps at the bottom of each shaft which helped alleviate the problem, but the effect was very local.

With the daily air raids, the dust churned up by the bursting bombs came down the shafts and into the tunnels. As the dry season continued, so the problem increased, and during a raid the laterals filled with a thick, choking dust; but for some even that was preferable to risking life and limb outside. In sustained raids breathing became an effort, almost to the point of suffocation. This was caused because the fans, which might spread a fire, had to be shut down. It was at times like these that the temperature inside the tunnels climbed to the limits of human tolerance.

Prior to the war, engineers had sunk twenty-two artesian wells for the sweet water supply of the garrison. The water from these wells was brought into a large concrete reservoir on Middleside. It was alongside a second reservoir filled with seawater, which was stored to meet the needs of the fire fighters. A particularly heavy air raid that day ruptured the dividing wall, and the sweet water became hopelessly contaminated. This left just one artesian well, which had been sunk about 100 yards down the road from the western entrance to Malinta Tunnel. Until the engineers could devise some desalination plants, this was all that was available to meet the needs of Middleside. The Japanese also hit the reserve water tank on Topside, which held 50,000 gallons and was filled to capacity. With a rush and a roar, water flooded over the parapet and poured down the hill in a raging torrent. Boulders and trees were swept along in its path, and the hillside with its revetments and weapon pits resembled a disaster area. All the men unlucky enough to be in the path of the torrent got a soaking, and a few suffered broken limbs, but there were no fatalities.

When General Drake surveyed the damage later he marveled that there had been no serious injury.

The Japanese bombers continued to concentrate on the surface structures, and by now, a month after the first raid, the whole of Topside was heavily pockmarked by craters. Although some of the buildings were constructed of reinforced concrete, not one had escaped intact. Many had received direct hits and were leveled to the ground, though, as we saw earlier, casualties would have been even higher had not the Japanese bombardiers continued to cut their fuses long for deep penetration. Only charred timbers remained of the wooden structures; the post theater and once-luxurious Officers' Club were gutted.

Bottomside too had been plastered with direct hits; the docks, warehouses, and repair shops were badly damaged.

Battery Chicago
Morrison Hill, Topside

With the destruction of the barracks, the gunners moved out completely into the field. Some built shacks among the trees, using the materials from the shattered buildings. They had to haul water from Bottomside in powder kegs to meet their daily needs.

Bressi saw his first suicide. The young soldier was a quiet man and only a few days before had been assigned to them for duty; so none of them really knew him. He worked as an ammunition loader, one of the unsung and anonymous members of the battery. During the height of one air raid, he left his post. They knew he had gone only because his absence meant more work for the others. For the first time they called him by name.

They found him after the raid sprawled in the bottom of a bomb crater, his rifle still in his mouth. He had taken his boot off, and his big toe was locked around the trigger. The new gun captain looked at the corpse and the mess on the crater wall. "Haul him outta there," he ordered. "Log him as a battle casualty," he added quietly.

On Morrison Hill the battery supply sergeant was named Hopkins. He had managed to salvage a mimeograph machine, an old hand-cranked model, but it served his purpose.

Each evening he would list the main news items from Radio KGEl, add some tidbits of local gossip, and run off a newspaper. They called it *The Morrison Hill Gazette*. The gunners, like everybody else in the garrison, lived off gossip, and the newspaper lifted their hopes and helped alleviate some of their worst fears. But the more sanguine appreciated that as time passed the chances of salvation became less real.

The hospital lateral
Malinta Tunnel

The hospital was extremely well organized, and facilities in the tunnel, though not ideal, were far superior to those on Bataan. The first lateral was the mess hall for the hundred staff—doctors, nurses, and orderlies. Then there was a surgical lateral, an operating lateral, and a medical ward. The last lateral was intended for the nurses, but they had been moved out to make room for the high commissioner, his staff, and their families. Mrs. Sayre used to spend her days, together with Mrs. Quezon and some of the other ladies, rolling bandages. The MacArthurs' son, little Arthur, had his lunch most days with the nurses. The three-year-old boy was a delightful child, an unwitting relief from the tensions of war, and a gentle reminder of another life and another world. He had become a sort of mascot to those who lived and worked in the tunnel, and Madeline Ullom kept devising new games for him to play. Ullom's day began in the wards where she bathed the patients and dressed their wounds. Lunch was eaten at eleven in the morning so that the nurses could be on duty in time for the air raids. The afternoon and evening Ullom spent in the operating theater. Dust fell in a steady stream from the concussion of the bombs, and for those who suffered from claustrophobia it was a terrible experience. At first the wards had beds, crammed seven to a row, but as the casualties increased from the air raids the engineers welded the beds, at first into double deckers and later triple-tiered. Even with a thousand beds, the hospital soon became overcrowded once the artillery bombardment began. There were no ladders, and so the nurses ministered to their patients by clambering up the foot of the bunks.

An early casualty of the raids had been the hospital laundry, and the nurses soon ran out of clean uniforms. General Drake found some bales of heavy-duty cloth called "West Point drill" in the stores, and these he issued to the hospital staff. The Marines had brought some Chinese tailors with them, and they set to work with needle and thread and fashioned two skirts for each nurse, and a one-piece coverall.

Ruby Moteley moved from Corregidor to Bataan. Her dietician skills had been used to prepare the special dishes for the ailing President Quezon until Colonel Cooper, the hospital commandant, called her into his little office to tell her that she was needed more on Bataan. He ordered her to report to No. 2 Hospital at Cabcaben, where there was a bad outbreak of malaria and dysentery.

There were tears in his eyes as he spoke, and she knew he thought she wouldn't survive.

She said her goodbyes, packed a small bag, and took the boat to Mariveles. She found the hospital a living hell. There was no cover for the patients; the cots, only a few of which had mosquito nets, were out in the open under the trees. There was precious little food of any kind for the patients, and very soon she was forced to make daily visits to neighboring units to beg supplies. Her feminine charms succeeded where the supply officer had failed. As a dietician, she employed her skills butchering horses and carabao, dressing and cooking the meat before the flies swarmed onto the carcasses.

Saturday, January 31, 1942
Naval headquarters
Queen Tunnel
Corregidor

Champlin made frequent visits to Bataan. Two or three times a
week he crossed over to see how the naval battalion was fitting in
with the Army. Despite their inexperience, they had done well in
the Battle of Longoskawayan Point and as a consequence had developed a new and more healthy relationship with the Army units.

Information of this sort was important to Rockwell, since he was
seldom if ever included in MacArthur's conferences, in spite of the
fact that he was the senior naval officer present and commanded
about a third of the American personnel in the Philippines.

The bitter clash of personalities between General MacArthur
and Admiral Hart had marred Army-Navy cooperation in the Philippines. This was to remain the case until MacArthur left for Australia. If MacArthur ignored the Navy, the same could not be said
for his principal corps commander on Bataan, General Wainwright. There was a significant maritime threat to Wainwright's
positions, and so he saw the need to have some expert naval advice
close at hand at his headquarters.

Wainwright sent a colonel from his staff to talk over the problem
with Admiral Rockwell and to request a naval liaison officer at his
corps headquarters and a much closer cooperation with the Navy.

The admiral called Champlin into his office and to the young
lieutenant's surprise and delight offered him the job. The colonel
explained the problem in detail. Though the Army had wiped out
the one landing, the Japanese were still holding on grimly to Quinauan Point. The area had been sealed off by the Air Corps and the
Philippine Constabulary, but it needed professional units to finish
the operation. In the close jungle terrain the enemy was infiltrating
snipers out of the bridgehead, and these were causing havoc in the
American lines. General Wainwright was afraid that the Japanese
might attempt to reinforce their troops by further amphibious
operations before the Scouts could deploy. Corps headquarters had
no clear idea of how many Japanese were holed up, though it was
thought to be a large force. What they did know was that if the
Japanese broke out of their bridgehead in strength they could
exploit inland through the Aglahoma Valley and cut Wainwright's

lines of communication. There was one road that wound its way from Mariveles and the ordnance dump at Little Baguio around the Bataan peninsula and along the western side of the South China Sea coast to the front lines. It passed across the head of Quinauan Point and not more than a mile from the Japanese outposts.

Champlin was ordered to leave the next morning. He packed a musette bag with a change of clothing, traded his .45 for a revolver, borrowed a Springfield rifle, and had it cleaned. He then spent the rest of the day briefing himself on the naval side of the war, studying the map and charts of Bataan and the coastal waters. The staff of the Inshore Patrol briefed him on the extent of the minefields, the role of the minesweepers and gunboats, and the nightly torpedo boat operations. Champlin rounded off his day of hectic preparation in conversation with Lt. John Bulkeley, who commanded the torpedo boat squadron.

Bulkeley was a wild man, daring, courageous, and admirable in many ways, but still to Champlin the Flag Lieutenant, a wild man. He reminded Champlin of a swashbuckling pirate in modern dress. Bulkeley wore a long, unruly beard and carried two ominous-looking pistols strapped to his hips. His eyes were bloodshot and red-rimmed from too many night patrols and lack of sleep, but his nervous energy was infectious. He walked with a cocksure gait and already had a reputation for raising hell among those Japanese who crossed his path. Highly strung, temperamental, brave, and gallant, John Bulkeley was one of the most colorful heroes of the Philippine war.

Champlin picked up a naval signalman and crossed to Bataan at dawn. They landed near the quarantine jetty in Mariveles and found a battered old sedan waiting to take them to General Wainwright's headquarters. About four miles up the road, they heard the steady hum of aircraft, and their driver pulled the car off the road and under the shade of some trees.

"What have we stopped for, sailor?" Champlin asked. "Those planes sound miles away." Hardly had he left the car when there was a terrific roar overhead. Champlin dived after the others into a monsoon ditch. A plane passed low over the trees, its cannons stitching holes in the dust, and dropped its bombs at a bridge a couple of hundred yards ahead. Two more followed in quick succession, and the ground beneath them shook and buckled to the blast of bombs, which fell wide of their intended target.

"That's why, Lieutenant, sir," said the driver, shaking the dust from his pants and holding open the back door.

Champlin, pensive and not a little shaken by his introduction to the war in Bataan, climbed obediently back into the car.

They left the car in the motor pool and walked up the hill into a grove of trees on the edge of a ridge. In the center of the forest glade were several tables, split bamboo poles lashed together with jungle vines, where they spotted the general talking with his staff. Wainwright, tall, lean, and every inch a cavalryman, had his back to Champlin as he asked questions of his staff who were pointing out enemy positions sketched on a map propped up against a tree.

Jonathan Wainwright, born in 1883 of an Army family, was a cavalry officer of the old school. His father had been a renowned Indian fighter, and Jonathan had seen action in France toward the end of World War I. His career thereafter followed the usual pattern: service with troops, attendance at Army schools, and the slow climb up the promotion ladder of a peacetime Army. He became a brigadier general in 1928, when he commanded the 1st Cavalry Brigade, and remained in that rank until he was given his second star in May 1940 and sent to the Philippines to assume command of the Philippine division. Tall and incredibly thin, forever wearing his Smokey Bear campaign hat in the cavalry style, he came to the Philippines with a reputation as a drinking man with a love for horses. For years he had been affectionately known throughout the Army as "Skinny."

When Wainwright had finished his briefing, Champlin stepped forward, saluted, and introduced himself. Wainwright looked tired and growled, "What do I have to do, go through God Almighty before I can talk to the Navy?"

Champlin didn't say a word. Then the general smiled and said, "I'm glad to have you here, son. Come over for a talk in the trailer when you are settled." He walked away.

They were soon assigned quarters, and Champlin talked to Wainwright's ADC, Captain Dooley, while he unpacked his bags. Champlin brought out a bottle of Scotch, one of the last from his secret hoard, which he had wrapped carefully in his towel. Dooley nearly fainted when he saw the bottle. Champlin asked whether General Wainwright would be interested in the Scotch. Dooley answered with an emphatic yes.

The two young officers walked up the track to the general's vine-covered trailer, and as they entered, Champlin handed the bottle to Wainwright.

"General," he said, "Admiral Rockwell sends his kindest regards and has asked me to give you this to cement Army-Navy relations." The wide-eyed general took the bottle reverently in his hands and held it up, the sunlight glittering on the clear golden liquid.

"Young man, do you realize that what you have here is the finest Scotch whiskey there is . . . and that I haven't had a drink in almost three months?"

That was the best apple that Champlin had ever brought to any teacher.

"Everything's quiet on the line right now, and I think we can safely have a snort," the general added. Despite the still early hour he poured himself a generous three fingers of straight Scotch and invited the two aides to join him. Dooley did the honors and diplomatically poured two small measures, which he topped with water.

The three drank in silence, and for a moment at least the war seemed a million miles away. "Well, we've cemented Army-Navy relations, son," Wainwright said at last. "Now stick with me, and I'll explain your duties.

"We used to think, in the old days, that an Army could anchor one end of its line in the mountains and the other end of the line on the seacoast, but this concept doesn't apply here. The front I have to defend extends not only from the Pantingen River in the center of Bataan, down the Bagac Valley to the sea, but around the coast, including all those scores of small inlets clear to Mariveles Bay. We not only have snipers behind our lines but also snipers who have landed from Japanese boats. The Japs have caught us out twice already, and it's imperative that I have the closest links with the Navy. I must know whether we are shooting at your torpedo boats or enemy landing craft."

The general paused and took the delicate pull of a professional drinker at his Scotch, savoring every drop. "Any thoughts, son?"

Champlin recalled the conversation he'd had with Bulkeley the night before. "Sir, we need to establish a naval observation post on a high point and near to the front line. From the chart, it appears to me that with a long glass, ships could be spotted and information relayed to Bulkeley for attacks with the MTBs and the artillery." Champlin added that he had brought a signalman with him with that job in mind.

Wainwright told him to talk to his staff artillery people, who would advise him on the best place, and the two officers took their leave.

Dooley introduced Champlin to Major Lindsay, the Staff Gunnery Officer whose opinion was that the best place would be the artillery observation post at the top of Trail 19. Since Trail 19 began just a few yards from headquarters, Champlin in all innocence slung the Springfield over his shoulder, tucked a long glass under his arm, and started off alone. The trail was wide and clearly marked but steeper and steeper as it went over the top of the ridge. Soon he came to an open area that ran straight for a couple of hundred yards.

Without really thinking, Champlin walked boldly across the open ground. He was getting a little tired by now, the sun was hot, and so he leaned up against an inviting tree to catch his breath before pressing on with his walk. Suddenly, and right next to him, a voice said, "Hello, Joe." Leaning against the same tree within a yard of where he stood was a Philippine Scout, festooned in tropical vines from head to foot.

"How long you on Bataan?" the soldier asked.

When Champlin replied that this was his first day, the soldier said, "I think so. I could shoot you right down there." He pointed down the trail. "I think you learn more soon, or you get shot. Where you go?"

Champlin told him he was looking for the artillery observation post.

"Post about a mile up the trail," the soldier said. "Snipers there this morning, but we wipe out. Now okay, I think. Goodbye, Joe."

The Scout disappeared into the undergrowth as quietly as he came, and Champlin unslung the Springfield and loaded and cocked the weapon before proceeding on his way—more cautiously.

The observation post was high in a tree, with stakes nailed into the trunk all the way to a small camouflaged platform in the upper branches. Leaving his rifle and helmet below with the outpost detail, Champlin tied the long glass to his belt and clambered up to the platform. The position was well chosen; 100 or more feet high, it overlooked the front line from the Pantingen River to the beach and around the shoreline to the entrances for Subic and Bingango bays. This was just what Champlin needed; connected by a field phone to the headquarters, it could provide immediate warning of enemy shipping. He did wonder how long it could be occupied, for the platform stood above the matted jungle, and a strafing plane could polish it off in short order if the position were spotted.

Champlin returned the next day with his signaler and arranged for him to work directly with the artillery spotters. The post controlled the fire of a battery of four 155mm "Long Toms" that were positioned high up on the same ridge but concealed so well that the guns remained in the same spot for over a month. They were never discovered by the Japanese in spite of daily searches by their reconnaissance flights. The Japanese did, however, discover the observation post, though its occupants were able to scramble clear before their platform was blown out of the tree. They were back in business a couple of days later with a new location farther to the east in the Mariveles Mountains. Meanwhile, Champlin had brought over two extra signalers so that the post could be manned continuously.

Monday, February 2, 1942
Headquarters, I Corps

At about 1600 hours that afternoon Champlin was called to the field phone; it was his signalman at the new observation position to the east. He reported that there was a Japanese cruiser in Morong Bay, anchored out of range of the artillery, and that there were a lot of boats around her stern.

"How many are there and what sort?" Champlin asked.

The sailor replied that it was difficult to tell, but that there appeared to be at least two dozen, and they looked like landing barges.

Champlin hurried to Wainwright's trailer and told the general that the Japanese were preparing for another landing. Champlin then phoned through to Navy HQ on Corregidor, relayed the information, and advised that Bulkeley be told immediately.

There was, indeed, a landing operation under way. General

Morioka, after persistent prodding from Homma, had decided to reinforce Kimura's beachhead with the remaining companies of the 1st Battalion, 20th Infantry Regiment.

At about 2330 hours that night, Champlin's lookout reported two small lights out on the water. Shortly after, rapid gunfire began. It sounded to Champlin like 8-inch naval guns. The firing seemed to be over a wide area near the front line, but it was wild and indiscriminate, and little damage was inflicted. Additional troops, Scouts and provisional Air Corps infantry, moved into position between the road and the shore and near where the lights had been spotted.

Three surviving P-40s took off from Cabcaben Field with orders to sortie the area. In the clear moonlight, they spotted two long lines of what appeared to be landing craft, loaded with troops. They strafed and bombed them at low level until both fuel and ammunition were exhausted. The Japanese had provided no air cover, and the slaughter was wholesale. Bulkeley's boats weighed in and added further to the mayhem. Artillery and small-arms fire from the shore opened up as the PT boats, their work complete, hauled off and headed out to sea.

Even so, Major Kimura, with about half his force still intact, staggered ashore. There he linked up with the surviving members of his advance company who had failed in their landing on January 27 to reinforce the troops on Quinauan Point. Against an alerted and aggressive defense, the Japanese had once again landed behind Wainwright's lines. All hope for an early end to the fight for Anyasan Point was now lost.

Tuesday, February 3, 1942
South Dock
Corregidor

The large fleet submarine *Trout*, Cdr. Mike Fenno in command, arrived from Pearl Harbor, bringing a load of the new 3-inch shells. For the first time in the war, the gunners would be able to punch the clouds at 20,000 feet and more. The shells were unloaded that night, and the submarine bunkered with fuel. By midnight Fenno realized that he would need ballast and lots of it, for his boat wasn't heavy enough to submerge.

Fenno rushed to the naval headquarters and asked the duty officer for some sandbags. Sandbags were worth their weight in gold on that beleaguered fortress, but Admiral Rockwell, who knew that the *Trout* would return to Pearl Harbor from her patrol, saw an answer to everyone's problem. He quickly arranged for the four key holders to the vaults to be roused while the naval staff organized trucks and a fatigue party. It seemed ages before the right people could be found and the gold delivered to the wharfside, and Fenno by this stage was beside himself with worry.

With the first gray light of dawn, a chain gang unloaded the gold from the trucks and straight down into the conning tower of the submarine. At $150,000 a throw it was the most expensive ship's ballast in history.

Sam Malick had been sent ashore from the *Mindanao* to work for a while on Rockwell's staff as a radio operator in liaison with Bulkeley's PT boats. He visited the *Trout* during that night of hectic activity. He had written a letter home and went down into the radio shack of the submarine to see if his opposite number would take it with him. There were many others milling around that night on similar errands. As he left the radio room Malick bumped into Commander Fenno.

"What's your rating, sailor?"

"Radio operator first class, sir," Malick replied.

"Do you know anything about sonar?"

"Yes, sir, I'm a qualified sonar operator."

"You're not leaving this ship," Fenno said. "I'm short a good operator."

"I can't do that, sir, not without permission."

"Look, sailor, by the time this sub docks at Pearl, you guys are gonna be eating rice. You come with me, and I'll clear it with the authorities at Pearl."

Tempting as the offer was, Sam Malick could not desert his shipmates and still live with his conscience. He refused.

"I admire your sense of duty," Fenno said, "but you're wrong."

Sam Malick saluted and left the submarine before his resolve melted.

Shortly afterward the last of the gold was loaded, and the U.S.S. *Trout* submerged out into the South China Sea. When the *Trout* eventually reached Pearl Harbor after a highly successful patrol it was rumored that Commander Fenno claimed salvage, as was his right, on the cargo. That particular naval regulation was coincidentally changed in March of 1942; but Fenno fought it through the courts and continued to claim his prize money!

Thursday, February 5, 1942
Anyasan Point
Bataan

The provisional Air Corps moved up to help seal in the Japanese battalion at Anyasan Point. John McCann and his comrades joined the expedition. They had spent four days waiting to move up to the battlefront with more than their fair share of false starts to sap their nervous energy before the order finally came to move.

Military police directed the trucks off the road and into a jungle clearing; as the men dismounted they could hear the sounds of battle in the distance. They shouldered their packs and moved north up the coast toward the rear area for the battle. After a couple of hours' march they found their camp located in an old railroad siding; the iron ties were still embedded in the ground. They hardly had time to settle in before a harassed officer called McCann's platoon together and ordered them to set up a defense line to the north, where they were to stop some Japanese who had broken out. From their new position they were to send out combat patrols as far as the beach.

The airmen gathered up their equipment and moved out. They drew C rations from a supply point and were told not to eat them unless the daily ration of hot food failed to make it up the line. The jungle was thick and almost impenetrable in places. As they dug in on that first night, John McCann had never been so scared in all his life. The huge trees had enormous roots growing high out of the ground, vines and creepers hung down to the soft matted floor, and the undergrowth seemed alive with rustle and scurrying movement.

He was convinced that unseen eyes watched their frantic efforts to prepare for night. The airmen called out to one another during the long, lonely night, seeking comfort in a friendly voice.

Then there were other voices in the darkness:

"Hey, Joe, come out with your hands up—I won't shoot you!"

McCann hugged the ground and shook with terror. All of a sudden war had lost its glamor; it was no longer a game.

"You damn fool, Joe, we're gonna kill you. Why don't you come out and surrender?"

It was the longest night he could ever remember. Occasionally they fired at the sound of voices. Mortars burst high in the trees, and bullets ricocheted in retaliation.

As the first rays of light filtered through the leafy branches of the high hardwood trees, the airmen were ordered to move forward. It was with extreme reluctance that McCann left the cocoonlike safety of his foxhole and crept stealthily forward. He followed in the footsteps of an Air Corps master sergeant who carried his Thompson like a seasoned warrior. The man still wore his coveralls, and John stared at the black wing and propeller emblem which stood out from all the grime on his back. No amount of urgency could persuade the airmen to fan out in a line. They moved forward slowly, a few yards at a time. They never once saw the enemy, but they did find the bodies of two Scouts; their arms had been wired behind them, and they had been bayoneted in the back.

The platoon spent two further nights of fear in the jungle, each a repetition of the first, before they finally pulled back to the relative safety of the railroad siding. Tired and hungry, they sat down and cleaned their weapons. There seemed to be few other men in the camp.

A couple of hundred feet below them, and on the edge of the jungle, there was a stream that flowed into a large natural pool. The group moved down, stripped, and jumped into the cool, inviting water.

Suddenly out of the bushes came a party of six small, brown-skinned men. There was pandemonium as the platoon scrambled out of the water and ran with lathered bodies for their weapons. They grabbed their rifles and turned to do battle. The intruders, however, weren't Japanese at all but tribesmen, Negritoes, who inhabited the hills around. The locals had wild honey, fruit, papayas, mangoes, and bananas. These they held out to the Americans and pointed to the bayonets. The airmen smiled in their relief and gladly traded for the fruit; bayonets were easy to come by.

The following morning they were relieved by the 1st Battalion, 57th Philippine Scouts. McCann returned south to the humdrum but safer job of guarding the dump at Little Baguio. It was to take the Scouts another week to annihilate the Japanese beachhead.

Unable to relieve his men, General Morioka finally ordered them to break out of the beachhead. Instructions were sealed in bamboo batons and dropped to Major Kimura from the air. He was ordered to bring his decimated battalion out by sea, on rafts or boats, and to try to reach the haven at Morong. Some of the batons fell on the American lines, where they were sent down to corps headquarters. Richard Sakakida translated them, and the Scouts deployed in readiness along the cliff tops. The riflemen fired at the swimmers, and the machine gunners blasted the homemade rafts of those who attempted to run the gauntlet.

0900 hours
Sunday, February 8, 1942
2nd Battalion, 57th Philippine Scouts

John Spainhower's battalion had been pulled out of the line after its successful operation mopping up the Japanese resistance at Longoskawayan Point and remained in reserve in bivouac. Spainhower had just returned to the battalion command post. He had been down to the rear area to see why breakfast had not been delivered on time. He was discussing the problem with some other officer when Photo Joe put in his customary appearance. The men paid no heed to the aircraft, as he seemed to be around at this time on most days. Without warning the plane dropped two bombs on the battalion headquarters. As the first bomb burst, men dived for cover. The second bomb exploded just a few feet from the command post, and there were screams and cries of pain. Spainhower jumped to his feet and yelled for an ambulance and medics. He had seen an ambulance coming up the track just as the bombs fell. As he stood up he found his trousers were around his knees. He hitched them up and saw that his hand was covered with blood. A bomb fragment had gouged through the small of his back. It had been deflected by his webbed belt, hence his trousers falling down. Pain stabbed through his back, and he staggered and fell. He had a deep wound across his lumbar region, and his legs had gone numb. A medic sprinkled some sulpha powder into the gaping wound and strapped a shell dressing around his waist; face down on a stretcher, he was loaded into the ambulance and together with three other casualties from the incident taken to the nearest aid station. There the wound was dressed and stitched, and Spainhower was evacuated to No. 1 Hospital. The journey took more than eight hours and, as the vehicle jolted over every rut and pothole, Spainhower couldn't decide which was worse, the excruciating pain in his back or the awful nausea as he lay on his stomach inside the hot and airless vehicle.

No. 1 Hospital had just one building, a nipa hut that served as the operating theater. Spainhower underwent another operation under a local anesthetic, the surgeons finishing by encasing him in a plaster cast. The ward to which he was later moved was out in the open, under the mango trees. Being an officer, he rated a cot and a mosquito net. Sanitation and living conditions were about as primitive as they come. Despite all the precautions, like most other battle casualties, the wound developed a secondary infection; abscesses started in the stitch holes. The plaster around the now festering wound had been cut away, and every morning the weeping sores were cleaned with swabs soaked in iodine. The pain was excruciating. John Spainhower was destined to be in the hospital for over a month, and along with the other patients he soon developed dysentery and malaria.

President Quezon's quarters
Malinta Tunnel
Corregidor

President Quezon held a Cabinet meeting that morning. It had become clear to the president and his advisers that the United States was not prepared to rescue the Philippines and that there now lay just one course of action open. Accordingly in the late afternoon he telegraphed Roosevelt.

Quezon proposed that the United States release the Philippines from the bondage of its commonwealth status and grant it immediate independence. The Filipinos then intended to make a separate peace with the Japanese. Since it was only the American connection that had brought the war to those shores, Quezon reasoned that it should be possible to become a Sweden of the Orient and, in return for certain concessions, reach a reasonable accommodation with the invader. On this occasion Quezon consulted MacArthur about the contents of his message. The general did not demur. On the contrary, he sent his own communiqué in which he, in an obscure fashion, appeared to agree with the Filipino analysis and ended by asking for orders in the event the Philippines became neutral.

The messages from Corregidor hit the Pentagon and White House like a bombshell. Roosevelt took a little while carefully phrasing his reply; his cablegrams reached Corregidor two days later.

The first wire was sent to President Quezon. The Philippine request was bluntly refused. Nevertheless, Roosevelt did go on to say:

> SO LONG AS THE FLAG OF THE UNITED STATES FLIES ON FILIPINO SOIL . . . IT WILL BE DEFENDED BY OUR MEN TO THE DEATH. WHATEVER HAPPENS TO PRESENT AMERICAN GARRISON WE SHALL NOT RELAX OUR EFFORTS UNTIL THE FORCES WHICH ARE NOW MARSHALING OUTSIDE THE PHILIPPINE ISLANDS RETURN TO THE PHILIPPINES AND DRIVE THE LAST REMNANT OF THE INVADERS FROM YOUR SOIL.

President Quezon interpreted this as a binding pledge, and in return this sick and dying old man swore an oath of loyalty to the United States.

To MacArthur, Roosevelt cabled:

> . . . THE DUTY AND THE NECESSITY OF RESISTING JAPANESE AGGRESSION TO THE LAST TRANSCENDS IN IMPORTANCE ANY OTHER OBLIGATION NOW FACING US IN THE PHILIPPINES . . .

IT IS MANDATORY THAT THERE BE ESTABLISHED ONCE
AND FOR ALL IN THE MINDS OF ALL PEOPLES COMPLETE
EVIDENCE THAT THE AMERICAN DETERMINATION AND
INDOMITABLE WILL TO WIN CARRIES ON DOWN TO THE
LAST UNIT. I THEREFORE GIVE YOU THIS MOST DIFFICULT
MISSION IN FULL UNDERSTANDING OF THE DESPERATE
SITUATION TO WHICH YOU MAY SHORTLY BE REDUCED.
THE SERVICE THAT YOU AND THE AMERICAN MEMBERS OF
YOUR COMMAND CAN RENDER TO YOUR COUNTRY IN THE
TITANIC STRUGGLE NOW DEVELOPING IS BEYOND ALL
POSSIBILITY OF APPRAISEMENT. I PARTICULARLY
REQUEST THAT YOU PROCEED RAPIDLY TO THE ORGANI-
ZATION OF YOUR FORCES AND YOUR DEFENSES SO AS TO
MAKE YOUR RESISTANCE AS EFFECTIVE AS CIRCUM-
STANCES WILL PERMIT AND AS PROLONGED AS HUMANLY
POSSIBLE.

Reading between the lines of his rebuke, MacArthur, the states-
man and strategist, recognized that the Philippines had been written off by the High Command in Washington. Their purpose in the
Allied grand strategy and contribution to the war effort lay only as a
heroic symbol of a last-ditch stand.

The following day MacArthur cabled his president that he would
fight to the last with his command and that both he and his family
would share the fate of his soldiers.

Quinauan Point
Bataan

As the final phase of the operation in the Battle of the Points
began, it became clear that numbers of the enemy had again holed
up in the caves. General Wainwright sent for Champlin and asked
his naval adviser whether a couple of minesweepers could be
brought around to fire into the caves. Champlin offered to check
the position himself, and Captain Dooley volunteered to go along
for company. They drove close to the front and then moved in with

an escort of Philippine Scouts. They passed the debris of war and moved down onto the beach, where they watched more Scouts shooting up into the caves. Champlin radioed back to headquarters that the operation was feasible for naval craft, and the decision was made to use the Mickey Mouse battleships from *Canopus*. The Japanese Air Force put in an appearance and sank one, though not before they had completed their task. Out of the eight hundred Japanese in the beachhead, less than forty made it to their own lines.

On his own way back to corps headquarters, Champlin thought about the battle he had just witnessed. "If I survive," he wondered, "how on earth can I describe to my family the horrors I've seen?"

It is hard to find words adequate to convey combat to those who have never seen the front. To a combat soldier the front is his particular hell. It is not merely a soldier pointing a gun and firing that gun. It is not merely a shifting of groups face to face, first one giving ground and then the other giving ground, with a few dropping cleanly and noiselessly, to be picked up later and given burial by their buddies. Not there, at any rate; not on Bataan. Not in the jungle.

War is sweat and filth and lice from the foxholes. It is unspeakable weariness and the fight to keep awake. It is, among other things, unclean. To the young Americans who had known the small unappreciated luxuries of home, it was having to live encircled by their own excrement, and this because dysentery made them too weak to stand, or danger too wary, or just afraid, to leave the foxhole. It was hunger, too, thought Champlin, ever-present hunger. It was the knowledge that the shortage of medicine could mean pain when you were wounded. It was the knowledge that their grenades didn't work because they were old and corroded, left over from another war and another age.

This was the front line. This was the jungle.

This was the reality that was Bataan.

4. The Battle of the Pockets: The Japanese Offensive Along the Bagac/Orion Line

Sunday, January 25, 1942– Tuesday, February 10, 1942

April 1980
Department of War Studies and International Affairs
The Royal Military Academy Sandhurst, England

During the three weeks that the Battle of the Points raged on the West Coast of Bataan, another hard-fought battle was taking place along the main front lines. USAFFE headquarters had been carefully monitoring the reports from the Abucay line, and MacArthur had become increasingly concerned over the situation. It was clear to the general and his close advisers that the line, with Mount Natib dominating the center and proving so hard to defend, was not the best position from which to fight the Japanese. As we have already seen, the disintegration of the 51st Philippine Army Division, coupled with the failure of the counterattack launched by the 31st U.S. Infantry and the Scouts to restore the line, had contributed to this decision to withdraw. However, disengagement from the enemy in battle and a withdrawal into new positions can be a dangerous business. It has to be carefully planned and coordinated, with reliable units to act as rear guard and every move carried out with precision; otherwise a retreat can easily turn into a rout.

The retreat into the new line took place by means of a phased withdrawal and mostly at night between January 22 and 26. The Japanese soon realized the defenders had gone and were quick to follow upon the heels of the retreating Allies. In Wainwright's corps, a gap developed in the line, and the Japanese poured through the hole before it could be plugged. They set up two strong pockets of resistance behind the line. Thus in the critical 26 days from January 23 to February 17, the American positions on Bataan were under strong attack in three places: the two pockets of resistance that developed behind the Orion-Bagac line, and the points along the West Coast beaches.

Let us look for a moment at the battleground in a little more detail. The main line of resistance now extended from Orion westward to Bagac. The Allied defense was more compact and certainly better organized. There was no Mount Natib in the way, so the two corps were able to link effectively and provide a continuous line of resistance across the peninsula. For the most part the line was to the south of the lateral highway, but artillery fire from the dominating high ground denied the Japanese use of the road. American combat engineers cleared the lateral trails behind their own front line, and this did help their own communication to a limited degree. Many of the units were reduced in size, shadows of their former selves, and there was a marked shortage of combat-experienced officers. Because of their example and their devotion, they had become early casualties in the desperate fighting along the Abucay line.

With these factors in mind, MacArthur's headquarters on Corregidor imposed a new organization on the corps battlefronts; instead of divisional areas, the line was divided into sectors. Wainwright defended some of the most forbidding terrain from his landward corps boundary on the Pantingen River to the coast. The front was covered by jungle and dense cane and bamboo. On small hills or knolls grew huge hardwood trees, 70 feet and more in height, trailing creepers as thick as a man's wrist. There were no reliable maps of the area for friend or foe, and under conditions such as these, with visibility through the bewildering jungle gloom no more than 15 yards, warfare became a hit-or-miss affair. Artillery could not penetrate; it would simply splinter the bamboo, and this was lethal in an infantryman's war. Nowhere on Bataan was the terrain less suitable for military operations than in the two sectors of Wainwright's corps.

To the east of the Pantingen River, the three sectors of Parker's front were dominated by the towering mass of Mount Samat, which afforded excellent observation over the low, swampy coastlands and river plains.

Fearful that the Japanese might try more amphibious operations, but with too many beaches and coves to be covered, MacArthur ordered that the main defense lines be held by the Filipino divisions in static positions and the regular units of the Philippine division be held as USAFFE mobile reserve. As the current operations along the West Coast demonstrated, these were the only troops capable of fighting mobile warfare.

There was a rumor in USAFFE headquarters that MacArthur had already decided that the battle was perhaps lost on Bataan and that he intended to withdraw the still intact elements of the Philippine division (the 31st U.S. Infantry and the Philippine Scouts) onto Corregidor. This would leave the Philippine Army divisions to their fate. The evidence for this rumor is murky, and in fact the Philippine division stayed on Bataan; but it is also true that MacArthur was concerned privately at the need to withdraw to the new line. There were, of course, the Marines, but they were on Corregidor watching the beaches against an enemy who couldn't attack until Bataan had been reduced.

Late afternoon
Sunday, January 25, 1942
41st Division artillery
Withdrawal to Mount Samat—
the Artillery positions behind the Orion-Bagac line

Everyone had been warned; movement was to be only by night. Japanese air power had by now become so predominant that the Zeros attacked even single vehicles. Anything that moved was fair game.

In the fading light, Winston Jones supervised loading of the vehicles with guns and ammunition, and had the trucks pulled into the shelter of a tree line until the MPs gave them the signal to leave. They were to move to their new deployments along a trail specially cut and strengthened by the engineers. It was dark when the word came to move out. The trucks swung into their allotted position in their mile-long convoy and slowly ground their way through the foothills. Ahead of them moved a battery of 155mm GPF, Long Toms, pulled by 10-ton Caterpillar tractors; even on good roads they had a top speed of less than 8 miles an hour.

They came eventually to the narrow bridge that crossed the Aboo River and found the road ahead jammed solid. Jones scrambled down from the cab of his lead truck and walked forward to investigate the delay. One of the Long Toms had slipped a wheel off the edge of the bridge, and its tractor had neither the purchase nor the power to pull it clear. The bridge was completely blocked while the Filipino officers and men gathered around their stranded charge and argued volubly on what course of action to take. Jones knew one thing: If they didn't move that monster, they would be stuck there at daylight and a plumb target for the strafing Japanese planes.

So Jones shouldered aside the Filipino committee and scrambled up into the cab. He had never driven a D-10 caterpillar in his life, but he soon got the hang of it. The Filipinos, only too relieved that an American had assumed responsibility, gladly followed Winston's instructions. They unhooked the tractor and ammunition trailer or limber, and the massive gun and towing bar or trail tilted and would have crashed through the parapet of the bridge and fallen into the river below had not the axle become embedded and held the gun, though now at a crazy angle.

Winston drove off the bridge, unhooked the limber, and spent the next ten minutes getting the feel, mastering the controls of the tractor and especially its powerful winch mounted up front. He drove back onto the bridge, and they hitched the tow hook to the gun. Pulling hard on the tiller bars, he locked his tracks alternately, first one foot one way, then one foot another while easing back a few inches at a time on the cable winch. It took them more than two hours but eventually the Long Tom was hauled off the bridge and the road cleared.

Jones brushed aside the gratitude of the gunners and hurried back to his own charges, who were all, to a man, fast asleep. He roused the drivers, and the convoy followed the Long Toms over the ridges and foothills to their new position in the shadow of Mount Samat. Jones drove them hard as they rushed to camouflage their guns before daylight. They established an observation post in an acacia tree high on Mount Samat, from where they could see all the way to Balanga and the Japanese troops moving down the main street in the little town.

Company H, 3rd Battalion
31st U.S. Infantry
On the road to Limay

It was now the turn of Garleb's company to pull out of its positions and retreat behind the new battle line into their newly allotted role as part of the USAFFE mobile reserve.

Hollow-eyed, gaunt-faced, and marching like automatons, the exhausted soldiers doggedly followed in the footsteps of the man in front. They were too tired to care whether they lived or died. For some, it had been more than a week since they last had either a few hours of undisturbed sleep or a hot meal. As fighting machines the battalions, for the present at least, were drained of their battle energies.

The company executed a Filipino during their night march out of the battleline. They caught him with a sack of contraband: American cigarettes, some canned food, and ammunition. The point section had stumbled across him in the dark. Captain Hunkins looked at the Filipino and his sack and asked, "Okay, who wants to shoot this sonofabitch?"

A couple of sergeants took him into the undergrowth beside the road, forced him to his knees, and shot him. They scraped a shallow grave, threw some earth over the corpse, and the battalion moved on down the road.

Garleb had watched the incident as if from a distance. Try as he might he could find neither pity or compassion.

General Homma, aware that the defenders had abandoned their

positions, urged his subordinates to follow quickly. He had no intention on this occasion of allowing the Americans time to dig in and organize their positions in strength. Accordingly General Nara drove hard for Limay on the East Coast, but again his Intelligence failed: They placed the American line 3 miles south of its true position. As a result, three battalions of Colonel Takechi's 9th Infantry stumbled into the main line of resistance before they even had time to deploy for battle. Once again Winston Jones's battery provided magnificent fire support in an engagement that lasted over three hours. He deftly shifted the weight of fire from point to point and covered all the concentrations that the infantry requested. The battle was brisk and at close quarters. The guns stopped firing as the Japanese advanced, heedless of casualties, up to the main line of resistance, but Filipino machine-gun fire kept the enemy at bay, and the next morning when a count was made they found more than a hundred dead Japanese within 150 yards of the main defense positions.

Nara pulled his beaten troops back and paused to regroup.

Winston Jones was pleased with the performance of his battalion. Now firmly in the chair as commander, he had kept a quizzical eye on the batteries. He realized that the workhorse 75mm field guns had done well in their deployment on the forward slopes. The real problems, initially at least, had been with the 2.95 pack howitzers in their positions farther back into the deep jungle. For the first time now, they fired the guns at their maximum elevation in order to have a clear field of fire. The gun jumped back in recoil, as it always did, but now the angle of the barrel made it unbalanced, and the gun tipped forward to bury its muzzle in the dirt. It required an alert and athletic crew to run forward, sidestep the crushing weight of the recoil, and still grab the beast before it tilted forward. Jones had them practice the maneuver until they could do it in their sleep.

The next morning Photo Joe introduced himself to the battalion. Jones was horrified at the absence of anti-aircraft fire and took it as a personal affront that this plane should be allowed to operate with such immunity.

"Nothing," he explained to his subordinates, "is likely to sap the morale of our boys quicker than their not being in a position to retaliate. I'm going to do something about the bastard."

He spent the rest of the day training Battery C in its new role of anti-aircraft. When Photo Joe appeared on time the following day,

Jones was ready. He had calculated the flight path of the plane, loaded the howitzers with shrapnel, and cut the fuse for 20 seconds. The battery fired as one, and before the first salvo had time to explode they had sent a second screaming skyward in its wake. The effect was nothing short of dramatic. The shrapnel shells exploded in a puff of white smoke and sprayed the surrounding sky with little balls and Photo Joe took all kinds of evasive action to avoid what he thought was heavy anti-aircraft fire. They didn't hit anything, but at least the gunners felt a lot better.

Monday, January 26, 1942
Surabaja, Java
Dutch East Indies

Roland McKnight and his crew arrived at the submarine base at Surabaja on board a Dutch corvette. Their submarine S-36 was a total wreck, and they reckoned they were lucky to be alive.

After their first success they had sighted nothing throughout the period of the patrol in the Sibuyan Sea. Close to the limits of their endurance, McKnight signaled his intentions to the Navy headquarters on Corregidor and headed south for the Malay Barrier and Darwin.

Trouble started on the fourth day. The port motor flashed and caught fire. The engineer and his mates took it apart, but it was to no avail. McKnight limped south with the port shaft out of commission.

On January 15 they were about 100 miles off the port of Tarakan, on the eastern coast of Borneo. McKnight was in the control room getting ready to go up on the bridge before diving at dawn when the intercom blared forth, betraying the note of urgency in the speaker: "Captain to the bridge."

McKnight clambered up onto the still darkened bridge, and there about 2 miles off on his starboard beam, and heading directly at the submarine, he saw the unmistakable V shape of a destroyer's bow approaching at high speed.

"Dive! Dive! Dive!" McKnight ordered, pressed the Klaxon, and the bridge lookouts scrambled through the hatch. He turned to follow as he saw a yellow flash light up the destroyer's bow. Her forward gun had fired.

"Captain, we can't." It was the engineer on the voice pipe. "I've lost lubrication on the starboard motor."

"We've got no choice. Dive!" McKnight shouted and pressed the Klaxon a second time before following the last of his crew through the conning tower hatch. Water cascaded over the bridge from the shell that fell just 100 yards off the port counter.

They dived. Just as the S-36 slid under, the Japanese destroyer ran right over it.

The first salvo of depth charges were set deep—they went off underneath the submarine's stern, tilted the boat, and sent it straight down to the bottom on one motor with no lubrication on the shaft and the bearings running hot.

McKnight gripped hold of the periscope stanchion for balance and looked across to the bulkhead at the depth gauges. They were already past their test depth, and, as the sub was still heading down, he didn't bother to look again. As the turbulence from the exploding charges settled they heard the ping of the sonar bounce off the hull. The destroyer had them in its clutches.

The engineers took the caps off the bearings of the starboard motor and poured oil out of 5-gallon drums by hand; each time the compartment filled with a puff of smoke. There was a rhythmic beat of propellers overhead as the destroyer ran in down the path of the echoing sonar. The crew heard the plop as the charges hit the water, but they exploded above them this time.

McKnight blew the main ballast. It was the only way he could stop their plummeting dive to destruction. This in turn brought fresh problems, since they were now bounding around like a cork in a whirlpool. Thrashing propellers signaled the return of the destroyer for its third run at the same time that the dive had been halted and the submarine was heading for the surface fast. Such antics must have thrown the Japanese skipper off his stride, since the third depth charges exploded well beneath the submarine.

McKnight flooded, or vented inboard the main ballast tank as much as he could; but there was still a bubble of air in the tank so they were unstable in depth. At least their mad charge to the surface had been brought under some control, but the abrupt movements of the submarine and the unremitting hammer blows of the depth charges had inflicted other damage. The gyrocompass tumbled and was unusable, and the magnetic compass was flooding, so they had no way of knowing in which direction they were heading. But the worst problem was the smoke from the engine-room compartment, which now threatened to fill the submarine with choking fumes. Unless the shaft could be repaired, McKnight realized he would have no choice other than to surface and fight it out with their guns. He passed the word to the gun crew, though he did not think much of their chances with a single puny 3-inch gun against the multiple 5-inch batteries that comprised the main aramament of most Japanese destroyers. He remembered, too, the bows-on shot they had tried before the submarine had dived. The Japanese had not been that far off target.

Fortunately the engineers were able to repair the shaft, so the immediate need to surface was avoided. McKnight continued to vary the submarine's depth to avoid the Japanese attacks, and their erratic course was probably what saved them. Obviously the Japanese sonar operators could not match the skill of their gunners.

After about four hours the Japanese destroyer gave up, or perhaps ran out of depth charges. Whatever the reason, it left. McKnight remained submerged. He knew conditions were calm on the surface, but in their crippled condition they were better below. He was able to get the air out of the main ballast tanks and the boat back in trim. By the end of the day the engineers even repaired the port motor. Thus it was with confidence restored that McKnight brought the S-36 to periscope depth, checked the surrounding waters, and surfaced with the onset of night into an empty sea. He set course by the bridge compass for Surabaja and handed the con over to the watchkeeper. Another ten minutes of this sea breeze, and McKnight then intended to get some sleep.

There was a loud bang from aft and a smudge of dirty black smoke came from the exhausts. The engineer wearily poked his head through the conning tower hatch and delivered the glad tidings: The starboard engine shaft had cracked. It took them three days to repair the fault, during which time they sailed slowly south on the surface at minimum revs, as McKnight was desperately afraid to overload the port engine. As he said to the navigator, "There're only sails left."

It was a great tribute to the combination of technical skills and dogged determination, the qualities that make a good marine engineer, that the motors were repaired and the S-36 was able to enter the last phase of the voyage more or less in one piece. They were now sailing into uncharted waters. All the charts for the Malay Barrier and Makassar Strait had been destroyed in the bombing of *Canopus.*

At high tide *S-36* piled onto the coral reef called Capabatang. McKnight sent off a distress signal, "AM AGROUND AND SINK-ING," together with his estimated position, and investigated the damage. There was a coral head caught under the port stern diving plane, and as the tide went out the submarine listed to starboard. The waves pounded her against the reef, and every time the waves lifted the submarine and smashed it down on the coral, the shaft and keel rattled all the way from the stern to the control room.

Early the next morning a small Dutch corvette came out from Makassar, and at high tide tried to pull them off the reef. When that had failed, McKnight transferred the bulk of the crew to the other ship, which then stood off as escort to the crippled submarine, and with a few key men awaited the arrival of a Dutch naval tug, which had been dispatched. However, before it could arrive on the scene, the sea rose, and the pounding got worse in the swell. The after battery room punctured and filled the compartments with chlorine gas and water.

There was nothing left for them to do except collect the confidential books, open all hatches and valves, and abandon ship. As the corvette pulled away from the scene, the *S-36* could still be seen, now listing heavily, her bottom plates ruptured and indecently exposed to view.

Thursday, January 29, 1942
The Big Pocket
Tuol River front
Western Bataan

In western Bataan General Kimura followed close on the heels of Wainwright's troops as they moved into their new defense positions. To spearhead his attack Kimura intended to use Colonel Yoshioka's 20th Infantry, or rather all that was left, the 3rd Battalion together with the headquarters and service companies. The total strength Yoshioka could muster was less than a thousand men. The other battalions of this once proud regiment (that was before their numbers had been decimated by the Allied defense) were fighting for their lives in the Battle of the Points.

The Japanese hit the main defense lines, more by luck than judgment, on the boundary between the 1st and 11th Philippine divisions, in thick jungle where it was extremely difficult for units to establish physical contact. The men of the 1st Philippine Division still had not really recovered from the drubbing they received at Mauban in the first Battle of Bataan. They dug trenches and cleared fields of fire, but the work was slow and difficult. The high summer noon temperatures sapped their energy even in the jungle gloom. They had neither entrenching tools nor axes. Most of the men dug foxholes with their mess cans and hacked at the bamboo with their bayonets in a futile effort to clear adequate fields of fire.

They were still frantically digging in when the Japanese struck, penetrated the line, and established a defense perimeter, or pocket, about a mile behind the main U.S. lines. In the thick, impenetrable jungle, Yoshioka's troops in turn prepared their foxholes and weapons pits, some of which they connected by a labyrinth of tunnels. It took the Americans a week just to identify the strength and location of the enemy.

Kermit Lay's outfit, provisional Military Police I Corps, was composed mostly of retired Philippine Scouts from the 45th and 54th Infantry. They were bivouacked about a mile in front of the corps headquarters. They spent their time either guarding headquarters and directing traffic, or touring the trails behind the front line picking up stragglers. It was the latter duty that Kermit disliked more. They used an old, converted, open-top bus for the job. Kermit was the duty officer that day when word came in that units of what was thought to be the 11th Division had broken in the battle against the Big Pocket.

After a couple of hours of searching behind the front, Kermit and his detachment came across what appeared to be about two companies' worth of soldiers. They were squatting in a jungle glade, clearly dispirited and beaten. Some had no shoes or uniforms, and many had discarded their weapons.

Lay dismounted, left the bus on the trail, and walked across to the group. "Okay, men, I'm going to take you back to your unit," he said.

Nobody paid any attention whatsoever, except for two American officers, who deliberately turned away. Lay put a hand on his .45 and tried a second time. "I'm gonna shoot the first one of you to refuse my order." He turned deliberately toward an American second lieutenant, the biggest and meanest-looking in the group. "Your original outfit is the 31st, isn't it?"

"What of it?" the big man asked sullenly.

"Well, you're a regular soldier, and know what it's all about. Why not start doing your job? They've made you an officer, now act the part."

"Shit," replied the man, spat at Lay's feet, and deliberately turned his head away.

Kermit realized that the whole group had suddenly taken a new interest in life.

Beat him, and I've got them, he thought. Lay walked over and confronted the man.

"I'm ordering you to get up on that tree stump and instruct these men to get back in the line. Go on! Tell them about face and lead them back where you've come from."

"Fuck off, policeman!"

Lay pulled out his .45 and pistol-whipped the officer, who crumpled to the ground without a murmur. He gestured at a couple of Filipinos and said, "Pick him up, and the rest of you follow me." The group meekly obeyed his instructions. Lay led the Filipinos out of the glade and back in the direction of the front line. He found their American adviser cowering in a foxhole. As he came up, Lay saluted.

"Lieutenant, get down, get down!" the elderly major said pointedly and then looked around. "Someone get that crazy lieutenant down!"

Lay calmly reported that he had about a hundred of the major's men back in the trees.

"Never mind them, get down quick!" the officer ordered.

"What do you mean, 'get down'?" Lay asked.

"You damned fool, don't you see that Jap plane up there?" Lay looked up at the sky and saw a P-40 Tomahawk circling to land at Cabcaben.

He turned around and walked away in disgust. "No wonder these kids ran with deadbeats like that around," he said to his Scout sergeant.

Sunday, February 8, 1942
12th Medical Battalion, Philippine Scouts
Sector D, II Corps
Trail 4 on the Orion–Bagac line, below Mount Samat

As a result of the reorganization that USAFFE had carried out among the Army formations and their deployment in Bataan, Paul Ashton's 12th Medical Battalion met those needs for the troops defending Sector D of the Orion–Bagac line. The soldiers in the front line belonged to the 41st and 21st Infantry divisions of the Philippine Army. By this time they were running very short of fuel as much as medicines, which made it necessary for Ashton to move the medical aid stations right into the very front-line positions. Every night he would send a group consisting of a doctor and litter bearers into the front line to stay with the men there. Two orderlies were to accompany any patrol that might be sent out.

Ashton frequently spent his nights away from the more comfortable bivouac in the rear area, where the battalion's headquarters was located, and moved into a front-line foxhole alongside the Filipinos. There was no particular requirement for him to do this. As adjutant he could find more than enough to occupy his time in administrative duties. However, Ashton was determined that the Filipino doctors should not be asked to do anything that he was not prepared to do himself, so he added his name to the roster for front-line duties.

Moving from the relative comfort of a secure rear-area base into the front-line positions was something that Ashton found particularly harrowing and often very dangerous. There was always the threat of the Japanese sniper in the tree, who had infiltrated through the front line and lay in ambush, waiting for the unwary to come along the trail. More often than not, however, the real threat that Ashton feared came from the Filipinos themselves. One thing the Filipinos were especially good at was digging booby traps. The particular favorite among the front-line soldiers of the 21st Infantry was a 30-foot pit that narrowed toward its base so that a falling body would be sure to slam onto the pointed bamboo stakes. Another and more sophisticated variety was a snare made from trailing creepers. The victim would be whisked high into the air by the ankle and impaled on stakes strategically located against the trunk of a nearby tree. It was a good idea to approach the front-line positions with a Filipino guide, since man traps did not discriminate between friend and foe. By this stage of the campaign there was no front line defined as such—just a series of foxholes with single strands of barbed wire in front of them, which the troops festooned with empty tin cans. This was as good an alarm system as any in the jungle. The foxholes too were not dug in a straight line but rather staggered in an irregular pattern so that the positions could have some depth to their defense.

There was something akin to a ritual as troops prepared to spend a night in their foxholes. Weapons were checked and loaded; knife, bayonet, and spare clips of ammunition laid out close at hand; water bottles were filled, and a final visit was made to empty the bowels. Except for those detailed as guards, most men tried to sleep in the early part of the evening, as there would be no chance later in the dark of the night. Artillery roared out, and an occasional machine gun chattered before a strange peace descended over the jungle twilight.

Once it got really dark on most nights the Japanese edged forward and attempted an infiltration of the position. Ashton found this the first bad moment of the long night—sounds all around, but what sounds were they—a crawling Japanese or some Filipino with loose bowels going to the john? Then a scream, perhaps a grunt, and the noise of Japanese falling into a foxhole followed by the muffled sounds of two men struggling for life in the bottom of a trench.

The middle of the night in the jungle is darker than the inside of a cow, Ashton thought. There are noises everywhere as unseen shapes slide by, man and creature, but who can tell? The moment of truth for the noises of the night comes when the black darkness gives way, and all of a sudden a man can see and identify shapes in the half light of dawn, but is it a friend or a foe in the next foxhole along the line? It is also the most dangerous moment, for both sides can see, and then the shooting begins. Pandemonium reigns, and many a man dies by the hand of his own comrades. Some mornings the dawn greets them with the sight of dead Filipinos sprawled across the top of foxholes and no sign of the enemy. This is the worst moment of all, for it means that they have infiltrated behind the lines to lie in ambush along the trails used by ration details and the wounded. A fighting patrol has to be sent back to search both the undergrowth and high in the trees, to kill on sight or risk being killed. In these encounters there is an important difference between friend and foe: The Japanese is resigned to death and seeks only to take at least as many of his enemy with him. The defenders fight to survive.

Monday, February 9, 1942
HQ, I Corps
Bataan

Word came that General Wainwright intended to visit the front line, and he asked whether Champlin cared to come along for the ride.

After a meager breakfast they got into a command car with Major Pugh, the G-2, and Captain Dooley. A Filipino corporal drove while two sergeants from Kermit Lay's outfit stood on the running boards scanning the skies for strafing planes. They drove down toward the beach but were stopped a little over a mile from headquarters by Lay, who flagged down the car and warned the general that the area ahead had been infiltrated by snipers the night before. Everybody in the car took note but showed little surprise. After all, this had become part of a regular pattern of activity on the part of the Japanese.

Champlin began to realize now just how close the headquarters was to the front line. He had known already that it was forward of some of their own artillery batteries. They drove along Trail 7 toward the forward positions occupied by the 11th Infantry and as the car neared a bend in the track a major flagged them down and hopped onto the running board. He pointed ahead to the curve and yelled to make himself heard above the noise of the engine.

"The country up ahead is wide open, general, and under enemy artillery fire. Take the bend fast please, sir."

The car surged forward in response, and they tore around the bend in a great cloud of dust. The driver slowed down as they reached the cover of the trees, and the young aides in the back kidded the major for his excessive caution.

"You'll see," he said. "Just be sure when you return to make a quick trip around this bend." He saluted and jumped nimbly off the car, and they drove on to inspect the more forward units.

Champlin could feel the tension among the front-line soldiers. Though he faced the enemy, the front-line soldier was cut off and isolated from the main sources of information in the headquarters behind the front line. Because they were so hungry for news, he understood now how rumors could start and spread so easily. Only the week before, one such rumor had started in the base hospital, where there was a tall tower with a couple of air raid watchers on top. One of them had seen some ships that appeared to be coming into the bay. The word had quickly spread that it was a gigantic convoy, a "mile long," which had arrived from the States. It was the news that everyone wanted and many expected to hear. What the luckless man saw were the ships of the Inshore Squadron, minesweepers and China gunboats, moving to their daytime anchorages under the protective umbrella of the guns on Corregidor.

After completing the inspection, the general's party returned to the command car and headed back. Nearing the same open curve in the road, the driver increased speed. Just as he stepped on the gas, they heard the crack and whistle of artillery, and it wasn't friendly. The first shell landed 100 feet and the second 200 feet ahead of the car. The driver tore around the bend and swung off the road. As a man the group was off, out of the vehicle, and sprinting for the cover of the undergrowth about 50 yards away. As they entered the woods, they ran into the forward command post for a nearby battalion. Since the artillery was still pounding away, they rushed to the nearest foxholes—that is, all except General Wainwright. He talked for a few minutes to the battalion commander, a major with a big grin, and the aides remembered him from the incident earlier. Then Wainwright recognized a captain who had been a sergeant under him in the cavalry school in prewar days. Wainwright took the captain by the arm and they walked over and sat down on a row of sandbags, deliberately turning their backs on the Japanese artillery. Shells whistled over the trees where the party had taken cover and burst less than 30 yards away. Champlin, peering over the parapet of his foxhole marveled at such conduct and wondered why the general chose to risk his life in this way. Never had he seen such coolness under fire; not once was the conversation interrupted except by the actual explosions.

When it was all over Champlin asked the question that was uppermost in his mind.

"General, why is it that you, commander of half the troops on Bataan, risk your life the way you did just a few minutes ago?" It seemed to Champlin to have been a foolish thing to do.

Wainwright smiled a little and answered slowly. "Champ, think it over for a minute. What have we got to offer these men? Can I give them more food? No. We haven't any more food. Can I give them ammunition? No. That is also beginning to run low. Can I send them supplies, equipment, medicines, or tanks? No. Everything has practically gone. But we *can* give them morale, and that is all I have left to give them. That is why I visit the front every day. Now do you understand, son, why it is important for me to sit on sandbags in the line of fire while the rest of you seek shelter?"

There was no need for an answer.

Provisional Air Corps battalion
Sector B, II Corps front
Orion, Bataan

The provisional Air Corps, some two battalions of ersatz infantry, held the coastal sector below the town of Orion. Those who had been involved in the Battle of the Points had learned fast, and they encouraged the others to dig in and site as many machine guns as they could lay their hands on. Good, deep foxholes afforded the best protection against Japanese mortar fire, and when the enemy did come, the only thing that could stop him was massed machine-gun fire. Crew chiefs made trips down to the *Canopus* and collected tripods on which they mounted the .50-calibers they had hacked out of the wrecked planes at Clark and Nichols. They packed the legs of the tripods with sandbags to give the bucking guns some stability in a sustained fire role to deny the Japanese their march on Limay.

Chaplain Zimmerman lived in the foxholes with the men of his battalion. The Japanese put in probing attacks most nights, so there always was plenty of call for his services. He slept on a stretcher outside the forward command post when it wasn't necessary for him to be in a foxhole. Zimmerman used to walk the line every morning and chat with the men. He collected their mail—they had worked out a system of managing without envelopes, as there were none to be had anywhere on Bataan.

The increasing shortage of fuel meant a particular problem for the chaplain, since they could no longer arrange to send the dead back down the line. Zimmerman took it upon himself to establish a cemetery just behind the front; he marked the ground and laid it out neatly. The first grave was dug under the shade of a big mango tree. It was while the chaplain was still completing the cemetery that word came in that a company of Filipinos on the left flank had broken. Zimmerman bumped into one of their number by the cemetery.

"My name is Rodrigues," the youth said. "I am the sole survivor of Company K. We were completely surrounded. Everyone else has been killed. I have had nothing to eat for three days, yesterday, today, and tomorrow."

About 50 "sole" survivors of Company K passed through their lines that day. The Air Corps rounded them up and escorted them back to their battalions.

By the middle of the month, the Japanese offensive began to die away. Despite their need to retreat to new positions, the Allied line had held firm no matter what the enemy had thrown at them. The Japanese had probed for weak spots along the main lines and even tried to outflank from the sea, but all to no avail.

Homma had never expected the Americans to defend Bataan in such strength or with such tenacity. His Intelligence officers had assured him that MacArthur would pull the Americans onto Corregidor and leave the Filipinos to their fate. Instead the Allies, Filipino and American, though they had to give a little ground, had fought the Japanese to a standstill. Failure in battle on this scale meant considerable loss of face for Homma, but such were his losses that he had little alternative.

Thus less than one month after the Japanese had opened the Battle of Bataan with a formidable artillery bombardment, Homma was ready to concede defeat and pull back behind his own defensive lines anchored on Balanga. Colonel Yoshioka, with considerable difficulty, was able to disengage his surviving troops of the 20th Infantry from the pockets and pull back behind the line. He had less than 380 men of the 1,000 who had begun the battle. When Philippine Scouts penetrated the bamboo they encountered a most gruesome battlefield. Some 600 dead lay buried in the most shallow of graves, from which limbs and torsos protruded, covered with enormous flies. Some of the dead held hunks of horsemeat in their hands. Fearing an epidemic, the American field commanders put the pocket to the torch.

Along the front, Homma's brigades had been severely mauled, and to their considerable battle casualties must also be added the sick. It is doubtful whether the enemy could have mustered more than three full-strength battalions, perhaps no more than 2,000 men, in the whole of Bataan by the third week in February.

In tactical terms the defenders knew they had inflicted a heavy blow on the enemy, and this was reflected in the fighting demeanor of many of the front-line regiments. They had instituted combat patrols and launched local counterattacks in places to straighten the line. Some of the divisional commanders favored a return to the offensive, but wiser counsel prevailed. Even if they had marched all the way to Manila, and they could have, it would not have altered the strategic position. The Japanese controlled the seas around Luzon.

The Filipino troops who had stuck it out on the front lines, and of course there were some who didn't, were now hardened veterans. Their own American field commanders and advisers didn't recognize them as the same formations who had performed so badly in the first days of the war. It is equally true that these officers had also improved with time and experience and that perhaps many of the earlier failings could in part be attributed to their own shortcomings.

The opposing armies drew apart, consolidated their positions, patrolled the no-man's-land, and prepared for the next round of battle.

More and more the American defenders on Bataan and Corregidor came to accept the inevitability of their fate. Their attitude was not that of a weary resignation but a grim, rock-hard defiance, not without a certain and peculiar gaiety. It seems an inherent characteristic of Western man that when his future seems hopeless, a wild humor emanates as he tries to make light of things. In Britain there was the Battle of Britain spirit, while in the Philippines, attitudes were best epitomized by Frank Hewlett, a war correspondent, who wrote a piece of doggerel that became famous:

We are the battling bastards of Bataan
No momma, no poppa, no Uncle Sam
No aunts, no uncles, no nephews, no nieces
No rifles, no guns or artillery pieces
And nobody gives a damn!

VIII. Siege: "The Battling Bastards of Bataan"

Wednesday, February 11, 1942–
Sunday, March 29, 1942

Fort Mills
Corregidor

Morale was still high on Corregidor at this stage in the campaign. MacArthur's headquarters had hailed the Battle of Bataan as at least a tactical victory for the Allies, and the island's garrison was convinced that it could give as good an account of itself if the Japanese should somehow bypass Bataan and attempt a landing on Corregidor.

Air raids were now a daily occurrence. Twin-engined bombers with meatball insignia on their wings flew leisurely across the sky, threading their way through the puff balls of exploding flak. The pattern of these raids was usually the same. During the morning a single photoreconnaissance plane, dubbed by the defenders as Photo Joe or the Lone Ranger, circled Corregidor and the other island forts. Shortly after, the bombers would appear, invariably at an altitude of 20,000 feet and a steady speed of 160 miles an hour. The bombers approached the islands in a tight V formation, then broke into smaller groups for the bomb run over their selected targets.

The raids produced a marked change in the attitude of the garrison toward the weather. The bright moonlight of the tropics, which had in the past aroused so many romantic memories, came to be feared because it carried the threat of a night attack. The muted light of a tropical dawn and dusk made it difficult to identify targets, and sometimes the Japanese would choose these moments for a sneak raid when they sought to catch the defenses unawares. Anti-aircraft gunners cursed when the sky above filled with broken clouds, since it was easier for the enemy to approach the targets, only heard but not seen. In stark contrast to the halcyon days of the peace when typhoons were hated and feared, they were now eagerly awaited.

The bombings had reduced the barracks on Topside to rubble. Already from the air it must have appeared as if the island had the pox. The lush greenery of the jungle had become dotted with scores of angry brown pockmarks where the bombs had scarred the jungle foliage into craters. The barracks and other buildings had been built in the days when the plane was not a menace, and, as at Singapore, the military architects of Corregidor had anticipated that the main assault would come from the sea. The seaward defense batteries had suffered comparatively little damage. The magazines and powder rooms had, in fact, been bombproofed before the war, either by being relocated into the sides of hills or dug deep underground, and so were virtually unscathed. The anti-aircraft guns were in more exposed positions, and these, as a consequence, suffered some damage and casualties. Neither was sufficient, however, to interfere with their operation.

The hospital was busy and fairly full, but the majority of the patients weren't battle casualties; they were suffering from illnesses such as bronchitis and influenza, respiratory diseases caused by confinement in the damp, dust-laden laterals under Malinta Hill.

Food was rationed. It was barely adequate and exceedingly monotonous. Everybody was on two meals a day, eaten early in the morning and just after dusk. Those in the tunnels ate better than the troops manning the trenches and gun positions. For those in the tunnels food consisted of canned salmon, usually, and rice with an occasional carabao or mule steak. For those in the front line, the fare comprised a couple of slices of bread if they were lucky, the inevitable rice and gravy, and dried fruit salvaged from the wrecked barges that lay in the shallow waters off the island's beaches. There was never quite enough food to fill the stomach. It was a monotonous and debilitating ration that did little to nourish the body, but the effects of a limited diet were not yet apparent.

Fresh water was another commodity that was in short supply. The power plants and waterlines by which it was pumped around the island were desperately vulnerable to bombing. On the many occasions when the system failed, units had to send a truck to the nearest point for their day's supply. The water was carried in 12-inch powder cans. They measured 2 feet by 5½ feet, a handy container but difficult to handle when heavy and full.

Wednesday, February 11, 1942
Headquarters, I Corps
Bataan

Richard Sakakida put the finishing touches to his propaganda message; it seemed strange sitting under a tree and composing in his mother tongue for his enemies to read. He checked the short message through carefully:

> IT IS CHERRY BLOSSOM TIME BACK IN YOUR HOMELAND, AND THE MILITARY HAVE SENT YOU HERE TO THE JUNGLES OF BATAAN. YOU OUGHT TO BE AT HOME WITH YOUR FAMILIES AND LOVED ONES ENJOYING THE CHERRY BLOSSOM. SO WHY CONTINUE THIS FUTILE BATTLE? COME AND SURRENDER WITH THIS LEAFLET AND YOUR SHIPMENT BACK HOME WILL BE GUARANTEED.

He took the finished product down to the orderly room in the grove of trees, loaded the field mimeograph machine, and printed a couple of dozen copies. When the ink had dried he walked along the trail that led to the field engineer company attached to corps headquarters. There he picked up an armful of ½-inch galvanized pipes, which the engineers had already cut into 2-inch lengths; he rolled and loaded the messages into the tubes.

Then Sakakida walked on to Kermit Lay's unit, where he picked up a vehicle, an escort, and a slingshot. The latter had been built by the engineers. It was a cumbersome affair and so, for convenience, he kept it with the police. The Y-shaped frame was made out of a two-by-four, and the sling was an inner tube fashioned from an old tire. The whole affair stood about 2 feet off the ground when properly dug in and "fired" from the sitting or kneeling position; on a good day it had a range of some 500 yards. The escort also brought along the loudspeaker and battery box that was an essential part of the performance. Richard felt quite lighthearted as they drove up to the line; this was to be his last propaganda mission over the enemy front. Tomorrow he would return to Corregidor, where he would work on the radio station propaganda service—a sort of male equivalent of Tokyo Rose.

The little group timed their arrival to reach the front just before dusk. They moved forward to the foxholes and dug the catapult base into the soft undergrowth. While one of the Scouts solemnly "loaded," Sakakida "pumped" the area to their front liberally with the metal tubes. There was silence for a moment, then a voice with a marked Japanese accent called out, "What the hell are you firing now, American? Are you out of ammunition?"

They moved to another part of the line, and there Sakakida set up his microphone and loudspeaker and spoke his message from the comfort of a foxhole. The Japanese as always were scrupulously polite; they allowed him to have his say before blasting the area with mortars. For this reason, Sakakida's was not a welcome face among the troops in the front line, for they always had to put up with the barrage of hate long after he had left. Sakakida, too, regarded the whole operation as an exercise in futility, and for that reason alone he was glad to be leaving; not that he thought his new assignment had much to offer, but at least men would not die because of it.

Saturday, February 14, 1942
Provisional Military Police Company
I Corps HQ, Bataan

They were bombed a few times that morning, and then Photo Joe came over and showered the front line with leaflets. One of Kermit Lay's Scouts collected a handful and brought them to the command post. They were all on the same theme, and most had a picture of a family in Manila, sitting around a big table with a couple of Filipino soldiers. The table was laden with good things to eat, mangoes and papaws, fried chicken, and a host of other delicacies. Underneath the caption read:

THIS IS NOT YOUR WAR. THIS IS THE AMERICANS' WAR. YOU SHOULDN'T BE IN IT. YOU SHOULD BE AT HOME WITH YOUR LOVED ONES. THERE WILL BE FURTHER INSTRUCTIONS IN A COUPLE OF HOURS.

An hour or so later, Photo Joe appeared a second time and more leaflets came fluttering down into the jungle and foxholes. The Scouts collected a selection, and they were all broadly the same. There were no pictures, just a message, written in English on one side and Filipino Tagalog on the other. The message was headed, "THIS IS YOUR SURRENDER CARD." Beneath were the detailed instructions:

> PLACE YOUR RIFLE ON YOUR LEFT SHOULDER WITH THE MUZZLE POINTING DOWN AND GO TO KILOMETER POST 147. REPORT THERE TO THE JAPANESE ARMY.

Kermit Lay picked two men and moved quickly to Kilometer Post 147 and the Japanese rendezvous. It was situated in no-man's-land, though nearer to the Japanese than the American line. They found a good position about 900 yards before the post on a small knoll that overlooked the trail and waited. They had been there about an hour when the first pathetic little group of Filipinos appeared. They moved forward cautiously; their rifles were on the left shoulder, muzzle down. Lay sighted his Springfield on the man he took to be their leader, a Filipino lieutenant, hesitated for a moment, and looked at his two Scouts. The old men, somber-faced, nodded their heads in stern agreement—they knew what had to be done. Lay turned back to the trail, sighted a second time, and fired. The lieutenant gave a piercing scream as the bullet smashed into his face. He was dead before he hit the ground. The others in the group fled back up the trail toward the corps battle line.

The policemen waited for another hour, but nobody else appeared. Obviously the word had spread: The propaganda was a Japanese trap. Lay and his Scouts returned to their headquarters. There was no telling how many would have gone if they hadn't been scared off, but that was poor consolation to Kermit Lay.

Sunday, February 15, 1942
The convent of the Sisters of Maryknoll
Baguio, Luzon

News arrived of the capitulation of the British garrison in Singapore. Sloth and smug complacency, born in part of a false conviction of white supremacy in fighting a machine-age war, had contributed to the failure of the British High Command to prepare adequately to meet the Japanese threat. General Percival in surrendering some 130,000 local, British, Indian, and Australian troops had not only lost for the Allies the western bastion of the Malay Barrier and given the British Army its worst defeat ever, but in so doing he also had effectively sealed the fate of the troops on Bataan and Corregidor.

That evening a Japanese officer arrived at the convent on the hill above Baguio. He ordered the Sisters each to make a Japanese flag, a square of white cloth on which they sewed a red sun, and to be ready to leave the convent the following morning.

The nuns were taken to Camp John Hay in an old alcohol-driven cattle truck. In the enlisted men's mess hall, one of the few buildings to survive intact from the air raids, they met all the other internees; it was the first time they had talked with outsiders since the city had fallen. Sister Louise was shocked by their appearance, the tragedy of recent weeks etched deeply into their faces, and then realized that they too must present a similar picture.

An American banker, the appointed spokesman of the civilians, told the nuns that they were all to take part in a Victory Parade through the streets of Baguio, hence the flags, and then they were to be interned in Camp Holmes. Sister Louise looked about her. There must have been five hundred people in the mess hall, Americans, Dutch, English, and Russians, men, women, and children. There were the elderly and infirm, pregnant women, children, and babes in arms.

"Surely the Japanese will not expect everybody to take part in this procession," she said.

"I'm afraid so," the banker replied. "We tried to reason with them, but all we got was a beating for our pains."

The march began when the sun was at its highest. An officer mounted on an American polo pony led the way, followed by two companies of soldiers with bayonets fixed. Then came the internees, flanked by guards, and another company of soldiers brought up the rear. Throughout the heat of that summer afternoon they "processed" the streets of the old capital, waving the little flags and intoning what their captors had ordered them to chant, "Fall, Singapore, fall." In this parody of a Roman triumph, the local population was forced to line the streets and witness the humiliation of the white man and the dawn of the new "Age of Asia." Filipinos sobbed and many turned their backs on the scenes of degradation. This in turn drove the Japanese into a frenzy. Though they beat and kicked the people, they were impotent against mass disobedience. Some Filipinos turned to the procession and took even greater risks to press on the parched marchers fruit and water.

Sister Louise stumbled along in the throng. Her white robes were stained and torn; her feet, shod in thin sandals, first blistered and then bled. She carried a little boy in her arms. Mercifully he slept some of the time, though by the end her arms had lost all sense of feeling.

After some hours the Japanese led the internees to the cemetery. There they took a number of men, Americans and Filipinos, perhaps a dozen in number, and while everybody watched they were forced to dig their own graves. The Japanese pushed the civilians into a wide semicircle facing inward and each man was ordered to kneel at the head of his grave. A priest in the crowd began the Lord's Prayer, the nuns dropped to their knees and reached for their rosaries. Sister Louise endeavored to shield the little boy from seeing the outrage. The Japanese first shot the Filipinos. An officer walked the line and fired his pistol into the base of the skull, and the bodies toppled forward. The Americans were beheaded.

The internees, struck dumb with the horror of what they had witnessed and weary beyond belief, were marched back to the mess hall in Camp John Hay. Their captors gave them a meal, bowls of thin rice stew with some fish, and provided lice-ridden pallets on which to sleep.

There was little sleep for Sister Louise and the other nuns that night. The events of the day, coming after weeks of deprivation, proved too much for some of the elderly and the sick, and during the night they succumbed. For the pregnant women it had been a horrific ordeal, and most either aborted or gave premature birth. The Sisters worked throughout the long hours of darkness. They had rigged a screen of sorts across one end of the hall, and there the babies were delivered.

The following morning a convoy of decrepit trucks loaded the living and took them to the camp that had by then been prepared inside the cantonment called Camp John Holmes.

Monday, February 16, 1942
41st Division artillery
On the slopes of Mount Samat
Bataan

A combination of offensive patrolling and painstaking Intelligence had identified what seemed to be a major Japanese headquarters in Balanga, 6 miles north of the American line. The town was out of range of the 75mm guns on the forward slopes of Mount Samat, and the angle was too steep for the 155mm GPF Long Toms that were dug in on the reverse slopes.

Winston Jones calculated that if he could move a battery about 2,000 yards forward, into the very front line of the infantry, and fire shrapnel shells, this would give him a range of about 7,000 yards, just enough to hit Balanga. It took him longer to persuade Divisional Artillery to agree to the scheme than it did to compute the range and distance required. Eventually Division agreed, provided that the operation could be done during the hours of darkness and the battery be back in its proper position by daylight.

Jones went down to that part of the front occupied by the provisional Air Corps, who were directly opposite Balanga. He talked with their officers, gained their ready support for the scheme, and they planned where the guns would be deployed. Jones surveyed the ground and positioned the aiming sticks. This would save precious time when it came to laying the guns on their target. By the end of the first night the gun positions had been prepared and the ready-use ammunition moved into place. Jones spent the day briefing his men thoroughly on the mission and overhauling the guns that had been selected for the operation.

The next evening the convoy of four trucks drove down to the Air Corps line. Extra men waited with block and tackle to haul the guns off the trucks and into their allotted positions. Jones moved quickly along the line to check that each gun was laid along its aiming stick and the barrels cranked up to their maximum elevation.

"Load!" he ordered. Four breechblocks snapped open, and the shells of point detonating shrapnel, guaranteed to do the maximum damage, were rammed home.

"Ready!" Four breechblocks slammed shut, and the gun captains, ramrod straight on one knee, raised their right arms in the signal. It was not every day that they had such an appreciative audience. The Air Corps had gathered around to watch the show.

"Fire!" Four barrels blasted aside the night, and before the guns rocked forward from the first recoil the breeches were sponged and the guns loaded again. The secret of the "French 75" and the mechanism that set it apart from all previous guns when it was invented in 1896 was the long recoil cylinder. This was a device designed to absorb the energy of the recoil and return the gun to battery smoothly and efficiently without disturbing the position of the gun's carriage. This removed the need to relay the gun after each shot and thus gave it the potential for a very rapid rate of fire, provided it was serviced by a good crew. Jones's men gave a faultless display of gunnery skill. They handled the 16-pound shrapnel shells like seasoned veterans, and as the guns spoke a second time the air crew cheered and applauded.

The battery fired twenty rounds from each gun before they packed up, loaded the trucks, and returned to the foothills of Mount Samat. As dawn broke the last gun was deployed back in its old position and the gunners manned their pieces for the dawn stand to. From their vantage points on the high ground, they could see the pall of smoke rising over Balanga.

Two days later Intelligence sources learned of the confusion and chaos the bombardment had caused. Apparently the Japanese thought the fire had come from warships in the bay. They retaliated by mounting some of their artillery on large floats and towing them down to bombard positions along the coast. The Americans were waiting, for artillery observers had spotted the whole operation. Corregidor was notified and Battery Geary, the only one on Corregidor that had the necessary traverse to support the land battle on Bataan, opened fire. It takes 1,000 pounds of powder just to push the shell out of the barrel, and when that bursts on water the lethal radius is more than 250 yards. Those barges that survived scuttled back to the safety of their own lines.

Battery E, 59th Coast Artillery
Fort Drum
South Channel, Manila Bay

For the men of the "concrete battleship," it had been a very strange campaign indeed. They had followed the progress of the war on radio, manned their batteries, stood their watches, and waited for the tide of war to reach them. They were largely self-sufficient, made their own bread, ate two meals a day, mostly corned beef and rice, though weevils had gotten into the rice. For breakfast they occasionally had cracked wheat instead, likewise infested with the ubiquitous weevil, and a little watery condensed milk. The technique for consuming this was well proven and simple: The men stirred the mixture furiously and the weevil floated to the surface, where it could be skimmed off.

Sol Fromer was in the lower handling room, where the shells and separate charges of explosives were prepared before being sent by means of a hoist to the battery, when a Japanese cruiser hit the fort with a single armor-piercing shell. A couple of salvos straddled the base and soaked the top deck with spray. The shell that hit had plowed into the top turret, Battery Wilson, and let in the daylight through 14 inches of armor plate. The crew had gone to action stations as soon as they had been hit, but it proved to be a hit-and-run attack. The cruiser must have fired from below the horizon and then after a couple of rounds made off at high speed. A repair party was organized, led by a civilian named Williams. They stretched some canvas over the gap, welded metal inside and out, and finally covered the outside with sandbags.

The attack was the portent of things to come, for shortly after the Japanese opened up from the southern shore of Manila Bay they had moved some 240mm mortars into position, and these began a regular bombardment of Fort Drum and Fort Frank. In the daytime the Japanese used smokeless powder, but at night the gunners saw a flash to herald the arrival of a round. The mortars fired from behind the shelter of a hill, and the sound of the discharge, depending on wind direction, gave the crew adequate warning—sometimes as long as fifteen seconds—in which to take cover. The men used to put bets on a board on how many seconds the next shot would take. The verdict of an elected "official timekeeper" was final, and the lucky man scooped up his winnings.

Once this shelling started in earnest, the garrison on Drum reversed the order of their day. They had breakfast in the evening, and the morning meal became supper, because they spent the night at full-action stations. Except for the duty watch on the AA batteries and a skeleton crew on the main armament, the men were free to sleep the day away. Sol Fromer dreaded the morning shift because for him that meant being exposed outside as a loader on the AA battery. Occasionally the mighty guns of Fort Drum would speak in defiance as the observers laid the batteries on the positions where they supposed the Japanese had deployed the mortars. For the most part they just carved enormous wedges out of the virgin jungle, but it did everybody's morale a lot of good, including those on Bataan and Corregidor, to see and hear those turrets belch forth their defiance. In return the forts took an awful pounding, and though no more shells penetrated the armored casing on Fort Drum, the crash of the exploding shells against the casements sounded like the clapper of a mighty church bell to the men entombed inside.

The Japanese were now hitting Corregidor with artillery. At first the island garrison had stood and watched in awe as the forts took the punishment, but then it was their turn. The enemy had found a way by which they could increase the range of their 105mm guns, for these now began to hit the island frequently. It was a remarkable achievement, for the range was well in excess of most field guns. Because the fire had to come from batteries on the southern shore of Batangas, the experts in the tunnels on Corregidor believed they had to be 155mm guns, but after some duds were found they accepted the word of the gunners on Topside.

The Japanese were aiming to hit the little dirt air strip, Kindley Field, located on the tail of Corregidor near Monkey Point. Most of their shells fell wide of the target and sent William Griffiths and his squad scuttling for cover.

U.S.S. *Canopus*
Mariveles Bay
Bataan

Ed Erickson had left the hospital and was assigned to the *Canopus* as the Air Corps liaison officer. Such a grand-sounding title meant that he did whatever jobs were required in meeting those needs of the provisional Air Corps battalions that could be filled from the resources of the depot ship. *Canopus* also fed the many Filipino refugees who huddled for safety in the caves and hovels of Mariveles. Commander King and his men had rigged up some empty 50-gallon oil drums, and twice a day they cooked rice on the wharfside, into which they would then empty canned salmon. The ship's stores had an abundance of canned salmon. The lines of hungry refugees formed long before the rice had come to the boil.

There was one teenage boy, a dockside brat, who intrigued Commander King. They had had the refugee relief operation working for about a week, and every time this kid walked past him with his mess cans full, he looked up at King and said, "Look at that! Hebrews 13, verse 8." It was the same every day. King thought that perhaps the boy was a little "bomb happy," so as the crowd gathered for the evening meal he warned the chaplain, who stood waiting with him next to the steaming cauldrons. The boy walked past, looked at King, repeated his words, "Look at that! Hebrews 13, verse 8," and disappeared into the night. The chaplain pulled out his pocket Bible and looked up the text. He read the verse to King:

Jesus Christ the same yesterday and today, and forever.

There were others, too, who came to partake of the bounty from *Canopus*. Ruby Moteley, still suffering after a severe attack of malaria, insisted on staying at her post in the hospital, and it was taking her a long time to recover. An officer from *Canopus*, a classmate of her fiancé, Carl, invited her to come for dinner. As soon as she stepped on board she had a real treat. The officer stood guard over the showers while she soaped and scrubbed away the ingrained dirt of Bataan. Then came the normal evening meal on *Canopus*, roast beef, potatoes, and apple pie, but to her it was the most beautiful meal in the world. It was served off snow-white linen, for the officers still lived like gentlemen and would continue to do so until the ship sank beneath them. As long as the refrigerator held some food, it would be well cooked and correctly served. As long as the laundry worked, they ate off clean linen and napkins.

When the time came at last to take her back to the hospital, the officers gave her packages of candy for the nurses.

Thursday, February 19, 1942
Darwin
Australia

After the fall of Singapore, the main base for the British Eastern Fleet was moved across the Indian Ocean to Colombo, in Ceylon. Deployed forward to defend Java and what was left of the Malay Barrier was a clutch of elderly cruisers and a modest posse of destroyers belonging to the ABDA (American, British, Dutch, and Australian) Command. This token force was totally devoid of air cover once it moved far from the shore.

A Japanese carrier strike force sailed unchecked through the length and breadth of eastern waters astride MacArthur's line of communications, striking at Rabaul, and at Amboina west of New Guinea. The strike force under Admiral Nagumo included four of the aircraft carriers whose planes had attacked Pearl Harbor, *Akagi, Kaga, Hiryu,* and *Soryu,* together with their crack air crews. Escorted by the battleships *Hiei* and *Kirishima,* cruisers and destroyers, they struck next at Darwin. Swarms of aircraft smothered the defenses, and then bombed at will. They destroyed valuable supplies and sank eleven freighters and an American destroyer. Twenty aircraft were destroyed on the ground and the air field flattened. Some 250 people, civilians and military, were killed and many more wounded in a town that believed the war still to be many thousands of miles to the north.

The Japanese were knocking on the door of the country that the beleaguered forces in the Philippines saw as the springboard for their own relief. Panic reigned in response to the Japanese raid. Emergency legislation was introduced, and there was an exodus of civilians. Vast herds of cattle were driven south, away from what the authorities believed would be the battleground of the Northern Territory. The federal government in Canberra, still reeling from the shock of losing twenty thousand men in the debacle at Singapore, recalled two of its veteran divisions from the Middle East to defend the homeland. It could spare no thought for the plight of the garrisons in the Philippines but rather saw in the expanding American presence the troops necessary to defend Australia.

Sunday, February 22, 1942
Oval Office
The White House, Washington, D.C.

Political pressure was being mobilized against the president. There was a steady decline in the popular confidence of the nation as the weeks passed and the pace of Japanese victories seemed to accelerate. Roosevelt had created the early euphoria, and now he had to confront popular reaction. Ever the eternal optimist, he had built up the nation's expectations from the first, unlike Churchill, who had safely warned the British of early "defeat, blood, and tears." Pressure came increasingly from those who now openly challenged not only the wisdom but also the morality and justice of a "Europe first" strategy. Why were war supplies going to the British and the Russians when American boys were desperately short in the Far East and the Philippines? To counter these attitudes, which Roosevelt interpreted as defeatism and disunity, he decided to use the occasion of Washington's birthday to address the nation. The people were warned in advance and asked to listen with a map of the world in their hands.

At the appointed hour the nation, and the troops all over the world, including the Philippines, gathered around their radios.

> This war is a new kind of war. It is different from all other wars in the past not only in its methods and weapons, but also in its geography. It is warfare in terms of every continent, every island, every sea, every air lane in the world.

As his audience followed on their maps, Roosevelt launched into a very blunt defense of his strategy of "Europe first," emphasizing all the while the need to counter the Axis objectives, which he saw as seeking to isolate the Allied powers from one another by the time-honored methods of divide and conquer. The president pointed to the interdependence of these centers of power and the global nature of the war. This last point was emphasized by the Japanese, for even as he spoke a submarine surfaced off the California coast and bombarded Santa Barbara. Most of the shells fell on ranchland and caused no material damage, though the psychological impact was something quite different.

When the president had finished, he had done much to repair the damage caused by the weeks of stinging defeat, but the men gathered around the radios on Bataan and Corregidor understood there could be no real hope of rescue. Against the "big map" of global war they hardly figured, and indeed the president only mentioned them in passing.

In another sense, however, the plight of the troops was very much on Roosevelt's mind. He had no intention of leaving MacArthur to become a prisoner of the Japanese, not just because he had skills that were unique, but also because of the propaganda triumph that would undoubtedly follow in the wake of his capture. Churchill had pulled Lord Gort, the British Expeditionary Force commander, out of Dunkirk in similar circumstances, thus depriving the Germans of a "needless triumph." With these precedents and considerations very much in mind, the president ordered that MacArthur and his family be rescued. The day before, Churchill and Roosevelt had reached an accord on the division of responsibility for the conduct of the war. The British were to assume control for the Indian Ocean, whereas the Pacific and Australia would become a prime theater of American responsibility. The president needed a general of stature and proven rank to become commander-in-chief in the South Pacific with headquarters in Australia.

Monday, February 23, 1942
Headquarters, I Corps
Bataan

Champlin was shocked and offended. He had just glanced through the dispatches that had arrived from headquarters in Malinta Tunnel. They included a copy of one of MacArthur's communiqués to the United States in which he claimed to have been on the front line in Bataan just two days before. The naval officer knew that he had not been there on that date, or indeed any other date since his first visit. To Champlin it seemed an unforgivable breach of an officer's code and honor to lie in such a manner.

His feelings were shared by many on Bataan and Corregidor.

Wainwright set out for one of his daily visits to the front. They now used a jeep, rather than the more thirsty command car, in order to save on gasoline. Major Pugh drove, and Dooley and Champlin sat in the back as "air guards." The naval aide cradled the general's personal Garand; Dooley preferred a Thompson.

It was clear and hot, a perfect day for Japanese planes, but the skies had been empty all day; a false sense of security descended over the group. As they reached the more open ground, beyond the foothills of Mariveles, the glare of the sun was terrific. Champlin put on his sunglasses and relaxed; except for the distant bark of artillery the war seemed far away. General Wainwright was indulging in one of his favorite pastimes on these occasions. Feeling that his naval aide's education had been sadly lacking, he discussed the great cavalry battles of the past. Champlin half listened as the general droned on extolling the virtues of Murat, Napoleon's dashing cavalry general; the rays of the sun beat down on his already tanned and weather-beaten face.

For no particular reason Champlin looked back at the sun. He could neither move nor speak; for a moment he sat there with his eyes riveted on that ball of fire spinning across the tropical sky. Directly in front of the sun a black speck was hurtling down in a direct line toward them. As he looked the speck became larger and then grew wings that dipped from side to side.

Champlin found his voice. "Aircraft! Get the hell out of the car! Everybody out! Out!" Champlin broke the safety strap across the general's waist as Pugh skidded the jeep to a halt under the trees. The group as one leaped into a roadside ditch, then scrambled through thorn and bamboo to the undergrowth beyond.

Champlin had hold of the rifle. As the ground around the jeep exploded into puffs of dust and the sky above filled to the sight and the sound of the screaming plane, he took aim through the trees and emptied the gun, yelling "Bastard!" with every bullet. As the plane zoomed away over the treetops, he looked around to see how the others had made out. Heads popped up from vines and bushes.

"Jesus," said Dooley, "that was a close one."

Champlin looked across at the general, who was sitting amid a clump of bamboo, an amused expression on his face and a twinkle in his eyes that could not be mistaken. "You kinda like that carbine, don't you, son?"

"Yes, General," Champlin replied, "I guess I do."

"It's yours, son. Take it and thanks for spotting that Nip plane. He'd have gotten us for sure if you hadn't seen him coming out of the sun."

"But General," Champlin protested, "this rifle is ordnance issue."

"Who's fighting this war?" Wainwright growled. "The pen-pushers in Washington or you and I? Keep it, son. It's yours."

When they reached the front line they toured the sector for a while and then tramped off into the bush to see one last battalion. They found it, the soldiers riddled with dysentery and malaria. Many of the men were dead where they stood, in the foxholes, festooned with bloated flies feasting on the feces that littered the ground. Their officers had left the dead in their holes, faces pointed to the enemy, rifles gripped in lifeless hands: Perhaps by these means the Japanese might be fooled into believing that the position was still defended.

"Don't say one word to a living soul about what you have seen in that battalion," Wainwright ordered. "God only knows the Japs could walk right through there, only my guess is that they're almost as badly off. Pugh, I want you to arrange for some reserves to move into the line and relieve that battalion."

The ground ahead was under artillery fire. Pugh stopped the jeep while the two aides observed the salvos and the pattern of bursting shells. Were the Japanese using the "Army method?" This is like a ladder system, first rung, second rung, third rung, as the shell bursts walked up the road. The alternative was the "Navy method"—one under, one over, and the third shell splits the difference. It was the Army system. They bided their time; then Pugh crashed the gears, and the Jeep surged forward as they outpaced the salvos.

It was late afternoon when they reached corps headquarters. Pugh hurried off to organize the reserves. There was a cavalry captain waiting for the general outside his caravan. He saluted and said, "We're just about out of fodder for the horses, General."

"Yes, Captain, I knew this was coming," Wainwright replied. "We've a lot of men who are also short of food, and horsemeat ain't so bad." He paused for a moment and gazed out over the South China Sea. Champlin standing there saw just how tired and drained he looked. Wainwright looked back to the cavalry man.

"Captain, you will begin killing the horses at once. Joseph Conrad is the horse that you will kill first."

He turned and walked slowly up the steps into his trailer. Champlin saw his eyes, which were filled with tears. General Wainwright was a cavalry officer of the very old school. He loved horses. Joseph Conrad was a prize show jumper and his own personal charger, which he had brought with him from the United States.

After dinner that evening Wainwright was in the mood to talk. He gathered his three personal aides about him and sat outside the trailer. They discussed the implications of Roosevelt's message, and the general, off the record, listed the three major errors that he considered had been committed by the high command:

> Failure of command officers to visit troops in the front lines, especially since there were shortages of everything else and all there was to offer them was morale.

> Failure to obtain more troops six months before the war at a time when such troops were available, on the assumption that the Philippine Army could then have been trained and made capable of defending the islands against Japanese invasion.

> Discarding the basic prewar plan of retreating into Bataan Peninsula for a gradiose scheme of getting the Japanese at the various beaches, but having only a paper Army with which to do it.

The discussion lasted well into the night. Champlin had never heard his general talk so freely or so frankly.

Friday, February 27, 1942
The Battle of the Java Sea

The mixed force of Allied cruisers and their destroyer escort tried to deny the Japanese invasion force Java. The squadron under its Dutch admiral, Doorman, tangled with the Japanese cruiser screen, and in a running battle that lasted over the following seventy-two hours was eliminated. The last vestiges of Allied naval power in that region had gone, and the Dutch East Indies fell like a ripe plum into the Japanese basket.

Those ships that survived had no choice but to make a run for it. This included the squadron's oiler, the U.S.S. *Pecos*. Besides the fuel oil that she had bunkered in Borneo, the *Pecos* carried sixty 300-pound-warhead torpedoes and shells of every caliber from 20mm to 8-inch crammed in her forward hold. Carl Armburst, Ruby Moteley's fiancé, was convinced the ship was the nearest thing to a Roman candle that had ever sailed the seven seas.

Japanese bombers had caught the aircraft tender *Langley* off Tjilatjap in the Indian Ocean. The *Pecos* was diverted to Christmas Island to transfer the survivors, who had been rescued by the escorting destroyers. The *Pecos* was under orders then to join the British Eastern Fleet at its base in Colombo. The exchange having been made, the *Pecos* sailed hurriedly from Christmas Island. Japanese submarines were rumored to be in the area and headed west into the Indian Ocean. The destroyers escorted them part of the way and then turned south for Darwin.

Four hours later Japanese carrier planes found the *Pecos*. Though the crew put up a sturdy fight, the air defenses were overwhelmed. Dive bombers caught her amidships and aft, and fires broke out immediately. Armburst directed the surviving guns at the Japanese and had the satisfaction of seeing more than one spin into the sea. Fire had taken a firm grip of the superstructure amidships and threatened to envelop the forward holds; the bosun played steam hoses on the holds to keep down the temperature. The radio shack sent Maydays until it was engulfed in the flames.

After an hour the unequal struggle was over, and the captain gave the order to abandon ship. Armburst climbed down from his director tower to the gutted and twisted steel that once had been the upper bridge. Very few lifeboats had survived the flames and the bombs, so the crew threw overboard everything that could float and jumped into the water.

Armburst moved back toward the stern and checked the gun batteries to make sure there were no wounded left behind; then, in company with the executive officer, he went over the side. They watched as the ship settled amidships, turned turtle, and sank. Carl could feel the suction pulling him back and struck out fiercely for a life raft. Armburst never saw the exec again. Eventually the destroyers appeared over the horizon. They had heard the Maydays and reversed course to effect the rescue, their second in less than twenty-four hours.

Sunday, March 1, 1942
Bataan

The hot season had reduced the amount of grazing for the carabao. The animals in the corrals waiting their turn for slaughter were becoming thinner and thinner. The veterinarians advised Drake that unless he slaughtered the remainder very quickly the amount of meat would hardly be worth the effort. There were five hundred carabao. divided into three great herds, and Drake ordered them killed and the fresh meat transported to Corregidor for freezing. The plant was by this time practically empty of fresh meat, which had been issued first in preference to the canned foods that had been kept in reserve.

The mammoth task began at once, and the quarters of carabao, eventually some 247,000 pounds, were shipped to Corregidor; it was to take four weeks to complete this undertaking. Once frozen, the meat was returned with the daily ration to the units on Bataan.

12th Medical Regiment, Philippine Scouts
Sector D, II Corps front
Bataan

Paul Ashton had acquired a Filipino orderly. The soldier was a Moro, dark-skinned, almost Negroid, with a face full of shiny teeth. He had just appeared at the bivouac one day and attached himself to the unit. He proved to be an excellent soldier in every respect except that he didn't like to use a gun, which he found far too noisy. Instead he carried a bola, the three-balled variety that the Spaniards had introduced into the southern islands more than a century ago. The stone balls were well grooved and polished, encased in carabao hide for stealth, and attached to long, thin tongs of supple leather. Intended primarily to trip the legs of wild game, he had developed its use into a fine art in throttling Japanese soldiers.

The Moro would steal out of the camp at night to get cigarettes for the soldiers in the hospital. Sometimes he attached himself to a fighting patrol, but more often he would go alone, find and kill the enemy, and rob them for their cigarettes. On one occasion, a couple of visiting doctors doubted his story; so the following evening the Moro returned with two bulging sacks, one full of cigars and cigarettes, the other with the ears of the Japanese he had slain.

Ashton found he was a useful man to have around, especially when he visited the units on the front line. On one occasion they walked along the trail that led to that part of the front manned by battalions of the 41st Philippine Division. They fell in with an old Filipino dressed in a plain, grubby coverall like a mechanic. He looked at least eighty years of age to Ashton. There was a sour-faced, seedy Filipino third lieutenant with him.

They walked together along the path, and Paul didn't ask who he was but was glad of the company as they chatted away. When they reached the battalion command post at the top of the ridge, Ashton found out the identity of his companion, for everybody stood at attention. It was General Vincente Lim, the West Point-trained commander of the 41st Infantry and one of the great Filipino field commanders.

General Lim asked the battalion commander how many machine guns he had.

"Twenty-three, General," stammered a flustered major.

"You're a damn liar. You got twenty-five. Two are back down the trail waiting for you to pick them up from ordnance. You had better get them back here damn quick," Lim replied.

Lim tramped the jungle from one outpost to the next all day and half the night and, though sometimes they got the rough end of his tongue, the men in his division loved him dearly.

Ashton looked at the condition of the battalion and wondered just how much longer they could continue. In any other theater of war most of these units would long since have been pronounced unfit for any duty, let alone combat. The daily ration of Bataan had been reduced to below 1,000 calories. It was just under 2,000 calories on Corregidor. The average requirement for a soldier in combat was 4,000 to 5,000 calories. As usual it was the troops in the front line, those farthest away from the points of distribution, who suffered the most. Vitamin deficiency accompanied the decline in diet, and this had a number of effects. People became snappy, irritable, and very short-tempered, with flare-ups and quarrels between good friends. It didn't help matters that the men lived in close confines with each other. Combat efficiency certainly declined. The eyesight of the range and height finders directing the anti-aircraft guns deteriorated. Battery commanders asked for an issue of cod-liver oil to correct the vitamins C and D deficiency, but supplies were soon exhausted. Soldiers found they could no longer tackle the sheer physical labor of reconstruction and repair from bomb and artillery damage. At the height of the Philippine summer, with temperatures in excess of 100 degrees in the shade, such work would have sapped the strength of even the fittest of troops.

Americans suffered more than Filipinos when rice became the staple diet of the garrison. Accustomed to potatoes and bread as bulk, they found rice a poor substitute. Consisting mostly of starch and with few vitamins, its nutritional value was low, and without seasoning or other additives it had little taste or flavor.

Trucks en route to the front line were robbed of their supplies by the Filipino police who had been instructed to guard them. On occasions the situation was close to anarchy. Fighting units fell back on their own devices in order to survive. Some continued to pad their ration returns: they would order more supplies from the stores than for the number of troops entitled to receive them. Others resorted to the private hoards they had first established in Bataan during the retreat. Soldiers began to eat dogs; cooked properly, the flesh tasted like lamb. The monkeys in some parts of Bataan were hunted almost to extinction. Ashton found that monkey stew was not bad eating, unless the hands turned up on the plate.

Some units developed an even more novel method of forage. Combat patrols would infiltrate no-man's-land, cross the enemy front line, and make their way to the nearby barrios, where they would purchase food at exorbitant prices. Species of jungle fruits that hitherto had been ignored now became very acceptable eating. One such fruit was called a pomelo; it was a primitive form of grapefruit, looked like a tomato, had fuzz like a peach, and tasted like cheese. Others experimented with various forms of jungle fungi, often with fatal results. One that resembled in appearance the large domestic mushroom contained a lethal poison.

Uniforms became ragged and threadbare. The greatest need was for shoes and underwear. The Americans were reasonably well off for shoes, but there were never enough of the smaller sizes to meet Filipino needs, so most went without. There were no blankets to spare. Few men washed, and none shaved.

The shortage of dependable combat formations and the need to keep a reserve in readiness to watch both the front and the beaches meant that units in the line were never relieved. There were no rest areas into which the men could be withdrawn. This, perhaps, was one of the worst features of the campaign. Except for the climate, the trench warfare conditions resembled the Western Front in World War I. In that campaign, however, units in the line were relieved after a spell at the front and retired to reasonable rest areas. It made all the difference then; at least it gave them something to look forward to and a target date to survive. There was nothing to look forward to in the Philippines except the mile-long convoy, and most had long since given up any hope of relief or rescue.

The Japanese had certainly recognized the changing needs of their opponents in the front line. Their propaganda leaflets no longer showed voluptuous blondes and the sex act; instead they sent over printed menus from the best hotels in Manila. Another considerable shortage was tobacco; hence the welcome forays of Paul Ashton's Moro orderly. Tobacco deprivation created a serious morale problem, and again it was the front-line soldier who suffered, for their supplies were frequently hijacked. They were rationed to less than one cigarette a day. On the front line a pack was worth five dollars, whereas in the rear areas cigarettes were sold for their market value of five cents a pack.

When the Army had withdrawn from the high ground of the Abucay line, their new defense positions ran through the malaria-infested Bagac Valley. So long as quinine was available, the illness was kept in check, but by early March they had practically run out and an epidemic of serious proportions occurred. The forces in Bataan needed a minimum of three million tablets a month to keep malaria in check. The total number available barely exceeded half a million. The few remaining P-40s that flew courier missions into Mindanao brought supplies of the drug back with them but never in sufficient quantity to meet the demand. Battalions in the line went from a 35 percent incidence of malaria to as high as 80 percent in two weeks. At first this meant perhaps 500 men a week down with malaria, but this became 1,000 hospital admissions a day by the first week in April. In part the problem was accentuated by the large number of civilians who provided the mosquito with a convenient breeding ground and were beyond the control of military authorities. The general hospitals were overwhelmed, and the medical units in the line had to establish their own field hospitals. Paul Ashton's battalion had one, in name only, of a thousand beds. Within a week he had to provide for an overflow. At first men lay on stretchers under the trees, but after a while they had nothing but the bare ground.

There was a frantic search from local sources for an alternative to quinine. Doctors experimented with the bark of the cinchona tree. Underneath the top hard crust was a soft brown sap, which they boiled into a thick, bitter syrup. Another drug called Atabrine was also used, but it was very hard on the liver and produced jaundice as a side effect.

Most Americans suffered from jungle sores. Some had "Guam blisters," a form of heat rash that covered the body in large white blisters about 3mm in diameter. They itched, stung, and burned enough to reduce the bravest soul to utter despair. Others suffered from a type of fungus, a soft mucus that men developed between their legs and under their arms. Those who began the campaign with ailments such as venereal disease or alcoholism didn't survive long.

A major problem was the debilitating effects of dysentery. They had exhausted the supplies of paregoric, so they turned again to local Philippine jungle lore. Hard woods were burned slowly to produce a type of charcoal. This in turn would be ground into a powder and given to the men to drink. You could always tell a soldier with dysentery, other than by the more obvious signs, because of his black lips and teeth.

Much of the dysentery was caused by the failure of the units to observe even the most elemental precautions in field hygiene. This was especially the case with the Philippine Army battalions, where soldiers drank unboiled water from the streams, constructed latrine straddle trenches next to cookhouses, and never cleaned their eating utensils. Even in American units, field hygiene broke down because the supply of Lysol was limited. The smell in the latrines became so offensive that men relieved themselves elsewhere.

All of these conditions and ailments, together with malnutrition and the environment of the battlefield, induced the prevailing mental and physical exhaustion of the soldier on Bataan. Rarely in the history of war had an army in the field deteriorated so quickly as did the troops on Bataan in March 1942.

Monday, March 9, 1942
USAFFE HQ
Malinta Tunnel

General MacArthur, in a message to the War Department, recommended all units on Bataan and Corregidor, with the exception of the Marines and the Navy, for unit citations. Indignant Marine officers and even Admiral Rockwell questioned whether this was an oversight on the part of their commander-in-chief. Richard Sutherland told them it was not. This slur was just part of the bitter interservice rivalries that had originated in the Philippines with the personality clash between General MacArthur and Admiral Hart in the prewar days. It was to prove a source of bitterness in later years that too often marred Army-Navy relationships in the conduct of the Pacific war. On Corregidor at times the relationship between the Marines and the Army—certainly in the command echelons, less so in the field—could best be described as one of mutual irritability.

Late evening
Wednesday, March 11, 1942
South Dock
Corregidor

General Drake stood on the bomb-charred timbers of the wharfside and said his goodbyes. He was among the few to know that MacArthur, his family, and an entourage of carefully chosen staff were to make a dash for freedom in Bulkeley's torpedo boats. Two days before, MacArthur had quietly handed his command over to Wainwright and in the utmost secrecy made plans to leave. The boats were to make the run through Japanese waters to Mindanao. There a flight of B-17s would rendezvous at Del Monte and fly the party to Australia.

As he surveyed the party gathered on the wharfside, Drake knew that they had not been chosen simply because of their skills and specialized knowledge, as some were elderly officers who were not standing up well, mentally or physically, to the rigors of the campaign. When the time came for the party to embark, one friend came up to Drake to bid him goodbye and said, "I'll be seeing you, Charlie, in about two weeks."

Drake had his doubts of that happening. The departure of the MacArthur party meant that those left behind were definitely out on a limb. Charles Drake knew that there would be no help coming from any source.

When word got out that MacArthur had left there would be a morale problem, particularly among the Filipinos, but Drake was determined to keep the flag flying on Corregidor to the bitter end.

For the first time he began to understand why MacArthur had been so insistent on holding Corregidor until July. It was not to allow time for the rescue to be effected but to take some of the pressure off Australia. They were, he reasoned, to buy time so that the Australian bases could be organized and strong forces shipped in from the States, not only for the defense of those bases, but also for future offensive operations. Perhaps, thought Drake as he watched the last of the three boats idle away quietly into the night, such operations might one day involve MacArthur's return to the Philippines.

Friday, March 13, 1942
Del Monte Airstrip
Mindanao
Southern Philippines

Dick Osborn and the others knew of MacArthur's arrival on the island. The Air Corps were billeted in plantation huts, and as the base was under frequent air attack they had taken up the floors and dug some foxholes. They lived about a quarter of a mile from where the commanding officer, General Sharp, had his headquarters and where MacArthur was now accommodated.

Some of the 19th Bomb Group had already been flown out, though nobody was very sure how the selections were made. Some thought it was alphabetically and by squadrons, others by trades and skills. Osborn was convinced that it was by religion. The unit in Australia that organized the shuttle was the 5th Air Base Group, a Salt Lake City outfit; the few that had left so far he believed were all Mormons. Anyway, he knew they weren't being sent alphabetically, because Sammy Boghosian was still around.

The airmen were in agreement in their attitude toward General MacArthur. They still blamed him for the loss of the B-17s on the first day of the war, and his behavior at Mindanao did not endear him to many or help to enhance his reputation.

MacArthur remained aloof and distant. He behaved almost as if the only inhabitants on the island were his immediate entourage. Men who had experienced the same ordeal as he, an escape through enemy-controlled waters, now sought guidance and leadership. General MacArthur gave them neither; he barely acknowledged their existence. Apologists for MacArthur might argue that after all he had been through he was entitled to rest and solitude and that to expect him to move freely among the troops was asking too much from the man. Perhaps this is the case, but then why are men chosen to be generals? Supposedly because they have exceptional and outstanding qualities. The garrison at Del Monte had the right to expect more of their general than he gave during his short stay at the base.

Four B-17s were sent from Darwin to pick up MacArthur. One landed at Del Monte, two turned back with engine trouble, and the fourth crashed into the sea off the cannery docks in Cagayan. Osborn helped service the one that arrived; it was flown by a good friend, Lt. Harl Pearse, a fresh-faced youngster who had the reputation of being one of the best pilots in the squadron. The plane itself was a veteran of the campaign and was very much the worse for wear. Its turbo superchargers would not operate, and the expander tube on the right brake had ruptured on landing. Osborn was helping to repair the plane when MacArthur strolled over with General Sharp. Harl Pearse saluted, and Osborn straightened up from the brake assembly and watched as MacArthur in a single contemptuous glance devoured plane and pilot.

"Bill, I'm not putting my family at risk in that broken-down crate and with this boy at the controls," he said. "I want three top planes flown by the best crews in the Pacific here as soon as possible."

MacArthur wired Washington and Australia and the latest Flying Fortresses, at that time stationed with a squadron in New Zealand, were prepared for the long flight. Pearse loaded up his plane with thirty members of the bomb group who were on the list and took off for Australia. Those who remained resented MacArthur's slight to their squadron. Attitudes were not improved when orders were given that for as long as MacArthur was at the base, there was to be no anti-aircraft fire, for fear of retaliation from the Japanese aircraft. This was an eminently sensible precaution on General Sharp's part, but for airmen on short rations, sleep, and tempers it made little sense.

The following afternoon three Japanese planes appeared low over the Del Monte plantation. One of the gunners could not resist the temptation and fired a burst. His actions stirred up a hornets' nest, for the Japanese turned, then bombed and strafed the area. One bomb burst near the huts where the MacArthurs were quartered, and some airmen around cheered loudly.

Two days later two B-17s stood ready to carry MacArthur and his party on the next stage of his journey to Australia. The first leg was a ten-hour flight to Batchelor Field in Darwin. Ground crews loaded cases of apple juice and pineapples, footlockers, and mattresses into the planes. Osborn checked the oxygen bottles on the flight deck and then stood by for the planes to leave. Lieutenant Fitzgerald, whose ship had crashed into the bay on the first flight, went up to the general as he approached to board the lead plane. "General," he said, "I want to get back to Australia to get another plane and back into this war."

"I'm glad to hear it, son," the general replied, "but I'm sorry, we don't have any room."

Osborn had overheard this conversation and seen what had been loaded into the plane, and he was incensed. He walked up to the frustrated flier and promised to get him out.

He grabbed an oxygen bottle, a mask, and a parachute from the service trolley and thrust them at the young officer and then led him around to the rear of the plane. Osborn took out a cloth and started to polish the rear turret. The gunner pulled back the side window. "Hey, fella," Osborn said, "when I give you the nod I want you to open the escape hatch, and this lieutenant here is going with you all the way."

The plan worked like a dream. The party climbed aboard, and a small crowd watched as MacArthur, "godlike," with a wave of his hand, boarded the plane, Dick signaled, the little escape hatch opened, and the pilot scrambled aboard.

The lead plane, piloted by Lt. Frank Bostrom, staggered into the night sky with its VIP passengers and a stowaway on board.

Wednesday, March 18, 1942
Headquarters, I Corps
Bataan

Champlin was called to the field phone. It was Captain Hoeffel, the commander of the Inshore Patrol, who ordered Champlin to report to Corregidor by 1800 hours. Champlin could not understand it—normally all his dealings were with the Chief of Naval Staff at Corregidor, Captain Ray. His first thought was that he had been deficient in his duty and was being relieved. Concerned and anxious, Champlin packed his few belongings and walked over to Wainwright's trailer. The general was finishing a letter as Champlin knocked and entered. Wainwright looked up from his desk; a slow, half-amused smile, that Champlin had come to recognize and love, appeared in Wainwright's eyes and spread over his face. He motioned his aide to a chair.

Champlin told him that he had been ordered back to Corregidor and asked the general if he knew why.

Wainwright did, and he explained to Champlin, "Admiral Rockwell told me a week ago when I went to Corregidor to relieve General MacArthur. You are to leave for Australia tonight to carry out your orders, and I wish you good luck."

He paused. "You can do something for me. Take this letter and mail it in Australia."

Tears moistened the eyes of the young officer. Wainwright handed him the letter, and they shook hands. "Godspeed, Champ. You've been a good officer and an excellent aide. We'll miss you. I'll say goodbye for the others. The fewer who know you're on your way the better."

Champlin saluted, stepped out of the caravan, and walked down the trail to the motor pool. His thoughts turned back to his first day at the headquarters, when he had trod that path with hope and confidence. Now with MacArthur gone he felt that the end must surely be in sight.

Champlin arrived on Corregidor and reported to the commander of the inshore patrol. The submarine U.S.S. *Permit* was expected that night. It had originally been sent to pick up MacArthur and his party, but now it would carry Rockwell's staff, Captain Morsell (Supply), Lieutenant Commander Grandfield (Operations), Lieutenant Commander Cheek (Intelligence), and Champlin as Aide and Flag Lieutenant.

At 2215 hours, the four slipped quietly out of the tunnel and made their way down to the South Dock, where they boarded a small launch that took them out to the Navy tug *Ranger*. There were a number of other officers and men on board, all radio specialists and cipher experts from the radio intercept tunnel. They had monitored and decoded the Japanese naval signal traffic in the southwestern Pacific, and now they were to continue this complex work from new locations in Australia. The tug steamed out through the marked channel between the minefields and waited the arrival of the submarine. To Champlin and all the others who walked the decks while the little vessel rose and fell on the gentle swell, the waiting seemed interminable.

Then the sea frothed and boiled, and the men rushed to the rails as a long black shadow slowly surfaced. Lines were tossed, and the *Permit* came alongside to starboard. Torpedoes were loaded into the forward hatch while the passengers scrambled across the saddle tanks, through the conning tower, and below decks. A voice called his name and Champlin looked up at the bridge. It was "Moon" Chapple, who had previously commanded one of the S boats that had been badly mauled in the Battle of the Lingayen Gulf when he had tried, harder than most, to break past the destroyer screen to the transports beyond.

It took an hour to load torpedoes, passengers, and dispatches. Lines were cleared, and the *Permit* pulled slowly clear of the tug. Chapple remained on the surface so that he could put distance between them and Corregidor before daylight. They headed west and then swung south toward the island of Mindanao. Down below, life was extremely cramped to say the least. The *Permit* had a normal complement of 50 officers and men, and there were 111 people on board. The wardroom, which measured 9 feet by 6 feet, was home for 14 officer passengers, as well as those who served on the submarine. When it came time to sleep, they took turns: Two officers slept on the table, one lined up three chairs, another slept under the table, and two slept in the bunks that folded down from the bulkhead. Another two could occupy the Exec's and OOD's cots when they were on duty. The rest sat in corners, reading books, or stood up, depending on whose turn it was. For food they had "Dutch hash." Chapple had provisioned in Surabaja before coming north and had acquired a shipment of this stolid Dutch meat and potato dish. It was stored all over the submarine. The engine compartments positively overflowed with the stuff, and elsewhere it was wedged behind every pipe and valve in the boat. For those who had been on half rations it was delicious fried, baked, or stewed. They couldn't get enough—at first. Thereafter the palate palled; fricasseed and casseroled were but variations on a theme. But it kept them going all the way to Australia.

On the evening of the second day they were bumped by a trio of Japanese destroyers. Chapple had not long surfaced into a mirror-calm sea after a day spent submerged. The destroyers came charging in for the kill, and then scattered in alarm as they tried to avoid the spread of torpedoes that Chapple unleashed from the bow tubes.

Champlin hung on as the submarine dived deep. Suddenly he heard a noise like a sledgehammer hitting a rain barrel, as depth charges pummeled the boat. The submarine shuddered violently to a first attack, which the Japanese then kept up for more than thirty hours. Chapple rigged the submarine for silent routine. Not a fan whirled to keep the heat down, and temperatures soared beyond anything the passengers could remember in the jungle. The wardroom resembled a Turkish bath, and the stench was almost unbearable. But bear it they did, resigned to their fate in a steel coffin, until the Japanese gave up and they were able to surface into an empty sea and head south. Hatches were thrown wide open and wonderful drafts of cool night air flowed through the submarine. All through that night officers and men came up to the conning tower in groups of four for 10 minutes at a time.

It took the submarine 23 days to reach Fremantle. The drinking water had to be rationed and with the auxiliary units damaged in the depth-charge attack, there was none to spare for washing. Lice spread and many developed the Guam blisters which had appeared in Bataan. The submarine submerged during the long hours of daylight, and then the air became thick and nauseous. However, they made light of their discomfort and considered it a small price to pay for their rescue from the besieged fortress.

All the passengers and the off-watch crew crowded the decks as the *Permit* came up the narrow channel that marked the entrance to Fremantle. A naval reception committee waited, complete with two bluejackets standing by with a freezer truck full of ice cream. Champlin, along with others, sat on the wharfside, lice-ridden and disheveled, and ate his fill of ice cream. It was the most delicious moment he could remember in a very long while.

Friday, March 20, 1942
Malinta Tunnel
Corregidor

After some initial confusion and a degree of political maneuvering by MacArthur and the Pentagon, Wainwright took up his new appointment as commander-in-chief of United States forces in the Philippines (USFIP). The new title and designation caused some distress among the Filipinos, but Washington rode roughshod over such national sensitivities. A separate and distinct Philippine government now existed, but only in exile. Washington maintained that the fate of the Philippine Commonwealth was indivisibly linked to that of the United States. More cynical observers noted that the new headquarters had been downgraded from a "theater" to a "local" command. In part this was entirely understandable given MacArthur's departure, but was not the reduction in status also a preparation for such future unpalatable options like disaster, defeat, and surrender? It was this feature as much as any other that caused so much distress among the Filipinos.

Wainwright was promoted to lieutenant general on his move to Corregidor, as befitting his new position as commanding general, but the headquarters structure that was created in Bataan was very confusing. A new organization came into existence called Luzon Force. This headquarters acted as Wainwright's forward command post on Bataan and coordinated the activities of the two corps headquarters. Maj. Gen. Edward King assumed command of Luzon Force. This red-haired gunner was very popular with the soldiers. He was modest, quiet, and polite to all he met. King was an intellectual, an extremely able soldier whose appearance was more like a college professor than a soldier.

Maj. Gen. Albert Jones, who had been Wainwright's senior divisional commander succeeded him at I Corps. This was a thoroughly deserved appointment. Jones had distinguished himself on a number of occasions in the campaign, notably when in temporary command of the Southern Luzon Forces during the retreat into Bataan and more recently in the Battle of the Pockets. One of Wainwright's first acts after handing his precious I Corps over to Albert Jones was to call a conference on Corregidor of his new senior advisers: Lewis Beebe (Chief of Staff), Col. Nicholl Galbraith (G-4), and General Drake as Quartermaster. The subject uppermost was the question of the food supplies on Bataan and what measures might be taken to relieve the situation. Drake estimated that if the rations remained as they were, some 16 ounces or 1,000 calories a day, then around the middle of April food supplies on Bataan would be completely exhausted.

Drake brought General Wainwright up to date on the progress of the blockade runners, both the local and the more distant operations. He revealed that all attempts to secure supplies from the southern shore of Batangas had now ceased. However, though the Japanese were tightening the noose around Corregidor, the short- and middle-distance operations were still feasible. Ships from Panay had brought in more than 6,000 tons of rice and a large number of livestock. The main problem was that few supplies had reached them from the advance base Drake had established some weeks earlier at Cebu. In fact, only one shipload, of about 700 tons, had gotten through. When Drake explained that the rest of the supplies that were stockpiled on the dockside at Cebu had been "frozen" by express instructions given by General Sutherland some two weeks before, Wainwright exploded into a rage. He immediately rescinded that order and at the same time increased the rice ration for the troops on Bataan to 10 ounces a day.

Before the conference dispersed, General Wainwright showed the officers a letter he had received from General Homma. A number of copies had been dropped over the lines in beer cans. It began:

> Anyone who gets this letter is requested to send it to the commander-in-chief of the United States forces in the Philippines.

Your Excellency:

We have the honor to address you in accordance with the humanitarian principles of *Bushido*, the code of the Japanese warrior.

It will be recalled that, some time ago, a note advising honorable surrender was sent to the Commander-in-Chief of your fighting forces. To this, no reply has as yet been received.

Since our arrival in the Philippines with the Imperial Japanese Expeditionary Forces, already three months have elapsed, during which, despite the defeat of your Allies, Britain and the Netherlands East Indies, and in the face of innumerable difficulties, the American and Filipino forces under your command have fought with much gallantry.

We are, however, now in the position to state that with men and supplies which surpass, both numerically and qualitatively, those under your leadership, we are entirely free either to attack and put to rout your forces or to wait for the inevitable starvation of your troops within the narrow confines of the Bataan Peninsula.

Your Excellency must be well aware of the future prospects of the Filipino-American forces under your command. To waste the valuable lives of these men in an utterly meaningless and hopeless struggle would be directly opposed to the principles of humanity, and furthermore such a course would sully the honor of a fighting man.

Your Excellency, you have already fought to the best of your ability. What dishonor is there in avoiding needless bloodshed? What disgrace is there in following the defenders of Hong Kong, Singapore, and the Netherlands East Indies in the acceptance of honorable defeat? Your Excellency, your duty has been performed. Accept our sincere advice and save the lives of those officers and men under your command. The International Law will be strictly adhered to by the Imperial Forces, and Your Excellency and those under your command will be treated accordingly. The joy and happiness of those whose lives will be saved and the delight and relief of their dear ones and families would be beyond the expression of words. We call upon you to reconsider this proposition with due thought.

If a reply to this advisory note is not received from Your Excellency through a special messenger by noon of March 22, 1942, we shall consider ourselves at liberty to take any action whatsoever.

COMMANDER-IN-CHIEF OF
THE IMPERIAL JAPANESE ARMY AND NAVY

March 19, 1942

To His Excellency, Major General Jonathan Wainwright,
  Commander-in-Chief of the United States forces in
  the Philippines

The staff agreed with General Wainwright that such a letter did not even merit a reply.

Central Railway Station
Adelaide
South Australia

General MacArthur, his immediate entourage, and family, stepped down off the quaint little narrow-gauge train that had brought them the 1,200 miles from Alice Springs. The news of his escape had become banner headlines three days earlier when their plane had reached Darwin. A crowd had gathered as he moved across the concourse to board a more luxurious train for the last part of the journey to Canberra. The press eagerly awaited some words from this international hero. MacArthur turned and read from a prepared statement:

> The President of the United States ordered me to break through the Japanese lines ... for the purpose, as I understand it, of organizing the American offensive against Japan, a primary target of which is the relief of the Philippines. I came through and I shall return.

Reactions to their chief's departure from Corregidor were very mixed from the men he had left behind. Some knew it was the end and thought it was only right that he should be taken out, as no good could be served by his suffering their fate. Others believed that he had gone to lead in the rescue force himself, and for a few days at least anxious eyes scanned the horizons for the convoy. Bill Massello had long since given up all hope of rescue, but he had learned very quickly that if you spoke the truth on Bataan then you were labeled a "doomsayer," and he knew that some of the young-sters who manned his lights searched the sea from their vantage points. Though weakened by recurring bouts of malaria he tried to visit his boys as often as possible.

"All we have to do is to stick it out for about another six months, men," he would say. "They'll find a way." His battery had a pet name for the rescue convoy—they called it "the good ship *Lollipop*."

Others, some of the Marines and the Air Corps, were unmoved by MacArthur's departure. Even those on Corregidor had rarely if ever seen him, and to most soldiers he was a distant, remote figurehead who, cocooned in his own high command, had little impact on their lives. The Marine cry on Corregidor took a new twist. "I'm going to the latrine . . . but I shall return!" It was an apt response to the pompous and arrogant tone of MacArthur's statement.

Once MacArthur had reached Adelaide, Wainwright was able to contact him and ask for warships to be made ready to escort the blockade runners into Corregidor from Cebu. MacArthur prom-ised that by April 1 the necessary ships would be at Cebu. Drake issued warning orders to his staff there to prepare the blockade runners for sea. Two American submarines arrived there that day, and they loaded up with food and medicines and headed for Cor-regidor. The Japanese invaded the island on April 10, and the loaded blockade runners were scuttled at their moorings.

Monday, March 23, 1942
The command post
Fourteenth Army Headquarters
San Fernando

Homma could not sit back and allow the defenders on Bataan to wither on the vine and simply be starved into submission. He had already suffered great loss of face, especially as Japanese force of arms had carried all before them elsewhere, in Singapore, Hong Kong, and now the Dutch East Indies. It was vital that he defeat them, decisively, in battle. It was a matter of honor for him as an officer. More important than the vanity of the Japanese officer code, however, was the foreign policy need. Tokyo had to prove conclusively to the people of Asia their superiority over the European overlords if they were to establish their dream of the Greater East Asia Co-prosperity Sphere. Thus the defeat of the American-Filipino forces in the Philippines would have repercussions that could vibrate all the way to the gates of Delhi.

If General Homma had been guilty of underestimating the Abucay line, he now swung to the very opposite extreme and grossly exaggerated both their defense capabilities and his own needs to take the rest of Bataan. From the latter part of February and throughout the month of March, reinforcements poured into Luzon from all over Asia:

- Seven thousand men came to fill the decimated ranks of the 65th Brigade and the 16th Division.
- Eleven thousand men of the 4th Infantry Division under Lieutenant General Kitano arrived from Shanghai.
- Four thousand men of the Nagano Detachment, a battle group from the 21st Division, arrived.
- Artillery reinforcements moved up to the front line on Bataan, and some deployed on the shores of Batangas. Homma was given four batteries of 240mm howitzers, a mountain artillery regiment, and battalions of 300mm and 150mm siege mortars.
- Sixty twin-engined bombers flew into Clark fresh from their success in Malaya, and the Navy, not to be outdone, dispatched an air brigade.

Homma called a conference of his senior officers to finalize the plans for the forthcoming battle. He was convinced that he was against upward of 60,000 men echeloned in three lines of defense from Mount Samat to the port of Mariveles. The Commander-in-Chief believed it would take a month of hard fighting before Bataan could be secured. The staff agreed that April 3 would be "D-Day." The plan called for a massive artillery and air bombardment, followed by an infantry and armored assault on a narrow front. The attack would be spearheaded by the 65th Brigade against I Corps, very much a holding and diversionary action, while the untried 4th Infantry attacked II Corps, with the 16th Division ready to leapfrog through to maintain the momentum of the main axis of advance.

In the meantime, Japanese combat patrols pushed forward an offensive screen to within 1,000 yards of the defenders' barbed wire. This kept the American and Filipino infantry fully occupied and thus allowed the Japanese to mask their preparations for the coming offensive.

Their efforts were not always crowned with success. Winston Jones was hungry and had already suffered three bouts of malaria, but he had acquired a Navy 36-power telescope, and there was plenty of fight left in him and his gunners. From the observation platform in its tree high on the forward slopes of Mount Samat, he could even identify the ranks of Japanese officers 3,000 yards away. This day he watched a large concentration of Japanese trucks and other transportation moving down the coast road.

Jones immediately called Division and requested fire from a battery of 155mm Long Toms who were deployed to his left. They belonged to another division, so he had to wait while permission was sought via Corps Headquarters. They agreed to allow him two guns to fire on the concentration, and he was connected directly to their battery commander. After the third round the guns under Jones's direction had the range and they opened up a sustained fire. Within a very short while there was a heavy explosion, and flames and thick black smoke signaled the jackpot. They had hit a Japanese oil storage point. Jones called down the cease-fire and scanned the target. Even though it was partly obscured by smoke, he could see the confusion and chaos his artillery had caused.

Jones continued to scan the front, and this time he looked carefully along the line of the Orion River. He saw some Japanese bathing, and immediately took a dim view of their enjoying themselves while he toiled away at the guns. He called up Battery A and gave out the concentration, and the point gun fired one round offset to land on a clifftop above the Japanese. He watched as the bathers ran naked for the shelter of an embankment.

He spoke into the receiver. "Down 200." A shell roared overhead, for all the world like an express train coming out of a tunnel, and burst against the cliff face. Rocks and debris cascaded down and engulfed the bathers. "Up 100." The shell screamed on its way, but he saw no effect. Jones was just on the point of calling for a repeat shot when the trees and the cliff face disappeared into the air in one white and gray-black mixture of smoke.

"That's cordite we've hit," he told the men on the battery. When the smoke cleared, the gunners stepped out from behind their guns, and men along the front watched the explosions, large and small, which continued for the next couple of hours. Division called to ask what had caused the smoke and flames. Jones explained with great glee that he had accidentally hit a Japanese arms dump, as well as a gasoline point, all in the course of the morning's work.

There were very few days like that for the defenders to cheer, and even Winston Jones's battalion later succumbed to the lethargy and despair of an Army ridden by disease, ravaged by hunger, and bereft of hope.

Despite such setbacks, the tempo of the Japanese preparations increased. They launched a major artillery offensive against Forts Frank and Drum, and the gunners on Corregidor watched in alarm, for they realized that if Bataan fell the same would befall them. At the same time, the air raids increased on Corregidor. Bressi felt as if they were one continuous affair, and many were convinced that the enemy had unlimited numbers of aircraft. The bombers flying out of Clark could make four or five sorties a day, and they were dropping bigger bombs too—1,000-pounders began to blast into the Rock. What was also worse was that the raids came at random times; day and night they had to man the defenses. There was no rest, and the constant raids took their toll, causing frayed nerves for those who stuck to their jobs. But at the same time, the population of Malinta Tunnel began to increase.

On March 28 the Japanese hit the cold storage plant on Corregidor. The refrigeration unit was built under 30 feet of earth and rubble and had been hit the first time around in one of the early raids in January, but little damage had been done and the crater was filled. This time the 1,000-pounder bored into the hill in exactly the same place, and the already weakened structure couldn't absorb another hit. There were still 247,000 pounds of carabao stored in the freezer rooms and it looked for a while as if they would lose it all as work parties ran the gauntlet of ammonia escaping from the pipes. In the end they lost just 2,000 pounds of prime meat, but the rest had to be eaten very quickly. Drake dispatched 1,500 quarters of fresh carabao to Bataan, and troops, even those on the front line who were fit enough, ate their fill for the first time in months.

Sunday, March 29, 1942
Provisional Air Corps Infantry
Sector A, II Corps front
Bataan

They had all the indications that the Japanese were preparing for a major offensive but there was little the troops could do to prepare themselves. They all had malaria, and most had vascular dysentery, which affected the glands and could cause heart disease. The unit doctor visited the bivouac and ordered Zimmerman sent back to the base hospital. He explained to them that he was not that sick, for with decent rest and medication he would probably be well in a couple of days. However, no matter how much he had helped them, he was now a liability, for they were expecting a lot of casualties very soon.

They took him on a stretcher to a collecting station and then on one of the worst journeys in his life by ambulance to the field hospital at Cabcaben. There the doctors treated Zimmerman with Atabrine, and the resulting jaundice nearly killed him. There were nearly six thousand patients in the hospital by this time, and it was due to the efforts of one doctor in particular that Zimmerman survived. The doctor took him into his own bed, fed him a syrup of tea and sugar, all that he could keep down, for a week, and gradually nursed him back from the brink of death.

IX. THE FALL OF BATAAN

Friday, April 3–
Thursday, April 9, 1942

Saved for another day
Saved for hunger wounds and heat
For slow exhaustion and grim retreat
For a wasted hope and sure defeat

I see no gleam of victory alluring
No chance of splendid booty or gain
If I endure I must go on enduring
And my reward for bearing pain is pain
Yet though the thrill the zest the hope are gone
Something within me keeps me fighting on

Lieutenant Henry G. Lee, U.S.A.
HQ company, Philippine division

Good Friday, April 3, 1942
41st Division
Sector D, II Corps front
Bataan

The weight of the Japanese artillery and air bombardment was directed against the infantry foxholes of the 41st Division. Behind the guns, the Japanese 65th Brigade prepared for the assault. The two battle commanders knew one another personally—Maj. Gen. Vincente Lim and Lt. Gen. Akira Nara attended the same course at Fort Benning Infantry School in Georgia in 1928. This was not the first time in the campaign, either, that their units had confronted one another. The Filipinos had inflicted grievous casualties on their foe in the first Battle of Bataan and had an enviable reputation as one of the best fighting formations in the Philippines.

The Japanese opened the battle with a massive artillery and air assault. With all the forces now at his disposal, Homma unleashed a rain of fire on the defenders that far surpassed anything they had endured before in the campaign. As the bombing increased further in intensity and gradually enveloped the whole front, it was the Filipinos of the 41st, hitherto the most steadfast of soldiers, who broke and ran. It wasn't just the volume of high explosives that did the damage, though that was bad enough. The telling blow came from incendiaries disgorged by the thousand from the bellies of Japanese bombers. Within moments the tinder-dry brush was a sea of flames engulfing the foxholes; those who didn't flee were incinerated. The soldiers fled back into the support line, which their wise old general had insisted they dig; but a sudden wind fanned the flames in their wake. A forest fire raged along the 3 miles of the divisional front. By now the Filipinos were completely unnerved and abandoned the front in confusion. Panic, particularly by units in the line in war, is contagious, and like a pulled thread on a sweater the whole of the Filipino II Corps front began to unravel. Japanese armor and infantry followed up their unexpected success and, instead of fighting hard for the forward line, simply mopped up the isolated pockets of defiance in the charred and blackened battlefield. By evening they had punched a corridor 3 miles wide deep into the foothills of southern Bataan.

Winston Jones had witnessed the debacle in the front line and watched as the Filipinos flooded back past his positions. Sickness and death had reduced his battalion to two batteries, and he worked hard to prevent his own men from becoming engulfed in the swirling panic.

Vincente Lim came on the field phone and ordered Winston to buy him some time while he tried to shore up the line along the apex of Mount Samat. The guns fired on the advancing Japanese, and for a while did cause them to waver in their resolve and lose some of their momentum. This, however, proved but a temporary setback, for the rate of fire soon became intermittent and desultory. The field pieces were so old and worn out that for any elevation over 1,500 yards it took ten men to push the gun back into battery from its recoil; wafer-thin springs and hydraulic systems had long since ceased to function, and one by one the breechblocks froze and the guns fell silent. A half platoon of self-propelled 75mm guns manned by the indomitable Scouts moved forward to provide covering fire while Winston Jones prepared to destroy his guns. He still had a fair amount of ammunition in the limbers, and this was difficult to destroy, for his guns fired the old fixed charges. There were no separate powder bags. The gunners dug pits to bury the ammunition while captains spiked their guns; they removed the breechblocks, took them apart, and buried the pieces in the surrounding jungle. Winston considered that even if the Japanese did find them it would be an impossible task to assemble all the parts. The guns were useless, but for good measure he took an ax and chopped through the wooden spokes of the wheel of the nearest gun. The gun captains followed suit, and their charges collapsed in a welter of splintered wood. Then the men were assembled and marched out of the batteries and along the east road, an island of discipline and good order among a sea of panic and confusion. About 2 miles down the road, Jones came across a holding area where General Lim and his divisional staff were attempting to reform the units in readiness for a counterattack. Some answered his bidding, but many, both officers and men, ignored the pleas of their general. The thin veneer of military discipline had gone, and instead the human instinct for survival reigned supreme. One complete regiment had disintegrated, and the other two wavered in their resolve.

Toward late evening Jones led a small fighting patrol forward with orders to reconnoiter the ground in preparation for a counterattack planned for the next day. General Lim, a soldier of the old school, was determined to obliterate the disgrace and salvage something of the now-tarnished reputation of the division. For the first 900 yards the small patrol had to battle against the human tide and Jones lost a few of the fainthearted, but then the road became ominously quiet. They had gone perhaps 1 mile when a flurry of mortar bombs burst in and among the point section. The survivors melted into the undergrowth. Another salvo of bombs hit the shoulders of the road and claimed more casualties. Jones recognized that the damage was being inflicted by the little knee mortars. The battlewise Filipinos had also identified the shot and understood its significance. Knee mortars meant the Japanese were less than 100 yards away, and demoralized and afraid, the Filipinos fell back. Jones had no alternative but to follow. Shortly afterward Japanese artillery opened up and carpeted the area with high explosives. The patrol sought what cover it could among the trees. Once dispersed in this fashion, the group lost first its cohesion and then its discipline. A dejected Winston Jones reported back to the divisional command post. General Lim ordered him to move south and try to assemble as many men as he could at the next line, which they hoped would stem the tide of the Japanese advance.

Saturday, April 4, 1942

The bombers were aloft with the dawn of another bright and clear day, sowing the front with the same lethal mixture of high explosives and incendiaries. Japanese infantry prepared to storm forward and seize the last slopes before Samat. From there they would advance toward the next objective, which they could already see, the towering peaks that marked the final range of southern Bataan.

Paul Ashton had established a field hospital in a grove of trees on the slopes of Mount Samat. Dive bombers had hit the hospital several times. The clearly marked Red Cross tent that served as his operating theater, together with a couple of the makeshift open-air wards, suffered direct hits. Of the two hundred patients, most of whom suffered with malaria, forty were killed and many more injured in those callous raids. Ashton collected a work party drawn from his orderlies and the more able-bodied patients and set them to digging a communal grave while he ministered to the injured. Operating out in the open on a makeshift table hewn out of bamboo and vines, he glanced up from his surgery and saw Japanese infantry swarming over the ridge line about a mile to his front. There was little he could do. They had one ambulance left and more wounded than he could count. "I'm a dead monkey," he thought and pressed on with the task at hand, saving the life of a young Filipino, his chest gouged by a ragged shrapnel wound.

The Japanese began to descend the slopes, and their first volleys smacked into the trees overhead. Then help came from a most unexpected quarter. A hundred or more American soldiers ran through the hospital and deployed their machine guns on the far perimeter. They were all that remained of two companies of the 31st Infantry, the raggedest, dirtiest soldiers Ashton had ever encountered. Their .30-calibers tore into the Japanese and sent them scurrying for cover over the ridge line. An officer came running up and advised him to remove the worst cases, as they would not be able to hold off the Japanese for too long.

Ashton hurried away, but it was not an easy task playing God as he selected the patients to travel in the ambulance and tried to ignore the appeal in the eyes of the ones left behind. With ten stretcher cases crammed into an ambulance meant to carry four he drove straight to No. 1 Hospital at Cabcaben and reported to the Bataan field force surgeon. From there he hurried to the corps headquarters close by and explained the crisis. They gave him a dozen old buses in which to evacuate his hospital and a few light tanks to reinforce the American line. By the time Ashton returned the Americans were barely holding the Japanese and welcomed the light tanks with open arms; shells were falling, and there were all the signs of a big attack. Ashton hurried to evacuate his hospital. Patients, staff, and all the equipment they could carry were loaded onto the buses. Bombed and strafed the whole way to the main hospital, they reached it just minutes after that, too, had suffered its first major air raid of the war. A scene of unbelievable carnage and confusion greeted Ashton as he drove into the hospital compound. There were bed sheets and pieces of people festooning the trees, and a mass exodus of patients was already under way. While many of the surgeons cowered in their foxholes, some of the wounded fled on crutches and sticks, many ripping the casts from their wounds. John Spainhower, along with most, lay in his cot and endured the bombing. He had no intention of joining the exodus even if he had the strength. His one thought was that the scheme he had used to let his wife know he was alive, increasing his monthly allotments to her, would now be finished. He was convinced he would die.

HQ, USFIP
Malinta Tunnel
Corregidor

Wainwright received a long and detailed instruction on what course of action he should take if the situation became desperate. He was ordered to mount an attack upon the Japanese along the following lines:

1. A feint by I Corps in the form of an "ostentatious" artillery preparation.
2. A "sudden surprise attack" by II Corps toward the Dinalupihan-Olongapo Road at the base of the peninsula, made "with full tank strength" and "maximum artillery preparation."
3. Seizure of Olongapo by simultaneous action of both corps, I Corps making a frontal attack and II Corps taking the enemy "in reverse" by an attack from the west, along the Dinalupihan–Olongapo Road.

"If successful," MacArthur explained from his new headquarters some 3,000 miles away in Australia, "the supplies seized at this base might well rectify the situation. This would permit operations in central Luzon where food supplies could be obtained and where Bataan and the northern approaches to Corregidor could be protected." The general concluded by suggesting that even if the attack were to fail, many of the troops would be able to break through the lines on Bataan and then escape to central Luzon to continue the war as guerrillas.

Wainwright and his staff studied the document with incredulity; could MacArthur have become so out of touch with the realities of the campaign on Bataan in such a short period of time?

In the meantime the Japanese pressure continued, and by the end of the second day of the offensive they had thrown the defenders back along the length of their main line of resistance. Three regiments of Filipino infantry were all that stood between the Japanese and the peak of Mount Samat. Headquarters Luzon Force under General King was charged with coordinating plans for a counterattack by the two corps. Slow and ponderous staff work in top-heavy commands, combined with a fluid situation of disintegrating Filipino regiments, meant that their planning started off out of date and never caught up with the war.

General King split the Philippine Division, which formed the only viable reserve he had, despite its weakened state, in readiness for the forthcoming battle. So he gave the 45th Philippine Scouts to the still relatively intact I Corps and sent the 31st Infantry to Lamao in support of Parker. He divided the remaining tanks and moved the 57th Philippine Scouts forward to support either corps if the need arose. Finally he kept the 26th Cavalry, now serving as infantry, for a last resort.

Easter Sunday, April 5, 1942

The Japanese were more than a day ahead of schedule and in some disarray, so they had paused in their headlong advance and had spent much of that Saturday night regrouping to meet the changing needs of the battle. Nevertheless, at dawn they resumed their devastating air and artillery bombardment. The infantry continued the advance and after a stiff fire fight overcame resistance and stormed the summit of Mount Samat. In the process, a second Filipino division was destroyed. The momentum quickened as the Japanese infantry rapidly overran the defenses on the reverse slopes of the mountain. They had driven a mighty wedge into the defense lines and separated the corps. If Homma moved quickly, first south and then east, he could be in a position to drive Parker's corps into the bay. With that very much in mind, the Japanese that night attempted to divert the attention of Parker's troops by launching a number of feint attacks, which took the form of seaborne landings on the beaches below Lamao.

The gunboats *Luzon* and *Mindanao* had been deployed north to meet such an eventuality. With lights out, they waited off the coast in ambush.

Sam Malick watched as a slow oil-burning tug came around the headland towing a string of small barges. They waited until the barges had been cut loose and started to drift in toward the shore. It seemed that they had no motors. At a range of under 600 yards, the forward 3-inch fired star shells and illuminated the target while the stern gun and the machine guns bombarded the flimsy wooden boats. The Japanese had some light weapon, probably a 1-pounder, mounted in the bows, and for a while attempted to return fire. They hit the flare bin on the deck immediately below where Sam Malick was manning his machine gun. The effect was spectacular— flares burst out over the sea like it was the Fourth of July, but no damage was done or casualties inflicted. The action was never in doubt, most of the barges were sunk, and the couple that managed to elude the gunboats in the dark ran straight into the now thoroughly alerted beach defenses. It was a small victory that could unfortunately, other than giving satisfaction to the sailors involved, contribute nothing to the overall battle and could not compensate for the disasters that were now about to overtake the defenders of Bataan.

Monday, April 6, 1942

On this day the fate of Bataan and ultimately Corregidor was sealed. MacArthur still demanded a last desperate offensive, and eventually Wainwright yielded. It was now his turn to give General King an order that the latter found incredible. Nevertheless, perhaps the only move left to stanch the onward march of the Japanese was a vigorous counterattack. Spearheaded by battalions of the Philippine Division, General King mustered every unit that was available and ordered that they march to battle. Every tank, every gun, every platoon of infantry were sent forward. Even the beach defenses were denuded of troops. In a coordinated offensive, King directed his corps commanders to take Mount Samat at the point of the bayonet and re-establish the line. It was a hopeless task from the outset. The Japanese anticipated that the Americans would counterattack soon, but Homma had no intention of allowing the initiative to be taken from him now and ordered his troops to maintain the momentum of their advance. So the day began with two armies advancing on a collision course.

The troops met head on in a contest of unequal forces. All the advantages lay with the Japanese. For the first time since the campaign had begun they held the high ground, and it was the Americans' artillery, such as could be found, that had to fire blind. Even more, the Japanese had undisputed control of the air, and they had their health and their vitality. Their generals had the scent of victory in their nostrils.

The defenders of Bataan were a scarecrow army with nothing but fire in their bellies. Many who marched into battle had risen from their sickbeds as desperate officers milked the hospitals for men fit enough to carry a rifle and help fill the decimated ranks. A goodly number never even made it to the battle line but died alone by the roadside. Men moved along trails subjected to constant air attack and cluttered with the flotsam of an already defeated army. Many advanced gripped by a mad despair, with only pride and a grim determination to inflict harm on the foe to sustain their ebbing strength.

Ben Saccone led four tanks and a half-track into battle in support of the 31st Infantry at Lamao. At times they found their route almost completely blocked by retreating Filipinos. Bataan had proved a disastrous campaign for the tanks. They were of little value in the jungle. They had neither the power nor the space to maneuver and, as some had already found, they could prove a death trap in the country, where the enemy could be upon you before you were even aware of his presence.

On the roads, though, it was a slightly different matter. They could at least cover a retreat or support an advance by acting as a mobile pillbox—provided they survived the constant attention of the Japanese Air Force. They turned off Trail 10, moved slowly up to Trail 2, and deployed into a forest glade under the shadow of Mount Samat to await the arrival of the infantry and the start of the counterattack.

A second lieutenant joined them that morning. He had been in the hospital since the start of the campaign with malaria and fever; the latter was an infectious eruptive fever that produced excruciating pains, especially in the joints. It spread like wildfire because of the primitive conditions that existed in the Bataan field hospitals. Today was his first day back with the battalion. The crews were getting their food when they heard the roar of artillery. As a man they dropped their mess cans and threw themselves to the ground or ran for the cover of the nearest tank. The young lieutenant had just stepped out of a Jeep, and his reactions were understandably slower than the reactions of those who had been in the line. He had not quite hit the deck when the first shells exploded right in the middle of the position. Shrapnel sliced the cheeks off his bottom. Frank Matson and the others had a hard time keeping a straight face as they bandaged his wounds and prepared to return the unfortunate young officer to the hospital. They could see the wounds were painful, but they couldn't resist odd ribald remarks at the expense of the officer who took it all in his stride.

"Quickest Purple Heart of the campaign, Lieutenant," one said.

"You'd be two inches shorter if they had caught you on your feet, sir," another added.

"Just as well you weren't on your back," said a third.

The tanks moved forward along the trail, dwarfed by the towering teak trees. Frank Muther manned the radio in the lead tank, which acted as scout and traveled about 100 yards ahead of the rest of the column. As they came around the corner, a white ball of fire flew right over the turret and they saw the antitank gun. The Japanese crew was still furiously trying to set up the piece. They must have heard the approach of the tanks and then deployed their little gun for action. Small-arms fire came out of the trees. The tank stopped, and Captain Moffat fired and hit the Japanese gun a glancing blow on its shield, which peeled back like paper. The gunners ran for cover, and the bow machine gun bowled them over before they could reach the undergrowth. There was no room to maneuver on the narrow trail, and this was certainly no place for a tank. The driver locked a track and on Moffat's orders turned quickly and headed back the way they came, pursued by a hail of small-arms and knee-mortar fire. Muther tried to radio a warning to the other tanks, but none had operators who could receive and they didn't have radios that could communicate on voice. Moffat hand-signaled the withdrawal as they squeezed by and the others followed suit. Then the Japanese opened up at point-blank range from both sides of the jungle: the Americans had been caught in a perfect ambush. The Japanese were hidden along the edge of the jungle for more than 200 yards but had withheld their fire until the unsuspecting Americans had moved right into the ambush position. Three of the tanks shed their tracks, and the crews abandoned their machines under the covering fire of the half-track and Muther's surviving tank. Saccone's half-track was hit by a second Japanese antitank gun. The solid shot came in low and took off the machine gunner's foot. The second gunner was hit in the shoulder by a piece of shrapnel from a knee mortar that burst against a teak tree.

They pulled out of the action and cared for the wounded as best they could, but some hours were to elapse before they could get them to an aid station. By that time the shoulder wound had developed gangrene, and the man died shortly after. The more seriously injured gunner, despite the loss of his foot, survived.

Muther's tank developed engine trouble that night; it had a suspension unit which had collapsed and was completely immobilized. He called up the recovery team, which arrived the following morning, and they towed him back to the repair shops at Cabcaben. They were strafed a number of times on the way to the base.

Company C, 57th Philippine Scouts, moved with great difficulty against the tide of defeat along Trail 8 to the junction with Trail 46, an approach march of some 9 miles. Loyd Mills was ordered to anchor the left flank of the corps attack. The rest of the battalion was to attack on his right and failing that to fight a rear-guard action as a new line was formed at Cabcaben.

The plan for the counteroffensive miscarried almost immediately. In most cases the Japanese advanced more boldly and beat the Americans to their jumping-off points. It was now the turn of the Japanese to catch the Americans before they had deployed for battle; by the end of the day the American commanders knew they had failed. The Japanese seized the initiative and scored decisive results. The Americans fell back in disorder and the Japanese pursued them relentlessly. A further great wedge had been driven into the line, and Parker's corps, with its flank open and unhinged, was ripe for complete disaster. It only required the Japanese to take a left turn and move south for the corps to be driven into Manila Bay.

Loyd Mills was ordered to cover the withdrawal of the battalion and buy as much time as he could while they struggled frantically to establish a new line inland from Lamao. The Scouts had to hold the Japanese until 2000 hours on Tuesday; then they would be on their own. Loyd asked his CO for advice, but got very little. After being warned that the Japanese were coming in thick and fast all down the line and that the Filipinos were breaking everywhere, he was told to try to hold the line and then fall back on the nearest friendly forces he could find. Then the harassed colonel wished him luck and with his command staff hurried off down the trail to catch up with the rest of the battalion.

Mills was down to eighty men in the company. He issued all the reserve ammunition, which worked out at a bandolier a man, and what very little food remained. He inspected the machine guns of the outpost line, posted his perimeter guards, and waited for the Japanese to attack. The last of the retreating Filipinos had gone, and the trail up ahead was quiet—but not for very long. The Japanese betrayed their presence, first with the cough, then the blast from the knee mortars, and they were upon them. The young captain still marveled at their extravagant waste of human life as they sought to bulldoze him out of the position with a charge en masse down the trail. The machine guns in the outpost line stopped them dead in their tracks. The second attack was more probing and deliberate, and Mills pulled in his outposts under the cover of the company riflemen. The seasoned veterans stood firm in the matted jungle and held the Japanese at bay throughout the afternoon and on into the evening. The Japanese tried everything, but the Scouts, on occasion at the point of the bayonet, denied them the trail. It is difficult to exercise command in the thick jungle and Mills had to delegate much of the control of the fire fight to his squad and platoon leaders. They did not let him down but handled their own part of the battle, invariably hidden from the other units by the jungle, like true veterans.

When the time came, Loyd Mills began the most difficult operation of all, breaking off contact with an enemy and retreating at night. Keeping his small company headquarters in the center, he leapfrogged his platoons down the trail, which took turns at rearguard. They had practiced this standard drill enough times in the hectic days before the war, and the Scouts could do it blindfolded, though of course against an enemy the drill book doesn't always cover every eventuality. They had been going for about half an hour, and Mills was just beginning to think that they might make it after all, when one of the men in the point platoon went beserk. He started to fire at jungle shadows in the darkness. It is difficult trying to be brave all the time under conditions of such relentless pressure, and the infection spread. Within a few moments everyone was blazing off indiscriminately. Mills rushed forward to restore order, and it was a wonder he was not killed there and then, because bullets were flying in all directions. Eventually he restored control and moved the company into another defensive position where they could rest; there had been a number of casualties, fortunately minor. The real concern now was that with Japanese possibly ahead of them they had given away their presence. There was no way of knowing what they could be walking into farther down the trail. The Japanese could even now be waiting in ambush.

The Scouts, now thoroughly ashamed and sheepish, sought only to make amends for their behavior. The perimeter lines were out and guards posted even before their captain had time to issue his instructions, and they settled down to see what the morning might bring. During the night a number of stragglers stumbled into the Scouts' outposts. One was an American colonel from the Philippine Regiment who had lost his battalion, and he was followed shortly after by a brace of sergeants from the 31st Infantry. They all had the same tale of woe to relate, of breakdown, rout, and men who had lost the will and the strength to fight.

The dawn revealed the true state of their predicament. Mills had less than fifty men left, and from their position (they were on a piece of rising ground) there was clear evidence of Japanese both in front and behind. It wouldn't be long before the Japanese realized their existence and mounted an attack to wipe them out. Mills decided that the only course of action was to split his men into small groups of four or five at the most and attempt to infiltrate the Japanese lines to reach the safety of the Cabcaben line beyond. The first couple of groups were about ready to leave when a Japanese patrol bumped into the outpost. Though they were quickly dealt with, it was the signal for all hell to break loose. In the mad fire fight that followed, salvation lay in taking action which was least expected. Using the .30-calibers, hand-held, to cover their backs, Mills massed his surviving troops against the line of encircling Japanese, charged the enemy, and chopped their way free. In the running battle that ensued, the Scouts scattered into the jungle undergrowth. Mills found that he had an American colonel, who despite his rank showed a marked disinclination to command, one 31st Infantry sergeant, and a few members of his own headquarters group who had stuck doggedly to their captain throughout the engagement. After they had put some distance between themselves and the Japanese, Mills stopped and held a council of war. There was no disagreement to the plan that he had in mind. He suggested that they break north into the mountains of northern Bataan, hole up in a Negrito village, and await the return of MacArthur. Mills was convinced that they would have perhaps six months at the outside to wait for relief.

At about the same time that Loyd Mills was reaching this decision, Kermit Lay was winning his Silver Star. He had a small detail, just three of his policemen, forward guarding a bridge, and despite all the chaos and disorder he was determined to bring them out. He knew they would stay there until the bitter end, directing stragglers, and that they would expect him to effect their rescue. His Filipino driver had fled and the rest of his Scouts were fully occupied, so he drove the bus alone up the trail and beyond the outpost line. An officer tried to stop him. "You must be crazy to go any farther," he bellowed as Lay drove past. The bridge, about 10 miles to the north, was under fire when he arrived. While he reversed the bus (on those narrow trails a herculean effort even under the most favorable of circumstances) the policemen gave covering fire, and then they roared off in the direction of their own lines.

Tuesday, April 7, 1942

The last two days of the campaign on Bataan exhibited all the manifestations of an army that has collapsed. The East Road was choked with men fleeing from the savagery of the Japanese onslaught. Wainwright on Corregidor directed King to launch an immediate and general counteroffensive. The order was insane and irrelevant to a situation that was running like a roller coaster out of control. Lines were formed and then abandoned even before they could be manned, and communications between battle groups and formation headquarters became severed. This grandiose scheme was to launch Jones's I Corps into an attack on the Japanese flank. The corps commander in a three-way phone link with King and Wainwright rightly pointed out that his corps was intact only because the weight of the Japanese attack had fallen largely against Parker's hapless troops. His men, he explained, hardly had the strength to get out of their foxholes, let alone attack an enemy across a mountain. While the High Command expostulated and delayed—perhaps some were more aware than others of the need to preserve reputations and keep at least one eye on the verdicts of history—those at the front sought to do their bidding. Men with fight left in them and units that still retained cohesion and courage formed around those field commanders who were still prepared to lead. One such man, General Bluemell, his original command in tatters but still more active than most, gathered an ad hoc battle group built around the 26th Cavalry and tried to shore up a line along the Alangan River, just 7 miles to the north of Mariveles. Another who still refused to admit that all was lost on Bataan was Bill Massello. He had already lost one of his outpost lights to the Japanese advance, and the operators had disappeared. As the Filipinos poured back in disarray he contacted the battalion commander and offered to move his boys in the hope that just the sight of some disciplined American troops moving into the line could rally the fleeing Filipinos.

"Well, give it a try, Bill," the commander said, "but don't tell Chase. The colonel is as stubborn as ever. He'll just say no."

Massello gathered as many of his battery as he had available, perhaps a hundred men, and prepared to deploy. Before they could move, however, Colonel Chase somehow heard of the operation—

probably through some indiscreet staff officer—and vetoed the plan.

Massello, nothing if not persistent, decided the next best thing to do would be to establish holding areas. He had his cooks prepare all the rice and hot food they had left, and his gunners directed the fleeing soldiers into the bivouac at riflepoint. There Massello fed them and allowed them to rest before he attempted to form ad hoc units. Some of the Filipino officers gave him a particularly bad time and repeatedly challenged his authority, while others ran off into the jungle. He had just about despaired of ever being able to restore some degree of order when instructions came through from Corregidor via corps headquarters: he was to evacuate his battery and take as much equipment as he possibly could to Corregidor. Orders went out immediately to the crews on the lights to blow up their equipment and head quickly for Mariveles; there they were to rendezvous with the rest of the battery on the wharfside and take passage for Corregidor. In the meantime the men loaded the more sensitive director sights onto a couple of trucks and destroyed the rest. Within the hour they had vacated the command post and were on the already heavily congested East Road to Mariveles.

Wednesday, April 8, 1942

Initially Wainwright had decreed that there should be no mass evacuation to Corregidor. He believed that the already over-crowded garrison could not absorb more men and still be in a position to withstand a lengthy siege. Thus only those troops who were part of the Corregidor command, such as Massello's battery and the nurses, were to be brought across. Then at this late hour Wainwright relented and agreed to have the naval personnel from Mariveles and one regiment of Philippine Scouts. The word was sent out to the 45th Infantry, who were at that time probably in the best shape in the Philippine division, but they were the farthest from Mariveles. Though they were pulled out of their line along the Binuangan River, the battalions failed to make it through the congested jungle trails and on the road to Mariveles in time to be evacuated.

At first light Japanese air reconnaissance had spotted the units hastily preparing their positions along the Alangan River line. Dive bombers appeared overhead shortly afterward and, together with squadrons of medium bombers flying out of Clark, saturated the line in the well-proven and lethal mixture of high explosives and incendiaries. Soldiers had to become fire fighters to save their positions and in so doing were exposed to the merciless strafing attacks of the Zeros. At the same time, other planes roamed over the rear areas bombing and strafing the more profitable targets presented to them along the packed trails that wound through the jungle to the sea. Even the most novice air crew could hardly fail to miss, and soon the ditches and undergrowth were littered with wounded and dead, abandoned in the haste of the rout.

Wainwright already realized that his troops could no longer defend, let alone follow, the directives from on high for a counter-offensive. He notified both the War Department in Washington and MacArthur in Australia that the end was in sight.

> IT IS WITH DEEP REGRET THAT I AM FORCED TO REPORT
> THAT THE TROOPS ON BATAAN ARE FAST FOLDING UP.

He received neither an acknowledgment nor a change in his orders. The last detailed instructions he had received had been those sent on April 4 by MacArthur. In the circumstances Wainwright felt that all he could do was transmit the same instructions on to King and the Luzon Force.

By the time that the first Japanese infantry had reached the Alangan line, the right flank of the defense had withered before the air assault. Detachments of Scouts and decimated companies of the 31st U.S. Infantry made a gallant stand, but against Japanese armor they stood little chance. By evening the scattered survivors were forced to give ground or risk being outflanked. The East Road, all the way to Cabcaben and Mariveles beyond, lay open. Bluemell deployed the remains of his battle group along the Lamao River as a stop line while the very last reserves that King could muster tried to reform at Cabcaben; but they failed to hold the Japanese advance.

Once the breakthrough along the Lamao line had occurred, Drake and the supply echelons moved quickly; all available barges and launches were dispatched to Mariveles and ordered to load equipment and the specified troops for evacuation to Corregidor.

The Bataan quartermaster depot cleared its supply dumps and issued all the remaining food to the starving troops; this included some forty-five thousand C rations and case upon case of canned fruit. Some men sat by the roadside and gorged on this unexpected bounty.

U.S. Naval base
Mariveles Harbor
Bataan

The Japanese had been bombing Mariveles almost without interruption for the past two days. They had finally seen through the subterfuge that was *Canopus*, and she came in for more than her fair share of attention, though no bombs hit. The constant air attacks on the harbor area took a substantial toll in human and material terms. Much of the Navy's remaining oil supplies, scattered in small caches in the jungle brush around Mariveles Harbor, were touched off by the heavy bombing. Commander King's repair shops on shore, the power lines, and few surviving warehouses were wrecked.

The decision was made to scuttle *Canopus*. The engineers got up steam for the last time, and, though tugs stood by, she proceeded under her own power, battle ensigns flying, into deeper water. There the crew opened all the valves, wrecked the equipment left on board, and abandoned ship. Defiant to the last, *Canopus* took her time to sink, and it was daylight before she turned turtle and disappeared beneath the waves.

Ed Erickson had been given the task of blowing up the ordnance stores at Mariveles before leaving for Corregidor. There were six partially completed tunnels bored into the solid rock of the Mariveles Mountains. They contained gasoline, torpedo warheads, 250-pound bombs, and various other supplies. Together with a small party of sailors, he wired the tunnels to dynamite charges so that a sequence of explosions would set them off from one end to the other. On the other side of the mountain was the Army ordnance dump; both were timed to be blown up at 0200 hours. Erickson was working on the sixth and last tunnel when at about 2130 hours the ground shook and rumbled alarmingly, the floor beneath his feet split, and a bottomless crack ripped its way to the tunnel mouth. Everything moved, and the roof caved in near the farthermost powder train. Nature had taken a hand, and an earthquake, with its epicenter near Cabcaben, shook the whole peninsula like a leaf. The tunnel that Erickson and his crew were in corkscrewed out of shape, and the men had to claw their way out to the entrance. Under these circumstances Erickson felt that he could not wait until the planned time to blow the tunnels. Once the crew was clear, he crossed the wires and pushed down on the plunger. Five tunnels blew according to plan but in the sixth, which had been so badly damaged in the earthquake, the force of the explosion traveled up rather than outward. Rocks and boulders were hurled all over the waterfront, and a number of smaller boats were sunk. A large slice of the mountainside slid down into the harbor.

The Army dumps contained hundreds of thousands of rounds of small-arms ammunition, Air Corps bombs, and artillery shells. The ammunition was blown up at about the same time as the earthquake, so people could not distinguish between the two. There were also a number of warehouses full of TNT, and when these were blown many were convinced that a second earthquake had hit Bataan. The immediate effect of this destruction was that the road into Mariveles had to be closed for some three hours while the ammunition and small arms exploded. Though this did ease the congestion in the port area and allowed the Military Police to reassert a degree of control over a situation that was fast getting out of hand, it nevertheless caused those who legitimately were to be evacuated to be delayed—some fatally.

Among those who now had to wait patiently for the inferno to burn itself out was Jerry McDavitt. Throughout the campaign he had serviced the needs of his artillery battalion and enhanced his reputation as an archscrounger of Bataan. Hardly a day passed when he did not make the long and dangerous drive from the supply dumps near No. 2 Hospital up to the battery positions on the line. As a result of these efforts his gunners were probably better fed than most during the siege. Earlier that day he had dropped by the hospital to visit some of his men. While he was there, one of the surgeons came up to him and told him that the colonel wanted to see him. McDavitt hurried over to the battered bus that still served as the administrative center for the hospital.

"McDavitt," the colonel said, "I want you to take the twenty-nine nurses I have here down to Mariveles. There should be a boat waiting to take them over to Corregidor."

McDavitt asked the colonel to clear it with his battalion headquarters and agreed to take on the task. While he hurried away to organize some transportation, Major Moffat got the nurses together. He found Ruby Moteley in the operating theater, where she was rolling bandages.

"Report immediately to headquarters, Ruby," he ordered. "Don't stop to pack anything. Just get over there as quickly as you can." Most of the nurses were under no illusions about what awaited them at the hands of the Japanese, but even so they were reluctant to leave. Some had to be forced into the two small trucks that McDavitt had found. It was desperately slow progress along the road to Mariveles, and at times McDavitt felt like taking a stick and beating a path through the crowd that cluttered the road. He was already in despair that the midnight deadline he had been given to reach Mariveles would not be met, when the ammunition dumps blew and all movement came to a stop.

Once the road was open again there were further delays while they waited to be processed through the police cordon that had been thrown around the port. Dawn was breaking by the time they reached the wharfside. It was a miracle that the two vehicles were still together, but of their boat there was no sign. The Japanese had already begun the first bombing raid of the day as McDavitt hurried to place his charges under the shelter of a large rock overhang. Moteley had thought that perhaps the *Canopus* could come to their rescue, but she saw instead the last moments of the old lady as she sank out in the bay. The best transportation that McDavitt could find was a small rowboat, though it did come complete with row locks and oars. He also found a case of canned peaches, and these he took to the nurses for their breakfast.

"Ruby, can you swim?" he asked.

"Yes, but I'm not going to swim in Manila Bay. There're sharks out there!" she replied.

McDavitt put her in the boat along with one of the drivers to help with the rowing and two other nurses whom he knew were strong swimmers. Then he returned to the remaining nurses, still huddled together under the overhang, though now starting into the peaches. He was worried because he had to leave them while he rowed to Corregidor to find a launch to pick them up, but they took Mc-Davitt's news in their stride. Some even joked about their predicament. Eunice Tyler, who came from McDavitt's hometown, Lockhart, Texas, warned him, "Jerome! If you don't come back and get me, I'm gonna tell your momma when I get home!"

The two men started to row the 3½ miles to Corregidor. They got about a third of the way across when a Navy lighter found them and took them aboard. On reaching Corregidor McDavitt rushed to Malinta Tunnel and reported the location of the nurses in Mariveles. A fast launch was dispatched without delay, and by 1600 hours they were happily reunited with the others in the hospital lateral. The group from the other general hospital had arrived in Mariveles before the dumps were blown. They had reached the harbor on time and made it to Corregidor without incident.

Paul Ashton had spent those last days helping to organize the medical services behind the II Corps line when he was ordered to report to No. 1 Hospital. It had been bombed again. The Bataan Field Force Surgeon appeared on the scene and directed Ashton to take over immediately as chief of surgery. The operating theater staff and the surgeons were overwhelmed by the number of casualties, and the bombing had completely unnerved them.

"We can't let things go on like this," he said. "Just get it moving. There are lots of casualties, and nobody is operating. It's all gone to hell."

Ashton put his own staff to work, and they cleaned up the debris in the operating theater. Gradually the hospital staff appeared to help, though some of the surgeons were so demoralized that it was some time before they were prepared to come out of their foxholes.

Orderlies restored some sort of order to the open-air wards, and patients drifted back into the hospital. Ashton succeeded in forming surgical teams and within a short time had four tables working in the nipa hut that served as the operating theater. They had been there for less than an hour when Japanese bombers appeared overhead for a second time that day. There was a white-coated movement toward the door.

"Nobody leaves. Nobody leaves," Ashton ordered. The surgeons turned back to their tables, and as the bombs fell the operations continued.

Ashton realized that he had inherited a bunch of fine surgeons but some of the worst soldiers he had ever encountered. As doctors, most believed that their day should still finish at 1630 hours. Paul was astounded to see a number of them later sitting around in silk dressing gowns and relaxing. "What the hell," he said angrily to them, "you don't stop work in this outfit. There are people out here who need to be fixed and helped. There are bandages to prepare and wounds to be dressed. So get back to work." One of them told him that he always stopped work at 1630 hours and threatened to complain to the Field Force Surgeon. Ashton had a ready response to such behavior. "You'll have to get by me, and I'll punch you in the nose, and I'll shoot you if I have to." Convinced, the surgeons donned their white coats and returned to the operating area.

Bill Massello had arrived on the Rock but with only part of his battery. His instructions had been to report to a Colonel Carpenter on the wharfside at Mariveles, but in all that chaos and confusion he could no more find the good colonel than he could "the Archangel Gabriel." However, this most resourceful of officers acquired a small barge and his men loaded what they could while he paced the wharf in search of his missing gunners. A Navy tug appeared alongside and made ready to pass a tow to the barge. Massello begged the captain to wait a little longer in case the missing members of his battery should appear. As the first gray tints lightened the sky and heralded dawn, the tug commander insisted on sailing. It tore Massello apart to leave his men behind, but he knew the commander was right. They docked at Bottomside at the height of an air raid.

McCann, Craig, and Brodemeyer had spent the night as part of a work detail loading barges at Mariveles. They had been dispatched to the wharfside late the previous afternoon when their job guarding the dump ended and the demolition squads had taken over. The trio was still together, though Earl Craig had been in the hospital with malaria and then had been wounded during subsequent air raids. A piece of shrapnel had sliced through his kneecap even as he fled the hospital, but though the leg was stiff and swollen the teenager resolutely refused to return to the nearest thing he had ever seen to what he imagined was hell on earth. McCann worked as hard as he could and tried to cover his friend's stumbling efforts. They labored throughout the long, hot, sticky night. As soon as one barge was full, a small tug steamed up, hooked on the barge, and towed it out into the bay. McCann noticed that as the night passed, the work party grew smaller, and by dawn there were less than a dozen of them left, and the barge they were then loading appeared to be the last. Just as they were about finished McCann grabbed Craig—Brodemeyer had disappeared in the course of the night— and they scrambled into the hold and settled down on top of the cases of food. Most of the others followed suit, though a few changed their minds and jumped back onto the wharfside. The hold had a sliding canopy, and this they pulled partly over and awaited developments. The tugboat steamed alongside, a crew member jumped across, fastened the tow rope to the bollard on the barge's bow, and cast them loose from the wharf. He never once looked into the hold but jumped nimbly back on board as the tug pulled away.

In the meantime, the stowaways investigated the cargo, broke open some cans of corned beef and pineapple, and settled down to eat a hearty breakfast. The sun's rays streamed in through the crack in the canopy, and they lay back and breathed a sigh of relief to have escaped the hell that was Bataan. McCann dressed Craig's wound and within a very short while joined the others in sleep.

It must have been the strange rocking motion the barge made that awoke McCann. The sun was high overhead, and he knew they should have reached Corregidor. He was thoroughly alarmed and roused the others, scrambling to the top of the crates and peering out over the cargo hatch. At first there was no sign of the tug. Then he saw it disappearing in the direction of Mariveles. It had cast them loose in midchannel, beyond the minefields; at least he now understood the barge's motion.

They drifted slowly, deeper into the bay, and closer to Manila. How far they drifted the now thoroughly alarmed and extremely frightened group couldn't tell, though it was close enough for them to see the harbor breakwater and Japanese fighters taking off from the new runway they had helped build on Nichols Field. One fighter peeled off and swooped low over the barge, but the fugitives had enough time to scramble down to the deeper recesses of the hold, which fortunately were in shadow.

In the late afternoon they started to drift out again, and shortly afterward, as if by magic, the tug appeared to take them in tow. It came alongside, a man jumped across, made fast the rope, and returned to the tug; again he did not bother to check the contents of the hold. The stowaways spent the time that it took the tug to pull them around Corregidor by the South Channel and into the South Dock trying to concoct a plausible story that could explain their being on the barge, but they need not have bothered. When the barge was tied up alongside a number of others and the group somewhat sheepishly stepped ashore, they were accepted as a matter of course, along with hundreds of others who had by fair means and foul reached Corregidor. They were marched down to Malinta Tunnel, given a meal, and mustered into new units. McCann found that he had been drafted into the 4th Provisional Battalion, 4th Marines. After all his abortive attempts in San Diego, it had taken a war and the military collapse on Bataan for him to realize the dream of his childhood and follow his father into the Marines!

Earl Craig was also to become a Marine, but when their company commander inspected his new recruits and saw the state of the youngster's knee he packed him off to the hospital. The two boys parted, they thought for a short while, but McCann never saw Earl Craig again.

Not everybody who was evacuated to Corregidor left from Mariveles. The gunboat *Mindanao* rescued some Americans from the 31st Infantry in the most dramatic of circumstances. They were returning to Corregidor after bombarding the Japanese positions north of Lamao. Patrolling close to shore, when they were abreast of Cabcaben Point the lookouts spotted a signal from a small rowboat. When they had come alongside, a young lieutenant scrambled on board. He was emaciated, weak, and close to exhaustion. For Sam Malick and the rest of the still well-fed crew it was their first encounter with the reality of Bataan.

The young officer explained that he had a party of some twenty men trapped on the beach. They were surrounded by Japanese and had just about given up hope when salvation in the form of the gunboat had steamed into sight around the headland. The coxswain and four sailors, including Malick, immediately jumped down into a 50-foot motor launch the captain had acquired from naval stores. It mounted a .30-caliber gun in the bows and was used as a picket boat. The young officer insisted on coming along to guide them to where his men were waiting. The coxswain ran the launch as close to the shore as he dared, but they were afraid to beach it in case they got stranded, for it was an ebb tide. Some desultory small fire came their way but that wasn't the real problem, which was the great difficulty the sailors had in getting the soldiers down the beach and into the boat. Malick was not alone in failing to disguise the look of horror on his face when they first approached the soldiers. Some were too weak to scramble out of their foxholes unaided, and all were starved and stricken with dysentery. But they still had plenty of fight left in them, and not one would discard his rifle as they were lifted into the launch.

The cooks of the *Mindanao* laid on the best meal they could manage while the sailors pooled all their spare clothing and afterward willingly surrendered their bunks. Fed and clean, the soldiers slept all the way to Corregidor.

The last three P-40s took off from Cabcaben airstrip just before dusk. The ground crews who had served them so faithfully throughout the campaign loaded them for the last time with fragmentation bombs and watched them go. They took off and circled back over the bay, then to swoop on the Japanese front lines. Their bombs gone, they flew low in formation over Cabcaben, dipped their wings in a final salute, and headed south to Mindanao.

Thursday, April 9, 1942
HQ, Luzon Force
Bataan

The sequence of events that led to the surrender of the forces on Bataan probably began on the evening of Wednesday, April 8, and history was made. General King, in what must rank as one of the most selfless acts of military courage, assumed the full mantle of responsibility for the destiny of the Luzon Force. Some would argue that he did this out of respect for the predicament in which Wainwright had been placed by the direct orders of MacArthur. Others maintain that General King could wait no longer for

Wainwright to face up to and then take the most unpalatable of steps for a professional soldier, capitulation. For whatever reason, General King did this in the sure knowledge that if and when he returned home he would likely be court-martialed for willfully disobeying the orders of his superiors in the field. Even exoneration from the charge would not remove him from that position in American military history which by his actions he was shortly to occupy. To General King was to fall the distinction of being the first general to surrender an army in the field in the history of the Republic. General King believed that in taking this course of action, he would be professionally disgraced and historically damned; however, what was more important was the fate of his men.

A commander in the field has a duty to his superiors to carry out the orders he has been given. He has a responsibility to ensure that the plans he prepares and the decisions he makes in the execution of that duty will result in the minimum casualties being inflicted on the men under his command. Duty and responsibility are synonymous in war, but they become irreconcilable when the prolongation of conflict becomes futile—then the demands of humanity transcend the needs of war. General King believed that events on Bataan had by then reached that critical stage. Even so, it takes a rare kind of military courage to make such a decision. It would appear that King's superiors lacked that same brand of courage. For him "the loneliness of command" must have come crushing down to overwhelm his resolve. Though fully apprised of the facts, Generals Marshall, MacArthur, even Wainwright to a degree, and the president, too, postured through ambiguous public statement or public silence. Such was their concern not to be closely associated with this military calamity.

General King informed his corps commanders that emissaries would be sent out at dawn under a flag of truce to negotiate terms for a cease-fire from the enemy. On Corregidor Wainwright knew nothing of King's actions. When they spoke by telephone at 0300 hours King made no mention of his decision. Wainwright first learned of the move from his assistant operations officer, Lt. Col. Jesse T. Traywick, Jr., as the emissaries, two bachelor volunteer officers, Colonel Williams and Major Hurt, drove across the American front line.

General Wainwright immediately sent a dispatch to MacArthur:

AT 6 O'CLOCK THIS MORNING GENERAL KING . . . WITHOUT
MY KNOWLEDGE OR APPROVAL SENT A FLAG OF TRUCE TO
THE JAPANESE COMMANDER. THE MINUTE I HEARD OF IT I
DISAPPROVED OF HIS ACTION AND DIRECTED THAT THERE
WOULD BE NO SURRENDER. I WAS INFORMED IT WAS TOO
LATE TO MAKE ANY CHANGE, THAT THE ACTION HAD
ALREADY BEEN TAKEN. . . .
  PHYSICAL EXHAUSTION AND SICKNESS DUE TO A LONG
PERIOD OF INSUFFICIENT FOOD IS THE REAL CAUSE OF
THIS TERRIBLE DISASTER. WHEN I GET WORD WHAT
TERMS HAVE BEEN ARRANGED I WILL ADVISE YOU.

The Japanese pressed on with the advance relentlessly. Though
all resistance had ceased, they opened fire indiscriminately. None
of the defenders could tell whether the Japanese knew of the
cease-fire. Their armored spearheads thrust out of the jungle trails
and onto the East Road above Mariveles, and war engulfed the two
general hospitals.

Paul Ashton moved forward to meet the Japanese as the tank
column stopped outside the entrance. A Japanese colonel climbed
out of the lead tank and saluted Ashton. He was both punctilious
and polite and he asked in halting English to be taken on a tour of
the hospital. During the tour, Ashton reported that they had 46
Japanese prisoners. All of them had been badly wounded and most
were in casts and traction. The Japanese officer walked across to
where they lay in an open-air ward; except that it was set apart, it
was no different than any of the others. The officer unsheathed his
sword and cut the ropes holding the limbs of the patients in traction. Though this act must have caused them unspeakable agony,
not one showed any sign of emotion on his face. Ashton tried to
remonstrate, but the officer held up his hand and everybody,
patients and staff, was forbidden on pain of death to leave the
hospital perimeter. Later in the day a couple of captured American
trucks drove into the area. The Japanese wounded were unceremoniously bundled into the back and driven away.

It was at about the same time that the Japanese occupied the
other general hospital, which was located just over 2 miles east and
nearer to Cabcaben. Bill Garleb was still in the hospital, but deep
into a recurring bout of malaria, he remembered nothing of their

coming. They were the first Japanese that Chaplain Zimmerman had seen close up. He wished he could have met them under more favorable circumstances, for they looted everything the patients possessed. One soldier took his lighter and a second traded cigarettes for his watch, though the chaplain did not think he had much option in the transaction.

The Japanese soldiers were short and squat—Zimmerman did not see one much above 5 feet, 2 inches—with round faces and shaved heads. It was difficult to guess their ages, though he formed the opinion that they were young, some barely out of their teens. Their uniforms were clean but had been laundered until the khaki had faded so much that it was difficult to make out the unit insignia or rank. They all wore the jungle boot of the Japanese combat soldier, unique in that the big toe is cut separately, like the thumb in a mitten.

There was one young American woman still left at the hospital. She had two young children and was married to a wealthy Filipino who had sugar beet interests in the United States. His father had died, and they had returned to settle his estates in Orion. They were stranded in the Philippines by the outbreak of the war. Just a few weeks previously the family had been caught in an air raid, the husband was killed, and her young son was badly injured. He had to have his arm amputated. The hospital had allowed this tragic figure to move into a small tent, where she was near to her son and had a ready supply of milk for the baby.

The Japanese came, and they raped her all night long. While some stood guard, they kept a circle going in and out of that tent. At first she screamed and moaned, but after a while all that Zimmerman could hear, and his cot was no more than 50 feet from the tent, were deep moans of pain and anguish. The Americans wanted to do something, but there was nothing that could be done. The Japanese officers had ravished her first, so there was little point in appealing to their sense of honor or human decency, while any form of physical interference would simply have put both her and her children at risk. The chaplain kept the children close by. They were at least too young to understand. He prayed the night away.

In the morning the Japanese released the woman. Zimmerman tried to comfort her as she looked after her children, and by midday she had gone. One of the doctors had been able to make the arrangements to get her and the children away from there, and she disappeared into internment.

* * *

During that last night on Bataan, word filtered down to both the troops in the line and those awaiting events in the huge holding areas that the Military Police had established on the outskirts of Mariveles, that surrender was imminent. Instructions on the action to take were frequently confusing and contradictory. Some were ordered to remain where they were and not to destroy equipment or weapons. Others were told to destroy all weapons and move down to Mariveles. Some of the artillery regiments used the most novel ways of destroying their guns. They took as long a lanyard as they could find, put a high-explosive shell in the breech, and forced another, armed with impact fuses, down the barrel. The effect was frequently spectacular. Soldiers in an orgy of fury and destruction gripped rifles by the barrel and smashed the butts against the trees. Bolts and what is termed in the manuals as "the working parts" were scattered in the jungle. As the holding areas filled, the Military Police gathered the men into columns and quietly shepherded them on toward the designated assembly areas in and around Mariveles. One of the biggest was on what used to be the Navy parade ground, but there were overflow points all along the East Road. When the Japanese arrived, they took their valuables—watches, rings, and wallets; and they appeared to be particularly partial to Parker or Shaeffer fountain pens.

Many of the Filipinos did not formally surrender as such. They stripped off what few vestiges of uniform they still possessed and tried to pass through the Japanese lines as civilians in the hope of returning home to their families. Some made it, but many failed. It seemed to depend very much on the mood of the Japanese they encountered. Those who were detained were either returned to the compounds or shot out of hand as escaping prisoners of war.

The remnants of Company C, 194th Tank Battalion were in a tank parking lot outside Cabcaben. They shot up the last of the half-tracks with the 37mm guns and dismantled the guns, poured sand into the fuel tanks, and immobilized what was left in a dozen different ways. By the time they had finished, the tanks and the other vehicles were just so much scrap. The men then formed up behind their officers and trooped off down the road toward Mariveles. They had not been on the road very long before they ran into a Japanese patrol, the roughest characters Frank Muther had ever seen. The soldiers appeared tired, dirty, and almost as weary as the Americans. Captain Moffatt, the company commander, went up, saluted the Japanese officer, and indicated that they wished to surrender. He was slapped, kicked, and, together with the other officers, stripped of all valuables before the company was taken on under escort toward Mariveles.

Shortly afterward they heard a column of tanks coming down the East Road. There was a familiar whine to the note of the engines. The tanks thundered by, and even in the dark there was no mistaking either the sound or the silhouette. They were Matildas, with Japanese crews perched awkwardly on the unfamiliar turret hatches.

Winston Jones was weary beyond belief. He had fought to the bitter end with the shattered remnants of his beloved division, and now he sat disconsolate and alone in the officers-only section of a big compound outside Mariveles. He reached inside his coveralls and pulled out a small pocket Bible given him many years before by the father of a close friend, and began to read. Some of the other officers gathered nearby asked him to read out loud. He turned the pages at random to the Book of Psalms and then remembered the words to one in particular. He read out loud from Psalm 7:

> O Lord my God in thee do I put my trust,
> Save me from all them that persecute me.
> And deliver me.

As far as anyone can be sure, General King surrendered some 76,000 men, including 12,000 Americans, on Bataan. It was the greatest capitulation in American history. There was terrible confusion everywhere, not least among the Japanese, who had anticipated that after another three weeks of combat perhaps 20,000 troops would surrender.

When MacArthur heard from Wainwright of the fall of Bataan, MacArthur wrote:

> The Bataan Force went out as it would have wished, fighting to the end [of] its flickering forlorn hope. No army has ever done so much with so little and nothing became it more than its last hour of trial and agony. To the weeping mothers of its dead, I can only say that the sacrifice and halo of Jesus of Nazareth has descended upon their sons, and that God will take them unto himself.

The men on Bataan deserved better than this mawkish sentimentality. If MacArthur had given Wainwright the authority to surrender, then he could have used his discretion rather than be caught in the military straitjacket of having to obey a legal command. The order to launch the final counterattack was totally wrong, and had it not occurred there would not have been so much needless slaughter, and the survivors would have been in better shape to face the ordeals ahead of them.

On the morning of April 10, the Marines on Corregidor witnessed a last tragedy from Bataan. Hundreds of desperate men tried to swim the 3½ miles to Corregidor. Others used small boats, dugout canoes, even bits of wreckage in an attempt to float across the narrow divide. Japanese artillery, after a couple of ranging shots, poured round after round into the waters of the North Channel, and where they failed, the sharks succeeded. Very few of those gaunt survivors made it safely through the oil- and blood-streaked waters to the dubious haven of Corregidor.

X. CORREGIDOR

Friday, April 10–
Friday, May 8, 1942

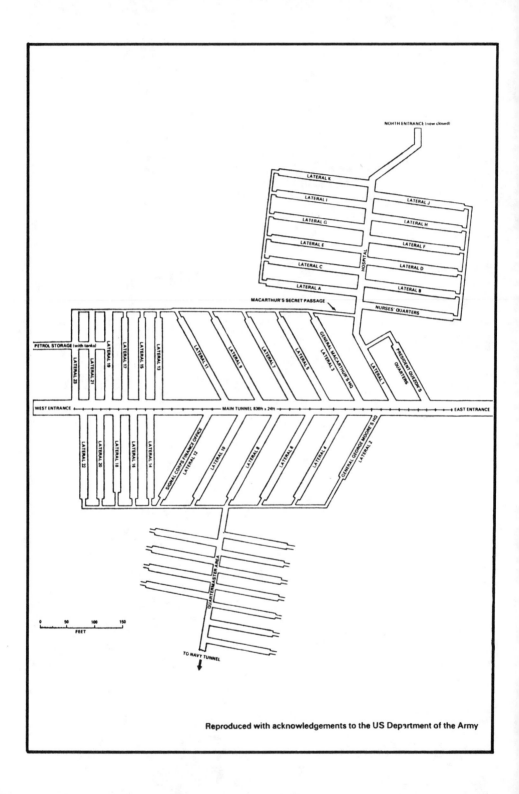

Reproduced with acknowledgements to the US Department of the Army

1. The Death March

If the Japanese can take the Rock they
will find me here, no matter what orders
I receive.

General Wainwright, April 1942

0100 hours
Friday, April 10, 1942
U.S.S. *Pigeon*
At sea

Lt. Cdr. George King shook hands with the captain of the
Pigeon and then prepared to board the submarine *Snapper*, which
lay alongside. It had been a hectic twenty-four hours since he had
left the doomed *Canopus* and arrived on Corregidor. No sooner had
he landed than he was told to be ready to leave that night, together
with twenty-five selected members of his crew, for Australia. It was
a difficult choice to make and even harder to face those to be left
behind. Once darkness had fallen (though with the fires still raging
on Bataan there was precious little night to blanket their movements) they attempted to rendezvous with the submarine. Three
times Japanese gunfire drove the *Pigeon* to seek shelter in the lee of
Corregidor. It was very close to the deadline before they were able
to elude the watchers on the opposite shore, negotiate the minefield, and sail into the South China Sea.

It was not the first time King had been aboard the *Pigeon*. As a youth in a Baltimore shipyard he had helped build her, and more recently, when a hurricane had driven the tender ashore on the China coast, he had brought her safely to Manila. At the time King had been en route to join the *Canopus*, but his orders had been changed, so he left the troopship at Shanghai to travel across to Singtow and assume command of the damaged *Pigeon*. The Japanese held the port at the time and gave him few facilities and little help. Nevertheless, with the pumps working all the while, he limped across to Manila Bay and docked safely in Cavite.

As George King made for the bridge ladder to join the others boarding from the well deck, the captain of the *Pigeon* turned to his yeoman of signals. "Say, Smithy," he said, "how many kids you got?"

"Three, sir," Smithy replied.

"Get down on that submarine and good luck, Smithy," the captain ordered.

The sailor did not need any persuasion, pausing only long enough to salute, and then in a display of emotion that overcame his years of training and discipline, clasped the hand of his captain in quiet gratitude and quickly joined the last of the evacuees. The submarine cast loose and submerged into the South China Sea.

King stood in the control room and talked for a short while with her commander, Hamilton Stone, a classmate at Annapolis, before going aft to check the passengers. He found there was a stowaway on board, an ensign from Corregidor, determined come what may to leave. The young man, a defiant and unrepentant Regular Navy officer, was placed under open arrest for the voyage to Fremantle.

Bataan

The Japanese contingency plan for handling the surrender and evacuation of the forces on Bataan had been prepared some weeks in advance, and at that time it must have seemed reasonable. The evacuation was planned with a number of intermediate staging points and from a Japanese viewpoint aimed to clear the front of prisoners in the most efficient manner with the resources at their disposal. The operation called for the prisoners to be gathered in groups of a hundred men and then marched under escort 19 miles from the battle zone to Balanga—no more than a day's march for a Japanese soldier. At Balanga trucks would take them to the railhead at San Fernando, where trains were to convey them to Capas, a small town north of Clark Field. There the men would be marched the 6 or 7 miles to Camp O'Donnell, a complex housing an old training center for the Philippine Army, which the Japanese were even then converting into three prisoner-of-war compounds. The Japanese calculated that they could clear the prisoners fairly quickly, and that for each party the journey could be completed in a maximum of four days. They planned to hold the men overnight at Balanga and San Fernando, both of which would require reception camps with food and some medical facilities made available.

The Japanese plan went hopelessly wrong from the start, and it was their failure to cope and adapt that sowed the seeds of disaster and allowed the operation to degenerate into one of the most horrifying atrocities of the war. In what was to become known as the "Bataan Death March," significant numbers of sick and diseased men from this beaten army were subjected to a heinously wicked ordeal by a callously indifferent barbarian horde. What went wrong?

In the first instance, Japanese HQ, Fourteenth Army, had grossly underestimated the number of prisoners. The staff anticipated some 10,000, of which the majority would be either from American or Philippine Scout formations. Second, though the Japanese had some indications of the defenders' food situation, they had not planned on capturing an army that needed medical help on such a vast scale. The state of health and the prevalence of disease, coupled with rampant and endemic malnutrition, made nonsense of the Japanese plans, even had they been right about the numbers. Almost all of the Americans and a goodly proportion of the Filipinos were incapable of walking half a mile without the greatest distress. Finally, the Japanese authorities did not consider, neither for the most part did they seek to curb, the brutality of their own soldiers. A peasant army, nurtured on violence and brutality as the means of enforcing discipline, was allowed to run amok and seek revenge on those who had inflicted harm, discomfort, and disgrace on them for so long.

Individual acts of cruelty were on such a scale that the honor of the Japanese Army was indelibly stained. Their crime against humanity defies description, and the acts of bestiality should be remembered if only as a salutary warning of the depths of depravity to which man is capable of descending in his blood lust.

In describing the fate of those who suffered in this way it is difficult to maintain a sense of detachment and proportion. At the same time it is important to keep the record straight. Many troops covered the march in an orderly manner and were humanely, and frequently sympathetically, treated by their guards throughout the journey. A fair number traveled the distance from Balanga to San Fernando in the trucks as planned, though they were in the minority and certainly the lucky ones. Finally, many men of Albert Jones's I Corps, who had capitulated high up on the South China Sea coast, had a shorter march, across country to Balanga, and were *in relative terms* in slightly better physical condition to endure the hardships.

There was no rhyme or reason to Japanese behavior, and this became apparent from the start. The Americans in No. 1 Hospital were protected and the conventions of war respected by the Japanese. Paul Ashton was to stay there until the end of April, sending his patients off a truckload at a time, until eventually he took the last remaining to Bilabid Prison in Manila many weeks later. The patients in the second hospital were subjected to deliberate cruelty after the surrender had been negotiated. There were 6,000 men in the hospital, mostly Filipinos, and they were encouraged by their captors to leave. Hundreds staggered from their beds and on make-shift crutches attempted to walk to the assembly areas. Bandages unwound as they marched, injuries hemorrhaged, and men died in the ditches, some within a few yards of the gate. Japanese guards ripped casts off Filipino patients and with bamboo lashed them out onto the road. It was a callous and deliberate act of brutality less than 900 yards from No. 1 Hospital, where in contrast Ashton and the surgeons received every cooperation from their captors. There is no clear reason for the difference in the treatment of the hospitals. Ashton's hospital did contain the wounded Japanese soldiers. But disgrace and dishonor awaited them, and it is unlikely that the Japanese Army would have felt gratitude for their care. No. 2 Hospital may have been so ferociously treated because the Japanese needed its jungle clearings to deploy their artillery in the coming battle for Corregidor. But such a military necessity does not excuse the Japanese Army behavior.

Kermit Lay had stayed in his provost company command post as he had been instructed at the time of the surrender. The area, which encompassed a number of formation headquarters, was rife with rumor. One of them was that every officer would have an orderly, the higher ranks two, and that all officers were to be taken to Manila by convoy. Indeed, that morning a number of command cars and trucks, driven by Americans and flying white flags, arrived at corps headquarters to take the officers, as they thought, to Manila and honorable imprisonment. Lay climbed into the front of a command car, an ordnance colonel named Peebles and two captains jumped in the back, and off they went. They had traveled perhaps a mile when a Japanese patrol, led by an officer, stepped out from the roadside, flagged down the convoy, and examined the documents that were presented to him by an interpreter in the first vehicle. Lay's car was third in the line. While they waited, a Japanese soldier strolled across and started to touch the colonel's silver eagle insignia on his collar with grubby, clumsy fingers. The American tried to shrug away such unwelcome attention. The Japanese officer saw what was happening and became very angry. At his instructions a couple of men pulled the colonel out of the car, dragged him across the road, and tied him to the nearest tree. While the officer stood by, the soldier who had been insulted bayoneted the colonel to death. The rest of the party were ordered out of their vehicles and marched down to Mariveles, where they joined the officers' compound.

At Mariveles Field the men were brought up in groups of a hundred and once again subjected to a thorough search by the Japanese. Some, but by no means all, were issued with a white armband by their captors. They were given orders to remain in their groups. Instructions were passed down the line initially from American officers who spoke some Japanese, or they came from Filipino quislings, some of whom had come into Bataan with the Japanese forces. Most American and Filipino prisoners got the word at the point of a bayonet, and that universal language was not difficult to understand.

Frank Muther spent a long and uncomfortable first night in the compound. Despite his exhaustion, he found it impossible to sleep on the hard, unyielding concrete. Like so many others, he sat on his haunches and whispered away the night hours with his friends, planning an escape. There were five of them: little Frankie Gabriel, Dick Longmeyer, and the Harrison brothers. They moved off shortly after dawn in one of the first groups and followed the road out of Mariveles toward Cabcaben. In places the undergrowth encroached to the very edge of the road, and they found it surprisingly easy to dart into the jungle, unnoticed by the half-dozen Japanese privates and an NCO who guarded the group. They planned to head north into the hills and hide out until MacArthur returned. They, too, believed that there were six months at the most to wait. They stumbled through the undergrowth and clambered over the elephantine roots as they hastened to put as much distance as they could between themselves and the road. The fugitives paused after a while and listened intently, but they could hear no sounds of pursuit; obviously their absence had not been detected. The men plunged deeper into the forest until, exhausted by their efforts, they came at last to a bubbling stream of clear, fresh water. As a man they flung themselves face down on the bank and drank deep and long before continuing. A well-defined path led away from the stream and unthinkingly they opted for the easier route, only to walk straight into the arms of a Japanese guard detail. Since leaving the column they had marched west rather than north and had stumbled into an artillery unit. The Americans had no armbands, nothing to signify that they had surrendered, and the sentry who took them down to the battery commander's CP certainly made no concessions to their status.

After a while, an officer came across to them and immediately launched into a long tirade of spitting invective. The group didn't understand a word he said, but the meaning was very clear. He became more and more agitated, and the Americans increasingly frightened. In desperation Frank Muther blurted out, "*Sprechen sie Deutsch?*"

"*Jawohl!*" the Japanese replied.

Frank explained that he was of Swiss-German parentage and then told him a lie about not being able to find anyone to whom they could surrender. The officer immediately became a little more friendly and gave them a guard, who took them down to Mariveles. They had ended up by walking at least a dozen miles or more, in a big circle, but they returned in plenty of time to be assigned a group and suffer all the pain and anguish of the Death March.

Saturday, April 11, 1942

Winston Jones left in one of the later columns for Balanga on the first stage of the march. Like many of the Americans, though he had been without food since the surrender he was not hungry. The shock of defeat and the enormity of their predicament deadened the pangs of hunger. He felt very uncertain and afraid. Despite the campaign, this was the first time he had come face to face with the Japanese, a race of people he knew very little about. None of the men knew what to do or how to behave as prisoners of war. It was not a subject that appeared on the prewar training schedules.

There were some in the group who were in very poor health. The others helped as best they could by supporting and even dragging them, though they were too weak to carry them. As they walked through the broad grove of trees and past the general hospitals along the road to Cabcaben, Jones saw the bodies of Filipinos sprawled in obscene death along the roadside. They had just come abreast of the dirt strip at Cabcaben Field when a battery of Japanese heavy artillery opened fire on Corregidor. The island replied in kind, but its first rounds were short, and they burst along the road and decimated the ranks of the column ahead. A Japanese military policeman appeared and motioned Jones's group off the road into a rice stubble field, directly in front of the guns and in plain view of Corregidor. The gun battle lasted an hour or more during which time the Americans were forced, along with other groups who happened by, to remain exactly where they were, though this had little effect on the rate of Corregidor's counter battery fire. At least no more rounds fell short. At the end of the gun battle, they were herded together onto the road to continue the march. Some of their number were now too ill to move, and the guards bayoneted them where they lay. A little farther on, Jones was at the head of the column when he stumbled over a head lying in the road. At first he thought it was a victim of the shelling, but the neck had been cleanly severed; with numbed horror he realized what it was.

From Cabcaben the road turns north and then straight up the eastern coast of Bataan. There were artesian wells every kilometer along the roadside. Their pure, clean water had been used to irrigate the rice fields. The ground around the wells was now littered with the dead, and in some the water had been contaminated. All the columns had to march against the tide of the Japanese Army still advancing down to the battlefront. The dust swirled up by the convoys added to the discomfort of the prisoners, while some Japanese soldiers found amusement in the cruel sport of attempting to knock men's hats off with long bamboo poles as the trucks thundered past. Many men were knocked senseless into the path of oncoming vehicles.

Temperature and humidity soared once the columns had left the forest glades. The weight of vehicles had broken through the macadam and made the road surface rough and uneven. This added to the men's pain and anguish.

Balanga

At Balanga, marching columns of prisoners from I Corps "collided" with the mainstream that had followed the coast road north from Mariveles and Cabcaben. There was chaos. The Japanese administration was in shreds, and there were no facilities prepared to meet the needs of these distressed men. Long lines of milling prisoners were herded into fields, and as darkness fell more columns arrived in the town to swell the numbers. Some lucky men were fed a rice stew, but the vast majority weren't, and the primitive sanitary arrangements the Japanese provided soon broke down.

There were only two hundred trucks available to move the prisoners to San Fernando, and most of these were in a dilapidated condition; they were the vehicles the Japanese Army had already rejected for its own purposes. The result was that the vast majority of the men had to walk the 44 miles to the railhead at San Fernando. The Japanese established enclosures along the roadside to serve as a form of staging post or rest areas for columns that were caught out at night between the main towns. There was one at Orani, 11 miles to the north of Balanga, and more at Lubao, a further 16 miles to the north. The conditions inside these stockades became progressively worse. There was no attempt to clean up after each group, so they became little better than open sewers. The bodies of those men who died in the stockades littered the ground. No attempt was made to bury them, and as the days passed the corpses expanded into grotesque, putrid, swollen shapes.

The columns were by now strung out and frequently out of sight of one another. The Japanese guards, perhaps seven to each group, became edgy and very wary of their charges, although the Americans were in no position, despite their numerical superiority, to offer any threat or challenge. Increasingly the roadside was dotted with bodies bloated and blackened by the sun. The Japanese guards would make a column march in double time, sometimes out of devilment, more often out of fear, to catch up with another group; for whatever reason it was agony for the prisoners. Men who could not maintain the pace would gradually drop back through the ranks until they fell behind, often a cruel target for the victors' sport. The Japanese soldiers they encountered on the road north of Balanga were low-grade, rear-echelon formations.

The cadavers along the road were picked over by carrion birds, and the smell of the dead is something the survivors carry in their nostrils to this very day.

Orani

John Spainhower had marched two days without water, and on the third, as they approached Orani, the guards allowed them to drink from a small creek that stank from the decomposing remains that floated in the water. Although the water had a sweet taste they had to drink, they were so dehydrated. John had some iodine, and he put a few drops in his cup before he sipped it through parched and cracked lips.

At Orani the Japanese found out that Spainhower had been an

adjutant of a Philippine Scout battalion, and they forced him to watch as they buried six Scouts alive. The men dug their own graves and then knelt down in the pit. Grinning guards hit them over the head with shovels and then piled the earth on top of their victims, who had only been stunned by the blows. This was just one of the many such instances in which the Japanese singled out the Philippine Scouts for especially brutal treatment. Spainhower was forced to stand vigil over the scene and later collapsed with sunstroke. Along with a number of other men whom even the callous Japanese recognized could not continue on foot, he finished the journey to San Fernando in the back of a truck.

Sergeant White was a crew chief who had helped service the P-40s on the strip at Cabcaben to the very end of the campaign. It took his column four days to reach Orani. On the edge of the town, they came upon an American officer on his hands and knees in the road. A Japanese officer drew his sword, brought it up, and swung it down two-handed in an arching curve that decapitated the officer in a single blow.

The column staggered on, each man who witnessed the outrage determined to remember what the Japanese butcher looked like. Shortly after they stopped for a rest close to a narrow balustraded bridge that spanned a ravine. Another group came around a bend in the road and marched by onto the bridge. As the leading ranks passed the midway point a Japanese troop convoy sped onto the bridge from the other end; it showed no signs of slackening its pace. Those who were able scrambled over the balustrade and hung on until the convoy passed—it was some 40 feet to the shallow waters of the rock-littered stream below. White and his column watched in horror as the trucks thundered over the bridge. The vibration was enough to shake some of the weakened men free, while those who hadn't the strength to get out of its path were crushed beneath the wheels as the trucks scraped the very sides of the bridge. Japanese soldiers in the back of the vehicles leaned out and swatted hands and wrists with their bayonets.

White's column was quickly reformed and marched across the bridge. They passed the survivors of this outrage under guard on the other side. Below, in the ravine, Japanese soldiers bayoneted those who couldn't walk.

Dinalupihan

Jones's column reached this small barrio at the neck of the peninsula and about 20 miles from San Fernando on the sixth day of the march. They reached a bridge that crossed a river, and on the other side was the junction that led to Olongapo and Subic Bay on the South China Sea coast. The column pulled off the road for a rest. While they were there, one of the officers asked Jones to read again from the Bible the passage that had given them so much comfort on their first night in captivity. He had enormous difficulty in croaking out the sentences, as his tongue felt many sizes too big for his mouth, but all who heard seemed to find strength from the words.

Eventually they were told to move onto the road. Earlier in the day Jones had fallen and had been severely kicked about the groin and stomach by a Japanese officer. He felt he could go no farther and, not wishing to cause the others any problems, chose to lie where he was while the rest moved on across the bridge. The guards either did not notice his absence or were too lethargic to do anything about him. It was something of a miracle, but as the column tramped slowly away he was left, alone and unmolested.

Some time later, a truck with soldiers in the back and an officer up front stopped across the road from him. They pointed at Jones, laughing and gesticulating. He was convinced this was the end and in a sense welcomed death. But nothing happened. The truck drove away, and Jones began to feel a little better. He had cooled down a little and knew there was water beneath the bridge. As he pulled himself across the bridge a guard on the far end watched him impassively. His progress along the bridge was painfully slow but the will to live had returned; the desire to survive was paramount. Sluglike, Jones hauled himself over the hot wooden slats, and when he judged that he had crossed the stream he heaved himself over the parapet and tumbled down the bank to the water. Jones still wore his belt, which had a canteen and a cup attached, and he drank some of the stagnant water from the creek and fainted.

Winston Jones recovered consciousness to the sound of voices on the bridge above. He looked up and saw a Japanese officer talking to an American and pointing down to him. The American, an Air Corps corporal, clambered over the parapet, scrambled down the bank, and joined Winston. The two men talked a little. Jones vomited up the putrid water, which caused him considerable pain because his throat was so swollen—it felt squishy like a sponge. A Japanese soldier stepped across the stones from the opposite bank toward them, and the two Americans wondered what was in store for them now. He took their canteens and disappeared under the bridge upstream. Shortly after he returned with the canteens full of clear, fresh spring water; it was like nectar. Later the soldier came again, this time with an officer's mess can. The bottom was full of rice, and there were a couple of small fish in a sauce in the top tray. The Japanese gave them the food and pointed to the bridge; they looked up and saw the officer gesturing to them to eat and smiling broadly. The two men tried hard to eat the food, though their throats were so dry and swollen that nothing tasted good, not even a share of a Japanese officer's lunch! They ate some and were both sick again; but they forced themselves to eat and eventually finished the meal.

Late in the afternoon the officer appeared at the parapet and motioned the two of them to come up to the road. They crawled up the bank very slowly until the Japanese started to yell at them; then they hurried. A soldier took their canteens and filled them, then the officer pointed up the road, smiled, and sent them on their way without a guard. Toward evening the pair reached a field of sugar cane and watched as a Japanese soldier escorted two Americans into the cane; then they heard the sound of shots. They passed another Japanese standing by a barrel of water placed on the roadside; he gave them each a cupful to drink. Jones believed that the water must have been contaminated, for shortly afterward their dysentery became more severe.

They caught up with the corporal's group just before dark, and the column stopped on the side of the road to find what sleep it could among the thorns and the ants. Jones and the corporal shared what water they had, though among 80 or 90 men it didn't go far. Like the others, they found more water by pulling out the blades of weeds and sucking them dry, though it made their mouths even more sore and irritated. The tropical sounds of the night were frequently punctuated by shots and screams.

In the morning the column reformed on the highway. The other men put Jones and the corporal at the front because they were the weakest. Throughout the heat of the day the column moved northeast toward the next staging point, at Lubao. They were still some distance from the town when darkness fell, and the guards allowed them a short break along the edge of a field of sugar cane. Jones knew he couldn't go on and decided to hide out in the field until his strength had returned. The corporal volunteered to stick with him. In the dark their absence was not noticed by the guards when the column moved on into the town.

The two men slept throughout the night, and the next morning they were discovered by the Filipino farmer who owned the field. He helped them deeper into the cane and hid them more securely from the Japanese patrols that swept through the part bordering the highway. He returned later in the day with food, water, and some blankets. The two Americans, much refreshed, spent their second night in the field. On the third morning the Filipino arrived with a large sled drawn by a carabao and used to haul the sugar cane. They scrambled on board, and the farmer covered them with cane.

So began the first part of a journey that was to take Winston Jones into the mountains to join and later lead a guerrilla band. He was still at large, albeit with a price on his head, to provide the beach parties that guided the American liberators ashore more than two years later.

Lubao

Lubao was a big town by Philippine standards. It had a population of some 40,000 people. But since the capitulation the population had been swollen by others who had traveled there from all over Luzon. They lined the streets and anxiously scanned the columns for loved ones and relatives. Throughout the march the local inhabitants had risked Japanese wrath and retribution to give comfort and succor to the prisoners as they marched by. If the Japanese had hoped by the humiliation of a public spectacle to weaken the Filipino regard for the Americans, they had sadly miscalculated. The Filipinos are to be honored for the help they gave the Americans. Many of the Filipinos living north of Abucay had been under the Japanese heel long enough to know what happened to those who dared to challenge authority; yet they made every effort to elude the guards and press food and drink into the hands of the needy men.

In Lubao it was the turn of many of the Filipinos to escape. Except for the Scouts, who in any case were closely watched, the majority wore tattered rags and had nothing that could identify them as soldiers. When the opportunity arose, men darted out of the columns, the crowd opened and closed ranks, and the fugitive was swallowed up in the heavy throng. Others slipped from the columns and grabbed a baby or held an arm around a woman to lend conviction to their being spectators. Despite their distaste, young women pressed themselves upon Japanese guards and allowed themselves to be fondled and pawed while men left the columns. Some Americans took a chance and also made a bid for freedom. Most attempts ended in disaster. It was difficult if not impossible for the willing Filipinos to hide them even in the most crowded streets.

Columns that stopped in Lubao spent the night packed tight in the town's rice mill. For many men the suffocating heat inside the corrugated iron sheds proved too much after all they had been through, and the death toll rose dramatically.

San Fernando

The last 9 miles of the march proved to be the worst for many. The road, devoid of cover and shade, shimmered in the heat as the temperature soared over 100 degrees. The macadam, distorted, scored, and rutted by the passage of a thousand trucks and tanks, melted into the paper-thin leather of those who still had soles on the shoes of their blistered feet. For some, the weight of the shoe seemed to increase a hundredfold; for the shoeless, hot tar burned deep gouges in already tortured feet.

Some men had become so emaciated and diseased that human degradation had lost all meaning. Men had dysentery so bad that they ripped away their trousers and emptied their bowels as they marched. In some columns the prisoners had little choice, for if they stopped to relieve themselves they were shot or bayoneted by the Japanese guards.

In the streets of San Fernando the scenes the men had witnessed in Lubao were repeated but on an even larger scale. Hundreds of Filipinos disappeared in one or another of these towns beyond Bataan. Confronted by the sheer magnitude of the problem and fearing the mood of an already angry and seething crowd, the outnumbered Japanese guards did little to stop the escape of the Filipinos. Neither did they prevent the people giving the Americans food and drink. It was the first real food that Bill Matson had tasted in the five days it had taken his column to march from Mariveles, for the Japanese had provided them with nothing. Along the way he had seen the Filipinos taking extreme risks, and he saw some families shot as a warning to others not to feed the prisoners. His own best friend, maddened by thirst, had been cut down for breaking ranks to try to get water from a roadside ditch already full of corpses.

The horror was not over yet. Most columns spent one or maybe two days at San Fernando waiting for trains to take them north. The majority were quartered in the large cockpit arena, which was close to the railroad station. They were packed in so tight that again many died in this Black Hole of Luzon. The Japanese very rarely bothered to clear the dead of the departing column from the building, let alone sweep out the feces.

Ben Saccone had made it thus far, but now malaria and dysentery struck him down, and for many days he hovered on the threshold of death. He always believed that it was only his sheer cussedness that had refused to allow his spirit to fall out. On two mornings he awoke to find himself lying alongside dead men.

John Taulbee's column took a week to reach San Fernando, and they lost 20 out of their group on the way. He had survived largely because he had learned early the Filipino trick of placing a small pebble under his tongue. This helped to alleviate the worst effects of thirst.

The boxcars that the Japanese provided at San Fernando were 7 feet high, 8 feet wide, and 33 feet long. They were similar to those that troops had used in World War I in France and were also marked "40 Men" or "8 Horses." Into these wagons the Japanese packed between 100 and 120 men, jammed shoulder to shoulder. If there were no guards, the doors were slammed shut. Men with dysentery were unable to control themselves, and the smell inside the black, airless, steamy boxcars became unbearable. Men vomited, some fainted, and many died. In John Spainhower's car there was a Japanese guard, and the men tried to move around so that everybody had a chance to breathe in some of the fresh air that came in through the open door.

The train journey took up to 3 or 4 hours, and there were frequent stops when the doors would be thrown open by angry and belligerent crowds that had gathered at the isolated stations. Again hundreds of Filipinos made good their escape, and even some of the fitter Americans seized the opportunity and ran off into the undergrowth while the guards, frightened in their solitude, were impotent. Even so, at the journey's end in Kermit Lay's wagon a dozen men fell over dead. They had suffocated.

It was a march of 6 or 7 miles to Camp O'Donnell, depending on which of the compounds the men were to be quartered in. When they arrived the camps were still incomplete and conditions Spartan in the extreme. In the ensuing months thousands were to die in those hellholes from disease, bureaucratic neglect, and incompetence of the Japanese administration or brutality on the part of the guards.

The statistics of the Bataan Death March make for horrifying reading, and the scale of the atrocity is difficult to comprehend. There are no definitive or precise figures, but the more reliable, which err probably on the conservative side, are as follows:

- Seventy thousand men started the march.
- Fifty-four thousand men reached Camp O'Donnell.
- Ten thousand died on the march from various causes—sickness, beatings, and execution—and of these, some 2,330 were thought to have been Americans.

Loyd Mills's bid for freedom in the mountains of Bataan lasted for about nine days. Three of the group were caught when they stumbled into a Japanese observation post directing the artillery bombardment of Corregidor. A couple of guards beat him pretty thoroughly before an officer appeared on the scene. The latter spoke some English and asked Mills whether he liked Roosevelt. The young American realized that he was bound to die. After all, he had been caught ten days after the surrender with a rifle and a bandolier, roaming the hills like a brigand.

"Roosevelt is my commanding officer," he said, "and I do what he tells me."

The Japanese officer laughed, slapped him on the back, and said, "You soldier, you OK."

The men were fed and allowed to rest. They stayed at the observation post for three days looking down on Corregidor as the bombardment increased and the island at times disappeared behind a vast, black, choking cloud, which the wind wafted over Bataan. Then came the time for the squad of observers to be relieved. When the officer returned to his battalion, Mills and his companions were driven by truck straight to Camp O'Donnell. They drove the route of the Death March and stared in horror and anger at the evidence of slaughter that still littered the roadside.

2. "As Goes Bataan So Goes Corregidor"

Saturday, April 11, 1942
Corregidor

With the fall and partial evacuation of Bataan, the population of Corregidor had now jumped from over 9,000 to 14,728 Army, Navy, Marine Corps, and civilians, men and women. The latter included Americans, Filipinos, Chinese, and some prisoners from Bilabid Prison in Manila. The prisoners were remnants of the Philippine Scout detachments who had mutinied some few years back and had been tried, sentenced, and confined in Bilabid. Fearful lest such men be recruited into an anti-American Army, and not wishing to present the Japanese with such a ripe propaganda plum, the authorities had them removed to a stockade on Corregidor on the outbreak of war.

It had been hoped that combat troops from the 45th Philippine Scouts would be able to make it to Corregidor, but most of the troops who were brought from Bataan were service formations, ordnance supply, and clerks from the proliferation of headquarters that had existed on Bataan. Some 900 troops from Bataan were absorbed into the beach defenses and came under the command of the 4th Marines. Most of these were diseased, dirty, and defeated. The regiment now numbered almost 4,000 men, but many of the new recruits had received no infantry training. All had to be equipped with weapons and at least partially clothed. In addition, the physical condition of these men, with their malaria and dysentery, made them next to useless for combat.

There was still a reasonable supply of food on the island. One of

Wainwright's first acts on assuming command had been to order that all the food be kept in a common pool. This was just as well, since there had been tension in the past caused by the belief that some services were better fed than others. However, this was only a matter of degree, since the garrison had supposedly been on half rations since January 5 though, with all the separate organizations on the island, this had proved difficult to enforce rigidly. It was true that until the end of March the Navy personnel with their own food stores had received a better and more varied ration than that of either the Army or the Marines.

Drake was able to issue half rations to the troops that amounted to a fairly adequate though unbalanced diet of around 30 ounces per man per day, or approximately 2,000 calories.

Unlike that of the refugees from Bataan, the health of the regular garrison on Corregidor was still fairly good in late March. There had been an outbreak of acute gastroenteritis among some Marines and there was a lot of jaundice about, but little malaria and at this stage no dysentery. Field hygiene was good, and all the men had been vaccinated against cholera.

John McCann joined M Company, 3rd Battalion, 4th Marines. It was a machine-gun company, and the new recruits spent their first night in the company command post before being assigned to their positions. McCann, in company with others, a private from the 728th Ordnance Company and a man called Flanagan from the 31st Infantry, was dispatched to man a .50-caliber machine gun. Since Flanagan was an infantryman with some experience, he was made the senior man of the squad. Their position was immediately in front of Battery Keyes and set into the clifftop above Ordnance Point. Battery Keyes was a beach defense position manned by regular gunners of the Philippine Scouts. They had 3-inch rapid-fire open mounts set into concrete casements. Each one had a separate pit with a stairway that led down into the ammunition bunker. The Scouts had been there a long while and their battery had become a real home away from home. There was a doorway set into the wall of the weapon pit, and around the edge of the parapet the Scouts had placed a line of powder cans filled with sand. These were the universal carriers of Corregidor. Six inches in diameter, about four feet high, and painted gray, they were used to carry water, store rations, and dump refuse. The cans provided the Scouts with a convenient firestep as well. They were small men and needed something to help them see over the parapet. A slit trench led out from the parapet to the edge of the cliff and a rope ladder, which was the only way to the beach, some 40 feet below. The Marines had already started work on the position that McCann and his companions were to occupy. They had dug a pit about 8 feet square and stacked it with crates of .50-caliber ammunition. The three men were ordered by the company top sergeant to dig down at least another 2 feet and line the bottom of the pit with the ammunition boxes. This killed two birds with one stone, for the ammunition was readily available and the boxes provided a solid base on which to rest their gun. The gun was a .50-caliber water-cooled beast, complete with its pedestal and a hook bar for the layer—a sort of shoulder strap that allowed the men who were firing to withstand the vicious recoil and still keep the weapon stable. It had come off a minesweeper that had been scuttled just a few days before.

They bolted the pedestal onto some crossed 2-by-4 and 2-by-6 timbers and piled extra ammunition on top for added stability. Behind their pit was a 50-gallon drum of water which McCann and the other two had to bury under huge mounds of rocks to protect it from shrapnel; it provided the coolant for the gun, and under no circumstances, according to the sergeant, were they to use it for drinking. It took them two days to finish the weapon pit, and then the company commander came to inspect the work. He suggested a few modifications and then gave them their orders. They were instructed not to give away their position but to remain concealed and not to fire unless ordered to by the company. The first targets they could expect would be invasion barges. The ration truck would meet them each night at the water tower on Denver Hill and issue the rations for the next day; if they chose to eat them at one fell swoop, that was their misfortune. The supplies included a breakfast ration, usually of a small can of sausage, a little coffee, and perhaps bread. The evening meal was a little more substantial: a can of salmon or meat with canned vegetables and rice or a gravy. Most of the men saved their bread to gnaw on during the long daylight hours between the meals. They were also given a seven-day pack of C rations, but these were for emergency use only and not to be consumed unless the enemy had invaded the island.

McCann went scavenging in the old quarters that had once housed the married men who worked in the Navy radio intercept tunnel. The houses were now bombed-out shells. To his delight he brought back a double-bed mattress. This they quickly carried down to the gun pit, cleared away an area in the jungle scrub, and then erected a shelter over the mattress out of pup tents. Since one man always had to be on duty, this meant the others could rest in reasonable comfort.

Immediately below and to the right of their position at the base of the cliff that marked Ordnance Point was a Marine emplacement. McCann would scramble down the Scouts' crazily swaying ladder to visit his neighbors. The Marines (there were eight of them) had two .30-caliber Brownings in a sandbagged position, behind which they had excavated a fair-sized tunnel into the cliff face. Once inside the narrow entrance passage, the cavern opened out, and there was room to stand. The Marines used this as living quarters and a shelter; it even had an emergency exit that led away through the cliff and came out farther up the beach.

Sunday, April 12, 1942

The Japanese had moved their observation balloon company from Abucay to the heights above Mariveles, from where it could direct the artillery fire on Corregidor. As the first of these two eerie monsters with their wicker baskets rose into sight the Americans laughed and called it "Peeping Tom," but its arrival heralded the new phase in the battle for Corregidor. Japanese batteries began a preliminary bombardment as they tried to range their guns on the targets on the Rock. They used the lighthouse high up on Topside as their main reference point to calibrate the guns.

Unfortunately, the Americans had just established the main plotting room for their counter battery fire on the ground floor of the lighthouse. Bill Hall, now promoted to sergeant but who had sat out the siege in his seaward defense battery waiting in vain for the Japanese Navy to put in an appearance, had been brought in to help run the plot. As the Japanese fire increased in volume, the communication lines to the observation posts were destroyed, and the plot could no longer function. Hall went out under fire and helped repair the cables, for which he was awarded the Silver Star. By the end of the day the building was a shambles, and it became clear that it was too hot a corner for the plot to operate effectively, so the men moved down the hill to the artillery tunnel complex below Battery Wheeler.

With 150 batteries deployed on Bataan and Cavite, the Japanese ringed the Rock and opened up a sustained and deadly crossfire that was to last for the next 27 days. From the heights of Mariveles, the Japanese could look down on the open weapon pits and gun emplacements of Corregidor. Captured maps gave them the precise locations of armament stores and headquarters. The unending barrage destroyed the defenses faster than they could be rebuilt and gradually chipped away at the taut nerves of the defenders. The few landmines along the beaches were exploded, and the little ships from the inshore patrol were sunk one by one. Al Broderick's beach wire was destroyed, and defenses built up after weeks of toil were flattened in a single crushing barrage.

The bombardment had an immediate result. This was now the height of the dry season when no rain fell, and the dust kicked up by the exploding bombs and shells had a crippling effect on the defenders. Water facilities and the power plants were early casualties. Fortunately the quartermaster had acquired some KW generator sets belonging to a civilian engineering company; they had been intended for use in mining operations in Luzon. There were three generators; one was kept in reserve and the other two were set up in Malinta Tunnel, one to provide the power for the hospital laterals and the other for the needs of the main tunnel.

In addition to the artillery, Japanese planes flew over the Rock every couple of hours from dawn to sunset, in groups of three to nine. At first the spirited AA defense forced them high, but in so doing the batteries revealed their position, and one by one they were knocked out by Japanese artillery. Thereafter the planes came in much lower and bombed with greater accuracy and effect. For the defenders there was no choice other than to crouch in their foxholes, cover their ears, and hang on until the bombardment lifted. The mind and the body cannot take such a strain indefinitely and along with the physical casualties, cases of shell shock began to increase, though nothing like that which was found in other theaters of the war, particularly Western Europe.

Throughout all the noise and tempo of the battle, Wainwright toured the island's positions. As on Bataan, all he had to offer the beleaguered garrison was to sit on the edge of a foxhole and talk for a while of home and other things that soldiers, even though separated by rank, share in common. For a few hours each day, this thin, emaciated, gaunt figure moved from foxhole to foxhole, and all felt better for talking to him.

At the end of a day of ceaseless bombardment large sections of Corregidor would be shrouded in clouds of smoke and dense, choking dust. These in turn were fed by grass fires and exploding ammunition dumps. The landscape of Corregidor, once jungle-clad, lush, and green, soon looked like the no-man's-land of World War I. Topside, with its stunted, shell-shattered trees, resembled Passchendale, and the James Ravine, an anticipated invasion spot, had all the appearance of the Argonne Wood.

After Battery Chicago had been knocked out, Bressi's CO, Captain Aimes, asked him if he wanted to become an artillery observer. Bressi agreed, seeing it more as an order than a choice. He spent a few nights dodging the shells and building his position on the northern face of Morrison Hill facing Bataan. It was manned by two men. They dug out a pit, put a couple of 55-gallon barrels inside, and filled them with sand; finally they camouflaged and roofed the position. They had to sneak into the position before dawn and stay there all day, knowing they would not be fed until dark. Under those conditions they quickly learned how to regulate bowel movements. They had a plotting board and compass and were linked in by field cable to the master plot, run by Bill Hall. The system had been devised on Corregidor and was simple yet effective. There were a number of such posts, and each time the observers saw the smoke from a gun firing on Bataan they called out "puff"; the master plot listened in and when two or more posts called together frequently it was clear they were watching the same gun. Angles were relayed, plotted on the board, and the information passed on to the mortars.

Counter battery fire, though brave, was largely ineffective. The big sea defense guns were irrelevant to the land battle, even had they been able to traverse onto Cavite or Bataan. Their weapon pits were smothered in shot and shell, and the crews were forced to take cover elsewhere. The 155mm Long Toms of the Scouts in Battery Kysor were hitched up to tractors and towed around the island in a mobile role, pausing long enough to fire two or three shots and moving on to the next location before Japanese counter battery fire could destroy them. By the end of the first week of the bombardment similar guns that were kept in their seaward defense emplacements along the north shore had all been destroyed. The only heavy weapons that had the ability to take up the Japanese challenge were the 12-inch mortars and Fort Drum's 14-inch batteries. The mortars had only one battery that was operational on Corregidor and that was Battery Geary. The other, Way, had been deactivated before the war because of a shortage of trained gunners. Geary could cause significant damage, but the mortars had to be used sparingly, for there were only 500 rounds of the 670-pound antipersonnel shells available. The mortars on Fort Hughes joined in too and fired on the Japanese batteries deployed in Cavite.

Kindley Field
Corregidor

Ed Erickson was given command of this small earth airstrip, which ran at an angle across the base of the tail on Corregidor. Occasionally aircraft made the hazardous flight in from Mindanao, trying to time their arrival over Corregidor at dusk. Erickson operated a bulldozer and made a one-blade strip for the planes to land on, though in so doing he created a dust cloud. With a small handling crew he tried to have the plane land and be airborne again in less than twenty minutes; by that time the Japanese mortars on Cavite would have zeroed in on his strip, which would prevent any further operations. If that happened, the whole operation, including the bulldozer's part, had to be repeated each time a plane managed to land on Corregidor. The nimble P-35s could manage the strip, but there was barely enough room for the Tomahawks to operate, and more than one that month crashed on take off. The planes flew in much-needed drugs and urgent dispatches, but as the month progressed such missions ceased to be merely hazardous and instead became suicidal.

Wednesday, April 15, 1942
Morrison Hill

That morning seventy Filipinos suffered a terrible death. They had taken cover from a particularly intense bombardment in the partially completed tunnels along the base of the reverse slope on Morrison Hill. A salvo of 240mm mortars burst along the overhanging rock face with devastating effect and started a landslide. The whole mountainside fell into the tunnel entrances. The Filipinos were entombed behind hundreds of tons of boulders and earth. It would have required very special equipment and mining knowledge to have mounted a rescue operation, none of which was available on Corregidor. After a few days the pathetic and muffled signals of the trapped men ceased.

Bill Massello and his battery had been unemployed ever since their return from Bataan. They lived in part of the regimental headquarters tunnel complex below Battery Wheeler, and by this time Massello was becoming very concerned about the morale of his troops. The men were hesitant, nervous, and increasingly reluctant to stray far from the cocoonlike safety of the tunnels. Massello had been down on a couple of occasions to Malinta Tunnel and was horrified by the scenes that greeted him. He saw people who had been in there day in day out since the start of the campaign—the pallor of their faces betrayed their molelike existence. Many, those who had no reason to be there, unlike the headquarters or hospital staff, looked on him as if he were a freak from the outside; tunnel existence had sapped their nerves.

The main concourse was a seething, swirling mass of humanity. Almost every space against the crates stacked along the tunnel walls was taken by some Filipino or American. The only time the crowd seemed to move in a disciplined fashion was when the siren installed in the roof sounded. This was the signal that another Jeep was about to drive in with its stretcher racks full of wounded.

There were many others, of course, who moved with purpose in the tunnels: officers of all services and ranks, nurses and war correspondents, and minor U.S. Government officials who were too lowly to secure a passage out of the beleaguered fortress to home and safety.

It was on a visit to the tunnel that Massello walked in on a discussion in the Coastal Artillery Command Headquarters lateral on the feasibility of reactivating Battery Way. Mortars were the first guns Massello had ever fired as a newly commissioned West Point officer, and he immediately volunteered his battery to undertake the task. It meant coming under the command of the

59th Coast Artillery, and Massello knew that his own CO, Colonel Chase, rigid and set in his ways as ever and twenty years out of date in his thinking, would never agree to such a move. So Massello and his great friend Harry Shank conspired to go over Chase's head and appealed directly to Colonel Bunker, who commanded the 59th, and to General Moore, the garrison commander. The ploy worked and with little grace Chase let his men go.

Massello's gunners and a host of volunteers who came forward moved in with Battery Geary to study the intricacies of the mortar. Meanwhile the ordnance artificers set to work reactivating the monster weapons at Battery Way. Restoring the neglected guns to a firing condition was in itself a formidable and highly skilled task. That the men also had to dodge enemy shot and shell is a further mark of their achievement in bringing the battery into a state of readiness in two weeks.

When Massello and Shank examined the shells for the mortars, they found that antipersonnel rounds were in short supply. However, they figured that the armor-piercing shells, of which there was an ample supply, could be adapted against land targets if they cut the delay on the fuses to produce instantaneous explosions. In their present condition the shells were of little value, since their weight and velocity caused them to be buried deep before they exploded.

The blueprints seemed to bear out the officers' theory, but there was only one way to find out. Shank and a couple of artificers unscrewed the shell cone, removed the delay in the fuse, and reassembled it ready for firing. It worked like a charm, and the word was spread to the mortar batteries on Fort Drum and Fort Hughes.

Thursday, April 16, 1942

As the bombardment continued unabated, the Japanese lobbed in a lucky round that hit the halyard in the 100-foot flagpole on Topside (the bottom portion of the pole was supposed to have come originally from the main mast of the protected cruiser U.S.S. *Olympia*, flagship of Commodore Dewey in 1898 at the Battle of Manila

Bay). The halyard was sliced through, and the flag started to flutter down to the ground and desecration. Captain Arthur Huff, who commanded Battery B, 60th Artillery, and three of his men dashed out into the rain of shells and caught the flag before it could touch the ground. They repaired the broken halyard, rehoisted the flag, and returned to safety, unscathed. All four were awarded Silver Stars for this act of conspicuous gallantry, and, even more important, the story spread throughout the garrison and gave a powerful boost to the sagging morale of the men.

Sgt. William Griffiths had been given some extra men—five Philippine soldiers, and two sailors from the *Canopus*. They had moved away from the beach defenses to establish a new observation post on the hogback immediately below Battery Denver. They dug slit trenches and sighted their weapons for all-around defense. Griffiths found the umpire's chair from the Officers' Club tennis courts, dragged it to the top of their hill, and from this exalted position watched the guns on Bataan. Instead of the umpire's score cards a plotting board was fixed to the chair, and the duty man sighted the flash of the gun and called out the bearings to another, who manned the field telephone. While the operator phoned in the bearings, the observer had to scramble out of his high chair and into a slit trench before the shell landed.

From this new position Griffiths was well placed to see the ration trucks, and they now seemed to have enough to eat of a diet that varied little—cans of salmon and peaches and, as always, rice. They also had a case of grated coconut in the command post, into which they frequently dipped. Eaten in that quantity, the very rich coconut proved too much, and most of the squad soon developed dysentery.

The Japanese completed the deployment of their huge 240mm siege mortars from Cavite to Bataan and lost no time in bringing these monsters into action. The heavier charge and high angle of fire exposed everything on Corregidor to their plunging shots. The shelling never really stopped. With over a hundred large guns deployed the Japanese were able to fire around the clock. Nevertheless, the thoroughly exhausted men learned to sleep through the bombardment; however, Bressi found, in common with others, that there was always one part of the mind that stayed awake and alert.

His mind would identify the whistle or shriek of an incoming shell that was likely to burst nearby, and then, instantly awake and alert, he would crouch low in his foxhole until the danger had passed and the shell burst. Thereafter it would be difficult to get back to sleep because the nagging fear and frayed nerves pounded the blood loud in the ears, enough even to drown the sound of the guns.

Most days Japanese artillery opened up with the dawn and fired steadily until noon when there was something of a lull, what became known on the Rock as the Japanese siesta. About midafternoon the bombardment began anew and continued till past midnight; then a random gun provided harassing fire through the night and robbed the men of rest and sleep.

At first the Japanese concentrated their efforts on the battery positions and beach defenses along the northern shore of Corregidor. Al Broderick's platoon, in trenches guarding the southern shore below Battery Geary, were left relatively alone for a while, though they did get one crack at the enemy. Late at night a raft was spotted and challenged off Breakwater Point. The Marines ran from the shell scrapes, small hollows scooped from the soil, where they slept to man their foxholes, and a light machine gun to their left, firing tracers, opened up on the raft. The Browning automatic rifles in Broderick's section joined in until the raft disappeared from view as the occupants landed. Broderick was duty officer that night and headed to the command post to find out what was happening. While he was away a young buck sergeant and a corporal scrambled down onto the beach to scout for the raft. Broderick returned to the trench and was furious when he heard that two Marines were now on the beach, and he passed the word to hold fire unless he gave the word. He leaned on the parapet of the trench and heard someone crawling up on him, so he called out, but there was no answering cry. Shortly afterward the two Marines returned by another path. They explained that they had found the craft and while they were inspecting it a figure rose up from behind some rocks, and the sergeant fired and killed the man. They moved cautiously over to the body, which was clad only in a loincloth and had no means of identification, so they returned.

Later Brockerick heard sounds of movement coming from directly below his trench. There was absolute silence along the line as men nervously strained to identify the source of the sound. Broderick called down again and again, but there was no response, just silence and then a scraping and scratching sound. In the inky blackness of a tropical night this was enough to set the nerves of even the most seasoned campaigner on edge. Broderick fired some rounds from his rifle in the direction of this unearthly noise, and thereafter there was silence.

In the morning after stand to, a small patrol moved down onto the beach to investigate. When they returned to make their report, a Scout who had been part of the patrol claimed that the loin-clothed figure was a Filipino. He was very angry at the Americans for shooting what to him was obviously an unarmed refugee who had belatedly sought to escape from Bataan. The Marines in the patrol were not convinced and as the body had already started to decompose, positive identification as to whether it was a Japanese or a Filipino, let alone friend or foe, was impossible. While the argument raged on the clifftop Broderick counted noses and suddenly realized that there was one more present than had gone down with the patrol. But by the time he had quieted everybody down and drawn their attention to this, the extra man had gone.

Sunday, April 19, 1942

Broderick moved his platoon down to man their foxholes in time for the morning hate, when the Japanese guns opened up, and as the men dropped into their respective holes he walked on down the line to report to the company command post. Suddenly a gun on Bataan opened up, and they all heard the now familiar roar, like an express train tearing out of a tunnel. There were still six or seven men in an exposed area, and they all hit the ground where they were, except for one youngster, who was near enough to his foxhole to make a dive for its sanctuary. Broderick cradled his head in his hands and watched through his fingers as the lad dived head first into the hole, just like a swimmer. His head and body were in the hole but not his legs when he started to come back out, for all the world as if someone had put a home movie into reverse. Meanwhile, the shell had burst 50 yards up the road, and as soon as the rubble and shrapnel had stopped falling Broderick ran over to his young

Marine to see what was wrong. The dazed boy was sitting in the road, stuttering something, and pointing with a shaking hand at his foxhole. Broderick walked over and saw a 240mm mortar shell at the bottom. Broderick and the others laughed for days, but the youngster concerned never really saw the funny side.

Gathered around their radios that night the men heard the news of the Doolittle raid. Sixteen B-25s had taken off from the deck of the carrier *Hornet* and in a spectacular low-level attack bombed targets in Tokyo and four other Japanese cities. Although most of the planes were lost over China through bad weather, Colonel Jimmy Doolittle and the majority of the air crews were rescued by Chinese Nationalist forces, and they returned home heroes. The raid had a heartening psychological effect on the Allies, caused the Japanese to withdraw fighters from the battlefronts for home defense, and made the men on Corregidor feel that there were others after all fighting in the war with them.

Corporal Finken, like a lot of the men, had lost touch with time by now and did not know which day of the week it was; many men were confused and had little idea what was happening. One of the Marines in his squad was a man named Sammy McEwan. He had been frightened stiff from the moment the very first bomb fell on Cavite. However, the two men had been firm buddies in China, and their friendship had survived more than one roughhouse in the bars of Shanghai. On these occasions McEwan had proved fearless and more than once had saved Finken from a beating and perhaps worse. So Finken covered for McEwan and tried to look out for him on Corregidor. Finken was half convinced that his friend would snap out of it and become his old self again.

Immediately behind their position was a steep cliff face thickly carpeted in lush jungle foliage. McEwan spent his whole time digging a bombproof shelter, and there he would stay most of the time. One evening the Japanese bombardment was especially heavy and the beach defenses of the northern shore once again came in for particular attention. Finken heard whimpering and moaning, and he climbed up the path behind the gun position that led to McEwan's shelter. It was a pitch-black night, the moon and stars blotted out by the swirling cloud of dust and smoke. He found the pathway blocked by fallen rubble, and as he leaned across the rocks his hands slipped in a pool of blood.

"Sam. Is that you, Sam?" he called.

"Help me. Oh, help me," a voice whispered.

Finken knew he could not manage without some assistance, so he called down to the third man at the gun, a Filipino, but he was cowering in the bottom of the trench and refused to come out and help even after Finken threatened him. The bombardment continued as Finken ran along the beach to the company command post, which was in a concrete bunker close to Battery Point. He found the medical officer sheltering there, and together they returned with a stretcher and some shovels to the cave. They dug desperately, clawing and pulling the rocks away until they had cleared the entrance. Finken groped his way forward and touched the still form of his comrade. Gently he edged back and pulled the silent McEwan along until both were able to lift him onto the stretcher.

There was no opportunity to dodge the shells or take any cover as they carried their burden to the aid station. Finken tried to tuck his head into his shoulders as he stumbled along mumbling all the prayers he remembered from his childhood. The ground shook and heaved beneath their feet to the concussions of the barrage, and twice they slipped and dropped the stretcher in that journey through hell. They reached the company aid station and lifted the stretcher onto the table. Finken hovered near as the orderlies went to work. The pale light cast by the battle lamp revealed the full extent of Sammy's injuries, and it took the doctor but an instant to discover his patient was dead.

"He must have died instantly," the doctor said by way of comfort.

"No, Doc, I talked to him. I know he was alive," Finken sobbed.

He turned and ran outside and oblivious to the lethal rain of shells that still fell, walked back to the gunpit, where he beat the hell out of the craven Filipino who still cowered in the bottom of the trench. Finken had never felt such anger and despair.

Friday, April 24, 1942

A large group of men had gathered outside the western entrance to Malinta Tunnel at dusk to take the evening air. Many were smoking, and they were in a lighthearted mood until a 240mm mortar shell burst a short distance from them. There was an immediate rush for safety.

Both the main entrances to the tunnels had by this time been fitted with gates 10 feet high, constructed out of galvanized sheeting framed by heavy timbers and rails from the disused rail track and weighted at the base with sandbags. The blast slammed the gate shut, and it could not be opened from the outside. As the men pressed against the barrier and pounded the steel with their fists, a second shell burst among them. There was carnage. Fifteen were killed instantly, and more of the 60 seriously wounded died later.

This sudden influx of casualties tested the capabilities and resources of the medical staff to the very limit. Madeline Ullom, trained at a big-city hospital used to emergencies, the Jefferson in Philadelphia, and not given to wringing her hands in despair, could no longer hold back the tears. Surgeons sliced through shattered limbs and repaired the wounds as best they could, though mortar and blast injuries at that close range create the most fearful damage to the human frame.

Casualties in general now began to rise, and the hospital was forced to take over more laterals and increase its capacity to cope with the numbers. There were more dead than before, and these could not be buried until dark. The smells from the hospital pervaded the laterals in the hot, humid air, and there were frequent breaks in the water supply, so the lavatories invariably overflowed. As the tunnel population continued to increase there was the fetid smell of unwashed bodies, sweat, and fear. Dust, too, became a major problem, and the quartermasters rapidly ran out of goggles in their stores.

A gift of huge amounts of new dollars and Philippine pesos at any time would seem like a welcome present. Some came the way of Frederick Howard that evening in the strangest of circumstances. He was standing in the food line and feeling, like so many others by now, depressed and weary beyond all measure. He knew that after midnight, once the bombardment eased, he would have to venture forth to repair the telephone ground lines that had been broken. It was a futile gesture, since the same lines would soon be knocked out when the guns opened up the next morning. He reached the head of the line and collected his rice stew and pineapple chunks before retreating to a niche in the rocks outside the main tunnel. A man came by whom he had never seen before, a supply sergeant with his mess can and a sack. It was obvious that the sergeant, bubbling over with excitement, was dying to tell his story to someone. He unburdened himself to Howard.

He had been cutting up money all day, millions of dollars he claimed, and pesos by the bucketful. The sergeant opened his sack to show that it was full of brand-new crisp dollar bills in various denominations. He plucked out a handful, gave it to Howard, and moved on his way, in search of a fresh audience. Howard counted his hoard; he had $6,000, more money than he had ever seen in his life. He quickly finished his frugal supper and hurried back to the solitude of his bunk deep inside the signal corps lateral. There with needle and thread he set about sewing most of his money into the waistbands of his two remaining pairs of trousers. He had a premonition that this might come in handy sometime in the future.

Tuesday, April 28, 1942
HQ, Fourteenth Army
Balanga, Bataan

Japanese headquarters published the field order for the conquest of Corregidor. The operation called for a massive artillery bombardment followed by a sudden blow, an amphibious landing. The troops earmarked for the assault were General Kitano's 4th Infantry Division. This was a strange choice, since most of the staff expected their commander to use the 16th Division, a battle-tested and now veteran force.

The Japanese possessed formidable advantages. They had a detailed knowledge of American defense positions and had located most of the heavy-caliber artillery on the island. Maps had been captured with the fall of Bataan, and it is fair to assume that the interrogation of prisoners yielded more up-to-date information on latest deployments. They had complete command of the air and, now that the American anti-aircraft batteries had largely been destroyed, were able to bomb with devastating effect from low altitude. The parade of Japanese aircraft in the skies above Corregidor had a significant influence on morale, and the defenders, like prairie dogs, never strayed far from their burrows, senses alerted to the first signs of trouble.

An invasion of Corregidor was not the only option open to the Japanese. General Homma could have chosen to starve the Americans into submission. The condition of those who were captured on Bataan gave him an indication of the plight of the island forts. He knew that neither rescue nor relief was possible; it could only be a matter of time before the defenders would be forced to capitulate. But a siege in the classic mold of military history, submission through starvation, was not the path that led to military honor for General Homma. He had to defeat the Americans by force of arms, massively and decisively, if he were to salvage his personal reputation and demonstrate the inferiority of the white man.

The British had been humiliated at Singapore before the Asians; now it was to be the turn of the Americans. Homma had to demonstrate Japanese superiority to the Filipinos, who for years had been restless under American rule. In such a manner, so Tokyo believed, a more solid foundation for the Greater East Asia Co-prosperity Sphere could be laid, based on the cooperation of the indigenous people. There was no choice; Homma had to bring the Americans to battle.

Despite their inherent advantages, it was not all plain sailing for the Japanese planners, and they did have significant obstacles to surmount. Amphibious landings are risky operations at the best of times, and the risk of failure is ever present for the invading forces. In this instance the Japanese had first to assemble all the landing craft, and this meant bringing them in under the guns of Corregidor from their moorings in Lingayen Gulf and Subic Bay. This took time, as it could be done only at night and under cover of a heavy artillery bombardment, needed to mask the sound of the tugboats' engines and to divert the attention of the defenders. In this the Japanese were largely successful, for, though Corregidor appreciated the significance of the nightly bombardments, there was little they could do to hinder, let alone prevent the operation. Some of the craft were concentrated at Lamao, just to the north of Cabcaben, and others moved across Manila Bay to Cavite. Smaller landing craft were hauled across country from Subic Bay to Hermosa, but this proved a long and tedious business.

Once all the craft had been gathered in Manila Bay, they had to be serviced and made ready for operations after months of disuse and neglect swinging at their moorings. The landing craft were handed over to General Kitano, busy training his infantry in their new role as assault troops, a few at a time. Practice landings, beach obstacles, and cliff scaling became part of the training cycle for the 4th Infantry Division.

Kitano was given specialist troops in the form of the seaborne operation units of the Army Engineers to man and operate the boats. These had been brought to the Philippines after their highly successful operations against the British in Singapore.

While the landing craft were being repaired and outfitted for the operation, additional boats—fishing smacks and other small craft—were converted to gunboats and artillery platforms to provide the close-in fire support for the landing.

While all these preparations were under way, an epidemic decimated the ranks of Kitano's troops. They were encamped in the malarial valleys of lower Bataan, and the disease spread like wildfire through the division. An emergency airlift of quinine eventually saved the day but not before some 60 percent of the assault troops had been stricken. Kitano needed all the time that Army headquarters could give him to prepare for the landings.

The operation was planned in two stages. An assault force of some 2,000 men drawn from the 61st Infantry Regiment under Colonel Sato was to embark at Lamao on May 5 and land at the tail of the island on the stretch of beach between Infantry and Cavalry Points. They were timed to hit the beach at 2300 hours; this was at high tide and an hour before the full moon. Tanks and artillery were to come ashore with the second wave to provide local fire support. Once the beachhead had been established, the Sato force was ordered to exploit outward toward Malinta Tunnel and to secure the tip of the island to Kindley Field. The next night a second and larger force, containing the rest of the division under its infantry commander, Major General Taniguchi, would embark at Limay, land on the beaches between Battery and Morrison Points, and storm Topside by way of the James Ravine. On the second day, both forces would advance on Malinta Tunnel from east and west. The operation was planned to be completed and Corregidor secured within forty-eight hours. In the meantime, the 16th Division practiced assault landings on the beaches near Cavite. This force would be available should the 4th Division fail or if a second series of landings were required against the other island fortresses.

Dusk
South Dock
Corregidor

Two Navy Catalina PBY flying boats braved the air blockade and landed on the bay 2 miles south of Corregidor. After medicine and artillery fuses had been unloaded, fifty people, chosen to fly south to safety—thirty nurses, three civilian women, and seventeen men—boarded the aircraft. The majority of the men were pursuit pilots. Ed Erickson was among the air crew. Ruby Moteley and Madeline Ullom were not with the nurses.

The two heavily overloaded planes seemed to skim the waves for ages before they had sufficient speed and lift to become airborne. The passengers sat facing one another on the side ribs of the hull, their feet braced along the central spar. The pilots flew low to avoid the Japanese fighters, since the flying boats had only the .50-calibers in the waist blisters for defense. It was a long and dangerous flight, which did nothing for the frayed nerves of the passengers, to Lake Taraka in Mindanao. The flying boat in which Erickson traveled damaged its hull on a submerged reef as it taxied to the landing dock.

Erickson and the other pilots escorted some of the nurses to Del Monte for the night. The next day when they returned to the landing stage they found it deserted. The plane had been repaired, and the pilot, afraid lest he be caught flat-footed on the ground at daybreak by marauding fighters, had no choice but to take off without them. Erickson saw this as yet another snafu in a long line of such disasters that had marked the campaign from first to last. The party had no choice but to return to Del Monte and wait for a flight out on a B-17, which they were assured would be sent to pick them up. There were a large number of other people there, all claiming priorities with similar assurances.

Wednesday, April 29, 1942

It was Emperor Hirohito's birthday, and the Japanese celebrated by firing the biggest barrage of the war; some 10,000 shells hit Corregidor. Despite this, the defense was still defiantly fighting back and indeed gained strength, for on this day Massello brought Battery Way into action. The Marines in their foxholes, who now lived each day as if it were their last, took fresh heart as the mortars roared their defiance at Bataan. Massello had a full crew of 16 men on each gun, and they fired 20 rounds apiece at the Japanese concentrations around Cabcaben.

It was a complicated affair firing these vintage breechloading mortars. The layer turned the wheel frantically and lowered the barrel level to the ground, then the breech was opened and sponged. At this point, and it did require careful timing, four men at a run pushed a trolley along the tracks that led from the magazine to the gun. Right on their heels were two men with the plunger. The gunners first loaded the 1,000-pound shell, with the "Massello fuse," into the breech, and the two behind rammed it home. The loaders then turned back to the trolley and lifted in the separate charge, a 96-pound sack of black powder, and packed the breech. The mortar then had to be elevated above 45 degrees to fire and the sight set by the layer with a gunner's quadrant. At this point, all but the gun captain retired while he, with the longest lanyard he could find (for nobody trusted this ancient piece or the sensitive fuses), pulled hard and fired the mortar. The blast alone was enough to rip the clothes from a man's back. A good crew could get a round off every two minutes, though this was academic since it was possible to fire only one mortar at a time. The concrete apron was so old and worn that Massello feared the concussion would shatter the foundations if all four fired at once in salvo.

Once the Japanese had gotten over the shock of this new battery coming into the battle, they poured everything they could at Massello and his gunners. For a while it seemed as if they were the only target on the island. He wisely withdrew his crew to the cover afforded by the reinforced concrete of the powder rooms and sweated it out. By the end of the day two mortars had been destroyed, and the weapon pit was full of masonry and debris. They worked through the night salvaging what they could and clearing the rubble in time to bring the two remaining mortars into action the next morning.

Saturday, May 2, 1942

The Japanese hit the powder magazine that served the eight mortars of Battery Geary. They feared the carnage those mighty shells would cause among the landing craft, and Homma had personally ordered its destruction as well as that of Battery Way. For days they had been sending in the solid rounds of 240mm mortar shells, and with their weight and velocity they shattered the reinforced concrete. Having created a breach in the time-honored fashion of solid shot, they poured in the high-explosive delayed-action shells. One entered through the breach, passed through the second, or curtain, wall, and exploded into the magazine. The entire island shook, and men were convinced it was an earthquake. Corporal Finken had been in California in 1933 and recognized the sensation.

John McCann and his group had taken shelter with the Scouts in their battery. They had dug an air-raid tunnel into the cliff above the gunpit and had three exits in case of a cave-in; the entrance looked out across the South Bay toward Topside. All of a sudden the tunnel started to shake. One man called out, "Look!" and pointed across the bay. Huge slabs of concrete rose high in the air, and they watched in awe as a long black tube turned end over end. It seemed as if the whole sky were full of debris and smoke. The strange thing was that there was no sound at first; and then a mighty roar bombarded their refuge as the concussion blasted their eardrums.

The mortars weigh over 10 tons each, and one complete unit, pedestal, traversing mechanism, and barrel, was plucked from its mounting and hurled out of the pit. It landed on the golf course, about 150 yards away. Another gun was blown bodily through the casement wall of 3-foot-thick reinforced concrete. The massive trunks of teak and mahogany, some 1,000 yards from Geary, that had survived the Japanese fire were scythed to the ground by great hunks of spinning concrete. Fifty-six men died outright. For the most part they were the ammunition handlers caught in the magazine, but scores of others were horribly injured, crushed beneath the tons of falling masonry.

The most effective means of keeping the Japanese at arm's length had been reduced to a mound of rubble by a single shell. Corregidor's firepower now depended on the two surviving mortars belonging to Massello and his crew in Battery Way.

Evening
Sunday, May 3, 1942

Twelve nurses and twelve Army and Navy officers boarded a launch and were taken to the edge of the minefield, where they rendezvoused with the submarine *Spearfish*. One of the officers was Colonel Irwin, from General Wainwright's staff. He took with him the complete roster of everybody on the Rock and in the forts. A pay officer carried the complete pay records for the garrisons. Ruby Moteley and Madeline Ullom had walked down to the dock to wave goodbye to their friends; both had become reconciled to their fate and knew that the end could not now be far away.

The hospital laterals were crammed to overflowing, and sanitation had become a major concern. At the best of times, the tunnels reeked of the sanitary fluids and lime that were used, but now there was so little water available, the air became fetid and almost unbearable.

The main tunnels were filled with men, the tunnel rats who had become shelter-shocked. Order, discipline, and their maintenance were becoming serious problems, made even more so by the marked reluctance of the staff to tackle the question. A rough balance was maintained essentially by those who cowered the days away in the tunnel. There was a tacit recognition that if they caused trouble, then the powers that be would be forced to take action. An armed guard was placed at the entrance to the nurses' lateral, as a precaution. Gambling was widespread and the stakes were fantastic. After all, everybody knew that where they were going promissory notes and IOUs would be worthless.

The *Mindanao* was scuttled that Sunday evening. All her fuel was gone, and she had defied the Japanese for the last time. The men moored the gunboat close to the South Dock and stripped her of everything that could be of value. Then they opened the sea cocks and she settled, slowly and with dignity, to the bottom.

The crew was taken to Fort Hughes, where they helped with the beach defenses, providing the ammunition parties and sweated labor for the second of the 12-inch mortars. Sam Malick made five journeys across those shell-tossed waters that night running crew, weapons, and supplies to the island. The mortar came into action against Cavite the next morning, and within a short while the crew were sent scuttling for safety to avoid the storm of shells that the Japanese fired in retaliation.

Evening
Tuesday, May 5, 1942

The Japanese artillery began the final phase of the pre-invasion bombardment. The defenders recognized it for what it was, partly because it did not ease, and it was so much heavier than anything they had had to endure previously. Soldiers develop a sixth sense for a battle, and everybody knew that "this was it"; the bombardment had the right feel to it. Gunners calculated that some 16,000 shells had hit Corregidor in the previous 24 hours. The noise was described as like being inside a blast furnace, a constant explosion with the sound and force from one running into the next.

By this time the Japanese had won the Battle of Corregidor without having set foot on the island. As on Bataan, there was a sudden and very marked deterioration in the health and resilience of the garrison. There was dysentery and even some malaria, but it was not disease that caused the decline. Malnutrition was a contributory factor, since the ration trucks had not been getting through to the more scattered outposts, and bureaucratic bungling had resulted in rations not being released during lulls in the artillery barrage.

Sergeant Bigelow, concerned that his men were starving, had organized raiding parties on the food dumps. The men held the MPs at gunpoint on Middleside while they took the provisions they needed. An order was published by the provost marshal that those caught stealing food would be shot, but the men were desperate and in any case did not take the order seriously.

The major cause of the deterioration was the cumulative effect of a month of relentless artillery bombardment. Lack of sleep, perpetual fear, and no hope of relief, when coupled to a meager diet, sapped the lifeblood of the garrison. Some who could not take it anymore, and found the thought of the same tomorrow unbearable, shot themselves; others simply voted with their feet and helped to swell the ranks in the tunnels.

The China Marines stuck it out, but now more than 10 percent of them had become casualties.

It was at about 1800 hours, at the very height of the bombardment, when the Japanese bracketed Battery Keyes. When the shrapnel and debris stopped, John McCann stared out from their machine-gun pit. It looked like cotton-picking time in the South. Their mattress had taken a direct hit, and the cotton filling was festooned on every bush and shrub around them. As soon as the shelling eased, the lieutenant from Battery Keyes came running down. He thought the three must have been dead and was obviously relieved to find them only shaken and otherwise unhurt. The young officer looked at the trees and told them to clean up the cotton lest the Japanese use it as a marker.

It took them three hours and, as the bombardment built up again, just about all the nervous energy they had left. McCann had never been so scared—except, that is, of not obeying the instructions of the officer! For the second night running they ate sparingly of their emergency C rations and prepared to stand their watch, though all three huddled in the weapon pit. The noise was so intense that there could be no rest for anyone on Corregidor that night.

In the meantime, Wainwright and his senior officers waited anxiously for news of the Japanese landing, which they were sure was about to happen. Though cocooned deep in their laterals, they were only too aware of the rising crescendo of the barrage.

2230 hours

Brig. Gen. Louis Beebe, who as a colonel had been one of Drake's principal supply officers in Manila and was now Wainwright's chief of staff, came into lateral No. 3, where the senior officers were all sitting on the edge of their chairs.

"It has happened, gentlemen," he said. "General Moore has just informed me that they are coming in near Cavalry Point and at James Ravine."

The greatest paper chase in history now began. In the headquarters lateral clerks were roused, files opened, desk and table drawers pulled out, and all the documents so meticulously collected over four months of siege torn to shreds by ink-stained, nerveless fingers until they were ankle deep in litter. Not a thing was missed; maps were ripped from the bare stone walls and destroyed. General Drake surveyed the scene. The headquarters lateral was only 15 feet wide and 50 feet long; he had never realized such a small place could hold so many records.

H-Hour

Battery Way received word of the concentrations of Japanese boats and landing barges, and the gunners ran to man the mortars. Massello broke out the antipersonnel shells. They were thin-walled shells weighing about 800 pounds, practically all TNT. They had a fuse 6 inches long, a complicated affair that unwound a tape as it went. The slightest little touch could set these monsters off, but their blast had a lethal radius of some 300 yards. Massello had been saving them for just this occasion. Rubble was swept from the tracks leading to the last two mortars, shells and powder bags rammed home, and the guns fired on the coordinates. At the same time the big guns on Fort Drum opened fire and at a range of 20,000 yards poured shell after shell on the craft of the Japanese second wave with deadly effect. On Fort Hughes, the mortar manned by the men of the *Mindanao* joined in, and the Japanese were caught flat-footed and exposed. They were already in some considerable confusion, for despite all their specialized knowledge, the planners had failed to take sufficient account of the currents along the northern shore of Corregidor. The first wave was carried more than 1,000 yards to the east of where they intended and hit the shore between Cavalry Point and North Point. The beach defense here included a 75mm two-gun battery that had never disclosed its position. They opened fire on the Japanese landing craft at point-blank range. The machine guns and small arms of the Marines of Company A joined in, and the carnage was sickening, even to the defenders. As the surviving Japanese struggled close inshore, the heavy mortars, fearful of hitting their own men, changed coordinates and concentrated on blanketing the waters between Cabcaben and Corregidor. They could hardly miss, for landing craft and auxiliary gunboats were strung out in confusion all the way to the shores of Bataan.

But it was not all one-sided, as the mortar pits came in for a fearful pounding from Japanese heavy artillery. Battery Way began to take casualties, and the third mortar was knocked out. Massello remained with the men who manned the surviving gun; his example and courage were an inspiration to them all. The piston rods that cushioned the recoil had snapped under the strain, and the mortar jammed. Massello liberally poured oil out of a 10-gallon can over the mechanism, and they were back in business. The mortars had never been intended for such a long and sustained fire. The barrel was so hot it blistered hands, and burning slivers of metal came spewing out with each round fired. There was no water left in the battery to cool the barrel, so Massello used his initiative, and that helped for a while. Chunks of concrete and rubble littered the pit and so intense was the Japanese fire that it was necessary to sweep the tracks clear each time the mortar was fired. Massello insisted on doing this himself.

"If they ever get me, what a hell of a way for a soldier to go, with a goddamn broom in my hand!" he yelled as he ran out from the powder magazine into a maelstrom of fire.

After a couple of hours of such use the recoil mechanism on the last remaining mortar was very shakey, and the chances of a misfire and premature discharge were considerable. Massello fired the gun himself rather than put his own men at risk. Casualties were mounting in any case. On each occasion the crew emerged to serve the gun, men fell.

H + 1
0030 hours

The Japanese were ashore. They came in on the heels of the barrage despite having suffered the most appalling casualties. Reliable sources indicate that of the 2,000 men in the spearhead battalions, less than 800 made it to land, while Homma lost some 60 percent of his landing craft and gunboats. But in one sense the Japanese were very fortunate, for the Marine battalion had 10,000 yards of shoreline to defend and only one platoon watching the beach on which the Japanese landed by accident. Once ashore, they quickly swamped the local defense and moved rapidly inland. Some deployed across the tail to Monkey Point, thus isolating the defenders to the east, while the rest of the battalion moved along the ridge line toward Malinta Tunnel. More good fortune came their way when the gunners of Battery Denver, who had nobly served their weapons throughout the campaign, unnerved at the prospect of an infantryman's war, abandoned their positions. The Japanese had the high ground; behind them the tanks and artillery started to come ashore.

Sgt. William Griffiths moved his platoon out to reinforce Company A along the northern shore; they were ordered to rendezvous on Battery Denver. It was only when he neared the battery and heard voices that "were not American" that Griffiths realized the enemy had reached that point. They dug in and opened fire on Japanese troops who were seeking to reinforce their own positions.

H + 3
0230 hours

The defenders were now in a perilous position, for there were only the survivors of Company A, about two platoons' worth of troops, that stood between the Japanese and the main entrance to Malinta Tunnel. Capt. Noel Castle, who commanded Company D, rallied his men and tried to lead them forward against the Japanese, now dug in around the base of the water tower on Denver Hill. The machine guns of Company D put down a vicious enfilading fire and for a moment the Japanese resistance slackened, but their snipers were still active. Captain Castle stood up and started to walk forward. Griffiths and a Marine with him yelled out a warning; as the officer turned he was cut down.

The Japanese had ample artillery, and their bombardment walked the short line back and forth, clearing the way for their advancing infantry. The only things the defenders could call upon were a few Stokes mortars without sights, and even use of these had to be stopped when the rounds started to fall on American foxholes. The first counterattack tried to move west along the ridge, but by the time the Americans got close to the water tower, the Japanese were in position in strength, with machine guns deployed. The fighting was vicious and confused. Grenades and rifles at 30 yards caused heavy casualties on both sides, but it was the Marines, open and exposed to the plunging fire from the high ground of Denver, who in the end had to concede. Griffiths lost touch with the rest of his squad as the men stumbled back over the broken ground and sought sanctuary in the foxholes of Company B along the southern shore. From these positions they fired up at Denver and tried to pin down the Japanese, but the position was confused by American units who were now behind the Japanese lines and Japanese units who in turn had been cut off by the Americans.

Colonel Howard at regimental headquarters grew more and more concerned. He dared not denude the beach defenses on Topside in case the Japanese attempted a second landing, and yet the enemy ashore had to be destroyed. The regimental reserves under Major Schaeffer and the sailors of the 4th Battalion (Provisional) 4th Marines moved down to Malinta Tunnel in readiness to launch a last desperate counterattack at dawn. Meanwhile, the Japanese began to exploit westward toward the tunnel, inching forward in the darkness past the isolated pockets of Marine resistance.

H + 5
0430 hours

Schaeffer and two companies of the regimental reserve moved out first and walked straight into a wall of high explosives and shrapnel. The Japanese laid down a curtain of fire on the line of their advance, and before they had moved 200 yards whole platoons had been decimated. Some had 5 men or less who were still on their feet. They reached the base of the hill and for a while even held the water tower, but before the first gray streaks of dawn lightened the eastern sky the counterattack petered out and the survivors found what cover they could.

Major Williams and the 500 sailors of the 4th Battalion, the men from *Canopus* and the naval base at Mariveles, in company column advanced out of the tunnel. They had been bottled up in there for two hours and were awaiting the order to move. They had endured the heat and claustrophobic discomfort, witnessing all the while the procession of wounded stream in from the battle for the beachhead. It did little to improve their morale when they learned that they were destined for the same battle. The sailors with bayonets fixed and rifles at the high port came out on the heels of Schaeffer's troops and swung into the attack on the left flank. The Japanese barrage caused heavy casualties, but the sailors doggedly pushed on. They cleared the Japanese outposts at bayonetpoint and came to within 200 yards of their main positions. Then withering small-arms fire from the well-sited Japanese machine guns brought them to a stop, and the most that Williams could do was dig in and form a skirmish line. The sailors had suffered fearful casualties, 100 dead and many more wounded. The latter lay where they fell, for no stretcher parties could be persuaded to venture forth from the tunnel. Some were wounded a second or third time where they lay, and others who tried to drag themselves off to the shelter of the tunnel fell victim to the remorseless barrage. There were no organized parties of stretcher bearers, nor did any leave the tunnel until after the cease-fire.

H + 6
0530 hours

At daylight Flanagan opened up on the water tower. John McCann and the others had spent the hours of darkness in confusion and fear, but once it was light enough to see they were able to swivel the gun around and join in the battle for Denver. The heavy .50-caliber bullets chewed up the ground, and the trio had the satisfaction of seeing Japanese infantry bowled over like tenpins as they came over the skyline. Flanagan, the senior man, dispatched a very unwilling McCann to Battery Keyes to find out what was happening. He reluctantly left the haven of their pit and scooted up the track to the battery. Even along the southern shore the air was alive with the whine of small-arms fire. He found the Scouts manning their handmade parapet and firing steadily on Denver with rifles and a couple of light machine guns. McCann arrived just after some Marines who had come scuttling in from Monkey Point. They reported that things were really bad on the tail with the Japanese in control of the landing field. The lieutenant in charge of the battery turned and beckoned to McCann. "You'd better abandon that gun of yours," he said. "Come up here and we'll make a stand." McCann scurried back to the others, and they quickly prepared to leave. Flanagan hurled the butt plate and firing pin over the cliff and joined the rest in the battery. They had lost their rifles when the mattress had been destroyed, but there were plenty lying around in the gun bays; they helped themselves and joined the battle.

For the next hour they engaged the Japanese as the latter deployed along the ridge line. It was a confused battle in which McCann never saw more than six or seven of the enemy at a time; small groups scuttled back and forth, moving from position to position.

To the Japanese on Bataan, the island looked like it was in a huge volcanic eruption, with billows of smoke and dust rising in columns thousands of feet into the blue sky. They had more than 400 guns blasting Corregidor and, with crews stripped to the waist and working flat out to service the pieces, it had to average a shell a second exploding on the Rock. The roar and vibration from the bombardment was continuous and unbroken.

H + 8
0730 hours

McCann watched two men come running down the road from the Navy tunnel. They had a light machine gun; one carried drums of ammunition, the other the gun and tripod. It was so funny that the men in the pit stopped firing and laughed hysterically at these characters until the lieutenant bellowed at them to give covering fire. They looked like a movie of a tactics and drill manual. Ignoring the dust being kicked up by bullets at their feet, they stopped, set up the gun, and fired at the Japanese on Denver. On each occasion others who watched from the battery were convinced they would die, for they made no use of cover at all. Methodically and with great deliberation they followed the drill book all the way and arrived at the battery unscathed.

The two men came in through the door and did not say a word. They just lay there and panted for a few minutes. After they had recovered, they told their story. They were writers from the Naval tunnel and except for a little basic training had never fired a gun in their lives. An officer had given them the Browning, and they had spent the night studying the manual to see how it worked and reading the drill book. They were elated by their success with the gun and the drills, which they had learned by heart for their break for freedom.

H + 9
0830 hours

The Japanese started to fire mortar bombs into the gun pit where McCann and the others had taken refuge. Three knee mortars dropped accurately along the parapet just as a couple of Scouts rose up to fire—they died instantly, and others were hurt, some seriously. The young officer in command decided that there were too many men crowded into the battery. McCann and a few of the others needed no urging to find another haven; this one had become decidedly unhealthy. They decided to join up with the Marines who were in the tunnels below Ordnance Point, about 500 yards west along the beach. Five of them made a dash for the shallow trench that led to the cliff face and the ladder down. The first part was easy; however, the group, huddled in the trench, had second thoughts about going down the swaying ladder. But Flanagan, who had a bad attack of malaria at the time and was out of his head with fever, shot past the others, vaulted the parapet, and went down the ladder like a scalded cat. McCann on impulse went second. He remembered his feet touching very few of the rungs, and rope burns laid bare the bone on the palms of his hands. The others came right behind, and it was a wonder that they did not pile up on one another at the bottom. The group caught their breath under the lee of the cliff and plotted their next move. There seemed only one way to reach the cover of the tunnels that were dug into the cliffs on the other side, and that was to make a dash for it across the beach. Their boots sounded like gravel in a bucket as they strove for purchase across the loose shingle before the sand beyond gave them a better footing and the chance for speed. Midway across they came into view of the Japanese on Denver, but Americans in the skirmish line on Malinta Hill gave them covering fire till they reached the shelter of the emplacements. Even so, with the Japanese fire never very far behind, McCann felt it was 100 miles across the beach. They reached the tunnel, and he flopped down in a corner, bound his burned hands in some cloth, and promptly fell into a deep sleep. He awoke four hours later to a voice saying, "There's a white flag flying from Fort Hughes."

H + 11
1030 hours

Massello came out of the magazine bunker, broom in hand, and started to sweep rocks and rubble once more from the tracks. There seemed to be no letup in the Japanese fire. As he turned to signal the track clear, he was caught by a hail of jagged-edged shrapnel. There were wounds in his legs, and one in his arm had severed the artery. Some gunners rushed out and dragged their battery commander back to the cover of the shell room. Massello had enough presence of mind to keep his thumb jammed hard against the artery while the men rendered first aid. For the rest of the morning he conducted the battle from a stretcher until the breechblock froze solid and they couldn't open the gun. Battery Way had fired the last shell in its short but violent part in the campaign.

Headquarters, lateral No. 3
Malinta Tunnel

Like many others in the tunnel, Drake had not tasted food since the evening before. His canteen with its precious water was nearly empty, and he was just about dehydrated by the heat. By now the yellow, suffocating dust that had been kicked up by the bombardment had become so thick he felt he was divorced from reality.

As the Japanese pressed hard for Malinta, more and more men fell back, and the tunnel became so full it was impossible to move. Earlier, Drake had tried to get from the headquarters lateral to his own quarters in lateral No. 10, perhaps 100 feet away, but had given up the attempt.

By this time information coming in from the outside confirmed their worst fears. The Japanese had tanks ashore, and advance elements of their infantry were not very far distant from the eastern entrance to the tunnel. General Wainwright sent word for his senior officers already in the headquarters lateral to assemble, and he told them that he intended to surrender at noon. The beach defenses were wiped out, he explained, and their defenders badly shaken. Practically all of the guns were either destroyed or out of action, communications were shattered, and the water supply was finished. The final blow had come when the Japanese sent the three tanks they had brought ashore into action. They had advanced along the ridge line beyond Denver and annihilated those defenders who tried to stay and fight.

They were a grim and haggard group who gathered to hear their commander pronounce the words that sealed their fate and spelled the doom of Corregidor. Drake watched the tragedy unfold as if he were in a dream. Wainwright was habitually thin, and the clothes sagged on his long, emaciated frame; tragedy showed in every line of his gaunt face and troubled eyes. To Drake he looked ages older than when he had first come from Bataan to assume command. He had had to carry the shame and humiliation of that defeat, and now he was about to repeat the process. There was no hope, and the time had come for humanity to displace strategy. With nothing to be gained by further resistance, he decided to sacrifice one day of freedom in exchange for several thousand lives. It was later estimated that by midmorning the defenders had suffered 800 dead and more than 1,000 wounded.

While the other officers planned the details of the surrender, Drake ordered the distribution of all the remaining food the quartermasters had in the laterals. As much as could be was moved into the main tunnel, and the men were allowed to help themselves.

Outside the battle raged, and the Marines had fallen back to the final defense line just yards to the east of the tunnel entrance. There the survivors of the China Marines prepared to make their last stand. In the meantime the regiment received the signal from General Wainwright via Moore's headquarters: "Execute Pontiac. Execute Pontiac." This was the code name for the surrender. Colonel Howard buried his face in his hands and openly wept. "My God," he said to Colonel Curtis, his executive officer, "and I had to be the first Marine officer ever to surrender a regiment."

Another signal was flashed to General Sharp in command on Mindanao. Wainwright told him of the surrender and ordered that he report directly to General MacArthur for further instructions. Wainwright's intention was clear: to surrender as few troops as possible.

1105 hours

General Beebe made the first broadcast, a lengthy affair to the Japanese that covered all the details of the surrender. Richard Sakakida then read the message in Japanese. At the same time, General Wainwright dispatched his surrender message to President Roosevelt and General MacArthur:

> WITH BROKEN HEART AND HEAD BOWED IN SADNESS BUT NOT IN SHAME, I REPORT... THAT TODAY I MUST ARRANGE TERMS FOR THE SURRENDER OF THE FORTIFIED ISLANDS OF MANILA BAY.... PLEASE SAY TO THE NATION THAT MY TROOPS AND I HAVE ACCOMPLISHED ALL THAT IS HUMANLY POSSIBLE AND THAT WE HAVE UPHELD THE BEST TRADITIONS OF THE UNITED STATES AND ITS ARMY.... WITH PROFOUND REGRET AND WITH CONTINUED PRIDE IN MY GALLANT TROOPS, I GO TO MEET THE JAPANESE COMMANDER.

While the defenders waited for some recognition from the Japanese, other messages went out from the Rock. Captain Hoeffel sent one on the Navy transmitters. Many radio hams in the Free World shared in the last hours of the island:

ONE HUNDRED AND SEVENTY-THREE OFFICERS AND 2,317 MEN OF THE NAVY REAFFIRM THEIR LOYALTY AND DEVOTION TO COUNTRY, FAMILIES, AND FRIENDS.

Ham radio operators along the Western seaboard of the United States listened also to the broadcasts of Sgt. Irving Strobing on the Army transmitters:

WE'VE GOT ABOUT FIFTY-FIVE MINUTES LEFT AND I FEEL SICK AT MY STOMACH. I AM REALLY LOW DOWN. THEY ARE AROUND NOW SMASHING RIFLES. THEY BRING IN THE WOUNDED EVERY MINUTE. WE WILL BE WAITING FOR YOU GUYS TO HELP. THIS IS THE ONLY THING I GUESS THAT CAN BE DONE. GENERAL WAINWRIGHT IS A RIGHT GUY, AND WE ARE WILLING TO GO ON FOR HIM, BUT SHELLS WERE DROPPING ALL NIGHT, FASTER THAN HELL. DAMAGE TERRIFIC. TOO MUCH FOR GUYS TO TAKE . . .

Beebe's broadcast was repeated, in English and in Japanese, at 45-minute intervals. The noon deadline came and went without the Japanese showing the slightest inclination to ease up in the battle. Col. Paul Bunker, under orders from General Moore, took down the American battle flag on Topside at noon, put up a white flag, and burned the American banner so it would not fall into the hands of the enemy.

Bunker secretly tore off a piece of the flag, which he intended to keep and present to the Secretary of War when he got back to the States. In a quiet moment he placed the strip inside a patch that he had sewn to the inner side of the left pocket of his cotton shirt.

White flags now flew from the entrance to Malinta and on Topside, but in international law that indicates only a desire to communicate with the enemy. The enemy for his part is under no obligation to cease fire.

Wainwright made a last attempt to reach the Japanese by radio and when that failed decided to send an officer forward with a flag of truce. He chose a Marine, Capt. Golland Clarke, together with a flag bearer (he carried a strip of white sheet from the hospital tied to a broom handle), a musician, and an American officer who spoke some Japanese. As the group passed through the defense lines, the bugler sounded forth. Captain Clarke suddenly remembered with absolute clarity a lecture he had attended five years before at Marine officers' basic school—the conduct of a *parlementaire* at a surrender.

The Japanese respected the flag and agreed to allow Clarke to conduct General Wainwright through to negotiate the terms of the surrender. There was a lull in the firing during which the Marine went back for General Wainwright together with General Beebe and General Moore from the harbor defense lateral.

By this time, early afternoon, Drake estimated there were more than 4,000 men crammed in the main tunnels, not including the 1,000 sick and wounded in the hospital laterals. The air became even more foul, eyes red-rimmed, and voices cracked with the dust. Over everything hung the smell of exhausted men, which renders one man intolerable to another. The situation was not improved either by the corpses stretched out at the eastern entrance to the tunnel. There was no way of disposing of them, and many had been there since the evening before. Drake, confused and weary beyond measure, didn't know what to do with his own pistol and the few clips of ammunition he carried on his belt. His exhausted mind persisted in forcing him to take elaborate steps to solve the problem of his personal weapon. He took the ammunition and hid it in his field desk and tucked some under a table. Then he took all the movable parts to his Colt automatic, smashed them on the floor, broke the grip, and bent the trigger. He vented his pent-up anger and frustration on the pistol as he stamped it into the earthen floor.

The firing and sounds of battle started up again as the Japanese renewed their assault on the eastern entrance to the tunnel and sought to mop up the remaining pockets of resistance. Drake, as senior ranking officer in the absence of Wainwright, Beebe, and Moore, became increasingly concerned. Perhaps the Japanese had refused the surrender terms, or perhaps Wainwright and his party had been killed. What was even more alarming was that he could hear machine-gun and rifle fire coming in from the western entrance, which indicated that the Japanese had passed around Malinta Hill and were now on the western side of the island.

Drake, standing at the entrance to lateral No. 3, discussed the problem with his executive officer, Lt. Col. Theodore Kalakuka, a West Pointer of Russian parentage and proficient in many foreign languages. He was a real soldier. The hotter the fight the more he enjoyed it, and he had already won two Silver Stars in the campaign. "Ted," Drake said, "we have got to do something quickly. These men here in the tunnel have about reached breaking point. We can't go on for much longer."

Kalakuka agreed and said, "Let me try, General. I have a feeling some Japanese officer there, if I can just get to him, will be able to talk my language. I will explain the conditions and tell him we are prepared to surrender. I've got a hunch I can put it over with those slant-eyed SOBs."

Drake agreed but first ordered the tunnel cleared for 100 feet from the east entrance, through which Kalakuka would attempt to contact the Japanese. The cleared space, he thought, would give them a better chance to control the men, and it would also give the enemy room to think as they entered the tunnel. An officer found a rope, and this they stretched across the tunnel near the entrance to the headquarters lateral. It took them some time to clear a space because it seemed impossible at first to crowd the men any more than they already were. Eventually Drake got some silence from the troops, and he stood on a box and yelled to lift his voice above the racket of small-arms fire from outside.

"Men, listen to me. We are going to try to contact the nearest Japanese troops outside this cleared entrance. We are going to tell him what conditions are like in here and that we have laid down our arms in surrender and ask that all firing stop so that we can get out of here properly and as soon as possible. I expect that if we can convince the Japanese that we will show no resistance they will come in here. If they do, I want every one of you to stand still. Don't move an inch, and keep absolutely silent. Any demonstration, any last-minute heroics, will mean the end of every one of us. We are helpless and at the absolute mercy of the enemy. If you want to live, don't move!"

With that Kalakuka, who had tied a piece of white cloth to a bamboo pole, disappeared through the barrier in the eastern entrance. Drake paced the area of the cleared space and waited anxiously for his return. Anxiety, concern for his men, and plain old-fashioned fear set his heart pounding. Suddenly all sounds of firing from outside the eastern entrance stopped. He looked up toward the entrance. The massive galvanized door creaked open, and Kalakuka came in with two Japanese officers. One was a major, the battalion commander, and the other a lieutenant who was to act as interpreter. Kalakuka quickly explained to his general that the language he had eventually found in common with the Japanese was Russian! The Japanese officers came up to Drake and stopped. The major looked him over, then he stared around the tunnel and at the men. There was not a sound—every man stood like a graven image. The Japanese lieutenant grunted some Russian at Kalakuka, who turned to General Drake. "He said that they are coming in and will give us ten minutes to clear everybody through the western entrance. If we are not out by that time it will be too bad."

"You tell him," Drake replied, "there are close to four thousand men in this tunnel. It will be impossible to get through the entrance in that short time. Also, there is firing going on outside that entrance, and it must be stopped before I will place the men in a position where they cannot protect themselves and could be shot down."

Drake allowed the lengthy process of translation to catch up before he concluded, "I guarantee to have every man outside this tunnel as quickly as I can if you will give us the time to do it."

Throughout his Army career, much of it in the Far East, Drake frequently had had dealings with the Japanese and had formed a strong aversion to them as a people. To Charles Drake, all Japanese had a poker face, and these were no exceptions. Drake watched the Japanese's face as Kalakuka told them the last of the message. Outside of a scowl not a change of expression could he detect. He hoped the delay indicated that they were turning the thought over in their minds. Since they are the biggest liars in the world, thought Drake, they never believe what they are told. Would this occasion perhaps prove to be the exception? The Japanese major finished speaking to his lieutenant, and Drake waited patiently for the message to reach him.

Kalakuka translated, "All right! You make a lane right through your soldiers immediately so we can get through to the other entrance and stop the firing."

With that, the two officers turned abruptly on their heels and taking Kalakuka with them headed out through the entrance. Drake turned to his own troops and gave them the orders to prepare for the arrival of the Japanese. "Squeeze back just as close as you can to both walls, men. Then open an aisle as wide as possible clear to the west entrance," he ordered. "Remember what I have said about absolute silence, and for God's sake don't even move a finger. These Japs will be as suspicious and jittery as hell."

Drake was right. The officers returned with Kalakuka between them and followed by a platoon of soldiers. Some had flamethrowers strapped to their backs. Others came with bamboo poles on the end of which were attached sticks of dynamite. Finally, two long files of infantry came in and immediately fanned out into the laterals that led off the cleared part of the tunnel. All the troops were dressed the same: black cloth shoes with rubber soles and the split big toe. They had camouflage suits in jungle green with hoods of green netting that had been thrown back off the face.

The major, through the interpreters, gave Drake his instructions. In neither manner nor bearing did he show the slightest respect for the other's general officer rank. "As soon as my men have passed through the far entrance, you will order your men to follow us and get them out as quickly as you can. I will stop the firing. You, the medical staff, and the wounded will remain here."

All this took time. After the last man was safely out, Drake turned and walked slowly back to his bunk in the lateral where all the generals lived and slept. Not a living soul remained in this dismal tomb except the rats who scampered over the piles of debris, seeking the scraps of food left from the last good meal the men would have for many a day. A chattering monkey, someone's abandoned mascot, ran ahead of Drake in fear that he too might be driven out.

Drake was dog tired, so he sought his bunk in the dim recess at the far end of the lateral. When he reached it he flopped down on the edge and sank his head in his hands. He was beyond the stage for rational thought. He had not slept for thirty-six hours and had consumed nothing but a corned-beef sandwich and half a cup of brackish coffee which Ah Fu, their Chinese cook, had brought to him.

As he sat there, more or less in a daze over the recent events, a feeling came over him that he was not alone, although he had heard no one enter the lateral. The tunnel outside was still silent as a tomb. Instinctively the general raised his head, and he was startled to see a Japanese soldier standing squarely in front of him, looking down through the slits of his little almond-shaped eyes. A smirk was on his swarthy face. Much to Drake's surprise it was the big burly sergeant who had been part of the Japanese detachment that had led Kalakuka into the tunnel. Undoubtedly he had had his eyes on the quartermaster, and when he had turned back from the exit he had followed along behind at a comfortable distance to see what he was up to.

Now the Japanese sergeant confronted the general, his legs spread apart in a splayfooted stance. His left hand fondled the hilt of his beloved samurai sword while he cradled his rifle under his right arm, the bayonet pointed directly at Drake's throat. The latter sat bolt upright. He had snapped out of his lethargy, and terror gripped him. He was convinced the soldier was about to kill him.

The ordinary Japanese Drake had met before the war was all smiles and bows and was overly polite in a meek way. But, Drake thought, put him in uniform and he felt clothed with the authority of his Emperor. This fellow was no exception to the rule. He looked pompous and most formidable.

Drake started to get to his feet, but he found the point of the bayonet too close for comfort, so he remained seated, and chills ran up and down his spine.

They looked at each other in stony silence for a fleeting moment. Drake knew that the Japanese would have to make some move first. What would he do? The suspense made him feel sick to his stomach, and his head reeled.

Suddenly in a gutteral voice, the Japanese spoke in broken English. "You sing?"

Drake nodded his head in assent.

"You sing American song!"

Drake did not know whether this was a demand or a question from the tone of his voice. In either case, it was incongruous in view of the situation. But it now called for a reply, and he managed to croak out a feeble "Yes" with a silent prayer that it was the right answer.

It was, and to Drake's utter amazement the Japanese stepped aside, rested his rifle on the edge of the bunk, and sat down alongside of him with his sword across his knees, the point in his direction. They were going from the sublime to the ridiculous.

Drake did not have to wait long for the Japanese to reveal his intentions. "You sing 'Old Black Joe.'"

There was no question there; he had to sing the song. In the bygone days of the amateur minstrel shows, Drake's father was an end man, and he knew all the old-fashioned songs. He had taught them to his son when he found that he had a good voice, and among them, of course, was "Old Black Joe." The general began to sing in a weak and rather wobbly voice, as he was still very shaken.

"Gone are the days when my heart was young and gay." How true that was in his present predicament. But as he sang his voice grew strong and resonant, and he gained in confidence. This was not so much because of his singing ability but rather the fact that the Japanese seemed to enjoy it and was intent on his every word, as if he were trying to memorize it to his own satisfaction.

"You very good," said the Japanese. "You sing again!"

This time the soldier kept time with his hands, much like a singing teacher would do with her class, his body swaying gently to the rhythm of the plaintive melody.

Outside the lateral General Drake could hear the faint murmur of many Japanese voices. The tunnel was filling up with those of the enemy who were on the prowl—for loot, maybe. Drake had a wild thought. What if some became inquisitive enough to poke their heads into the lateral (the entrance was boarded and screened) to find what all the singing was about? He did not relish the thought that he might become the center of attraction of a lot of curious-minded Japanese bent on mischief.

The affair was becoming ludicrous, and Drake prayed that it would be over soon. This plea went for naught as his captor demanded another encore. This time the sergeant joined in the singing. He was a little off key, but he knew all the words, down to the last doleful, "Old Black Joe."

When the song was finished, the Japanese held up his hand for silence. Then to Drake's surprise and inward amusement, he sang the song alone in the same discordant tone. When he had finished he turned to the general and said, "Not bad, eh?"

Drake nodded in enthusiastic approval and judiciously replied, "You good singer. Much better than I can do."

With that the Japanese bobbed his head in assent, delighted as a little boy. It seemed to be all over at long last. He had made his point. The sergeant got up slowly from the bunk as if he wanted to stay and hear some more singing. Somewhat reluctantly he picked up his rifle and again stood in front of the general, this time with his rifle in carrying position, and his heels together; Drake remained sitting on his bunk. The soldier bowed from the waist in Japanese fashion, made an about-face, and prepared to leave.

Without thinking Drake ventured a remark. "You speak English very well. Where did you learn it?"

The soldier spun around and with the back of his hand gave Drake a stunning blow to the face. "You no speak to Japanese soldier without permission," he rebuked.

Later in prison camp Drake learned, frequently to his own regret, that a prisoner never asks his captor or guard a question. The guard asks the question, the prisoner supplies the answer; and it had better be good.

The Japanese looked hard at Drake, then, in an abrupt change of mood, smiled and said, "I learn English in high school in Tokyo. I also learn American songs. I like 'Old Black Joe' the best."

The soldier left as quietly as he had entered, and Drake was alone again with his thoughts. The tunnel had quieted down; evidently the Japanese guard had run everybody out who had no business in there. Drake waited patiently for the other generals to return and marveled at this strange quirk of fate whereby his life had been spared by song.

H + 17
1630 hours

Outside the battle still raged. The Marines in the tunnel where John McCann had found refuge had established a strongpoint out of rocks and sandbags. Every time the enemy appeared, the Marines sent them scuttling for cover with their accurate fire. In the late afternoon the Japanese sent over a low-flying plane. The men retreated inside and heard the "plonk" of an exploding canister as smoke gushed in through the entrance. Everybody thought it was gas, and pandemonium reigned as they struggled furiously to get out through the carefully constructed emergency exit. Once outside in the clear air they lay gasping for breath, and only then realized that it had indeed been a smoke canister.

This last episode had, however, knocked all the fight out of them, and nobody appeared to contemplate a return to the battle. There was a lot of firing all around them, and this confused the group, since they could now see the white flags flying everywhere. A few even believed the Japanese were shooting all the prisoners. Eventually they decided to head in the direction of Malinta Tunnel. The men climbed the cliff stairway that Filipinos had built in a quieter day and came out near the 92nd's parade ground. As they walked across the sun-bleached concrete, a voice called out, "Come up here!"

They looked up and saw a Japanese officer, arms akimbo, standing on a hill above them. They clambered up the slope, and the officer motioned them toward a group of his soldiers.

"Where are you going?" he demanded.

"To the tunnel for some food," a Marine replied hesitantly.

"No. You stay here now," the officer replied.

They were searched by the Japanese and lost everything of value they owned—rings, watches, and wallets. Then the guards took them a little farther along the track until they came to a fold in the ground in which there were some forty or fifty prisoners squatting in a line. A Filipino looked up as they approached and tried to signal to them by pointing to their tin helmets, but it was to no avail. His gesture appeared meaningless—that is, until an old Japanese soldier came up to them. He had a gray, stringy beard and was obviously a seasoned veteran with campaign bars on his faded tunic. He didn't waste any time knocking the tin helmets off their heads, and then he motioned to them to join the others. There were the sounds of battle in the distance but otherwise silence among the prisoners.

McCann, tired and dazed, felt he was sitting at the end of the world, with nothing but a vast expanse of nothing, a void, stretching ahead. One of the Japanese soldiers came over to him and motioned for him to stand up—a clear enough signal, two grunts from his foul-breathed mouth, a prod with the bayonet, and a mighty kick in the small of his back. The Japanese pointed to the Red Cross pack that was fastened to his webbed belt; he wanted it open. This was one of the old World War I-type belts with two snap fasteners, one of which was jammed, and McCann, with his hands still bandaged, couldn't manage it. The Japanese brought over a Filipino to help; the latter, beside himself with fear, fumbled and sweated at the stubborn catch and even tried to pry it open with his teeth until his gums bled. When even this had failed the guard took the bayonet from his rifle and stepped forward. The Filipino was convinced that this was the end for him, and he screamed and ran off down the track as fast as his little legs could carry him. The guard did not pay any attention. He stuck the bayonet through the clasp and yanked the case open. McCann was too petrified to move and was convinced that his moment had come. Inside the pouch there was a small metal case sealed by a ring clasp. McCann started to pull it when the Japanese soldier stepped back and yelled in fear; he thought it was a grenade. McCann opened it up and showed the Japanese the bandage stored inside, whereupon the latter grunted and swung his rifle. The butt caught McCann a vicious blow to the stomach. As the young American folded into the ground the soldier, his dignity and face restored, walked away.

It was now close to dusk, and an occasional squad of Japanese soldiers doubled past at a run in the direction of Monkey Point, from where there was still the sound of firing. One group came by covered with dirt, their uniforms showing the clear signs of having been in salt water. One soldier swung his rifle at a Filipino who squatted next to the still groggy McCann, missed, and hit McCann across the head. McCann collapsed in a heap for the second time, his skull split and covered with blood; the guards unconcernedly looked in the other direction.

Shortly after, they were arranged in formation and marched out along the North Shore Road toward the sounds of battle. They passed by groups of Japanese wounded, many seriously, and the ground was littered by the dead of both sides. One man McCann could never forget; he was a young American medic who must have been caught by shell fire. There was a gaping wound in his side, and the contents of his medical satchel were strewn all over the road. The blast had blown off his trousers, and his buttocks were bare. There were no shoes on his feet.

The Japanese stopped every now and then, and the group was ordered to collect abandoned weapons. McCann carried a broken flamethrower and some poles with warheads tied to them. Then they were turned back along the island and through Malinta Tunnel to the South Dock, where they piled up the equipment and then joined hundreds of other men who had been penned into a temporary stockade in the ruins of the San José barrio. As they moved in, a

Marine detached himself from a group and came up to McCann. "God, Johnnie, what are you doing here?" he asked. It was the man who had been sweet on his sister in San Diego and had persuaded John to enlist.

Sgt. William Griffiths had heard of the surrender as the word was passed down along the skirmish line in front of Malinta Hill; by that time he had assumed control of an ad hoc squad of nine men in the confused battle that had raged all morning. Griffiths was very angry at the news, but at the same time relieved.

After Bressi's observation post had been knocked out, he had manned a beach defense foxhole above the James Ravine. His head and arms were heavily scored by shrapnel wounds, but he was fit enough to surrender with the rest of his battery, unlike Massello, who had been taken into the main hospital by his caring gunners. Bressi had acquired a Navy handkerchief, and once he had seen the Japanese rob and steal he took off his high school ring, the last thing of any value he possessed, and concealed it in a knot around his neck. The Japanese took his wallet and his watch.

As a prisoner, he was put in the stockade established at the 92nd's garage. The hangar nearby had once housed the boats and equipment for the Philippine Scout's Sailing Club.

Sergeants Bigelow and Broderick, Corporal Finken, and others, like so many Marines of the 2nd and 3rd battalions, never actually fired a shot at the enemy. While partly trained sailors and ill-assorted Filipinos had provided the island's mobile reserves, the Marines had sat in their foxholes and prepared for a landing that never came their way. It was yet another example of the incredible misuse of these highly skilled troops that had been a hallmark of the whole campaign from the very first day of the war. First a political football in an internecine service squabble and then a generalissimo's Praetorian Guard, they had been misused and abused. The 4th Marines ended the campaign sweating it out in their foxholes taking all the Japanese artillery could throw at them, losing men, and refusing to bend. When word came through to destroy all their weapons, some men took more kindly to that instruction than others as they smashed rifles that, after 5 months of constant combat, had never actually held an enemy in their sights.

No sooner had this been accomplished than the Japanese opened up the most tremendous bombardment on Topside. This was intended to persuade General Wainwright to surrender all the Philippine Islands rather than just Manila Bay. Most of the Marines got low down in their foxholes, covered their ears, and finished off their C rations. Many ate better in the last 24 hours than they had in the previous month.

Richard Sakakida refused the opportunity to leave Corregidor and instead gave his place, which had been allotted on the last submarine, to another Nisei. This man had been interned in the Philippines originally because although an American citizen he had worked as a lawyer in the Japanese consulate in Manila. He had even sent his family back to Tokyo along with the others as the war clouds gathered. If the Japanese had ever caught him he would have been in real trouble. Since he had actually worked in the consulate, the Japanese would have been convinced he was a spy.

Now that Sakakida had decided to stay, Colonel Pugh instructed him to revert to his old role as an undercover agent and to try to get into the Japanese forces somehow and bring any intelligence he gathered to the guerrilla units, which even then had started to form. At the surrender he was listed as a civilian, and they had done their best to fabricate a cover story. Sakakida claimed to his captors that he had been forcibly abducted from the internment camp and made to work for the Americans. However, the Japanese did not believe his story for a minute, and he was handed over to the tender mercies of the Kempeitai for interrogation.

For the nurses in the hospital lateral the surrender as such made very little difference except that the cease-fire meant that they were flooded with wounded who had not been able to make it to the tunnel during the bombardment. They tried to ease their suffering, but all they could administer was a half grain of morphine while the wounded men waited for surgery. The next morning ten of the nurses, Madeline Ullom among them, posed for photographs outside the tunnel. They were told that these would be sent to MacArthur to show that all the nurses were safe.

Fort Drum spoke to the very end. On the last day of the campaign, more than a thousand shells hit the fortress. Some 15 feet of its concrete had been chipped away by shell fire during the siege. While the white flag flew, the gunners blew up the 6-inch and 14-inch guns by loading them with sandbags, taking off the nuts from the recoil cylinders, and firing them from the remote-control center. Other men took the bases off the remaining shells, the tops off the cans of powder, opened the sluices, and let the seawater pour into the magazines.

The Japanese came the next day, and Sol Fromer was among those prisoners who climbed out through the 6-inch casements in the first batch that were taken to Lubac on the Cavite coast.

Sam Malick was taken to Corregidor when Fort Hughes surrendered.

Malaybalay
Mindanao

Amid much later rancor and recrimination, Wainwright was forced to surrender the southern islands and then persuade General Sharp and the others to accept the legality of his position, having earlier released them from his command. The result for Sammy Boghosian, Dick Osborne, and Ed Erickson was that they went into the bag when the Japanese occupied the plantation of Del Monte. There just were not enough aircraft making the shuttle to Australia to get all the men out before the capitulation overtook them.

U.S.S. *Porpoise*
At sea

The crew of one of the many planes that crashed was rescued by Roland McKnight. He had sailed from Fremantle on Anzac Day in command of the U.S.S. *Porpoise*, a large oceangoing submarine and a far cry from the antique but much-loved *S-36*. McKnight was ordered to patrol the Molucca Sea and then set course for Pearl Harbor and home. That evening he received instructions to proceed at his best speed to the island of Yu, a small atoll practically on the equator and lying between Halmahera and New Guinea. The pilot had given this island as his position in Mayday distress signals that had been picked up by another plane.

The ditched plane was an LB-30, the cargo version of the Liberator, and the first that the crew knew of the surrender was when anti-aircraft fire hit them as they came in to land at Del Monte. Crippled and on fire, the pilot had nevertheless been able to elude the barrage and had reached this far south on his flight home before being forced to ditch.

McKnight was close to the limits of his endurance and about to head for Pearl when he received the signal. He unhesitatingly diverted to Yu on this mission of mercy. They rescued three officers and two crewmen from the downed plane, then set course for Pearl Harbor and home.

Erickson had spent a couple of days after the surrender hiding out in a pineapple warehouse and then turned himself in because the guerrillas refused to accept him. He did not have the price of a guerrilla ticket, a hundred tablets of quinine and small arms. All he had was a pair of shorts and two packs of cigarettes, no shoes, nothing else.

The Japanese in the meantime had found two P-40s at Malaybalay—an outlying field which had not been destroyed. The Japanese interrogated some staff officers and tortured them into identifying Erickson and another man as pilots, and they were ordered to deliver the planes to Manila.

The two planes were in very poor shape, even by Philippine combat standards, and barely staggered into the air. Erickson, in particular, had very real troubles, and every time his engine misfired he lost altitude. On such occasions two of the nine Zeros, which had problems enough in escorting the lumbering American machines, would dive down and fire at him. It was enough of an inducement for Erickson to manage to get the engine going again until eventually Manila Bay came into sight. He passed low over Corregidor. A thick pall of smoke still obscured much of the fortress, though the waters below were busy with small craft scudding among the islands.

It was when he made his final approach into Nichols that Erickson hit upon a scheme whereby he could sabotage the aircraft without risk of discovery or injury to himself. He changed the mixture in the fuel in such a way that the heat became so great on the pistons that they swelled up and froze. The motor burned out just at the right moment when he had barely cleared the perimeter fence and was able to make a dead-stick landing. At first Japanese officers believed that he had deliberately sabotaged the plane and would have killed him had it not been for the timely intervention of his flying escort. They were able to testify that he had enough problems flying to Luzon and had nearly crashed on a number of occasions.

Erickson's adventures with the P-40 were not over yet. The Japanese had captured intact six brand-new P-40s in Singapore and had shipped them to Manila. Still in their crates, they came complete with their TAC orders.

Erickson and a number of other pilots were taken to a large warehouse on the Manila waterfront where the crated planes were awaiting assembly. The Japanese had set up a long table, extending the length of the warehouse, and gathered together their own engineers and interpreters to supervise the pilots, who were ordered to assemble the planes!

It took three months of beatings and harassment before the Japanese gave up on the scheme and shipped the still incomplete planes to Japan. The pilots had soon learned not to admit that they were unable to do the job. This simply roused the wrath of their captors, who would beat them senseless. Instead they pretended that certain vital components or special tools were missing and that they had to improvise. This still caused the Japanese to become angry, but an occasional slapping was easier to take. Eventually the Japanese lost interest in the scheme, and Erickson was taken under escort to join the other American prisoners at Cabanatuan.

Even as the last act was being played on Corregidor, the tide turned in the Pacific war. Aircraft carriers cleared their flight decks, and in the Battle of the Coral Sea the United States gained a strategic victory in halting the Japanese advance. The men in the Philippines had not fought and died in vain. Had their surrender followed the Japanese timetable, then the enemy would have had a spare capacity in men and materials that might perhaps have tempted them into a bolder thrust south, to Australia. What is not in doubt, however, is that the men of Bataan, Corregidor, and the island forts showed by their example that the Japanese soldier was not invincible in battle. As at the Alamo, their spirited defiance of an enemy obsessed with their destruction was the shining light that spurred others on to prepare for their fight against a bestial foe.

EPILOGUE

One Dollar a Day

Introduction

The Japanese chose to deal with their prisoners according to their own centuries-old code known as *bushido*, which literally translated means "the way of the warrior." It was the deep commitment to the code that led Japan to refuse to ratify the Geneva Convention on prisoners of war. The convention and the code were contradictory, since *bushido* equated compassion with weakness. Thus Japan's prisoners of war encountered a totally alien culture. These men had survived the battle, and far from feeling disgraced they were delighted to be alive. For the Japanese soldier surrender was forbidden, and suicide was the only honorable course of action. To surrender meant, at best, permanent disgrace in the eyes of the country and dishonor to the family. To their captors, Americans such as those taken in the Philippines merited contempt.

Adherence to the code of *bushido* can explain to a degree the absence of compassion, but it cannot explain the abuse and the inhumanity of the treatment that the prisoners so often received. Japanese officers and men assigned to prison duty were either of the lowest quality or equally inadequate Formosans or Koreans. Their guards were looked down upon and derided by front-line units, who reserved for them the contempt that combat troops show to rear echelon formations. Such emotions are to be found in all armies, but in the oriental world it also involved loss of face. The guards, infuriated perhaps by this behavior, suddenly found that for the first time there were people who were lower down the pecking order than themselves and over whom an uncaring state had given them power of life and death.

• 475

These remarks are not intended either as a theory to explain the actions of men, or as an excuse, for Japan stands condemned in the eyes of the world because of the deeds carried out under its banner in war.

In all, Japan maintained about 300 POW camps throughout the conquered territories and home islands, and there was no consistency in the way they were run. There were those camps where prisoners were reasonably well treated, at least for some of the time, and where discipline was lax under a liberal regime. At other times, in the same camps and elsewhere, soldiers of the Imperial Japanese Army were cruel captors. Indeed, so bitter and ingrained are the memories of some of the veterans who are part of my story that they have preferred not to recount or record their experiences. I have respected their wishes.

On the whole, the 3,500 civilians who had been captured as the tide of conquest swept over the Philippines did not experience the physical brutality inflicted upon military prisoners. In some respects theirs was a more subtle form of torment. The Japanese simply dumped them behind the guarded gates of internment camps and left them to fend for themselves. Tokyo felt no obligation to see to their needs or comfort, and the mood of the camp commandant determined whatever meager fare came their way.

The entire period of imprisonment was one of dismal misery interspersed with frequent periods of acute suffering. Men were humiliated and systematically tortured on numerous occasions. The behavior of the guards was cruel and brutal to the point of sadism. Starvation rations were the standard fare. Naturally, all also suffered from acute anxiety and worry concerning their families at home. The constant harassment created a nervous tension that for many proved as hard to bear as the actual physical punishment.

The Years of Despair

Following the capture of Bataan, most of the prisoners of war were sent to Camp O'Donnell, where crowding, disease, and starvation, coming so soon upon the trauma of the campaign, the shock of defeat, and the agony of the March, caused an immediate and very high death rate. At first the only water available was that drawn from an already polluted river. Men developed amebic dysentery, and many vomited to death. Prison existence soon reduced human nature to what it was without the conveniences of civilization, without the props and veneer. Yet the same set of variables that would cause one man to go into shock and die would motivate another to fight for survival. Even so, the death rate in the early months proved to be calamitous. Precise figures are impossible, but it is generally accepted that by Christmas 1942 some 2,700 Americans and 29,000 Filipinos died in that hell on earth.

Many officers above the rank of captain captured in Bataan were segregated from the rest and in time dispatched to Karenko POW Camp on Formosa. Those officers who were left in the Philippine Islands were reduced to unranked laborers.

After the fall of Corregidor, most of the prisoners were assembled at the 92nd's garage, formerly an amphibian aircraft ramp that had been paved over. Here the men, under fairly loose supervision from their captors, foraged for scraps of lumber and blankets to provide shelter against the hot sun. Open-air slit trenches were the insanitary excuses for toilets and were much in use by those with diarrhea and dysentery. When heavy rain fell, though it must at the time have seemed impossible, things got even worse.

Large numbers were deployed by the Japanese on work details. Art Bressi formed part of the burial detail. Groups were sent out with handcarts to recover first the Japanese dead. These they gathered from the beach defense areas, along the shoreline, and from the battle inland, and piled them up at the entrance to Malinta Tunnel. The bodies were then arranged in stacks of about fifty, and, in a quaint little ceremony, a Japanese officer poured what Bressi described as some "sweet-smelling stuff" over them. This liquid had a highly inflammable nature, for when fired the bodies burned fiercely. The remains of these warriors of *bushido* were then scooped up into scores of little boxes or caskets for shipment home.

By the time they got around to collecting the American dead, it was anything but pleasant. They were badly distorted in the tropical heat and blown up perhaps to double life size. The stink was terrible, and the bodies were burned as quickly as possible and without any ceremony.

Most of the prisoners were employed in clearing up the battle-field and salvaging the discarded weapons and ammunition. In this, as in all other labor details, the Japanese made it abundantly clear that they had no intention of observing the recognized code of behavior; they worked all the prisoners hard and fed them little.

Sergeant Bigelow was drafted to work with a Japanese engineers detail. Their officer had a complete set of finely detailed and scaled plans of the laterals that led from the main Malinta Tunnel. Under the officer's direction, Bigelow paced off the steps into a particular lateral and marked a point on the rock wall. He was given a pick and shovel, and within a very few moments had pulled away what proved to be a thin crust of rough cement to reveal a complete new lateral. This process was repeated at a number of other places in the tunnel complex. These secret laterals were packed full with materials, foodstuffs, even canned water. There was a field hospital complete with stores and tentage, together with large quantities of medical supplies, including quinine and sulphur.

Bigelow and other Marines, including Cpl. Bill Finken and Sgt. Bill Griffiths, and Pvt. John McCann, worked in the chain gangs the Japanese then formed to move this and other war booty to the South Dock. There three small freighters were loaded by the prisoners, and the ships sailed across the bay to Manila Harbor.

Toward the end of May all the able-bodied prisoners were herded together, and they, too, were dispatched to the docks and loaded onto old freighters. The men were battened down into the holds overnight. Neither food nor water was provided, a foretaste of things to come.

As soon as he realized what was happening, Bressi slipped away from the crush of men around the hatch and crawled along the top deck as far forward into the bow as he could go. There he found a large piece of hemp cordage and coiled up inside; in this way he managed to avoid spending that awful night down below.

The following morning the freighters anchored off Dewey Boulevard. Rope net ladders were let down over the side, the battens lifted off the holds, and the men clambered over and waded ashore. In full view of the Filipino people, for this was intended, the men were formed into columns of fours and marched along the boulevard to Bilabid Prison. Their feet were wet and their shoes full of sand and gravel. Under these conditions blisters soon formed and burst. There was no letup to their agony, for the guards allowed them no respite in the march. However, the Japanese plan backfired, and their crude attempt at the humiliation of the Americans failed. The Filipinos stood and watched and wept; some raised two fingers in the Churchillian victory salute; others tried to sneak food to the men, even though many were caught and brutally beaten for this act of simple charity. Eventually, after a march of some 5 miles, they limped in beneath the forbidding portals of Bilabid Prison, notorious in its day, since it housed lifers, murderers, and rapists. These and other kinds of scum had been let out by the Japanese to make room for the new prisoners. Given its reputation, the use of Bilabid was also intended by the Japanese as an act calculated to humiliate and denegrate the Americans in the eyes of the Filipinos.

The prisoners were in most cases kept at Bilabid for only a couple of nights. From Bilabid the men were marched to Manila Station and shoehorned into boxcars, a hundred or more crammed into each, for their journey northward to Cabanatuan. By the time that Bressi's train arrived it was already dark, and they were marched into a schoolyard. There was a cauldron of rice for those who could reach it, but most went without and slept where they could find a place to lie down. The next morning guards formed the prisoners into columns and marched them the 6 or 7 miles to one of the three designated camps at Cabanatuan. It was here that the garrison of Corregidor was reunited with the defenders of Bataan.

Bill Massello made the same journey, but not until July. At the time of the surrender, he was in critical condition. The ulnar nerve and artery of his right arm had been severed, and his left ankle shattered by shell fragments. He had numerous other wounds and had lost a lot of blood. The doctors had done the best they could with the limited supplies available. Even so, when July came and the Japanese decided to move these last Americans to the mainland, Massello's wounds had not healed, and his right hand was completely paralyzed. In the long years of captivity that lay ahead, he made but slow progress from his appalling wounds. Despite the best of medical attention after the war, Massello, along with so many other veterans of the campaign, never fully recovered from his wounds and ordeal.

The seriously wounded were hauled down to the dock by the more able-bodied on handcarts and loaded into a Japanese freighter. The men spent the night lying on bare wooden platforms in the insufferably hot and foul hold. Their freighter tied up alongside the wharf at Manila, and the next morning the men were disembarked and formed into columns. They were emphatically told that nobody except the extreme stretcher cases would be allowed to ride, and then the column moved off into the town. The vast majority of men in this group had wounds that still had not healed. Massello's wounds opened, blood and pus soaked through his grimy bandages, his leg was weak and pained him extremely, and his crippled arm and paralyzed hand were useless.

In such condition and worse, the column was compelled to march 6 miles without pause for rest or water during the heat of a tropical noonday. The shortest and most direct route would have taken them to Bilabid in under 2 miles, but instead the Japanese sought to humiliate them, too, before the people of Manila. They were no more successful than they had been on the first occasion, but unfortunately this only riled the Japanese, who in turn took it out on the poor unfortunate captives. They were goaded along with club and rifle butt.

At Bilabid they were given a scanty meal and crammed into small cells, where they passed the night lying on the bare concrete.

The Japanese made no concessions when they transported the wounded by rail to Cabanatuan the following morning. With a hundred men to a car they could neither sit nor lie down. The guards stood at the open doors but refused to allow any prisoner to come within 2 or 3 feet of them. By this time Massello's bandages were filthy and had worked loose, and his leg was swollen with infection. Within a very short while they were all drenched in their own perspiration and their neighbor's urine. After a train journey that lasted ten hours, they arrived, in a distressed and sorry condition, at Cabanatuan to face the march to their camp.

As with others who had trod that path before to camp No. 1, they were quickly divided into groups, with no distinction made between officers and enlisted men, and assigned to *behais* (straw shacks). The huts themselves were divided into a number of bays, each about 8 feet square, and there were 6 men to a bay. The first night was a miserable one. Heat exhaustion, sour rice, and hardship took their toll from the weak and wounded men. Diarrhea was rampant, and men too weak to move vomited and defecated all over the *behais* and the area around the shacks. For Massello, sleep was out of the question.

For all but a select few this was the route taken by the men from Corregidor. Madeline Ullom, Ruby Moteley, and the other nurses were taken in just a little more comfort, once the hospital had been closed down, to the civilian internment camp at Santo Tomas in Manila.

General Drake remained in his room in lateral No. 10 in Malinta Tunnel until May 20. Then together with most of the officers of field grade and above he was loaded into a large landing craft, taken to Manila, and lodged in what was then an empty but still filthy Bilabid Prison. After a few days of waiting while 20 generals, including Wainwright, were assembled, they were moved to a guarded schoolhouse on the outskirts of the city.

On June 3, 1942, the generals were taken by truck to Tarlac, 40 miles north of Manila, where they were lodged in the constabulary barracks. They were allowed to occupy the whole second floor. While at Tarlac, Colonel Ito, a liaison officer on the Japanese general staff, came from Manila to visit the prisoners. He brought them some bread, coffee, and a little brandy, and told them they would not stay at Tarlac long but would go to a beautiful mountain resort. He did not say where. For the most part, the diet at Tarlac consisted of rice with an ounce or two of beef or pork once a week. Wainwright lost 40 pounds in the first 4 months of imprisonment.

They had been at Tarlac for only a short time when the Japanese commandant ordered a full inspection of all the Americans' belongings. Drake had an officer's field bag in which he carried everything he possessed. He took the bag outside and emptied out the contents along with the others. In going through one of the side pockets Drake was horrified to find some .45-caliber bullets he had placed there when he loaded his automatic on the first day of the war. Not really knowing what to do with them, he held them out in his hand when the inspecting guard, a corporal, came by. The corporal looked down at the outstretched hand, drew back, and struck Drake a blow over his heart that knocked him off his feet. Drake struggled up, expecting to be hit again, but instead the guard began kicking his things all over the ground. After this tantrum had passed, Drake gathered his possessions together and went back to the barracks. His breast was sore and bruised, but there were no bones broken.

A couple of days later the interpreter approached Drake, bringing with him the Japanese corporal. Through the interpreter the corporal asked how Drake was feeling.

"I'm all right now," Drake replied, a little confused.

The guard went on to apologize and added that if he had not struck the general, he in turn would have been beaten by his own officers.

Colonel Ito was right. It was not long before the general staff took a train for Manila. The trip to the capital was like a triumphant procession. Crowds of people filled the stations as they passed. The train stopped at one station where there were so many people that the Japanese guards could not keep them back as they crowded around the train cheering and clapping.

When they arrived in Manila, the officers were taken straight to the docks and onto a freighter, where they had to sit and sleep on the upper deck. While waiting to sail, Drake watched a guard of honor as it formed up on the dockside. As the Americans peered down on the spectacle, hundreds of little wooden boxes, with due ceremony, were brought on board.

The next day, August 12, their ship sailed out through Manila Bay, past the now seemingly deserted and ominously silent Corregidor, and turned north into the South China Sea. Their destination was to be Karenko, a prison camp high in the mountains of Formosa.

There was one American still on Corregidor. Richard Sakakida was kept there for six months and interrogated by the Kempeitai, the Japanese Military Police organization. Just before the American surrender Richard had been given clear orders by G-2 Intelligence and CIC officers to infiltrate the Japanese forces in the Philippines and then somehow to feed information back through the guerrilla chain. Sakakida had a cover story, and it was this, in a lateral off Malinta Tunnel, that the Kempeitai interrogators were testing. Sakakida maintained that he had been dragged out of internment camp by the Americans and made to work. He had been forced to wear a uniform because those were the only clothes his oppressors would make available to him. Though some Japanese were brought over from the mainland and testified to the truth of his claims about internment, others, liberated prisoners, identified him as a willing and effective interrogator. Richard Sakakida was tortured regularly and systematically. He was strung up like a side of beef for hours on end with his back arched over a beam and his feet dangling. They tried a variation of the water treatment. He was force-fed water, then spread-eagled so that his tormentors could jump on his stomach. Despite this and even more hideous torture,

Richard stuck to his story and so the Kempeitai moved him to the mainland.

Taken first to Fort Stotsenberg, Sakakida was subjected to a further period of interrogation and torture, but still he did not break. Eventually his captors announced that he would be charged with treason. Insofar as the Japanese were concerned he was of Japanese ancestry and as such could not be an American citizen, even by birth.

In December Richard Sakakida was moved to Bilabid Prison to await trial. He was placed in the same cell block as the Japanese soldiers who had surrendered on Bataan. They were serving long sentences for their act of foolishness. It was 15 years for a private, while an NCO got life. Many of them had been interrogated by Sakakida, and they all remembered him and lost no time in paying their respects. On three separate days the Japanese took Sakakida out of prison to the court at Fort McKinley where he was due to stand trial. On each occasion his case was not called. After that Richard was locked up in solitary confinement at Bilabid and left to rot.

For the American civilians, internment had begun much earlier, but for those who had moved into Santo Tomas life did not seem quite so bad at first. Ever the optimists, none thought they would be there for more than a few months at the outside. It was only gradually that the truth began to sink in that it was going to be a long affair.

Santo Tomas sprawled over 52 acres, and survival for its inmates became a matter of individual initiative and stamina. For the first 6 months the Japanese provided no food at all. If it had not been for the help and charity of Filipino servants and friends (the Japanese allowed them to bring food to the captives), death would have been inevitable.

The camp had a management committee, and the Japanese allowed the inmates to run their own affairs, up to a point. They published a newspaper (called *Internews*), they grew vegetables, and from their reservoir of talent ran classes and courses on almost every subject under the sun. Shows and variety concerts were held in the evening.

Sister Louise, together with some of the other members of the Maryknoll community, had been brought down from Little Baguio in July and after an overnight stay in Santo Tomas had moved on to Los Biños. This was a new civilian internment camp that had been established in what had formerly been a government agricultural college situated on the outskirts of Los Biños, a fishing village on the southern shore of the inland water called Laguna da Bay. The camp was about 50 miles from Manila.

The college had consisted of 15 concrete school buildings, 5 large, two-story dormitories, 30 small cottages for the teaching staff, and a sugar mill. The Japanese erected additional huts with wooden frames, *suwali* walls, and a nipa roof. The camp was surrounded by a perimeter fence liberally sprinkled with watch towers. When Sister Louise arrived there were 1,200 internees in the camp. Within a year the numbers had swollen to over 2,000 American and Allied civilians. There were nine nationalities of men, women, and children.

Each barrack was divided into sixteen cubicles measuring 20 feet by 15 feet, open to the center aisle but cut off by *suwali* partitions from adjoining cubicles. There were 6 beds in each division and 96 internees to the barrack. Toilets and washhouses with sinks and a primitive shower were in separate buildings between each two barracks. The camp was in beautiful country. It nestled on the slopes of a valley. Mount McKieling, with its summit wrapped in a mantle of fog, rose on one side, and Mount Banahao on the other. The hillsides were covered with luxuriant forests, and the colors shifted and spilled as the sunlight and shadows of the clouds played over the greenness of the trees and the valley. Yet within a very short period of time this camp, set in the midst of such idyllic country, was to become a place of distress, despair, and eventually death. As food became ever more scarce, with the Japanese guards callously indifferent to the plight of the civilians, the mortality rate rose, first from disease and later from starvation.

By the following year, 1943, the Japanese had consolidated their POW establishment in the Philippine Islands to three main centers. The largest was at Cabanatuan; then there was Bilabid, which served a number of functions; and the third was in the old penal colony at Davao in the southern islands. The survivors from Camp O'Donnell were transferred, and that hellhole was closed down. The vast majority of the Filipinos were sent home.

While the Japanese systematically pillaged the Philippine Islands and the people, the Americans were used as slave labor.

There were farm camps and forestry schemes at Cabanatuan and Davao, dock work and salvage at Bilabid. There were work details at Nichols where the runways were enlarged. A particularly ruthless work detail was established in Tayabas Province, where the men were sent to construct a jungle road. The story of this operation, resulting in the death of 90 percent of the POWs in 6 weeks, reveals the effect of the callous treatment as well as the particularly ruthless means the Japanese employed to force the prisoners literally to work themselves to death.

Because of the large number of sick and wounded, the position of the doctors was a very special one in the story of the American POWs. Many of the camps were under the doctors' direction.

Another detail was sent to Bataan to salvage the wrecked and rusted combat vehicles abandoned there. It was a specially selected group of men, mechanics and the like, who dragged the remains of trucks, tanks, half-tracks, and artillery out of the jungle and loaded them onto Chinese junks at Mariveles Harbor. From there they were taken to Caloocan near Manila, where the salvageable parts were used to repair and even construct serviceable vehicles. Bill Hall worked on this detail. He helped collect metal, any metal, ammunition, empty shell cases, and rusty rifles. There were several thousand vehicles that had been abandoned on Bataan, many originally commandeered from Manila showrooms. These the prisoners carved up with acetylene torches and carted away as scrap to feed the hungry furnaces in Japan.

Working parties went out each day from Bilabid to the port area of Manila and the airfields driving trucks, while others were sent as cooks to the homes of Japanese officers. Some Americans were even *topans,* "dog robbers," or orderlies for Japanese officers. They and the cooks stole parts from radios on a planned basis, and in time they were able to build a set in Bilabid to receive the news from the United States.

Bressi worked for a while at Nielson Field. The Japanese intended to extend the runways at Nichols and Nielson fields and so convert them into a single airfield. For Bressi the effect of disease and malnutrition, especially the lack of vitamin C, was that, in common with so many others, his testicles had swollen to the size of small grapefruits. The Japanese cure for this complaint was a mixture of creosote and water; those who suffered had to stand in line, squat over the tub, and dip their testicles into the solution. The pain was excruciating. He was returned to Bilabid and the prison hospital where Paul Ashton ministered to him, and then after a couple of months, when he was on the road to recovery, the Japanese sent Bressi back to Cabanatuan.

Paul Ashton, the surgeon from Bataan, had survived that ordeal, and from 1943 on he was confined to Bilabid. In Bilabid the food situation at first was not so bad. Inmates could buy a few articles in the prison commissary, a banana, sugar, a little coconut, and occasionally eggs. In time both food and money became scarce, and this was really because under Japanese rule the Philippine economy was wrecked. Filipino farmers grew enough to eat, but any extra was commandeered by the Japanese. The sugar industry, a staple product of the islands and the main source of revenue, was brought to a halt, and the Japanese substituted cotton. The experiment was a dismal failure. The Filipinos refused to use the Japanese occupation currency, and so the economy simply fell apart. The Japanese were forced to bring in their own food by sea, and as the American submarine blockade became more effective, even the occupiers had to go without. However, the result was that the American POW, the lowest man on the totem pole, was soon starving. There were distributions of Red Cross packages, but the vast majority of the men saw only two issues during their time in the Philippines, and by then the packages were old and had been pilfered.

Prison camp No. 1, located about 7 miles north of Cabanatuan, was on about 50 acres of rice land. Before this old Philippine Army depot was converted by the Japanese into a prison, it had been ransacked by the local Filipinos. Most of the huts had their flooring ripped out, and the plumbing was taken too. The campsite was generally level but crisscrossed with rice paddies, which made walking off the main paths rather difficult. Drainage was very poor. In wet weather, the mud was knee deep, and the camp became a bog. The entire camp was divided roughly in half by a road. One side of the road was the hospital area, and the other side was the main camp.

Sleeping quarters consisted mainly of straw shacks (*behais*) with an occasional wooden hut. All living quarters were crowded. The straw shacks had a dirt corridor running through the center with two tiers of bays along each side. These bays were about 8 feet square and floored with bamboo slats. From four to eight prisoners were assigned to each bay. No beds or mattresses were provided or allowed. Seats of any description were prohibited. In the wooden shacks, prisoners slept on the floor; under these conditions, men soon developed kidney disorders. The only blankets were those they brought with them, and these had to suffice as cover from the mosquitoes. Any makeshift bunks or benches constructed by the prisoners were confiscated and destroyed by the Japanese whenever discovered. All the shacks were completely devoid of shelves, so the prisoners were forced to keep such articles as they possessed in a barracks bag or piled against the wall. No lights of any sort were provided or permitted in the *behais* or in the confines of the camp except in a very few administration buildings. During moonless nights, a latrine run was a hazardous adventure. All the buildings leaked.

Sanitation just did not exist. The latrines were open trenches located at the far edge of camp. Since water was invariably struck at about 2 feet below the surface, these latrines were never deep enough. With the great amount of diarrhea and dysentery present, latrines were filled about as fast as they could be dug. They dug straddle trenches but these too were unusable because maggots by the millions dug into the sides of them, and they collapsed. The Japanese provided only a few shovels and tools for latrine digging. All the latrines were crawling masses of maggots and filth. The occasional bag of lime furnished by the Japanese was useless. Flies were numerous, and the horrible stench pervaded the entire camp.

The camp's population was ever changing, but at times it exceeded 10,000 men. Shortage of water made bathing almost impossible. There was one trickling water spigot for every 1,500 men. To obtain a canteen of water meant a very long wait in the line, and containers were very rare. In general, bathing was done under the eaves during heavy rains—a chilling and most uncomfortable method. There were no soap, toiletries, or toothpaste provided by the Japanese.

Kitchens were unsanitary. Floors were of dirt, work tables crude and rough, water and cleaning facilities inadequate. Kitchens were unprotected against the swarms of ever-present flies. Cooking was carried out in large cast-iron cauldrons called *kawas*. Rice was served from crude wooden troughs with improvised scoops. Each kitchen served about 1,500 men. The men were normally fed twice a day. In the morning they had *lugow*, a watery rice stew, and in the evening a canteen cup of polished rice with maggots and vegetable tops. Occasionally, and therefore regarded as a special treat, a fish head was included on the menu. Proteins were very rarely served and then only in microscopic quantities. Prisoners existed on less than 1,000 calories a day, and this poor diet quickly led to malnutritional diseases such as scurvy, beriberi, and pellagra in epidemic proportions. All had dysentery, malaria, and jaundice.

Most of the POWs were employed in hand tilling the large farm. They planted rice and sweet potatoes, onions, beans, and tomatoes. Most of the produce grown was for the Japanese troops in the area and the guards at the camp. After the feudal due had been paid, a small amount was left for camp consumption. Even this was carefully controlled, and if any man was caught stealing the punishment was either one or both arms broken on the spot, depending on the amount of food involved.

The men made their own entertainment at camp; music and variety shows in an improvised camp theater were popular, and gambling schools flourished, though often the stakes were the very passport to life: a few root vegetables, a cigarette, even an occasional quinine tablet.

Many of the men did not even have any clothes because with dysentery they had soiled themselves and dropped them by the side of the road. One of the tasks of Chaplain Zimmerman was to take the clothes off the dead men, wash and fumigate them as best he could, and then issue them to those in need. There were no shoes available, so most of the men went barefoot. Others fashioned sandals from pieces of 2-by-4 with the tops of old shoes used as straps.

In general, the Japanese stayed outside the enclosure. However, punishments and beatings, when administered, were severe. Bill Massello watched as a group of about 6 prisoners were summarily shot after a day of torture, allegedly for smuggling in food. They were given no trial. Day after day, large numbers of his comrades, many of them close personal friends, died. His immediate commanding officer and intimate friend was brutally tortured to death. Three officers from his regiment who attempted to escape were cruelly tortured for two days and finally taken out and shot, but only after they had been forced to dig their own graves.

To discourage any attempts to escape, the Japanese divided the men into squads of ten, or "blood brothers," as they were called. If any man did escape, the Japanese instructions were that his blood brothers should be shot. As a consequence, the prisoners took a fairly rational position on escape. There was no place to go, and even if they did escape they were dependent upon the Filipinos to hide them. If the Filipino was caught the whole village would be punished. Zimmerman could see only one purpose behind escaping, and that was the prestige of getting away from the Japanese. So, instead, men fit enough volunteered for work details, if only to escape the sheer monotony of prison camp routine and perhaps to scavenge if the opportunity presented itself.

The Japanese worked assiduously to break the spirit of the men. They received no pay or mail, nor were they permitted to send any mail out. Protests as to their treatment were answered by the evasive comment that the men were not recognized as prisoners of war by the Japanese Army, and a beating.

Living conditions in the hospital area were even worse than in the main camp. The hospital itself was divided into two sections: one for those expected to recover, and the "zero ward," for those expected to die. The filth in the hospital was indescribable, and little care could be given to the sick. Medical supplies were very short, and thousands who might have been saved by proper food and medicine died. The Philippine Red Cross tried to bring medical supplies into the camp, but the Japanese flatly refused to let them enter or to deliver any supplies. In general, the hospital was so bad that even seriously sick men preferred to take their chances in the main camp rather than go to the hospital area.

In the zero ward, men waited to die. They lay in their own filth on the floor, too weak to care, too full of tropics-induced sores in their mouths to eat. At about 1600 hours each afternoon, the dead were taken to the cemetery. They were piled into long, shallow ditches, one on top of the other, 15 or 20 to each grave, and covered with a little dirt. Because of the level of the water table, some men would have to bail even as the hole was being dug. Before they could cover the bodies over, the water would seep back, and they would float on the water. So those who had bailed now held the bodies down with shovels until the others had thrown on enough earth to weigh down the dead.

Zimmerman or one of the other chaplains would say a few words and stand for a moment in silent grief at the conclusion of the simple ceremony. Most of the graves had less than a foot of soil on top; the men were too weak to do more. A good rain would frequently wash away this thin covering of soil, leaving the dead exposed to the sun and putrefaction.

Bill Massello spent four months at the camp, and the death rate at this time was about 6 percent per month. Many of the others in this account, Bressi and the Marines from Corregidor, Garleb and the survivors of Bataan, were there for considerably longer.

The Hell Ships

Bilabid was used by the Japanese as a transit camp throughout the whole period of their occupation of Luzon. It was a convenient staging post for work details en route from Cabanatuan to the southern islands. Sergeants Bigelow and Griffiths came through on their way to work in the Palawan Islands. This was in July 1942, when in company with about four hundred men they were used to build an air base in the jungle. Sergeant Griffiths was there for two years, and then he was returned to Bilabid.

Others passed through Bilabid on their way to Davao Penal Colony (known as Dapecol). Loyd Mills left on this detail in October 1942, and Bill Garleb left Cabanatuan for the same camp a year later. There they were forced to work in the rice fields, on the camp farm, and in the rice mill. Sammy Boghosian went to Dapecol directly from his first prisoner-of-war compound at Malaybalay, as did other men who surrendered on Mindanao.

The Japanese evacuated Dapecol in the summer of 1944 and moved the men north once again to Bilabid. Here the prison functioned in its other role, namely as a staging post for men awaiting a ship to take them north to Japan. The first ships left within months of the American capitulation. Richard Osborn was brought north from Mindanao in October 1942, spent two nights in Bilabid Prison, and sailed in company with a thousand men.

Bill Massello left a month later, as did Sam Malick from the *Mindanao*. For all the men who made the journey, it was a gruesome ordeal of filth and misery. Massello sailed in the *Nagato Maru*, an old coal-burning hulk of about 10,000 tons. In its three dirty holds some 3,000 men were crowded. The upper deck of each hold held

Japanese troops, a total of some 1,500 men. The lower, fouler, and filthier decks held the Americans, about 500 in each hold. It was so crowded that only about half of the men could sleep on the bare deck at one time, so sleep was organized in shifts. No ventilation was provided. In the tropics, the heat was insufferable, and the stench was nauseating. During the nights, large rats frequently ran over the sleeping men.

Experiences varied according to the ships, but only with regard to the degree of agony suffered. Food was issued in buckets, invariably by the simple method of lowering them into the hold on a rope. On some ships the men were allowed on deck, perhaps fifty at a time for exercise and toilet; on others they were kept below and spent the whole voyage in darkness. The Japanese word for latrine is *benjo*, and so many of the hell ships were christened *Benjo Maru* by the Americans. The situation was so acute that prisoners had to use the same buckets in which they drew their rice for latrine purposes.

The already starved and weakened Americans sickened in large numbers, and many died. Their doctors did what they could, setting up sick bays in the crowded holds; but without the necessary medical facilities, which the Japanese obdurately refused to provide, they could do nothing.

There were no markings whatever on the ships to indicate that they were carrying prisoners of war. Hence they had to take their chance in convoys and were subjected to attack by American submarines and, later, aircraft. Osborn's ship, the *Totori Maru*, was attacked by an Allied submarine, and two torpedoes narrowly missed them. For the men entombed in the hold, the whirl of the torpedo propellers resounded throughout their prison. On Massello's ship there was a submarine alarm. The ships in the convoy zigzagged while all their guns blazed away. The Japanese officers and men became frantic and ordered all Americans below at once. The narrow hatchways were a bottleneck around which the prisoners crowded. Without giving the men a chance, some Japanese officers seized rifles and began to beat the Americans viciously over the head and back. They were battened below for 18 hours without food, water, or latrines.

Bressi sailed to Japan in September 1943. His hell ship stopped en route at Takao in Formosa, and they were landed at the Japanese port of Moji (these days it is called Kita Kyusha) a month later.

Bressi was the world's worst sailor in any case, and on this trip he was so sick that he would have welcomed death a dozen times and more.

After nearly two years in the penal colony at Davao, Sammy Boghosian was moved north to Manila and Bilabid to wait for a ship to take him on to Japan. On July 14, 1944, they sailed in the *Canadian Inventor*, a war prize built in Vancouver. There were 1,200 men on board; Bill Hall was a member of this group. They joined a convoy of eleven ships, but soon lost a tanker in Manila Bay, probably due to a drifting mine. The *Canadian Inventor* blew a couple of boilers in the South China Sea, and the rest of the convoy deserted them. The ship eventually docked in Japan at the beginning of September. Sammy Boghosian, like most of the POWs, lost over 15 pounds in weight during the voyage alone.

In the spring of 1944, Chaplain Zimmerman was caught by the Japanese trying to smuggle food into Cabanatuan. After a period of torture and punishment, he was moved to Bilabid, where he stayed for more than 6 months while American aircraft sank every ship in sight in Manila Bay.

In October, more than 1,200 POWs were loaded onto an old coal-burning freighter. Sgt. William Griffiths and Chaplain Zimmerman were part of the same detail. The men were crammed into two holds. Griffiths spent the first few days crowded onto the coal-dust beds, which were still carried as ballast. Later as the number of dead rose and more space became available, he found he could straddle the planking on the sides of the hold and get some relief from the crowding. Zimmerman was less fortunate. One night he was trying to sleep in a sitting position up against a bulkhead. He counted the bodies of 14 men touching him at any one time. The man on the bottom would stay there as long as he could, then he would kick and they would all move and shuffle around, and somebody else would be on the bottom so that the "instigator" could stand up.

At first the Japanese demanded a roll call each day. This became an unmanageable task, for the majority were disabled by sickness. It was found to be much simpler to deduct the number of dead each day from the total. On this ship they were battened down for the whole voyage. Men died of heat exhaustion and of suffocation. Every time they had a meal in these crowded holds the temperature soared. The prison ship spent 11 of the 40 days it took to reach

Formosa eluding American submarines and waiting for an escort in Hong Kong.

The conditions on the ship were so bad by then that even the Japanese were moved to show some compassion. The survivors were taken to Shirakawa Camp on Formosa. As prison camps go, this one was better than most. The climate was temperate, and the men were given a little fresh fruit from time to time. The rice portions were larger, and they had a ration of meat once a week. The men were moved into the senior officers' quarters. These had only just been vacated by Generals Wainwright, Drake, and the other members of USAFFE who spent a short while at Shirakawa while waiting to be flown to Japan. From there the generals were taken by ship and train to Tienti Tung Camp in Manchuria.

Both Zimmerman and Griffiths left Shirakawa in the New Year. They sailed in a Japanese troop ship that even served hot food. It was equipped with small wooden bunklike pallets for crowded sleeping. The prisoners discovered below them a cargo of sugar (*sato* in Japanese) and the ship became known as the *Sato Maru*. The sugar gave them energy but exacerbated the ever-present problem of diarrhea and dysentery.

Loyd Mills left Bilabid, in what must have been one of the last of the hell ships, on December 14, 1944. There were 1,600 POWs on the *Osyaka Maru*. The next day their ship was hit and sunk by U.S. Navy carrier planes off Bataan Peninsula, and 400 Americans died. The survivors were taken ashore and loaded onto a second ship; it had once been a cattle boat. The ship docked, as most of the hell ships did, in Takao Harbor in Formosa, where it was hit by U.S. Navy planes, with again heavy loss of American life. Loyd and the survivors joined a third ship, which docked in Moji at the end of January 1945. Mills suffered appalling treatment on the third ship. The men had to exist on half a cup of water a day and just a small portion of rice. Perhaps half the men on this final leg died, and Loyd had to be carried off the ship.

Liberation

There was a time when some among the Joint Chiefs of Staff questioned the wisdom or the strategic need to liberate the Philippines in the American drive for Tokyo. General MacArthur, however, having made his much-publicized promise to return, never wavered in his resolve. Whatever the strategic arguments, he believed it essential to American prestige in Asia that the Philippines should be liberated.

In the event, even the detractors came by force of circumstances and the shifting pattern of the war to accept the need for the Philippines in their strategic blueprint. In the summer of 1944, the largest amphibious force ever seen to date in the Pacific was assembled. General MacArthur had overall command of all the forces directly allocated to the assault. By the end of that year his forces numbered more than one and a half million men. Admiral Halsey and his command, the fast battleships and carriers of the Third Fleet, would provide the distant screen should the remnants of the Imperial Navy seek to intervene.

The campaign opened in October 1944, when four divisions from General Krueger's Sixth Army landed on the southern island of Leyte.

By now there were very few able-bodied men left in Bilabid Prison. It had become one big hospital, full of men with scurvy, severe beriberi, pellagra, malaria, and numerous parasitic infections. Everybody had dysentery. Paul Ashton and the small team of surviving doctors did the best they could, but it was a combination of deadly disease and the absence of medication, with less than 1,000 calories a day of polished rice, that caused the mortality rate to soar. If this combination was accompanied by anything else—for example, punishment for an infraction of some petty rule—then the result was inevitably death. Prisoners were brought in daily from the outlying details because of beatings and illness. Others whom Ashton had to administer to were the special prisoners from the Military Police Prison next door, too sick or weak to go through the daily torture sessions, broken in body and often in mind. Richard Sakakida was not among them. He had been told earlier that the Imperial Army was to give him amnesty. He was to work in the judge advocate's office of the headquarters, Fourteenth Army. Though his body was bruised and battered after his treatment. Richard was mentally sufficiently alert to play just a little hard to get. "Look," he said to his inquisitors, "I'm getting tired of this treatment. The U.S. Army did the same thing because they considered me to be an American citizen. What if the Americans should capture me? Must I go through the whole damn thing again?" Sakakida tried to sound adamant and convincing. Even his Kempeitai tormentor permitted himself a wry smile, but was equally adamant. "This is an order of the Imperial Japanese Army."

Sakakida went on his way to work for his new masters. He had already endured imprisonment, torture, and finally solitary confinement for close to two years.

Sakakida was employed as an English translator, but he spent most of his days as the orderly and servant to the headquarters duty officer. The Japanese were incredibly lax over their security, for whenever the officer went off to make his evening rounds Sakakida had the run of the office. Whereas the Americans secured sensitive documents in filing cabinets and locked them away, the Japanese used captured footlockers that were left open.

The Imperial Army even provided him with couriers for his espionage. There were many Filipino guerrillas and other suspects held in Martin Luther Prison. Their wives and families needed a pass to visit their menfolk, issued by the judge advocate's office. Sakakida acted as interpreter on these occasions, and it proved easy to slip sensitive documents to the women, who in turn passed them down the line.

The prison situation had reached a hopeless and helpless level, starvation was with them, and still conditions continued to deteriorate. But then their morale was suddenly elevated by new events. Ashton was up early one morning and making his rounds. He had to climb a few stairs to enter the door to the large room in which all the British cases were kept, and this allowed him to look out over the high wall that surrounded the old Spanish prison. It was dawn, and the city was quiet. Quicker than he could relate it, there appeared three twin-engined fighter-bombers screaming over the city at roof-top height. With a terrific roar, they came over the prison wall from the front to the back, where Ashton stood. Ashton watched as they opened up with their tremendous firepower once they had passed by the prison. And then they were gone . . . but he did notice a peculiar insignia on their wings, one that he had never seen before. The idea that they might have been Japanese entered his head only for a second, and by that time he wondered if it had been a dream. Had it happened at all? But it had, and everyone was awakened, and in that minute everything changed. The Japanese guards who had dived under the stairs and benches were a bit sheepish, while the Americans stood and discussed the new situation that had unfolded. Now they were adversaries again.

The Luzon campaign began on January 9, 1945, when four infantry divisions stormed ashore at Lingayen Gulf. There was a stiff defense by the Japanese, but sheer weight of firepower forced them to give way. Japanese HQ fell back on Little Baguio, where in the ensuing confusion Richard Sakakida was able to make good his escape. He stayed long enough to loot an abandoned store and then ran off into the jungle; he planned to hide away until the American advance reached him.

Richard very foolishly rolled some looted tobacco leaf, and the odor attracted the attention of an outpost, which bracketed his position with a highly accurate barrage of knee mortars. Sakakida was badly wounded by mortar fragments in the chest and stomach. He crawled away and tended his wounds as best he could. On a couple of occasions in the next week he hid when he spotted patrols of Americans. In their jungle fatigues and new helmets (he was used only to the frying-pan helmet), he thought they were Germans!

At the end of January 1945, American forces in their drive for Manila had liberated Cabanatuan, and they reached the outskirts of the capital a week later. However, the Japanese had no intention of declaring Manila an open city. Instead the garrison, some 25,000 naval personnel, intended to fight. A fierce battle for every house on every street began. Bilabid Prison and the Santo Tomas internment center were on the very front line.

Paul Ashton was by now under sentence of death. He had killed a Japanese guard, though in self-defense, and was awaiting his sentence by looking after the sick in what became known as the prison within a prison. This special compound was the contagious-diseases area, for none of these inmates were welcome in Japan as forced labor. Besides all the usual diseases, there were those with tuberculosis and diphtheria, poliomyelitis and even rabies. There were many chronic and advanced cases, particularly of amebic and tuberculous dysenteries. Bill Garleb was in the hospital at this time. Earlier, 50 British prisoners had been shipped in from Singapore with suspected cholera.

Japanese rations were now so reduced that the prisoners were eating sweet-potato vines, grass, the poorest quality of moldy rice, and rats when the wily beasts could be captured. Ashton would occasionally shoot one with a slingshot made with the rubber tubing from an old, used, blood plasma kit.

American aircraft were now an everyday occurrence for the prisoners in Bilabid. Groups of 75 bombers would appear over the city, and some would unload their bombs even as close as just across the street. The target was Far Eastern University, used by the Japanese as their Air Force headquarters. The flights of bombers were often shepherded by P-38 Lightnings and P-51 Mustangs looking for Japanese Zeros, but there were none anymore.

The battle for Manila rolled up into an ever louder and dustier crescendo. Some days it was continuous, and, long after dark, searchlights would scan the sky with spider-web patterns.

As the American advance reached the outskirts of the city, flying columns were dispatched to rescue the prisoners and secure the metropolitan water supply. Manila by this time was a city of **800,000** inhabitants. If the water supply became a casualty of the battle, the result would be plague.

While the prospects for eventual rescue of the prisoners were excellent, Ashton was concerned for those who were so ill. It was too bad to make it this far and then die. Most of them were too weak to walk and remained in their filthy, infested bunks. Then one night in February the prisoners began to hear at some distance sustained gunfire coming closer until it resolved into the unmistakable clatter of tanks. They had come to the walls of the prison and were in position at each corner of the square compound. Occasional bursts of automatic cannon and machine-gun fire could be heard. They remained there all night. The next morning Ashton, Garleb, the British, everyone was expecting something, anything. The Japanese guards, all 28 of them, had goose-stepped out of the front entrance of Bilabid to their death the day before. Small-arms fire could be heard outside, all over town. The bombing and strafing had not begun for the day when Ashton realized that someone was trying to remove the heavy boards from the iron-barred apertures in the southern wall. Soon one, then another were pried loose and two obviously tired, dirty, rumpled soldiers from some army stared down on them. Dressed in unfamiliar uniforms and helmets and carrying strange grease guns, they looked at them with some disdain and asked, "How the hell did you guys get in there?"

Ashton then knew that they were Americans. He told them they were Japanese prisoners and advised them to come to the front gate on Azcaraga Street.

As Ashton walked around to the front and watched, a patrol headed up the street to the main gate. It came under sniper fire from the Ideal Theater building opposite, and one of the Americans, with what looked like a stovepipe, obliged the prisoners with a show of firepower. There was no more sniper fire from the rubble that had been the Ideal Theater building.

So they were rescued, and the tanks took off for better opportunities. More soldiers came and went, but Ashton had to get back to his patients. Rations arrived later, and they ate the manna called K shared by their new friends. By this time the bomber crews had breakfasted and were out and around. The battle for Manila was reaching its crescendo. There were a thousand heavy-artillery pieces in the old North Cemetery firing over the heads of the liberated prisoners at targets in the walled city, and the main advance linked up with the column that had rescued the men at Bilabid. The noise was deafening and the reports uncountable. The unaccustomed sound of the shells going over was unnerving. Some mortar fire was falling into the prison, and it became temporarily untenable, so the prisoners part walked and part rode in trucks to the Ang Tibay Shoe Factory, where they stayed the night, close to the artillery positions.

The trip there and back to Bilabid the next day was like New Year's Eve in Times Square. Ashton saw the war being fought, the costumes, the unfamiliar weapons, the strange vehicles, boats with wheels, all sorts of tanks and weapons carriers . . . and he was glad to get back to the security of the world he knew, Bilabid Prison.

But they could not remain for long in the destroyed city, amid the stench of Japanese and civilian dead, who were lying all around and in some areas being incinerated by masked men with flamethrowers. So Ashton and the other able-bodied were placed in trucks and driven back through San Fernando to Lingayen. Bill Garleb was taken to the shell-like building that had once been the Quezon Institute and was now the home of the 54th Evacuation Hospital.

The rescue of the civilians and Army nurses in Santo Tomas had been even more dramatic. Though they had not suffered the privations and systematic torture of the soldiers, the civilians had had a terrible time, and food throughout was scarce. Initially everyone had been crowded into the classrooms and dormitories, but when these became too full the Japanese allowed the building of shanties—huts, really—in which married couples and children lived.

The little children fared reasonably well under the circumstances because the adults tried to ensure that they got as much as possible. But the older children, especially those in their early teens, lost as much as 20 pounds, and at their age that was a lot. The children suffered particularly from glandular disorders, and this in turn affected their teeth. By the end, many of the children and most of the adults had beriberi. Most of the men had lost 50 to 60 pounds in weight.

As with the soldiers in Bilabid, the arrival in the skies over Manila of the first American planes had been the cause of many rumors for the civilians. On February 3, American planes flew low over the camp, and one pilot dropped his goggles, to which he had tied a message. The note read simply, "Roll Out the Barrel." Later in the evening gunfire could be heard, and though it was by now dusk, the internees could hear people cheering.

Clay Seitz hugged Lilla and said, "That has to be the Americans. The Filipinos wouldn't cheer that way for anybody else!"

The flying column of the 2nd Squadron, 8th Cavalry used a Sherman tank as a battering ram to break through the perimeter of the camp. Inside, the guards, most of them Formosans, put up little fight, and within a few minutes some 3,500 internees were liberated amid scenes of pathos and joy which none of those who were there will ever forget.

In the education building, however, the camp commandant, Lt. Col. Toshio Hayashio, and 65 men held hostage 275 other internees, mostly women and children. A fire fight ensued, and this lasted intermittently throughout the night.

The next day under a flag of truce some food was sent into the education building. The divisional commander, General Chase, had by now arrived on the scene, cleared most of the combat units out, set up field kitchens and a hospital, and begun to negotiate with the Japanese.

At seven in the morning of February 5 terms were at last agreed on. The enemy was given a safe conduct to the Japanese lines, which had by then been established in the southern part of the city. The prisoners were set free. On February 7, General MacArthur arrived to visit the internees and to receive their adoration, recorded for posterity by the Allied press corps in his retinue. The camp was still under Japanese observation and intermittent fire. About 15 minutes after the general left, Santo Tomas was shelled.

Though the American combat units moved out of the camp and hospital companies arrived to take care of the internees, it was shelled frequently over the following days. Madeline Ullom and Ruby Moteley found their old skills being pressed into service as casualties mounted. On February 8, some 45 internees were killed and over 100 injured as a result of the artillery fire, and many of the buildings were destroyed.

The following day the camp was shelled again. This time the Japanese hit the water tower. The inmates, both liberator and internee now under siege, had to use water drawn from the Pasiq River, heavily chlorinated from Lister bags. A hundred Army nurses arrived that evening, and Ullom and the others were relieved of their duties.

A couple of days later Ullom, Moteley, and the other surviving "angels" from Bataan and Corregidor were taken out of Santo Tomas. Two trucks drove at breakneck speed through Japanese sniper fire to a temporary airstrip that American ingenuity had established on Dewey Boulevard. There they were packed into a C-47 Dakota, which, having dodged the rubble and fallen masonry, clawed its way into the sky.

The nurses were taken first to a rehabilitation center that had been established on Leyte and then by easy stages to the United States. The civilians were evacuated group by group in the succeeding days.

But perhaps the most dramatic rescue of all was that of the civilians at Los Biños. It was one of the most remarkably audacious and successful operations of World War II. They were rescued from deep behind Japanese lines, all 2,147 of them, men, women, and children.

In many respects the condition of these poor souls was far worse than that of the internees in Santo Tomas. The camp was practically out of food, and the internees were existing mostly on palay, unmilled rice. People were literally dying of starvation.

On January 6, the Japanese commandant had handed the camp

over to the American committee and marched away. Excitement reigned amid unconfirmed rumors of a landing on Luzon. A few internees wandered away from the camp, but most heeded the Japanese warning that a war zone existed outside the perimeter wire and civilians would be shot on sight. They were too weak to go very far in any case. Food was brought to them by the local Filipinos, and some of the guerrilla units sent what they could spare, but it was barely sufficient to bring but temporary ease to their suffering.

Their freedom lasted barely the week. On the morning of January 13, Konishi, their brutal commandant, his staff, and guards had all returned. Now the regime was even more sadistic than before, and the death rate rose alarmingly.

The great fear of the American forces was that as full-scale operations began in southern Luzon, the Japanese garrison at Los Biños might massacre the internees. The corps headquarters had a complete picture of the camp and the number of its inmates based on photographic intelligence, the local guerrillas, and an internee who had broken through to American lines.

The plan was to launch a raid by a specially constituted force some 25 miles behind the enemy front lines, overpower not just the guards but also the enemy forces in the immediate area, liberate the hostages, and bring them all back to safety. Other formations would launch deep-penetration strikes into the vicinity of the camp to distract the Japanese forces in the area and so prevent them from reinforcing the garrison. They could also provide a backup escape route through a land corridor should the main plan of operations fail. In many respects the secondary force, men of the 1st Battalion (188th Glider Infantry, 11th Airborne), together with their support forces, were the unsung heroes of the operation.

On the evening of Friday, February 23, the pathfinder or reconnaissance platoon of the 11th Airborne, guided by guerrillas, moved into position, some around the camp and others on a beach some 2 miles away.

On Nichols Field six Dakota C-47s sat waiting for the dawn, and in tents nearby Company B went through the well-practiced drills of the last-minute preparations for battle. Just before dawn the next morning the Sisters of Maryknoll gathered in their little chapel, one of the stalls in a converted cattle shed, to say Mass and wait for the gong to sound roll call at seven.

As the gong began to strike, the sound of planes was heard. One of the Fathers in passing a window saw a parachute. There was a dash for the windows and the door. To Sister Louise the sky seemed full of white parachutes, glistening like angels' wings in the early-morning light. Almost immediately the nuns heard shots, and the battle for the camp was on.

The paratroopers had timed it to perfection. Company B of the 1st Battalion, 5th Parachute Infantry dropped from their C-47s while troops on the ground set off smoke pots to mark the dropping zone and stormed the perimeter wire. The vast majority of the Japanese guards were at early-morning PT and separated from their weapons. The internees rushed out and embraced their rescuers, but they knocked them away. Sister Louise was bowled over by one young, blond paratrooper.

These men are as mean as the Japanese, she thought.

The battle intensified, and the internees ran for cover.

After about an hour the paratroopers reappeared. With tears in their eyes they embraced the internees and explained that their orders were to kill the Japanese before they could turn their weapons on their captives. It was just about at that time, when everyone was milling around in excited groups, that the first of the 54 amtracs, armored amphibian tractors, came crabbing through the gates carrying the rest of the battalion. The troops quickly threw out a defensive screen around the camp and secured the route to the beach.

The sounds of battle could be heard in the distance where the glider infantry, having marched in over incredibly difficult terrain, was now busily engaged in tying down the enemy forces in the vicinity. This in turn gave an added sense of urgency to the evacuation of Los Biños.

The nuns quickly gathered together whatever belongings they could carry in their hands, took a last look around those Spartan quarters that had been home for so long, and hurried down to the lower camp where the amtracs were drawn up, engines idling, ready to make the return trip. As they passed down the road, the barracks on both sides were burning, for the troops had been ordered to destroy everything. The soldiers and guerrillas helped with their bundles as they clambered into the holds of these strange and wonderfully terrifying machines.

The hospital patients were taken out first. The nuns helped to get them ready and gave first aid to the few who had been wounded in the battle, though no one was seriously hurt. Each vehicle could hold about 30 people, and the first contingent quickly rolled down to the lake, about 2 miles away. The column had to run the gauntlet of Japanese sniper and machine-gun fire as the enemy tried to stop the progress of this strange procession, but the rapid-fire cannon of the amtracs fired back, and thus they made their way to the water.

After a journey of about two hours, the tanks waded ashore and deposited their precious cargo on the beach. While waiting trucks took the internees on to a specially prepared reception center, the amtracs returned to Los Biños. By the time the flotilla had reached the camp it was past midday, and the remainder of the internees had been escorted to the beach by the troops. The rearguard was called in and the last of the amtracs retraced its route along the lake shore to their base.

In the distant hills the gliderborne infantry retreated, their services no longer needed.

It was truly a remarkable operation. Everyone had been rescued, one American soldier and a Filipino had died, while three internees were slightly wounded in the battle.

The adventure was by no means over for the internees. Their home was now the new Bilabid Prison at Muntinlupa, which had been liberated just a short time before by one of the flying columns. Already, however, the road to Manila was closed by Japanese roadblocks. So they were prisoners still, of a kind, but very willing ones. The paratroopers could not do enough for the internees. As the nuns entered the compound, their names were checked off a list, and they were given chocolate bars, and cigarettes, too, before joining with all the others in a temporary dining room where steaming bean soup was served. It was midafternoon, and they all had a good appetite for their delayed breakfast. Some complained about the plainness of the fare until it was explained that until they had recovered a little it was better to eat simple things. They were taken to their sleeping quarters, where despite the front-line conditions, engineers had rigged lights and all the hot water in the world. Sister Louise was too afraid to sleep lest she wake to find it all a dream. Their last freedom was but a bubble—that lasted only 5 days—and this one was so wonderful that it might be still more fragile.

Supper that night lasted almost 8 hours, not because the menu was particularly exotic (K rations of meat and vegetable stew with tomato juice), but because many of the internees were so famished that they went through the chow line 3 or 4 times. The paratroopers, for their part, showed a sympathy and understanding way beyond their years, but even they could not help but be amused at the way the internees scrambled to salvage the empty tin cans. They had been prized dishes for so long in Los Biños.

Each morning the paratroopers drove off to war until the road to Manila was opened. Supplies were dropped to the beleaguered forces, and in the evening the troops would mix with the internees and play with the children. Some of the nuns met boys from their hometowns. Sister Marion Cecilia was overcome when a handsome, athletic paratrooper introduced himself as her nephew. She had last seen him when he was 5 years old.

By the end of the month, the road was open and temporary passes were issued to those who wanted to go to Manila. Gradually the internees began to drift away. Once they had been medically cleared and could prove to the military authorities that they had a home to go to or a country to return to, they were allowed to leave. The Sisters of Maryknoll, for their part, resumed their work in the Pilippines.

For many of the men who survived the hell ships, there were even more hard times to follow in the work camps to which they were sent in Japan, Korea, and even Manchuria. Many of them arrived in winter. In their already weakened condition and having spent the years in the Philippines, the northern Asian winter took its toll. Most incoming groups had a very high death rate for the first two months or so and then gradually became acclimatized. Loyd Mills was at a camp called Kukioka No. 1, where 90 men died very soon after arriving. Loyd was at his lowest ebb—he weighed only 80 pounds.

The work on which the men were engaged varied enormously. Some like Bill Finken were given rough-and-ready training as riveters and sent to work in the Osaka shipyards as *kyo-byo*— literally a "hammerer." The majority worked in factories, warehouses, and docks as unskilled laborers doing the most menial of tasks. Long, punishing hours in a cruel climate and harsh living conditions sapped the reserves of what little strength they had left.

Richard Osborn was in Japan through three successive winters, working in a steel strip mill and later as a stevedore on the docks.

Albert Broderick worked in a steel mill in Osaka. Here he was beaten innumerable times. On one occasion he was made to stand on the edge of a curb and hold a pile of bricks above his head until he fainted—or at least convinced the guard he had. The strange thing is that during the slappings and the torture, he had no sensation of pain—only the determination to beat them. "Don't let the bastards knock you off your feet. Don't flinch. Laugh in their faces. Make sure you are conscious enough to fall forward, otherwise they will stomp your groin into pulp."

All, in their own ways, continued to fight the enemy, if only by simply surviving.

Sammy Boghosian went to a POW camp near Nagoya where he worked in a copper foundry, the fumes from which added further to the discomfort and distress. Temperatures were down to -20° C in midwinter, with perhaps the majority of the camp suffering from influenza and dysentery. The living quarters were almost always without either light or heat of any kind.

Bill Massello began his time in Japan at Umeda Camp in downtown Osaka, where the emphasis was on getting the most work out of the prisoners as cheaply as possible. Sam Malick was in this camp as well. Here officers and men were employed on the hardest of physical labor, such as shoveling coal and ore, handling heavy scrap iron, loading and unloading freight cars and barges, and carrying heavy loads on their backs. After about a month, the men were issued cast-off Japanese Army clothing, which though poor and ill-fitting was something of an improvement over their torn and threadbare cottons. Their clothing and bedding crawled with lice. Recreation of any kind was strictly forbidden. Books, improvised chess and checker sets, and other forms of amusement were confiscated, and their owners were beaten mercilessly.

Bressi went to Hiro Hatu and worked in the local steel mills. There he met Americans who had been captured on Wake and Guam.

Conditions varied from camp to camp; in some the discipline was more lax and the regimes more liberal. In August 1943, Massello was sent to Zentsuji Camp, where life was a little easier.

Many men found themselves drafted into the mines in the ore-rich island of Honshu. Paul Kerchum, who now weighed 90 pounds, was sent to a lead mine in the south, while Bill Hall, over 6 feet tall and down to 108 pounds, was sent to a coal mine. Here his draft of 200 men met up with some British POWs who had been captured in Singapore. The camps were established near the mining villages which in turn were owned by the big corporations of the day, such as Mitsubishi. Chaplain Zimmerman was there.

The men worked 12-hour shifts in the mine, 6 days a week. The first shift began at 0400 hours and the second at 1600 hours. After two weeks the men changed shifts. The only good thing that Bill Hall found about working in the mine was that underground there was a more constant temperature, cool in summer and not so cold in winter. They had considerably better barracks, but there was no heat except in the mess hall and the large communal bath, which they were allowed to use after coming off shift. This and other camps were in very remote areas, and so the discipline was easier and the vigilance of the guards practically nonexistent; after all, there was nowhere for the Americans to go. Often the gate to the camp would be left unattended and open at night.

William Griffiths reached Japan in one of the very last prison ships to beat the American submarine blockade. He was sent to a camp at Kawasaki and worked as a laborer for the Suzuki Company shoveling coal and carrying sacks of flour. Some of the latter always seemed to get broken. The earlier British arrivals at the camp had made a crude hotplate, concealed it within the walls of the warehouse, tapped the electric wiring, and were actually baking bread. Some was eaten by the prisoners, but much of it was used to trade with the prison guards.

At every opportunity newspapers were smuggled into the camp. A Dutch officer translated the Japanese into Chinese, and from this a British POW translated it into English. By reading between the lines the men were able to tell that the war was reaching its climax.

Many lived and worked in the towns, and all can remember the first raids by the B-29 Superfortresses. The flights of these machines was a wonderful sight and lifted the spirits of the men higher than ever before. But if a couple of days went by without a raid, morale would slump.

The prisoners were bombed out of their factories and shipyards. Many witnessed at first hand the horrendous fire raids launched by low-flying B-29s on Osaka. Some of the prison camps were hit, and there were obviously casualties. Men were employed creating firebreaks and in clearing rubble, and others were moved inland to the remoter regions of Japan.

Loyd Mills was sent with a detail of 140 POWs to Jinsu in Korea.

For those men who were still in the urban camps and along the coast, the real indicator that the war was coming so much closer was the appearance of swarms of carrier strike aircraft. Morale soared to see such planes fly with impunity over the Japanese cities.

Richard Osborn was by now working in Niigata, a port in the northern part of Honshu. There he worked on the waterfront unloading ships and barges. There were sorties by B-29s, filling the sky with their shape and sound as they came in low to mine the harbor, and Navy F-6 Hellcats strafed the dockside. In the very last days of the war. Osborn probably had the luckiest reprieve of them all. Niigata was one of the four possible target cities for the atomic bomb.

But, of course, the bombing raids and submarine blockade produced another side to the picture. Food became even more scarce in Japan, and the POWs experienced much of what those who were left in the Philippines suffered. On Honshu the inmates in the camps were starving; they lived off fish entrails, rice, and dogs if they could catch them.

Men heard of the end of the war in many different ways, but most got the message when they awoke in their camp to find the guards had gone and the gates were open. Neither did the glad tidings come for everybody on the same day, because even the Japanese authorities in some of the more remote areas did not receive word until often as much as a week after Tokyo's formal acceptance of a cease-fire. There were camps where B-29s appeared promptly, their bomb bays loaded with crates of food and medicines that were then dropped, as low as the pilot dared, to the starving men below. Undoubtedly some men died from overeating.

For Bill Hall, Paul Kerchum, and others in the mining camps on Honshu it took up to a week for the B-29s to find them. Bill thought they looked like the Empire State Building—he had never seen anything so big in his life. Even at this stage there were casualties. Kerchum saw two men killed by falling crates, one by a case of peaches and another by a barrel of chocolate bars.

At Bill Hall's camp the containers were parachuted in, and men gathered in groups around the silk and opened the food, butter, cheese, and fruit cocktails. This food was far too rich for their starved systems, and they got sick, whereupon they started all over again. To this day Bill Hall cannot stand the sight of fruit cocktail.

Instructions were also dispatched, and the message to all the POWs was simple: "STAY PUT." Those in the mining camps and elsewhere had nowhere to go and in fact had to wait a number of weeks before the bomb damage to the railroad (it was the only means of communication in the region) had been repaired and a train sent to evacuate them. Nearer the towns, however, it was a different story. Many of the men simply got fed up with waiting and took off into the cities. Bill Finken was part of the group that moved into Osaka and took over the one remaining decent hotel and waited for the Americans. Sam Malick was one of a party of 60 Americans who also became fed up and so they caught a train to Tokyo. It proved a dangerous game, for the train was full of discharged Japanese soldiers. Nevertheless, they arrived more or less intact, only to be picked up by American MPs within minutes. After the reunion was over, they were very firmly escorted to a POW reception center that had been established at Yokohama.

Doubtless, too, there were reprisals and revenge, though some would call it justice, but also there was kindness and incredible generosity on the part of the POWs to the Japanese. In many camps the men had worked alongside Japanese laborers who were not much better off themselves. So with the arrival of the "K manna" from the B-29s, the men took food into the nearby villages and fed the local people. In other areas when the camps were finally vacated, untouched rations were left for the civilians.

Generals Wainwright, Drake, and other members of the higher command, together with some 1,700 men, were in a prison camp in Mukden, Manchuria. They were liberated on September 5—by the Russians. Two days later, elements of the American 7th Infantry Division arrived in Korea; Loyd Mills and his camp were liberated. Until that time they had been sustained, since the cease-fire, by the B-29s.

It was also about that time that Richard Sakakida walked out of the jungle in the Philippines and surrendered to the Americans. It took a little while before they accepted his story. Then a couple of CIC officers appeared and whisked him away—the CIC had kept track of him until the end of 1944.

In Tokyo Bay were moored two new hospital ships. The U.S.S. *Consolation* and *Sanctuary* were but recently commissioned and were intended to deal with the casualties that had been anticipated if the Americans had to take Japan by storm. The atomic bombs helped save all that, and instead these hospital ships were used to succor and transport the POWs. Most were taken in slow and easy stages by sea to the Philippines. There they were housed in reinforcement depots, and the vast majority sent by slow transport via Honolulu to the United States mainland.

The men were convinced then, and still are, that this was to fatten them up a little before they met with their families. The officers, senior and middle-ranking, were flown home. Some of the men were promised flights from Manila, but their seats were given instead, the men believed on the intervention of MacArthur, to Filipino students who were off to study in the United States.

When the POWs arrived home, by whatever means, it was their sole desire to be reunited with their families. Many chose to make light of their ills and to spend as little time as possible in the hospitals and as a result failed to have their ailments registered with the authorities. Consequently, in years to come when they have applied for disability pensions, the authorities have proved to be less than sympathetic.

Faith that he would eventually see his loved ones again had kept Sammy Boghosian alive, but when he arrived home in October he was greeted with the news that his father had died of a heart attack. The following day they told him that his 19-year-old sister had died from polio and that two of his brothers were crippled by the same disease. It was then that Sammy Boghosian went to pieces.

Returning POWs were allowed a two-week vacation with one dependent at the expense of Uncle Sam, and most were promoted one grade. They also received back pay less deductions.

A year or two after the war, the POWs were also given a dollar for every day they had been a prisoner. This money came from the Japanese reparations. Chaplain Zimmerman got $1,274.

SELECTED BIBLIOGRAPHY

Bateson, Charles. *The War with Japan: A Concise History*. East Lansing, Mich.: 1968.

Beck, John J. *MacArthur and Wainwright*. Albuquerque, N.M.: 1974.

Belote, James H. and William M. *Corregidor: The Saga of a Fortress*. New York: 1967.

Burns, James M. *Roosevelt: The Soldier of Freedom*. New York: 1970.

Collier, Basil. *The War in the Far East, 1941–1945*. New York: 1969.

Dull, Paul S. *A Battle History of the Imperial Japanese Navy, 1941–1945*. Annapolis, Md.: 1978.

Eyre, James K., Jr. *The Roosevelt-MacArthur Conflict*. Chambersburg, Pa.: 1950.

Ganse, William A. *The History of the United States Army*, rev. ed. New York: 1964.

––––––. *MacArthur Close-Up: Much Then and Some Now*. New York: 1962.

Hayashi, Saburo. *Koqua: The Japanese Army in the Pacific War*, trans. Alvin D. Coox. Westport, Ct.: 1978.

Hersey, John. *Men on Bataan*. New York: 1943.

Hough, Frank O. *The Island War: The United States Marine Corps in the Pacific*. Philadelphia: 1947.

––––––. *Pearl Harbor to Guadalcanal*. Washington, D.C.: 1958.

Hunt, Frazer. *MacArthur and the War Against Japan*. New York: 1944.

Ind, Allison. *Bataan: The Judgment Seat*. New York: 1944.

Kelley, Frank Raymond, and Ryan, Cornelius. *MacArthur: Man of Action*. New York: 1950.

Liddell Hart, Basil H. *History of the Second World War*. New York: 1980.

Long, Gavin M. *MacArthur as a Military Commander*. New York: 1969.

Lowenheim, Francis et al., eds. *Roosevelt and Churchill: Their Special Wartime Correspondence*. New York: 1975.

Manchester, William. *American Caesar*. New York: 1978.

Mayer, Sidney L. *MacArthur*. New York: 1971.

Miller, Ernest B. *Bataan Uncensored*. Minneapolis: 1949.

Morison, Samuel E. *The Rising Sun in the Pacific, 1941–April 1942*. Boston: 1948.

――――. *The Two-Ocean War*. Boston: 1963.

Morton, Louis. *The Fall of the Philippines*. Washington, D.C.: 1953.

Parrish, Thomas. *Encyclopaedia of World War II*. New York: 1978.

Richards, Norman. *Douglas MacArthur*. Chicago: 1967.

Romulo, Carlos P. *I Saw the Fall of the Philippines*. Garden City, N.Y.: 1942.

Rutherford, Ward. *Fall of the Philippines*. New York: 1971.

Stamps, T. Dodson, and Esposito, Vincent J., eds. *A Military History of World War II*. West Point, N.Y.: 1953.

Toland, John. *But Not in Shame*. New York: 1961.

――――. *The Rising Sun*. New York: 1970.

Waldrop, Frank C., ed. *MacArthur on War: His Military Writings*. New York: 1942.

White, William Allen. *They Were Expendable*. New York: 1942.

Wittner, Laurence S., ed. *MacArthur*. Englewood Cliffs, N.J.: 1971.

Wohlsetter, Roberta. *Pearl Harbor: Warning and Decision*. Stanford, Calif.: 1962.

INDEX